LEE TAKES
COMMAND

LEE TAKES COMMAND

by CLIFFORD DOWDEY

With Maps by Samuel H. Bryant

BARNES
&NOBLE
BOOKS
NEW YORK

Originally published as *The Seven Days: The Emergence of Lee*

Copyright © 1964 by Clifford Dowdey. Copyright renewed 1992 by
Carolyn Dunaway.

This edition published by Barnes & Noble, Inc.
by arrangement with Harold Ober Associates.

1994 Barnes & Noble Books

ISBN 1-56619-455-5

Printed and bound in the United States of America

M 9 8 7 6 5 4 3

*For my dear friend and battlefield
companion McDonald Wellford
and his wife Margaret*

Contents

List of Maps

The Year of the Settlement

IN THE SMOKY DUSK outside Richmond on May 31, 1862, a general was knocked from his horse by a shell fragment and a stray minié ball. It was one of the rarities in the history of warfare for a general commanding an army to receive a wound during battle, and Joseph E. Johnston was one of only two commanding generals to be wounded in action in the Civil War. The other general, Albert Sidney Johnston, had bled to death at Shiloh two months earlier.

Joe Johnston's wounds came at the Battle of Seven Pines, a crossroads seven miles from Richmond, where the general was commanding in an area separated from the main action. Johnston's part of the field spread out from a clearing at Fair Oaks Station, a stop on the Richmond and York River Railroad where it crossed Nine Mile Road. The flat countryside there was mostly wooded and heavily brushed, with entangled vines growing close to ground that, naturally spongy, had been turned into a bog by rain the night before. It was bad terrain for assaulting troops whose officers held no clear idea of the enemy's dispositions, and the scant information possessed by Johnston happened to be wrong.

The counterattack at Seven Pines was Johnston's first aggressive action since he assumed command of the Confederate forces in Virginia after First Manassas nearly a year before. By a series of anticipatory moves, the slight, sprightly commanding general had evaded the advances of George B. McClellan's big army. Then, backed up on the flat, damp farm country on the outskirts of the Confederate capital, Johnston had been forced to make a stand. Though the dandified little general was a scholar of warfare, he was a lazy, hazy thinker on the details of battle preparations. The result

was, as seen by Alexander, his analytical chief of ordnance, "a phenomenally mismanaged battle."

Johnston's personally directed action late in the day was really an
effort to salvage the deranged plans of his first counteroffensive. He
hurried forward his brigades of unseasoned troops with neither
reconnaissance nor guns for support. The soldiers, innocently eager,
deployed in battle lines from the mud of Nine Mile Road across the
quagmire of a wide yard. In front of the snug Adams house, the men
were swept by a gale of lead balls and jagged-edged slugs of canister.
Their doomed fellows led forward as supports were sent slushing and
threshing into the dense, dripping woods that enclosed a cleared field
on three sides. By then the light was fading, and the supporting
troops could only locate the Federals by the flashes of their rifles
from the woods.

All three brigadier generals of the supporting troops were struck
by enemy fire. One fell dead; one, left unconscious on the field, was
later captured; and huge Wade Hampton, the South Carolina grandee, stood on one foot beside his horse calling for the surgeon to
come and extract a bullet from the other. Major General Gustavus
Smith, second in command, was off trying to advance more supports
to the already lost action.

Into this disorder and anguish, Joe Johnston went galloping
across the cleared field on some frantic mission. Almost simultaneously, a partially spent musket ball struck him in the right shoulder
and a fragment from an overshot shell lodged in the chest. He fell
so heavily from his horse that at first he feared a spinal injury. Two
staff officers hurried to the commanding general where he lay on the
wet field. The light figure was carried toward the farther woods beyond range of the random fall of metal.

When the litter-bearers arrived, Johnston was conscious and
asked if someone could fetch his sword and pistols. "That sword
was the one worn by my father in the Revolutionary War," he said,
"and I would not lose it for ten thousand dollars."

The lean, erect figure of Jefferson Davis approached through the
dusk. The Chief Executive and the commanding general had been
steadily, sometimes bitterly, at odds for the past months, but Davis
leaned solicitously over the wounded man. Johnston, his conscious-
ness failing, merely shook his head when Davis asked if he could do

anything. Manifestly Johnston would be out of action for some time.

Davis returned to his horse, remounted and rode to find General R. E. Lee, the "Military Adviser to the President." Lee had left his cheerless office in Richmond during the afternoon and ridden to the field to try to discover from Johnston what was going on. Though the two Virginians had been intimates since they were classmates at West Point (sharing the bond of knowledge that their fathers had served together in the Revolution), Johnston had refused to divulge any of his plans. Davis joined Lee, and together they rode to find Major General Smith and learn from him his superior's intentions.

The handsome second in command knew little more than they. Johnston had told him, Smith said, of a "misunderstanding" between him and assault commander General James Longstreet, who had attacked on the wrong road and piled up the bulk of the assault force at Seven Pines. No one knew what was going on across country at Seven Pines, though it was obvious the enemy was not being driven. By then the rattle of firearms was dying off in the gathering darkness. Whatever Johnston's plans may have been, the day was over without change in the oppressive situation confronting the defenders of Richmond. McClellan was unimpeded in the methodical advance that threatened the city with heavy siege guns the Confederates could not match.

When Davis and Lee rode back through the night to Richmond, the President was forced to the decision he had long avoided: the soldier he preferred to keep as his military adviser must be given the army and put into the field the next day. This escape from the desk, the dearest wish of Lee's heart, marked the end of more than a year of thankless, frustrating chores remote from the major actions of the war, while Confederate centers fell and Confederate forces retreated from the Atlantic to the Mississippi, from the Ohio River to the Gulf. For the war, it marked the end of the period of attempted settlement between the sections — the year that began with McClellan's assumption of command after First Manassas in July, 1861, and ended with Lee's mounting of a counteroffensive in the Seven Days Battle Around Richmond.

From the night of May 31 when the President and Lee returned to Richmond, the course of the settlement by arms began to change, leading to a change in the nature of the war and finally in the ultimate objectives. More than any combination of causes or moral abstractions, the turn the settlement now took was determined by a stray piece of metal fired by an unknown battery whose gunners overshot their target. Joel Cook, a reporter for the Philadelphia *Enquirer*, wrote that "this was the saddest shot fired during the war," for it changed the Confederate command. It brought to the test by arms the first single, controlling hand on either side.

2

Lee did not exert his profound effect on the war by the full flowering of military genius, nor yet by the harmony of the powerful elements in his nature which gave the quality of grandeur to his character. A professional soldier who, serving long in the engineers, had never led men in combat in his life, he did not assume command completely developed, as "sprung from the forehead of Jove."

In the techniques of command he was a novice, inexperienced in the tactical arrangements necessary for moving in battle the separate masses of men whose actions must be coordinated over miles of obscuring terrain. The units he was to move were indifferently organized, a crude and makeshift machine compared to McClellan's masterpiece. In committing himself to the destruction of the invading force, Lee would be using an unfamiliar and imperfect weapon.

But he did commit himself to attempt to destroy the enemy outside the city. With Lee the long retreats came to an end. Immediately discarding Johnston's strategy of evading the enemy, Lee planned to seize the initiative and fight the enemy *at points of his own selection*. Although he operated within the Confederacy's defensive policy, he abandoned its static aspects and arranged to strike a decisive counteroffensive. What he brought that changed the pattern of the armed struggle was strategy, the first introduced by the Confederates in their defense.

Since this strategy was adapted to the administration's general policy of defense, Lee also brought to the war in Virginia the first instance in which the military objective perfectly expressed the political purposes. In this way, Lee illustrated Napoleon's maxim, "Nothing is so important in war as an undivided command."

The chance to test his strategy before he was practiced in command or his army ready to take the offensive was presented Lee by the division in command that subverted McClellan's objectives. Without this division, McClellan's superb army could have taken Richmond regardless of Lee. Indeed, with an undivided command McClellan could have forced the evacuation of the city before Lee assumed command. As it was, McClellan's commander in chief, Abraham Lincoln, seemed dedicated to the proposition that Napoleon was wrong.

The political purposes which McClellan was to implement were not nearly so simple as the Confederacy's purpose of proving its right to independence by a successful defense of its land. From Lincoln's decision to employ armed coercion as a solution to secession, unforeseen and undesired developments began to move of their own chartless momentum. As one of the most astute politicians produced on the continent — perhaps only Jefferson and F. D. Roosevelt were his equals — Lincoln was a bold improviser who never shrank from the consequences of his improvisations. Instead, he managed to provide a sense of ordered inevitability to even the most uncontrollable events and his most demonstrable expediencies. He did this with the ambiguities of his wonderfully evocative prose, in which he used the politician's technique of avoiding reference to earlier statements that appeared contradictory. However, in that year of attempted decision, none of his gifts — many of which, like Lee's, were in a formative stage of development — served to bring a clarity of purpose that the military could execute.

3

The unpredictable elements began to gather when force was first tried on the modest scale of "suppressing a combination" formed of the seven states of the Lower South. At the outset, Lincoln miscalculated the effects of coercion when he demanded that citizens of the border states participate in the invasion of the seceded states. A Midwesterner, he failed to interpret the emotional content of the political principle of States' Rights — that passionate attachment of a people to a place — and failed to appraise the strength of conviction that supported the principle of "a federated republic" of sovereign states.

When the relatively populous states of Virginia, North Carolina and Tennessee, along with Arkansas, then seceded and joined the new confederation, the "combination" became a nation. It was small and pitifully poor, but the new states brought, with their manpower, an industrial nucleus, military leadership and a battleground. On this battleground twenty miles from Washington, the "suppression" ended with First Manassas on July 21, 1861.

Thus committed to force as a solution, the Lincoln administration was compelled to the next step of mobilizing the nation's manpower and resources. Five days after Manassas, young George McClellan arrived in Washington to disperse the armed defenders in the Southern states and to reestablish the authority of the United States in the territory embraced by the Confederacy. With McClellan came the crucial period, the one year when a "settlement" by arms was possible.

A more realistic appraisal of the Southerners' determination to defend their homeland caused the Lincoln administration to concentrate its might to overwhelm the hastily improvised compact of agricultural states before they could provide adequate organization, supporting services and military material for their outmanned volunteers. However, before McClellan felt his mighty army was ready to assume the offensive, the general and the administration were at cross-purposes.

Lincoln had the sound instinct to leave the military as free from civilian interference as possible, but he was himself divided by a conflict of purposes. Along with the larger objective of restoring the Union, he held the narrower one of retaining his own party in power. A regular party man in the new Republican Party, composed of diverse elements and occupying a tenuous position in prosecuting a war that lacked popular support, Lincoln was committed to the dual objective of winning the war and securing the future of his heterogeneous party.

Among the factions in his own party, the powerful bloc of Radicals was not motivated by a desire to restore the Union as it then existed. Their purpose was to use the war to establish their party's ascendancy in quite a new United States. In this the society of the Southern whites would be destroyed and four million slaves would be freed and enfranchised as potential Republican voters.

For their purposes the Radicals were supported by sincere abolitionists who, unaware of the political implications, permitted the zeal of moral coercion to direct their immediate goals against the Southern whites. As John Randolph, who wrote off half a million dollars in property when he manumitted four hundred slaves, observed: "Southern abolition was reform and appeal to the master; Northern abolition was revolution and appeal to the slave."

Whether or not the Radical leaders were conscious of all the implications of social revolution in the forces they sought to direct, for self-interested reasons the group was more realistic than Lincoln. He was essentially trying to restore by arms a national structure which had collapsed under the stresses of peace. The Radicals, welcoming the collapse, aimed for a Union composed of the loyalist sections in which their party operated and to which the South would be added as a conquered appendage, stigmatized by rebellion and slavery. To this end, destruction must come before reconstruction. The war must be prolonged until the forcible abolition of slavery could become a reality.

Directed by the same passions that impelled the extremists of the French Revolution, the Radicals advocated extending the war beyond traditional battles between soldiers to punitive action against the civilian population. Military leaders were encouraged to run off slaves or provide sanctuary for runaways under a policy to deny any rights to those who had seceded from the old Union. In Washington, the group tried to force or persuade Lincoln to declare abolition as an objective of the war.

While McClellan prepared his invasion, Lincoln was resisting the Radicals' importunities. Like the nonslaveholding majority of Southerners, Lincoln recognized that the abolition of slavery was not merely a moral issue but one that raised complex sociological problems of the freed Negro in a white society. The problem of the deportation of freed slaves was a stumbling block to passing abolition legislation in the 1832 session of Virginia's General Assembly, and Lincoln himself had said that sudden emancipation would present a worse evil than slavery itself.

At the time of McClellan's appearance, Congress passed a resolution that restricted the objectives of the war to the restoration of peace and specifically disavowed any purpose of changing Southern society. All of Lincoln's cabinet except Secretary of the Treasury Salmon P. Chase, the career abolitionist, supported him in keeping the issue of slavery out of the conflict.

Yet, though Lincoln officially refused to accede to the Radicals' demands, privately he was careful not to antagonize that skillful, determined bloc. He controlled them by adroit appeasement. It was Lincoln's extemporizations in relation to this appeasement, designed to present a unity of political action, that undermined the singleness of his objectives and led to a divided command.

What obscured the area of exchange between the administration and the general was the fact that McClellan personally believed in the official policy stated by Lincoln and thought "the restoration of peace" was the objective he was supposed to achieve. As a conservative Democrat, he naturally supported the government's objectives of restricting the invasion to the defeat of the armed defenders and preserving the Union. Since Lincoln expressed the same views, and the Radicals vehemently pressed for a different policy, McClellan assumed that Lincoln was opposed to the Radicals.

When McClellan took command, though Lincoln was opposed to the Radicals' policies, he was not opposed to the Radicals as a strong bloc in his party. Along with this distinction, which McClellan missed, Lincoln gradually changed under the mounting pressures during the year of the settlement and the growth of the Radical influence.

For his part, McClellan proceeded with a deliberateness that antagonized the Radicals, as well as arousing criticism in segments of the press and the general public, and this placed a strain upon Lincoln. While the President, improvising and ambiguous, did not deal forthrightly with the general, McClellan could not deal forthrightly with either Lincoln or himself. For as Lincoln was committed to a dual purpose, so was McClellan: he wanted to restore the Union and gain recognition as the hero who accomplished it.

During the course of their undeclared conflict, neither McClellan nor Lincoln was the man of his historic image. Lincoln, of course, experienced later growth, and the postwar apotheosis tended to present a somewhat mythical character. McClellan experienced the misfortune of being presented to the future by his enemies.

The ambitious general provided them with ammunition by his

vainglory, his arrogance, and his undiplomatic treatment of politicians. In a winner, the same traits would have been presented as color, dynamism and the scorn of a forceful character dismissing unqualified importunists. But McClellan was not only a loser: to the Radicals he had the wrong attitude.

Though circumstances and his own ego make it easy to judge McClellan by his less admirable traits and actions, the fact is that the complex, extraordinarily gifted man was wholly right in his idea for crushing the resistance in Virginia. His campaign, from July to July, was the only imaginative offensive ever mounted against Richmond. Beyond that, it was the military execution of a clear political objective and held the possibility, as one of Lincoln's cabinet members said of McClellan's strategy, "of preserving the Union without destroying the nation." And he might even have achieved that, despite the government's interference with his army and his plans, except for the stroke of bad fortune that removed from Confederate command the general whose defensive techniques were ideally designed for the triumph of McClellan's methods.

4

Before Lee took command, McClellan did not have to fear the enemy's exploitation of the internal conflicts in the Federal command. Also, the Confederacy's static policy of resistance negated the natural advantages of defense. With interior lines of communication, with nearly one thousand miles of front and another thousand miles of coastal line pierced by rivers offering inland passage to amphibious forces, the Confederates undertook the stultifying assignment of defending everywhere. Though this policy was a true expression of the new nation's political objective, as operated under Jefferson Davis it ignored the broader strategies of counteroffensives possible within the defensive system, and continually yielded the initiative to the invading forces.

This policy was supported by nearly all civil and military authorities, except Lee, who was not consulted. The troubled men in Richmond, like their Washington counterparts, were not the figures of the historic image as they groped their way from new problem to new problem in the uncertainties of that year. Many Confederates wished to return to the Union, on good terms for the South. Davis had been deeply sorrowed when his state, Mississippi, left the Union, and he accepted the undesired office of President with no aggressive intent.

As Jefferson Davis was the leader of the Confederacy, many failures were attributed to him that were inherent in the young nation's political structure and slim resources. In establishing a nation from nothing, and maintaining it under powerful attack with very little, Davis was forced to spread his attention over an enormous and complex range of problems. In conscientiously struggling with a succession of crises from all sides, Davis was most remarkable for the consistency of his adherence to the principles at issue. Yet, this preoccupation with principles — with his well-reasoned theories of constitutionalities and abstract justice — reflected the man's fundamental weakness as a revolutionary leader. An inner insecurity, an unadmitted fear of inadequacy, caused Davis to hold rigidly to anything that gave him a sense of security.

Thus he clung to an established operation whether or not it achieved the desired results. In this way the unpragmatic man established a bureaucratic system, wasteful and inefficient, that only a rich nation such as the United States could afford. Within this system he could never delegate real authority to anyone because of an instinctive fear of the operation getting out of his control.

Extended into military policy, this need made him establish departments to bring all field operations into an orderly system in which he could plan to meet every contingency. The antithesis of confident improvisers, such as Lincoln and Lee, Davis was like McClellan in feeling he had to provide against the possibility of unforeseen contingencies. As war is dealing with infinite combinations of the unpredictability of human behavior in the greatest concentrations, successful command requires quick reactions to the unexpected and the ability to exploit the unplanned. Lee acted on this by instinct. By instinct Davis sought to protect himself against the unpredictable. He arranged to contain the enemy's movements within a fixed system of preparation.

The resulting inflexibility in the Confederate defensive system reflected the personal inflexibility which many of Davis's contemporaries criticized in his character. This rigidity was not, as his detractors presumed, an expression of overbearing egotism, though he was certainly not modest. It was the defensiveness of a proud man whose need to be right went too deeply into his character for him to consider opposing positions or to consider the consequences of the tactlessness with which he asserted his authority.

During the year when all leaders were testing procedures and methods in unprecedented situations, neither president had determined on a satisfactory, effective relationship between civil and military authorities. In a nation without the tradition of a military establishment, and in which two of its greatest heroes, Washington and Jackson, had been civilians, both presidents in their different approaches acted on the assumption that they were at least as well qualified as the generals.

Lincoln, without military training, concentrated in the realm of decisions, and only used the authority of his office when he grew dissatisfied with McClellan. Davis, with a military background and actually preferring to serve in the field, took literally the title of commander in chief and concentrated on the army's organization. Because of Davis's preoccupation with details and Johnston's uncooperativeness in conducting the passive defense, the Confederacy's command was worse than divided: it was a vacuum.

5

During the period when McClellan was permitted to construct his great army at leisure, Lee, off on mundane assignments, was no factor whatsoever in the war in Virginia. In March, 1862, with the gathering threat to Richmond, Lee was hurriedly recalled to the capital for advice and for what amounted to staff work in the emergency. In this ignominious capacity Lee managed, by an unsuspected guile, to introduce some cause-and-effect tactics in the Shenandoah Valley front. Without his knowledge, the larger effect was to widen the breech between McClellan and Lincoln. In turn, this produced an even larger effect on McClellan himself. Lacking his government's confidence, the "Young Napoleon" ponderously inched his armored forces forward to within sound of Richmond's church bells.

While Washington politicians grew frantic at the absence of

thrilling battles in his campaign, deliberate McClellan, without risking a major engagement, had approached the position from which he could force the evacuation of Richmond. Unlike Washington as a symbolic capital, Richmond was more like Paris and London as a true center. Containing the largest industrial operations in the South, at that time it was the only producer of heavy ordnance, the major producer of light ordnance and ammunition, and, as a transportation hub at the top of the South Atlantic tier, it served as the center of operations for supply and other supporting services.

Beyond its importance as a city, Richmond acted as a fortress for the food-producing region from the Atlantic Ocean to the mountains west of the fertile Shenandoah Valley. In turn, this swath served as a buffer for the vast territory from south of the James River, at Richmond, to the Gulf of Mexico. Finally, railroads at Richmond connected the northeastern Confederacy with Tennessee and the country west of the Alleghenies. McClellan was right in believing that the capture of Richmond would mark the beginning of the end — an end that, as he desired, would come with a minimal dislocation to Southern society and a minimal bitterness between the contestants.

For McClellan to win this glory, to become literally the savior of the Union, was the last thing the Radicals wanted. A Democratic hero would immediately threaten their tenure in Washington. Then, with no possibility of promoting forcible abolition and enfranchising the freed Negroes without the existence of a national emergency, the political abolitionists would lose their cause for being.

At this stage Lee stepped into the vacuum and achieved in one month what the Radicals could not have achieved without him: he prevented a settlement in the year of the limited use of force for restricted political objectives.

Lee had won his position of influence by a subordination of self not in the character of McClellan and Johnston. He gained the trust of his government by a deep assurance that, like Lincoln's, gave him no need either to prove himself or to assert his own ego in personality exchanges. There was a kinglike quality in his leadership, as if by divine right, and he was the product of a society that had trained its superior individuals for authority. That society of Colonial Virginia, which produced the post-Revolutionary dynasty in

Washington, began to wane when Lee was growing up, but it formed him — a product of the last late flowering of Virginia's "golden age."

Again, like Lincoln, he was a product of the "old America." But also like the Radicals — though for wholly different reasons — he accepted the end of the seventy-one-year-old political union of that older America. It was not that he wanted anything new any more than Lincoln did. He simply wanted his region of the old America established outside a union which, as he said, had to be held together by bayonets. As a professional soldier having no stake in the institution of slavery (he was engaged in the "distasteful" chore of manumitting the slaves of his late father-in-law, foster-son of George Washington) and disbelieving in secession as a political remedy, his course was determined solely by reaction to coercion.

With his aggressive strategy reduced to the simple truism, "A good offense is the best defense," Lee made the Seven Days Battle the single most significant military engagement of the war. The decisiveness of the Seven Days lay in its effect on the course of the resolution by arms: as a climax, a culmination, of the year of the attempted settlement, it heralded the end of the effort to restore the Union as it then existed. By preventing a settlement in 1862, the Seven Days prepared the way for the war of subjugation according to the Radicals' purposes, chief among which was the introduction of the slavery issue in the preservation of the political Union by armed force.

Without Lee's counteroffensive the Union could have been restored without slavery becoming an issue and establishing a course in which, under the resurrected banners of moral coercion, the Negro again became a political issue one century later. Though the Radical leaders in Lincoln's government never claimed Lee as an ally, nor have histories mentioned his unsung contribution to their plans, the tragedy of the Virginian was that, in preventing a settlement in 1862, he served the purposes of those elements who ultimately brought the rule of terrorists to the South.

The Divided Command

CHAPTER ONE

"Passion Spins the Plot"

W HEN thirty-four-year-old General George B. McClellan
arrived in Washington on July 26, 1861, after the debacle of
First Manassas, the streets, bars and hotel lobbies were clogged
with soldiers wandering aimlessly in defeat. Five days after the
battle, demoralized federal officers and men continued to limp across
the bridges into the city. Across the river on the rolling plains of
Northern Virginia, the Confederates had advanced outposts to
within ten miles of the bridges to Washington. Upstream, cavalry
patrols had appeared near the river, led by a red-bearded, twenty-
eight-year-old colonel — lately a lieutenant in the U. S. Army —
J. E. B. Stuart. The troopers were fine-looking outdoorsmen,
mounted on blooded horses and lounging carelessly in the saddles
as if watching a sporting event instead of surveying a system of
forts.

These were the results of Lincoln's attempted quick suppression
of the "combination" of seceded states when McClellan was en-
thusiastically welcomed as the savior of the nation. Fresh from his
triumph in Virginia's western mountains and, as was said, "a gallant
figure," the handsome young general fitted the image of a man of
destiny. Unawed by public adulation and the deference of Washington leaders, he showed only confidence when conferring with
President Lincoln, the venerable general in chief Winfield Scott,
cabinet members, senators and swarms of highly placed opportunists
who saw the nation's first hero of the war as the architect of the future.

Though outwardly unimpressed, McClellan was by no means
unaffected. A shining success both in the army and in civilian life,
McClellan recognized that circumstances had given him the greatest
opportunity that could come to any man in his generation. "By

some strange magic I seem to have become the power of the land," he wrote his wife. "All tell me that I am responsible for the fate of the nation, and that all its resources shall be placed at my disposal."

McClellan assumed his role with the conviction that the nation's resources were indeed at his disposal and that he could use them in his own way. Lincoln gave tacit support to this attitude when he accepted without comment the general plan McClellan submitted on August 2. This paper was a development of a plan McClellan had submitted to Scott in May, and which had attracted the old general's attention to him.

McClellan's suggestion held the same military objectives and political purposes as Scott's own disregarded Anaconda Plan. Both plans aimed at a settlement between the dissidents by building a broad-fronted military force beyond the capacity of the Confederates to resist. While Scott's emphasis was on an interior blockade — with control of the Mississippi a primary objective so as to exploit the rivers that sliced into Confederate territory — McClellan's emphasis was on the strength of the ground forces. Both planned a concentration of power capable of overwhelming any resistance with a minimum of fighting on the Southerners' land. Both felt that defense of their homes would harden the spirit of dissidence and, as General Scott, the old Virginian, warned, "If you invade the South, I guarantee that at the end of a year you will be further from a settlement than you are now."

In calling for nearly three hundred thousand men for the main army in the East, McClellan justified the immensity of his project by saying, "I understand it to be the purpose of this great nation to reestablish the power of the Government and restore peace to its citizens in the shortest possible time."

While Lincoln evidently did not then accept the necessity for this grand scale advance, he showed a desire to support McClellan as far as he possibly could. In those midsummer days the President sought McClellan's company, appeared often at his house on H Street, and offered "George" every evidence of support. The men had been acquainted before the war when Lincoln was attorney for the railroad of which McClellan was president. Lincoln's attitude of trust and approval caused McClellan to assume that lack of comment on the plan implied acquiescence. He could do what he wanted.

2

While George McClellan believed his plan was accepted, his own motives were not restricted to restoring peace by amassing an irrestible force. By his method, McClellan risked no defeat himself. His plan was a perfect product of a union of conviction and ambition, and McClellan had a habit of success.

Born of a Philadelphia family of modest means, he had been blessed by good looks, a brilliant mind and a charming personality. Directed by ambition and supported by energy, McClellan's native gifts formed a quality at once colorful and dynamic, a force which opened the way all his life. He received special dispensation to enter West Point two years before the prescribed age and graduated before twenty at the head of his class. Brevetted in the Mexican War, where he served with Lee as an engineer on Scott's staff, he was appointed by Jefferson Davis, then secretary of war, to a commission of military scientists to study the Crimean War. Leaving the army to enter the lucrative field of railroad engineering, at thirty-four he was earning the impressive salary of $10,000 a year as railroad president.

He came into the war as major general in charge of Ohio volunteers and was soon promoted to major general in the U. S. Army. For his first campaign in western Virginia, McClellan had organized his force of twenty thousand with characteristic attention to detail. The deliberate advance of his compact forces, superbly equipped and supplied and avoiding all risks, had proven irresistible. In contrast to the luckless General Irwin McDowell's campaign in the environs of Washington, McClellan's decisive victory caused him to be hailed as the "Young Napoleon." The significance of his victory appeared greater at the time than it does today: he had conquered a part of Virginia and had freed it from the Rebels.

The public was ignorant both of the small numbers of crudely equipped and poorly organized Confederates opposing McClellan and of the deep-seated political disaffection in the region that was to become West Virginia. Native loyalist leaders in the northwest counties seized the opportunity to sever ties with the Old Dominion (an antisecession convention in Wheeling would lead to the formation of a separate state) and formed alliances with the Union forces in Ohio to clear the way for McClellan's advance. Until the scattered Confederates, totaling not more than five thousand, neared the area in the Alleghenies which is now the border between the two states, they had been fighting in country at best neutral and at worst more hostile to them than to McClellan's soldiers. McClellan naturally did not emphasize the enemy's deficiencies in his dispatches, but he could not have been unaware of the weak opposition he had faced.

In the main theater, McClellan obviously planned to repeat on a larger scale the methods that had worked so well in western Virginia. Nevertheless, he recognized that a Confederate army entrenched on Virginia's homeland would be a different proposition from the bands in the western mountains.

Having known Southerners intimately at the Military Academy and in the Old Army, he appreciated the passion with which they would defend their land. He was personally acquainted with many of the officers, whom he knew to be soldiers of skill and courage. The Confederates were comparatively well armed — partly owing to the rifles, ordnance and equipment captured at Manassas — and at least as well trained. Their ranks contained a high proportion of hardy, self-reliant country types who had been familiar with weapons all their lives. Then, too, the army commanded by Johnston possessed the morale created by victory.

McClellan had inherited some fifty thousand infantry, whose state of morale, discipline and training was indicated by the need to dismiss more than two hundred officers. In forming his troops, including fresh recruits, into twelve divisions, McClellan could appoint only novice generals to command. Scarcely half of these were potentially more than adequate, and at least two were unfit. McClellan himself had been no more than a captain of engineers and had as much to learn as his subordinates about coordinating large bodies in battle and in maneuver. Little more than half the men he requested came to him, and by the end of the year he could not have fielded more than one hundred thousand combat troops.

Though these were enough to drive Johnston's army, which

numbered less than fifty thousand of all arms, it was unlikely that a decisive battle could be won. No more impetuous than McClellan, Johnston was not apt to commit his troops to battle against unfavorable odds. Johnston had one hundred miles behind him in which he could withdraw by stages. In that withdrawal would come the skirmishes, the rear guard actions, the small battles, which would take McClellan deeper and deeper into the enemy's country, until the Confederates could turn to fight on conditions of their choosing. This, above all, was what McClellan wished to avoid. Even if his career had not been at stake, McClellan could not have justified an advance on solely military grounds for at least three months.

During those three months until November 1, while Johnston showed no aggressive intent, McClellan's personal ambitions became more involved with the retirement of General in Chief Scott. Seventy-five-year-old Scott should have retired without any prodding. His huge body, once an impressive monument to his pride, was wracked by disease and infirmities of age, and, unable to mount a horse, he could only spend his time propped on a sofa at army headquarters. In no condition to direct the details of proliferating armies, the vain former hero clung to his nominal authority and refused to leave the scene of his triumph. After briefly bearing the indignity of McClellan's making minor dispositions without consulting him, in early August he had exploded when his subordinate sent a memorandum on the Washington defenses directly to Lincoln.

Scott wrote the President an outraged letter, accusing McClellan of having continually operated as if he, Scott, did not exist. The accusation was apparently justified. McClellan did regard the ancient Virginian as an "incubus" from another age. But Lincoln did not know what to do with him. Nobody did. When McClellan continued to disregard him, and when the embittered old man could rally no support for his case, Scott made use of a new law which permitted him to retire on November 1 with full honors. Not until then did the "Young Napoleon" assume the title and full duties of general in chief.

Before this immediate ambition was fulfilled, McClellan began to be criticized for not taking action against Johnston's army. Both Radical politicians and segments of the public had grown impatient for McClellan to drive the Confederates away. In their growing security from the Confederate threat, and having learned nothing from McDowell's defeat, the civilians began to stress the element of time which McClellan had ignored in the statement of his plans.

While Scott remained general in chief and in command of the Federal forces on the South Atlantic and in the West, no significant action had been taken anywhere. But McClellan was the new hero ·to whom the government and the public looked for action, and Virginia was then the all-important front. By the end of October, just before Scott retired, Radical leaders visited McClellan at his house to try to persuade him to move out against Johnston. They also attempted to force Lincoln into ordering McClellan to advance.

At that stage, Lincoln refused to be a party for a second time to forcing a general to mount an offensive before he was ready. He did remind McClellan that the public could not be ignored indefinitely. Evidently he did not then, or ever, point out the peculiar sensitivity of Republican politicians to the presence of Rebel soldiers within marching distance of Washington. As it was the Republican Party's responsibility to suppress the secessionists, each day the proximity of the Southerners' army mocked the administration's power.

Besides the indignity of their presence, Lincoln and his advisers were haunted by the threat of the Confederates' capturing Washington. If the Rebels ever took the capital, Lincoln could foresee the quick collapse of the war and, with it, the Republican Party.

It was not that McClellan was insensitive to political considerations, or that, as accused, he was politically purblind. McClellan played small politics when it suited his purpose, but he was thinking in the larger political meaning of restoring peace to a united nation and that objective was the star to which he hitched his wagon. With this purpose, he was not so unmindful of party politics as he was indifferent to the political future of the Radicals. He certainly had no intention of risking his own future to secure the tenure of the Republican Party in Washington.

This was not something he could explain to the President, nor to anyone else, even if he articulated it to himself. So, as Lincoln had not committed himself to McClellan, in turn the general did not tell the President the reasons for his slowness — what his critics were beginning to call his "procrastination" — in attacking Johnston. Instead of explaining why he was preparing a campaign that contained no margin for error, the new general in chief developed the habit of demanding more men, more material, and more time for preparation.

Most of what McClellan asked for was necessary, and was certainly necessary to his plan. The misunderstanding between McClellan and the government, as well as the public, arose partly over the contradiction between his deliberate methods and the impression he gave of the man of action. It was a time of romantic concepts, and the dark young general with the dramatic movements and the flash in his eyes captured the essence of the prevailing ideal.

A vigorous and graceful rider, accompanied by a resplendent entourage, he personified the image of boldness when he galloped by on a black horse, even on his way to a social function looking as if about to rise in his stirrups, swing a saber over his head and call, "Follow me!" In those days people envisioned a general leading troops, sword in hand, in the glory of a charge. No soldier ever glimpsed in Washington so suggested the heroic dream of the assault, its awful beauty and its predestined victory as George McClellan.

While the aura of his presence, the attitude by which men knew him, epitomized the ideal of the era, McClellan was in fact the most modern of generals then active: he was an executive. His talents were in organization and administration. This accounted for his quick rise in industry, his postwar success as a state government executive, and the organizational structure he built in the Army of the Potomac. This structure permitted the army to continue functioning through successive failures in command, changes of command, inner political divisions and crushing defeats inflicted by a physically inferior enemy. But, as a combat general, McClellan hated to go near a battlefield.

This dynamic soldier who disliked battles obviously was unaware of the contradiction between his "image" and the reality. Very much of his own time in expressing its sentiments, McClellan loved to speak and write in a charged prose that evoked deeds of valor, and no other Federal general ever stirred men's hearts as did "Little Mac."

Perceiving no contradiction between his attitude and his methods, McClellan did not see that his promises and his demands were partially becoming excuses for a reluctance to commit himself. He did know that everyone assumed he would advance against Johnston during the fall, before winter weather made the Virginia roads impassable. It is possible that McClellan was preparing a tentative advance in late October. Then occurred one of those actions whose importance now seems small, but whose effect at the time, particularly on McClellan, was immeasurable.

3

A lull descended upon Confederate military operations after First Manassas. Johnston's forces were no more than observers of McClellan's preparations for overwhelming them. The future leaders of the Army of Northern Virginia held subordinate ranks, some no more than obscure colonels of volunteer regiments, and Lee was off in the western mountains on the bootless assignment of creating harmony between several politically appointed generals. In the bleak isolation, Lee let his beard grow and wrote his wife of the depressing effects of the rain. In Richmond the first discord arose in the government as cabinet members resigned and the President grew resentful of P. G. T. Beauregard, one of the five full generals, for advocating an offensive to break the inactivity. On the plains south of the Potomac, Johnston's idle troops enjoyed the mild September days by extending outposts from Fairfax Court House to within seven miles of the Long Bridge across the Potomac into Washington.

The Confederates were almost due west of the city. The Potomac approached the city at an angle flowing southward, and along those stretches detachments of Johnston's forces guarded river crossings actually north of the capital. From Washington for a stretch the Potomac flowed directly south, passing the old port city of Alexandria, and in that area McClellan's camps extended from the system of forts on the Virginia side of the river to Alexandria. In this position, McClellan's forces on the Virginia side of the river were as close to Johnston's outposts (near Falls Church) as the Confederate advanced line at Fairfax Court House was to these outposts.

On October 19, when McClellan's growing army showed signs of movement, Johnston abandoned his outposts. Then he abandoned the Fairfax Court House line and fell back to Centreville, which had

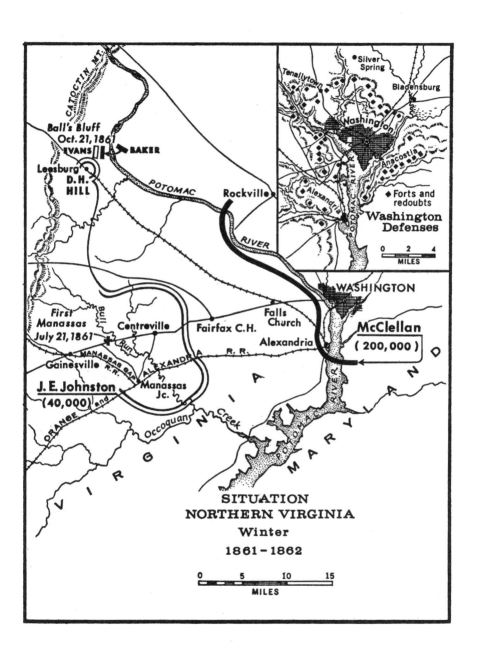

CATOCTIN MT.

Ball's Bluff
Oct. 21, 1861
EVANS   ⟩BAKER
Leesburg
D. H.
HILL

POTOMAC

Rockville

RIVER

POTOMAC RIVER

Tenallytown   Silver
Spring

Bladensburg

Washington

Anacostia

Alexandria

◆ Forts and
redoubts

Washington
Defenses

0   2   4
MILES

WASHINGTON

First
Manassas
July 21, 1861

Centreville

Fairfax C.H.

Falls
Church

Alexandria

McClellan
(200,000)

Bull   Run

MANASSAS GAP.   R.R.

ALEXANDRIA   R. R.

Gainesville

J. E. Johnston
(40,000)

Manassas
Jc.

ORANGE   and

Occoquan   Creek

V I R G I N I A

POTOMAC   RIVER

M A R Y L A N D

SITUATION
NORTHERN VIRGINIA
Winter
1861-1862

0   5   10   15
MILES

served as the Federal base in the battle of First Manassas. Since this was a strong position, Johnston kept his troops spread over a relatively wide area, reaching back to his supply base at Manassas Junction. The detachments along the Potomac, north and west of Washington, remained where they were. In McClellan's tentative movements, detachments from his army in division strength began to make gestures toward crossing the river to the northwest.

One of these divisions was commanded by a professional soldier, Major General Charles P. Stone, and contained a brigade led by a political appointee, Colonel Edward Baker. Colonel Baker had been a senator from Oregon and was a personal friend of President Lincoln; he was one of those civilians who derogated the need of special military training and was eager to win glory by demonstrating how the Rebels could be driven. Baker's brigade was patrolling the Maryland side of the Potomac across from Leesburg, Virginia, where a Confederate camp was located.

As McClellan prepared to put troops across the Potomac between Washington and Leesburg, he directed General Stone to observe whether the crossing of the Union troops farther east had caused the enemy to withdraw on his front. McClellan also suggested that "a slight demonstration" might help induce a Confederate withdrawal from Leesburg. Since a small part of Baker's brigade had already crossed to the Virginia side, General Stone gave Baker the choice of either pulling this force back to the Maryland side or supporting it with the rest of his brigade for "a demonstration." Baker seized the opportunity to advance on the Virginia side with his full brigade.

In his eagerness, Baker advanced without reconnaissance or preparations for crossing the river. He also suffered the same misfortune that had overtaken McDowell at First Manassas by encountering General Nathan G. ("Shanks") Evans, the finest unsung combat soldier the Confederates fielded in the early operations. This wiry, cold-eyed professional from South Carolina was too open about refreshing himself from the keg carried on the back of his orderly to win high regard from teetotaling superiors, and Evans was shunted off to other fronts. But outside Leesburg at a point overlooking the river, called Ball's Bluff, Evans wrecked Baker's brigade in one of the most savage actions of the war.

Baker had crossed the river to attack the Confederate camp supposed to be near Leesburg. Finding neither a camp nor immediate opposition, his troops took up a weak defensive position and waited for developments. Responding to the threat promptly, Evans brought up three regiments and a cavalry unit and proceeded to envelop both of Baker's flanks and drive him back to the river. Caught between Evans and the river (whose bank was a cliff one hundred feet high), Baker's troops were cut to pieces, and Baker himself was killed.

Newspaper reporters, hungry for stories of combat, rushed to the grisly scene where corpses of the Federal soldiers floated in the Potomac, over which they had tried to escape. Secretary of State William Henry Seward, as part of the policy of presenting the "suppression" as a simple matter of dispersing the Rebels, declared a censorship of the news stories. However, misguided Baker had been killed in the action, and somebody had to pay for the death of the President's friend. General Stone was a made-to-order victim for the Radicals who controlled the powerful Joint Committee on the Conduct of the War.

A career officer without political interests, Stone had operated his forces in enemy country with scrupulous regard for the rights of civilians, according to the current official policy. As this also represented McClellan's military policy, the committee's persecution of Stone as a Southern sympathizer was aimed indirectly at the general in chief. Divided by his loyalty to a subordinate and his fear of the committee, McClellan finally chose to protect his ambition and sacrificed the innocent man to the Radicals. Stone was thrown into prison without trial and refused a military court of inquiry; when he was released in 1862, his career and life had been ruined.

The vindictiveness and ruthless power displayed in this affair impressed McClellan with the high cost of failure to those who tried merely to preserve the Union. So recently hailed as savior of the nation, McClellan found himself operating in a hysterical political climate that chilled any burgeoning plans of assaulting the entrenched Confederates. Politicians would find a scapegoat for lives lost in defeat, and if he failed to defeat Johnston he could be the next victim of the extremists' cabal. In addition, a victory appeared considerably less than certain when McClellan, along with everyone else, accepted exaggerated estimates of Johnston's strength.

McClellan lacked any cavalry suitable for reconnaissance, but he was in advance of his time in attaching an intelligence section to the commanding general's staff. It was unfortunate, however, that he selected the Pinkerton Detective Agency, whose methods were not appropriate for gathering military intelligence. These bold-faced, derby-hatted civilians operated, as was their custom, among civilians, and none was trained to estimate the numbers of military units. The fanciful figures the detectives gave McClellan represented Johnston as commanding more men than the whole Confederacy had under arms.

It can never be known when McClellan decided he would not open a fall offensive in Virginia, but somewhere between late October and December — when weather prohibited the movement — he knew he was not going to advance. This decision, perhaps never articulated, McClellan did not communicate to Lincoln, except in tacitly admitting his abandonment of an offensive against Johnston in reply to a proposal from Lincoln.

Lincoln had been forced to the public defense of McClellan against the clamors for action, and when Congress met on December 1 he urged the government and the people to heed the wisdom of leaving the ship to one captain, the general in chief. On the same day Lincoln sent McClellan a suggested invasion route to Richmond which would eliminate a frontal attack on the Confederates' fortified position. Ten days later McClellan answered the President by dismissing altogether the Confederate line at Manassas, and wrote that he was considering "another plan of campaign that I do not think at all anticipated by the enemy."

His new plan was undoubtedly the amphibious operation he developed during the winter and which was opened in late March as "the Peninsula Campaign." In this plan he would avoid the one hundred miles of ground fighting by transporting his army to the Virginia peninsula east of Richmond. When McClellan wrote Lincoln in early December the plan could not have progressed beyond its formative stages, and it is possible he had turned to it simply in order to avoid attacking the enemy in works outside Washington. Unexplicit about details, McClellan continued to feel too assured to need to explain, and the turning point in his relationship with the President came with this somewhat airy announcement of a shift to a waterborne offensive.

4

Lincoln, along with his growing distrust of McClellan's willingness to attack Johnston, personally opposed the waterborne route. An amphibious operation that removed the main army to the vicinity of the enemy's capital conflicted with his obsession with the safety of Washington. The overland route from Washington, seemingly the shortest distance between two points, would keep the army between the Northern capital and the Rebel forces. (Lee, after he was established in command, always tried to operate his army in Northern Virginia in order to keep the Federal army near its own capital and away from his.) McClellan, as a strategist, knew that if his army threatened Richmond, the Confederates would be forced to follow him there.

Unconvinced by this cause-and-effect strategy but as yet unwilling to impose the authority of his office on the general in chief, Lincoln sought a solution by conferring with cabinet members and McClellan's senior generals. While the civilians unanimously supported the direct overland route, a majority of the generals, eight to four, supported McClellan's waterborne route. Still dissatisfied, Lincoln by then wanted to exercise authority without a certainty of how to proceed in the amorphous area of high command.

On January 11 the important post of secretary of war was taken by a strong man who, scornful of the nuances between civil and military authorities, began at once to goad Lincoln into directing the operations himself. Edwin Stanton, a forty-seven-year-old Washington lawyer from Ohio, was the most power-driven and least understandable operator who maneuvered for the Radical purposes.

A Democrat by party affiliation and an abolitionist by sentiment, Stanton possessed such devious skill that he persuaded both Radicals and Conservatives in the Republican Party to believe him their friend. He cultivated a useful intimacy with Conservative Democrat McClellan while worming his way into a post of power in the administration he regarded as "imbecile." No sooner had he assumed office than the emotionally bilious man turned on McClellan and worked against him with the President, though he privately referred to Lincoln as "the original gorilla."

An irascible sufferer from asthma, given to maniacal rages at subordinates, Stanton seemed to find no gratification except in a frenzy of work, and his unprincipled drive to power is properly a clinical study. Hating slavery, he hated all Southerners along with it, and was one of the most vindictive of the Radicals who justified destruction by equating slave ownership with disloyalty.

Once established as an absolute despot in the War Department, Stanton made decisions and gave orders that remain unexplainable. If he did not wish to thwart McClellan in order to prolong the war — as McClellan came to believe — the interferences with McClellan after his ascendancy could not have been better designed to achieve that end.

Around the time of Stanton's assumption of power, McClellan began to be referred to as "not a good Union man." As viewed by such as Stanton, Benjamin Wade, Zachariah Chandler, Thaddeus Stevens, and the transcendentally self-righteous Charles Sumner, McClellan certainly was not a good Union man with his purpose of restoring peace and preserving the Union. Within this suspect purpose, McClellan was further adjudged guilty of not disliking Southerners.

On the contrary, McClellan disliked the fanatics — those so-called "fanatics for freedom" who were also fanatics for total war carried to other people. McClellan, with all his weaknesses of vanity and the afflatus from popularity, was directed by a native decency which caused him to doubt that acts motivated by hatred could achieve a moral or political good. As he did not bother to be diplomatic with this attitude, whisperings soon translated "not a good Union man" into an untrustworthy man. These calumnies reached Lincoln at about the time he was deciding to take over the reins, and coincidental with Stanton's appearance. From then on, the relationship between the President and the general in chief deteriorated rapidly.

Lincoln began a series of authoritative moves into McClellan's realm of operations that were awkwardly, even harshly made, as by a man not entirely approving of what he was doing. It was as if, once he decided to ignore the tenuous balances of authority and to deliver mandates to the commander of the military establishment, he could find no graceful way of going about it. His gift for improvisation failed him as Lincoln went from general directives to interference in the details of McClellan's command structure, and he showed the least adroitness of any time in his administration.

5

The President's first move in asserting the prerogatives of commander in chief came little more than two weeks after Stanton entered the War Department. Shortly before, Stanton had warned McClellan that a Radical cabal was plotting against him because of his slowness to commit himself to definite action. Once in office, Stanton began to urge Lincoln to force McClellan to move out immediately. On January 27 the first such directive was given — but not to McClellan. The amazing document called General Order No. 1 was published in the newspapers. Along with the reading public on both sides, McClellan read that his army was to advance against Johnston on February 22.

The arbitrary date was chosen for the sentimental reason that it fell on the birthday of an earlier Virginia Rebel, George Washington. No regard was given the weather conditions in late February nor the condition of the roads. Four days later an additional directive, Special Order No. 1, defined the routes the troops under McClellan's command would follow. At this unexpected turn, the general bestirred himself and asked that he be allowed to submit his counterplan in detail. In agreeing, Lincoln sent him a catechizing letter which McClellan was to answer as a means of explaining why his plan was better than the President's.

However far McClellan's plan may have progressed before he was forced to defend it, his February 3 document was written with the clarity and conviction of a professional elucidating the techniques of his craft. The letter was long, much too long, and its unnecessary preamble could be interpreted either as defensiveness or as the natural response of a man convinced of the justice of his position. In his specific answers to Lincoln's questions, he developed areas beyond anything the civil leaders had considered.

Moving by water to a position east of Richmond rather than fighting mile by mile with ever-lengthening supply columns would transfer the theater of war from Virginia's border — with its potential threat to Washington — to "the heart of the enemy's power in the east," where he would be struck "when least prepared." If successful, the operation would yield "the capital, the communications, the supplies of the rebels; Norfolk would fall; all the waters of the Chesapeake would be ours; all Virginia would be in our power and the enemy forced to abandon North Carolina and Tennessee."

To achieve this objective, McClellan planned to establish a naval supply base at Urbanna, on the south bank of the Rappahannock, one of the tidal rivers flowing into Chesapeake Bay. Along with transporting the army from Washington down the Potomac and Chesapeake Bay, McClellan — with a broader view of the employment of the navy than any other Federal general — planned to avail his land forces of the support of U. S. gunboats on the rivers reaching into Virginia as far as Richmond. He explained that a river would serve as his flank. McClellan's presence at Urbanna would immobilize the Confederate batteries on the York and James rivers to the south, and his army would be little more than fifty miles, in a direct line, from Richmond.

Lincoln made no reply to McClellan's presentation, and the general in chief and the army assumed his silence meant assent. In appearing to give acceptance to the plan by not rejecting it, Lincoln seemed like "the man who convinced against his will is of the same opinion still." It is clear now that he should either have insisted upon his own plan or given wholehearted support to McClellan's. Without history's perspective, the President found himself involved in what was becoming a civil war, and he seemed to be trying to establish control of its direction by reducing McClellan's role to that of a technician.

During February, while McClellan continued his preparations, action opened in West Tennessee under Ulysses S. Grant and Admiral Andrew H. Foote in a joint land-naval advance. Before the end of the month, loss of river forts caused the Confederates to evacuate Nashville, Tennessee's capital and a large supply depot, and retreat to the northern border of Mississippi. On the Atlantic Coast, an amphibious force under Ambrose Burnside captured the strategic position of Roanoke Island in the North Carolina sounds. These unrelated actions were no part of the total front offensive recommended by McClellan on assuming command. This grand design seemed to have been tacitly discarded by everybody, as Lincoln grew determined that McClellan commit his army to action in its own theater. To this end Lincoln demoted McClellan as general in chief and restricted his command to the Army of the Potomac.

Before the demotion order was issued, Lincoln made two preliminary moves asserting the government's authority over the army. On March 8, the President's General Order No. 2 directed McClellan to organize his army into four corps under the command of division commanders appointed by the government. Except for forty-four-year-old Irwin McDowell, the professional soldiers were in their fifties and sixties; none of them advanced on performance during the war and two would resign before the end. Three had voted against McClellan's amphibious plan in the poll taken by Lincoln.

On the same day, McClellan was ordered to move out by March 18, in a directive which stipulated that Washington must be protected "by such a force as in the opinion of the general in chief and the commanders of army corps shall leave said city secure." The political touch fell heavily in ordering that an army's offensive operation be directed *in committee.*

Three days later, on March 11, McClellan learned that he was no longer general in chief by reading General Order No. 3 in the newspapers. At the same time, Stanton ordered all army departments to report directly to him. When Stanton moved into the vacuum left by the removal of the general in chief, the division of authority was officially established.

Stanton's order was incomparably more far-reaching than it appeared on the surface. As McClellan's control was now limited to the specific objective of the Army of the Potomac, his authority was removed from the other military units in Virginia whose operations interrelated with the movement on Richmond. The troops in front of Washington were placed under separate command, responsible to Stanton, as were the troops under General Nathaniel P. Banks in the Shenandoah Valley.

Banks's mobile force had been designed by McClellan to contain any quick thrust northward from west of the Blue Ridge or to move eastward in the unlikely event of Confederate forces appearing in front of Washington during the advance on Richmond. Stanton evidently convinced Lincoln of the perils of depending upon McClellan's strategic contingencies and insisted on immobilizing forces in front of Washington to conduct a static defense unrelated to McClellan's operations. Thus, the offensive was opened with split objectives — one under McClellan and the other under Stanton.

Stanton even went so far, during an absence of McClellan from Washington, as to move the telegraphic communications center, which McClellan had established in army headquarters, to his own office in the War Department.

In this atmosphere of hostility and distrust, with military operations in control of two peacetime Midwestern lawyers, and before McClellan could embark his armada, a new, unsettling element was introduced by the Rebels. Johnston's army vanished from the plains of Northern Virginia.

6

The prolonged inactivity of Johnston's forces across the Potomac had caused McClellan to regard the enemy as a static and predictable quantity in the time schedule of his plan. He was right in assuming he had nothing to fear from attack, for Joe Johnston was a general who did not want to fight battles any more than McClellan. But it is likely that Johnston never held any more intention of defending his lines than McClellan of attacking them.

The fortifications that loomed so formidably in Federal estimates were indifferently constructed, and even the winter quarters were crude, primitive affairs that gave poor protection from the damp cold lancing across the plains. Johnston was not an energetic general. While social life at headquarters was genial and relaxed, Johnston was a slovenly administrator and careless about details. He liked to be liked.

As a soldier, his fundamental gift was his accuracy in appraising the enemy's intentions against him, and he could always move his army out of harm's way. As this skill in evasion was not accompanied by any purpose to inflict injury on the enemy, he could never lose a battle. Of course, he could never win one either, but at fifty-five, a lifetime spent in the Regular Army had thoroughly imbued him with the doctrine that avoiding mistakes was the way to promotion. Though the goals were different in a rebellion, he was not among those soldiers from the Old Army who changed with the new conditions. He directed his army as if engaged in a contest without stakes.

With the first signs of the coming spring, Johnston began watching for indications of a Federal movement. Being himself a cautious general, Johnston did not anticipate the offensive which the politicians were trying to hurry McClellan into making. Nor did he think it likely that such a student of military science as McClellan would follow McDowell's unprofitable overland route against a fixed position. Johnston's concern was for a maneuver that would flank him out of his lines. When Johnston suspected that such a movement was imminent, without waiting for *his* President's permission or to remove supplies, he hurried his men out of their cheerless winter quarters unobserved and hustled them southward to Fredericksburg.

Equidistant (fifty-five miles) from Washington and from Richmond on the Rappahannock River, at Fredericksburg Johnston was in a position to move in whichever direction McClellan moved. More significantly from McClellan's viewpoint, Johnston was established on the same side of the Rappahannock as the projected base at Urbanna and could readily interpose his army between the Federal advance and Richmond.

Johnston's troops moved on March 8 and 9, when Stanton and Lincoln were too preoccupied with a simultaneous event to recognize that McClellan, instead of flanking Johnston out of position, had by his delays permitted the enemy to anticipate him.

On March 8 the former U. S. frigate *Merrimack* reappeared in Hampton Roads as the C. S. A. ironclad *Virginia* and tore into the wooden vessels of the U. S. Navy like a wolf among sheep. In startled Washington panic-stricken Stanton envisioned an apocalyptic sea monster steaming up the Potomac to force the evacuation of the capital.

The next day brought news that a countering ironclad, the *Monitor*, had been hastened to Hampton Roads and engaged the *Virginia* in a draw. Strategically, the continued presence of the unconquerable Confederate ironclad would have a long-range effect. By blocking the entrance to the James River, it closed this avenue to McClellan's amphibious uses. Though such considerations were remote from Stanton in his relief from destruction, the fright caused by the enemy's new weapon entered into the complications surrounding McClellan's campaign.

During the respite from interference, McClellan held a council of war to consider alternatives to the Urbanna-based invasion. In originally presenting his plan, McClellan had offered as a less desirable route the eighty-odd-mile approach to Richmond over the flat Virginia peninsula from the base of Fort Monroe. The oldest continuously fortified position on the continent (since 1609), the powerfully constructed fort had remained in Federal possession when Virginia seceded and offered complete facilities for McClellan's purposes. Its wharves fronted Hampton Roads, into which entered the James River, flowing between Norfolk and the peninsula. Though the James River was blocked by the *Virginia*, the U. S. naval supports could use the York River on the northern side of the peninsula.

At that time the York was also blocked to the navy by land batteries at Yorktown and, across the river, at Gloucester Point. McClellan, however, anticipated no difficulty in overrunning those positions and opening the York River. He conceded the Richmond approach from Fort Monroe would lack the speed and "brilliancy" of the Urbanna route, but his officers agreed that it was preferable to the overland route.

McClellan had just read of his demotion from general in chief and he had not then absorbed the implications of Stanton's new authority over army departments. In fact, the general was very slow to accept the reality of Stanton's actual use of separate and conflicting controls, and he obtained permission for his shift to the Fort Monroe route on the assumption of direction of operations between Washington and Richmond.

On March 17 the magnificently organized and equipped army of 150,000 troops began embarking at Alexandria, and on April 1 McClellan boarded the steamer *Commodore* for his date with destiny.

CHAPTER TWO

"We Are Betrayed by What Is False Within"

T HE COMMANDER on Virginia's lower peninsula, Major General John Bankhead Magruder was not regarded as one of the Confederacy's dependables. He was greatly admired for his pleasing personality and courtliness (President Davis called him "knightly"). A bon vivant and gourmet, he was nicknamed "Prince John" in the Old Army for his sumptuous style of living. It was by chance that the colorful Magruder, with his appealing strains of immaturity, occupied the line that suddenly became the vulnerable front in McClellan's waterborne shift to the peninsula.

The peninsula is formed by the roughly parallel York and James rivers which empty into Hampton Roads. From the Federal encampment at Hampton, the flat tidewater land stretched about fifteen miles to the Confederate lines outside Yorktown, the old Colonial port on the York River. From Yorktown to the James River the marshy peninsula was little more than twelve miles wide. A defensive line was established there by General Lee in May, 1861, when he commanded the state forces before the Confederate armies and leaders came to Virginia. Magruder commanded there at the first action in Virginia, then called the "Battle" of Big Bethel, when the Federal political general, Benjamin F. Butler, made a quickly repulsed effort to advance on Richmond from Fort Monroe. When the main action shifted to the Manassas area, Magruder was left with about twelve thousand troops in the unglamorous assignment of guarding where no man threatened.

Though many soldiers would have chafed at being shunted off on the periphery, Magruder enjoyed himself thoroughly as sole commander of a district where the life was bland. In this way, the post surpassed his choicest assignment in the Old Army when he had been a social lion at Newport. He never thought of himself as slighted here any more than he had ever seemed to mind his slow advancement in the Old Army.

A Virginia contemporary of Lee and Joe Johnston, he had graduated one year behind them at West Point, after spending a year at the University of Virginia, where he was a classmate of Edgar Allen Poe. While Lee had resigned from the Old Army with the regular rank of full colonel and Johnston with the staff rank of brigadier, Magruder resigned with the regular rank of captain and brevet rank of lieutenant colonel. Yet, he was recognized for his contributions to the artillery arm, having commanded at the artillery school at Leavenworth, and was frequently decorated for gallantry in action. Evidently, however, his personal life suggested some instability.

The year after his graduation from the Military Academy, Magruder had married the daughter of a prominent Baltimore merchant, Berend Johann von Kapf. The couple had three children. However, the well-endowed Mrs. Magruder found him an unsatisfactory husband and father, and moved with her children to Italy. Magruder saw his family last in 1853, when he was in Paris as a military observer. The trait objected to by his wife was the same that caused his fellow officers to call him "Prince John" — living like a *grand seigneur* on a line officer's pay. He was frequently in debt and, foolish as well as careless about money, sometimes tried to recoup with ill-advised speculations. On occasions he drank too much.

With these traits, Magruder not unnaturally was a man of great charm. He was tall, of fine bearing and handsome face, his dark hair and mustache untouched by gray, and, the most magnificently turned-out officer in the army, a truly impressive figure. Though his manners were florid, he was courteous in the deep sense, possessed native kindliness and ready sympathies and was totally without guile. His childlike qualities made him take vast pleasure in dress parades and fancy affairs, and in addressing his troops and expressing himself in highly individualistic letters to the unappreciative war office. Magruder was the only general officer who wrote reports with drama, and he generously singled out for praise more subordinates than the generals commanding large armies. He had taken to signing his official correspondence "J. Bankhead Magruder," though he entered college as John Magruder.

The character of this naive hedonist was scarcely of a nature to make a fearsome impression on an opponent, and McClellan was probably influenced in his planning by the factor of facing "Prince John" on the peninsula and not a military student with the reputation of Johnston. Magruder was left at the Yorktown line in the face of the armada gathering at Fort Monroe because the Confederacy's departmentalized high command was not organized to do anything else. With all the bureaucratic divisions of districts, no single general was responsible for the defense of Virginia.

As Magruder commanded the peninsula, across the three-mile-wide James at the tip of the peninsula old garrison soldier General Benjamin Huger commanded the district of Norfolk, and Johnston, waiting at Fredericksburg to see what McClellan was going to do, commanded the Department of Northern Virginia. In the middle of March, Lee had been hurriedly called to Richmond from his duties of building the South Atlantic defenses between Charleston and Savannah, but he was given no authority. As military adviser to the President, he was not asked to introduce any general plan of coordinating the separate forces and could only advise commanders in local situations who asked for advice. Magruder, alarmed and excited, did turn to his former fellow-cadet. And it must be said for Magruder that he was not a man to ask for advice and then not follow it.

When Lee took the loathed desk job in Richmond, no one was certain of the Federal plan of attack. The transports sailing into Fort Monroe could have for their final destination the support of Burnside, for an offensive into the interior of North Carolina. If they remained at Fort Monroe, the objective could be the port city of Norfolk or a march up the peninsula to Richmond. With tens of thousands of Federal troops in the area between Alexandria and Washington, those at Fort Monroe could be designed for a diversionary attack to be mounted in conjunction with a major offensive from the north. With all these possibilities, and too newly in Richmond to be familiar with any details, Lee could only advise Magruder to hold fast where he was and to calm down.

Once relieved of the oppressive responsibility, Magruder immediately acted with boldness. While on the peninsula, Magruder had used his time for more than dress parades and dinner parties. Personally stirred by nervous energy, having to do something all the time, "Prince John" was an active commander.

Magruder's line ran west of the Warwick River which, flowing into the James, extended most of the twelve or so miles across the peninsula from Yorktown. Innumerable tributaries wandered off from the Warwick, and Magruder kept the naturally boggy ground inundated by building dams at each of five fords across the river, which also served as water barriers at the crossings. At strategic points, Magruder had erected gun positions.

The old artillerist had trained a number of well-served batteries, around the nucleus of a company of the Richmond Howitzer Battalion. This prewar militia unit, largely composed of educated men of well-to-do backgrounds, had been organized by George W. Randolph, a grandson of Thomas Jefferson's, who became Magruder's chief of artillery.

For his infantry brigades, Magruder had only two officers from the Regular Army to serve as subordinate generals but was developing a group of volunteer officers, several of whom showed promise as colonels and brigadiers. With half his force in the works at Yorktown and, across the York, in the river battery at Gloucester Point, Magruder could place no more than five or six thousand troops along about ten miles of front south of the fortifications at Yorktown. Since this force stretched out would provide no more than a skirmish line, Magruder concentrated small forces in support of the guns at points most readily bridged by the enemy.

Since he rightly suspected that McClellan's whole army would be advancing against him, Magruder placed considerable faith in the morale of his largely inexperienced soldiers. Though Magruder's waterline was not a very formidable barrier, and his fortifications at Yorktown were far from models of engineering skill, he had achieved well in building morale in green troops enduring the ennui and discomfort of garrison duty in a miasmic, debilitating climate and exposed to dreary tales of defeat — territory abandoned in the West, Burnside to the south threatening an inland invasion from the coast of North Carolina, and Johnston falling back north of them. Not only did "Prince John" expect his recruits to stand steady to the grim work assigned them; the men expected to hold their positions.

The one person who did not anticipate resistance was George McClellan.

2

When McClellan occupied his new quarters in the picturesque, hexagonal fort on April 2, he was thinking with wounded vanity and not his usual deliberation. Following his demotion and the restriction of his authority, the day he arrived at Fort Monroe he was handed a telegram from the adjutant general's office advising him that the fort's ten-thousand-man garrison, under General John E. Wool, was removed from his authority and not subject to his orders. The detachment of his base of operations from his area of command could only be regarded as a gratuitous and senseless reduction of his position, and he reacted with the decision to move against the enemy at once.

Little more than half of his army had disembarked, and barely sixty thousand men and one hundred guns were ready to move, but a vitalized McClellan issued orders for an advance the morning of April 5. Not only did the Yorktown lines have to be carried to clear the way for the land advance to Richmond, but — with the *Virginia-Merrimack* blocking the James — the York River had to be opened for the passage of the naval support. Though land batteries were rarely successful against gunboats, Yorktown was situated at a narrow waist of the river across from Gloucester Point, where a crossfire could be brought and the high shores made a difficult elevation for the ships' guns. To achieve his double objective, McClellan's plan was designed with a simplicity that placed no complicated maneuvers on his troops.

From Hampton, the site of the Federal encampments outside the fort, the main road led west bearing north to Yorktown. The only main road leading out of Yorktown, it cut southwest toward Williamsburg. Several miles out of Yorktown the road passed Halfway House, and this was McClellan's objective.

Sending one column along the road directly at the entrenched positions at Yorktown — some of which survived since the Revolution — McClellan planned to advance a second column to his left,

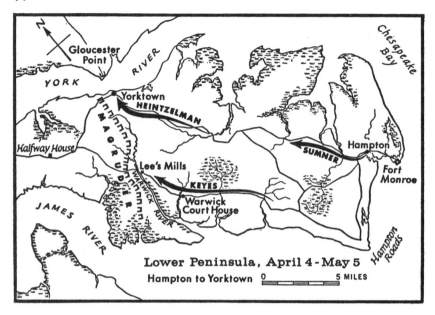

Lower Peninsula, April 4 - May 5
Hampton to Yorktown   0   5 MILES

turning Magruder's flank and pushing on to Halfway House. Once McClellan's troops gained the road in the Halfway House area, Magruder would be forced to a hurried evacuation of Yorktown. In fact, if not sharp, he would be in danger of having all or parts of his command captured.

The plan was wholly sound according to conditions as McClellan assumed them to exist. Where McClellan was unlike himself was in assuming that Magruder's flank was open and — without reconnoitering the enemy's position — in accepting the maps drawn by the ancient General Wool. What McClellan had to contend with was ground, and ground that was most inaccurately mapped. Wool's maps did not suggest Magruder's dams that flooded the ford crossings nor the inundations by which the Warwick River and its tributaries turned the marshy, heavily wooded flatlands into a bog. Nor were Magruder's gun positions shown on the maps. Knowing only that no heavy works extended southward from Yorktown and that the defenses were manned by an Old Army *magnifique* famous for his festivities, McClellan briskly advanced one column on the road to Yorktown while Keyes's corps swung to the left to turn the works and reach Halfway House.

The first check to the advance came from the skies: clouds opened in a steady downpour, turning the dirt roads into canals. On Keyes's movement off the main highway, the bottomless roads became useless for the passage of artillery. Off the roads the foot soldiers, soft from months in camp, floundered through quagmires in some places deep enough for men to drown in.

Late in the afternoon, Keyes's advance column came under sudden shellfire blasting from guns posted where the maps showed an innocent depot. Supporting infantrymen in rifle pits poured in a sharp fire which, if not heavy, indicated that the Confederates were making a determined stand along prepared lines. At dusk the assault force slithered to a disordered halt among the wooded swamps in front of the Warwick River.

It was Keyes who reported, "Magruder is in a strongly fortified position behind Warwick River, the fords to which had been destroyed by dams, and the approaches to which are through dense forests, swamps and marshes. No part of his line as far as discovered can be taken by assault without an enormous waste of life."

Keyes, an uninspired career soldier who had been placed in corps command by Lincoln and Stanton, was an alarmist to estimate that heavy loss of life would be required to bridge the Warwick River for the advance. Had he been placed in that position by Stanton solely for the purpose of drenching McClellan's offensive flare, he could not have been more effective. Once McClellan learned that Magruder occupied a fortified position between Yorktown and the James, he lost all interest in any laurels that might be regained by "rapid movement."

A persuasive legend grew up around Magruder's defense. He supposedly "imposed" on McClellan with a great show of strength, using his bent for amateur theatricals to provide a spectacular demonstration. While a role of "the Great Demonstrator" fitted Magruder's personality, it fitted the facts less well.

McClellan made a close estimate of Magruder's force, judging it to be fifteen thousand, and he was so little imposed upon that he ordered his only impetuous assault of the war. McClellan had first been "imposed" upon by Keyes and his own imagination. That night, without announcement of his intention, he abandoned maneuver and committed himself to a siege operation.

There is no element of assumption about this decision. His chief of artillery, Brigadier General W. F. Barry, reported, "The army having arrived in front of the enemy's works April 5 went into camp, and preparations were at once commenced on the siege. From this date until April 10 active reconnaissance of the enemy's lines and works were pushed by the commanding general . . . for the purpose of selecting a suitable place for the landing of the siege train."

Later, in rationalizing the brevity of his forward movement and the immediate adoption of siege tactics, McClellan stated that reinforcements from Huger and from Johnston (the first of which appeared on April 10) swelled Magruder's numbers to proportions that made direct assault unfeasible. After April 5 Magruder, in nervous expectation of McClellan's resuming the advance, paraded his troops menacingly back and forth, trying to give the impression of double his strength while waiting for the reinforcements. Though these threatening gestures may have exerted some effect on McClellan, a communication from Washington on the night of the 5th removed any intent of an active campaign from McClellan's mind.

The laconic wire from the adjutant general's office announced that McDowell's corps was to be held at Washington for the protection of the capital. The detachment of McDowell, following the enemy's resistance at a position unexpectedly fortified, came like a blow on a person already shaken at being struck. While the discovery that Magruder had fortified lines only stilled McClellan's urge for rapid movement, the withdrawal of his largest corps was incalculable in its effects on McClellan in his role as the nation's hero.

3

McClellan now began the sequence of moves the reasons for which became involved with his later rationalizations and his known, though unadmitted, purposes. In a one-hundred-page report written the following August, McClellan said that he had planned to employ McDowell's corps of forty thousand men to clear the Gloucester Point batteries on the north bank of the York in the event the works at Yorktown "should offer a serious resistance." He moved quickly against Yorktown, he said, in order to overwhelm Magruder before reinforcements could arrive from Huger's command, at Norfolk, or Johnston's army on the Rappahannock. This sounds logical enough. The troublesome point is that McDowell's capture of the Gloucester Point batteries would have forced the evacuation of Yorktown regardless of reinforcements, and McDowell's corps seemed not to figure prominently in McClellan's plan until he thought about it later.

Obviously a siege operation had been in the back of his mind from the beginning, since he had shipped a siege train of 101 heavy guns to Fort Monroe. Yet, once he was informed that McDowell's corps would be withheld, McClellan began to write Washington that his entire campaign depended upon McDowell silencing the Gloucester Point batteries and forcing the evacuation of Yorktown.

It was not that McClellan consciously seized upon and later used McDowell as an excuse. Rather, McDowell became the symbol of the frustrations caused by the government, and all of McClellan's unconfessed anxieties became focused on McDowell's corps. McDowell began to grow in McClellan's mind as the obsessive contingency: *if* he only had McDowell's corps, everything would fall into place.

Whether McClellan was dishonest with himself or with the government, or both, McDowell was used to obscure the fact that McClellan intended to act according to his own preferences while assuring Lincoln and Stanton of his intention to engage quickly in an active campaign. Over McDowell the estrangement between the civil and military leaders became complete.

Lincoln did nothing to bring understanding into the collapsed relationship. He admitted in a letter to McClellan that political considerations directed his interference with the army, but the President could not take McClellan into his confidence to the extent of admitting the dominance of political consideration in summarily detaching nearly one third of a general's army while it was being transported for an invasion. He could not explain that acute concern over the defense of Washington caused him to listen to civilians in protecting the Republican Party's tenure from what might appear, even to unqualified observers, to be a lack of proper precautions for the safety of the capital.

When McClellan left Washington, he had loosely conformed to the requirements of designating fifty thousand troops for the protection of the capital. Though the powerful system of forts, containing 408 guns, was manned by twenty thousand admittedly second-line troops, McClellan had included in the Washington defenses the mobile force under Banks operating in the Shenandoah Valley. Other troops in the general vicinity of Washington and along the Potomac in Maryland brought the total to seventy-three thousand, about equal to all the Confederates then gathered in Virginia.

On March 23, before McClellan himself left Washington, Jackson's small force in the Valley attacked General James Shields's division, attached to Banks, on the outskirts of Winchester. In his repulse at the Battle of Kernstown, Jackson achieved his objective: Shields's division, instructed to join McDowell, had its orders canceled and remained uselessly with Banks in the Valley.

Far beyond this limited objective, Jackson's show of agression (though he fielded no more than five thousand troops of all arms) called Stanton's attention to what he saw as a potential threat from the Valley. Whether in military ignorance or, as McClellan believed, in obstruction to McClellan's plans, Stanton contended that Banks's whole army was necessary to protect the Valley route north and refused to count Banks's thirty-five thousand as part of the Washington defenses.

Then, on April 2, Stanton received a communication from Brigadier General James S. Wadsworth, a wealthy Hudson River patroon, Republican Party leader and political appointee who had been placed in command of the Washington defenses. Wadsworth had waited until McClellan was en route to Fort Monroe before complaining to Stanton that McClellan had ordered him to transfer two good regiments to Sumner's corps and two other regiments to other corps in the Army of the Potomac. Wadsworth stated that his command was "entirely inadequate to and unfit for the important duty to which it is assigned," though he said in the next sentence, "I regard it very improbable that the enemy will assail us at this point."

Two days later Wadsworth wrote Stanton again: "I have now further to state that, after a careful inspection of the troops under my command, I do not find any regiments fit to take the field." Then, asking for Stanton's instructions "under these circumstances,"

Wadsworth pointed out that Sumner's corps would embark for Fort Monroe the next day and, hence, "it is desirable that I should receive your command at once."

Stanton's response to Wadsworth's protest was to withdraw the largest corps in the army from active operations. He then wrote McClellan that the force of Banks and Wadsworth was "deemed by experienced military men" (a fifty-five-year-old farmer) to be inadequate for their assignments, and that McDowell's corps had been detained by the chance of Sumner's corps having begun its embarkation.

Along with this, the adjutant general's office informed McClellan that McDowell would command his forty thousand men in a newly created Department of the Rappahannock, and Banks would command his thirty-five thousand in a separate Department of the Shenandoah. Wadsworth would continue command of the Washington defenses. No Confederate general could have accomplished more than did Republican Wadsworth with a letter that immobilized ninety-five thousand troops in three separate departments for the protection of Washington, with not one Confederate north of the Rappahannock River.

To these orders Lincoln added an insensitive message. Ignoring the possible consequences of McDowell's detachment on McClellan's total plans, he reduced the campaign to the immediate objective of breaking Magruder's Warwick River line. On April 6 he wired the general to get on with that and added the sarcastic line, "This will probably use time as advantageously as you can."

Several days later, Lincoln, evidently recalling the adage about catching more flies with honey, wrote a friendly letter. Explaining in effect that political considerations had caused him to preempt the direction of the army, Lincoln stressed the need of action. "It is indispensable that you strike a blow. I am helpless to prevent this." He pointed out that the public suspected McClellan of repeating the reluctance to attack entrenched works he had shown at Manassas, intimating that any strategic plans McClellan might have for taking the Confederate capital were to be secondary to satisfying the public.

McClellan did not reply that his purpose in coming to the peninsula was to take Richmond, as a decisive stroke in suppressing the rebellion and affecting a settlement, and that his campaign had been designed to avoid the profitless fighting for ground which Lincoln advocated. His opinion of Lincoln, Stanton and the administration had grown so low, and his determination to go his own way so fixed, that he abandoned any inner pretense of trying to work with common purpose. He began to put them off with empty promises and to protect himself against further derangements of his command by high-sounding assurances that he intended to fight as they wished.

McClellan had become unrealistic in demanding, as he wrote his wife, "if they will simply leave me alone . . ." He was undoubtedly "shocked," as his friend, General Alexander S. Webb, reported, by the authoritarian interferences that continually diminished his status and strongly implied Washington's lack of confidence in him. But still regarding himself as the savior of the nation, he was not concerned (as Webb thought he should have been) with restoring himself in the Republicans' confidence: his purpose was only to circumvent those whom politics had placed in positions of authority. Like any brilliant, self-assured subordinate working around a superior in whom *he* had no confidence, McClellan regarded the Lincoln-Stanton combine only as an obstacle.

With all his ambition, McClellan, with the invading forces on Virginia soil, already observed the pillaging and hoodlumism in defiance of his orders, the physical expressions of a hatred he sincerely wished to prevent. Colonel Wainwright, of a New York volunteer regiment, recorded his support of McClellan in his diary and wrote, "Whatever may be the crime of the inhabitants, it is not right for individuals, whether officers or privates, to judge and punish them . . . and the inhabitants [are] our fellow citizens though they are rebels. Our object is to put down the rebellion, not to widen the breach of estrangement, or to impoverish our own country."

Dedicated to this proposition as well as to the avoidance of casualties in indecisive fighting, McClellan most probably (as indicated in a letter he wrote) preferred to restore the peace with no fighting at all. Certainly his plan for forcing the evacuation of Yorktown — which he did not divulge to Lincoln and Stanton — was designed to avoid bloodshed.

Only half of McClellan's siege train was composed of regular siege guns, those pieces on a two-wheel carriage too heavy for the mobility of field guns. The other half was composed of seacoast guns weighing up to eight tons. These could not be moved at all in the field, and could be fired only from stationary platforms. The platforms, derricks, blocks and tackles, and other equipment required to haul and lift seacoast guns into position had been brought along with the siege train. Though these huge guns — 100- and 200-pounder Parrott guns, 10-inch and 13-inch mortars — were included in McClellan's meaning of his "siege train," such monsters could not be employed in a break across Magruder's Warwick River line. Nor did McClellan plan any attack against Magruder's line, as Lincoln urged. When his guns were placed in position, he calculated the weight of their metal itself would force the evacuation of Yorktown and the whole peninsula front.

Since Washington was demanding an attack — to satisfy what Francis P. Blair had called "the carpet-knights" — McClellan pacified Stanton with one of his most grotesque circumventions. He wrote that he was "impressed with the conviction that here [Yorktown] is to be fought the great battle that is to decide the existing contest," and promised to open the attack as soon as he could bring up his siege trains. Manifestly he expected no great battle at Yorktown. Richmond remained his objective, and obviously its defense was the major objective of the Confederate forces.

4

During that rainy April, while the bedeviled Federal army commander was floating his seacoast guns to the front by barges at night, Joe Johnston arrived with his army from Fredericksburg to supersede Magruder at the new main theater in Virginia. With Johnston came the premonitions of retreat. The day he arrived he took one look at the lines behind which Magruder's five thousand men had dared to stand off McClellan, and the next day rushed to Richmond to tell Davis that defense was impossible.

For the only conference he ever requested of the President, Johnston, small and spruce, flanked himself with two large and impressive major generals. Gustavus W. Smith was his haughty-faced second in command, and laconic James Longstreet was his most highly regarded division commander. Johnston needed to muster support in making a demand on the President, for during the preceding month his behavior and attitude had done much to bring their relationship to the stage of restrained hostility.

While McClellan fended off his superiors with elaborate assurances, Johnston used a simpler method: he ignored Davis. Before the army's withdrawal from the Manassas line, Davis had badgered Johnston about forming his brigades of regiments (usually four) from a single state. In this obsession Davis was considering the self-awareness of the individual states as well as indulging his fancy for organizational details. Johnston, concerned with the efficiency of his units, avoided compliance on that point by procrastination. But when, as Johnston's move became imminent, Davis's directives grew contradictory — the inelastic mind trying to provide for every contingency — Johnston resolved the confusion by withdrawing his army without advising Davis or even communicating with him until Johnston was camped on the Rappahannock a week later.

Davis was further antagonized by Johnston's wholesale abandonment of guns and supplies and destruction of mountains of food when he made his leisurely withdrawal, for which he had had two weeks to prepare with no enemy in sight. Though Johnston, as usual, presented excuses, Federal soldiers moving into the abandoned camps were surprised, after hearing tales of the pinch suffered by Confederates, to discover a carelessly strewn abundance of corn, cornmeal and fresh meat, cooking utensils and ovens, entrenching tools and axes. All of these articles represented the sacrifice of private citizens.

The point was that Johnston was a man of the organization, acting as if the Confederacy possessed established machinery of operation, and never assumed personal responsibility for the whole. He brought a more intense rank-consciousness from the Old Army than any general officer in Virginia, and many of them, especially among the older men, retained an acute awareness of the finest gradations of seniority. At the same time that he depended on the makeshift organization, he grew to regard the employment of his army as his own affair. In brief, he wanted it both ways. Claiming he refused to take the commander in chief into his confidence because of leaks in the war office, Johnston implied that he considered the President should know only what he saw fit to tell him.

Davis had tacitly, though never openly, admitted the hopelessness of cooperation between them when he gave Lee the ticklish assignment of dickering with Johnston over the piecemeal transfer of Johnston's army from the Rappahannock to the Yorktown line. When Lee opened the correspondence, Johnston seemed to be pleased to be dealing with his old classmate and friend. However, as soon as Johnston perceived that he would not get his way, he became as uncommunicative with the newly appointed military adviser as with the President. Showing primary interest in his areas of authority, Johnston divorced himself from the total preparations to meet the Federal threat and never once inquired about the conditions on the peninsula.

When the Confederate authorities in Richmond grew convinced that the main threat was coming from the east, and the bulk of Johnston's units were moving to Yorktown, Johnston received, on April 13, all he had ever asked for in authority. Retaining command of the forces left in middle Virginia, and also given command over Magruder's forces and Huger's at Norfolk, Johnston became the nearest approach to a general in charge of Virginia's defenses. Yet, when he hurried to Richmond after one day at Yorktown, he was concerned only with saving the army gathering at Yorktown from a fight.

To hear the coldly courteous general's proposition, Davis had also buttressed himself with two supporters: Lee, whose dark mustache had grown into a gray beard since Johnston saw him last, and Brigadier General Randolph, Magruder's former chief of artillery, recently appointed secretary of war. Both Lee and Randolph had been given their posts in an attempt by Davis to counter Congress's demand for a general in the war office with the right to take field command — in effect, a general in chief.

It was not that Congress was dissatisfied with the President's policies or the majority with his leadership. As the military tide began to run against the Confederacy, Congress felt that operation of the armies should be a full-time job entrusted to a trained soldier. As Davis, with a West Point education (a class ahead of Lee and Johnston) and some army experience before he entered politics, considered himself a soldier, he regarded a general in chief as an encroachment into his sphere of supreme authority. The post created for Lee and the appointment of Randolph, who had early in life served as a midshipman in the navy, was the less than felicitous compromise.

To these three men Johnston stated that it was obvious that McClellan planned to use "artillery and engineering," weapons the Confederate forces could not match, in the development of a siege approach against which they would be helpless. Since retirement was an eventuality, Johnston proposed to make an immediate withdrawal all the way to Richmond. There a concentration of force could be massed by stripping coastal garrisons from North Carolina to Georgia.

Davis listened in silence, his good eye as unblinking as his glass eye, and allowed Lee and Randolph to enter their strong objections. They opposed both the withdrawal from Yorktown and a concentration at Richmond as moves unrelated to the complex of military factors of which Johnston's force at Yorktown was only one element.

Randolph, sensitive to the Hampton Roads area from his service with Magruder, opposed the evacuation of Yorktown on the grounds that Norfolk would be uncovered, forcing the *Virginia* to be scuttled. As this ironclad presented the only obstacle to the Federal navy in the James River, gunboats could be at Richmond by the time Johnston was. Though Johnston could scarcely have been unaware of the threat of the gunboats, which could force the evacuation of the capital, he persisted in his argument.

Then Lee came in on the point of stripping coastal garrisons. With Burnside occupying New Bern, North Carolina, removing troops from that area would invite an inland invasion aimed at the Weldon Railroad, and protection of Richmond's lifeline with the coastal South was basic in all military thinking emanating from Richmond. As for the coast south of North Carolina, Lee had recently returned from organizing state troops and posting them in ingeniously arranged defensive systems, while holding off the enemy's amphibious forces from Charleston to Florida. He opposed a plan that negated his own efforts and exposed three states south of Virginia to invasion from the coast. Also, he knew from his recent experiences in diplomacy with the Southern governors that a sudden removal of state troops from North Carolina, South Carolina and Georgia would precipitate something close to another secession.

Though these were the reasons Lee gave at the chilly conference, fundamentally his concepts were the antithesis of Johnston's. He wanted always to engage the enemy as far from the capital as possible, and he would never by choice concentrate for a purely defensive stand that could exert no military effect beyond the local repulse of the enemy. As Lee was not a policy maker, his recorded objections, as his recorded words in other instances, did not provide an accurate guide to his purposes.

His purpose was to delay McClellan as long as possible, while he rearranged other fronts, seeking favorable developments. A military opportunist, he saw no advantage in following Johnston's primitive notion of concentration. If the Confederates abandoned all positions to mass in one place, nothing prevented the Federals from doing the same thing — and they not only had more men and guns to concentrate, but shorter distances and superior means of transportation.

Lee's arguments, supported by Randolph, probably confirmed Davis in his own opinion, and Johnston's proposition was rejected. He was given the definite order to defend Yorktown as long as possible.

When Johnston left the meeting to return to Yorktown, he had no intention of obeying the intent of the order. As he wrote, "the belief that the events on the peninsula would soon compel the Confederate government to the necessity of adopting my method of opposing the Federal army, reconciled me somewhat to the necessity of obeying the President's order."

In the sense of holding Yorktown indefinitely against McClellan's superior armament, Johnston was wholly sound in predicting that he would be forced to withdraw when McClellan's siege guns got into position. But Johnston intended to use the enforced withdrawal from the Yorktown line to adopt his own "methods of opposing the Federal army" — that is, at Richmond. Since the government did not plan to make the defense at Richmond, Johnston's intention was in conflict with the interrelating operations based upon the government's plan. When Joe Johnston returned to Yorktown the two armies confronted each other in the unique situation in which each was commanded by a general planning operations contrary to his government's orders.

5

The difference between the two generals' plans was that McClellan's, if successful, would accomplish a major advance toward his government's ultimate objective — suppressing the resistance of the states in rebellion. His evasions were over the matter of the means toward ends that were, at least officially, desired by his government.

Johnston was conducting a private campaign with no objective beyond the immediate purpose of avoiding combat until he retired to Richmond. No advantage would be gained by making a stand at Richmond, where no significant fortifications were erected and no forces would be concentrated, since his government did not expect to fight near the capital. Johnston could not even be helped in evacuating supplies and heavy guns from the peninsula and Norfolk, which would be uncovered by his withdrawal, as the government had ordered him not to withdraw.

While the two generals went their secret ways, Joe Johnston, like McClellan, commanded the affection and respect of his troops. To many observers he appeared the "beau ideal of a soldier," and he talked so intelligently of the science of war that his admirers believed him the greatest general of them all. It was partly because, when not stiffened in protection of his ego, he was so attractive a person, that men wanted to believe in him. His subordinates never saw the prickly aspects of personality he presented to Davis and in correspondence to Lee, and never experienced the smallness he could act upon when his reputation was involved. They were exposed to the engaging manner of a warm nature. He wore a spike-shaped chin beard that gave piquance to an intelligent, high-bred face, and his bright eyes reflected a humor rare among Civil War heroes. To his intimates at headquarters he was an unforgettably good companion. Also, he never worked anybody hard.

In command of the army he had brought from Manassas for as long as McClellan had commanded the Army of the Potomac,

Johnston fielded a relatively loose organization. This was partly because of Davis's refusal to permit Johnston to form his divisions into semiautonomous units of corps. (One President denied a general's wishes for corps formation, while the other President forced the formation of corps before his general was ready.) Within the somewhat sprawling structure of his army, Johnston had sensibly spread his professionals from the Old Army throughout the brigades; on the whole he had made sound choices in the men he advanced in command, and his regiments — the basic unit in the Confederate armies, then averaging from three hundred to five hundred men — had a high proportion of good, or potentially good, leadership in colonels drawn largely from civilian life.

Fundamentally, Johnston's slothfulness about details created a laxness in the operation of the complementary services such as ordnance and supply. The artillery units were poorly organized and badly supervised. Staff work was mostly primitive, and the commanding general's personal staff, highly agreeable socially, was worthless for serious work. Throughout the whole, among officers and men, the tone was slack.

During the last two weeks of April, while waiting for McClellan's siege guns to be engineered into position, Johnston showed no interest in correlating the action on the other fronts — Norfolk, the Rappahannock and the Valley — with his planned evacuation. His thoughts seemed to turn to a gradual preparation of the government for his withdrawal. On April 24 he wrote Lee about collecting some wagons in Richmond, "in the event of our being compelled to fall back . . ." On April 27 he went a little further, and two days later came right out with it: "We must abandon the peninsula soon. As two or three days, more or less, can signify little, I think it best, for the sake of the capital, to do it now . . . I shall therefore move as soon as it can be done conveniently."

However, later the same day, he advocated a change of strategy to a grand offensive: "Collect all the troops we have in the East and cross the Potomac with them, while Beauregard, with all we have in the West, invades Ohio . . . Please submit this suggestion to the President."

In the interests of harmony Lee did not submit that airy abstraction in strategy to the President. He acknowledged Johnston's proposition as if it were reasonable, and ended by tactfully saying, "It is feared at this time it is impractical."

Johnston apparently forgot his proposed change of Confederate policy, for two days later he sent a wire directly to the President announcing that he was evacuating Yorktown at once.

Though shaken by the news, Davis accepted the accomplished fact with good grace. Saying mildly that the announcement took him by surprise, Davis asked Johnston by wire if the safety of his army would allow them time to remove the public property from the Norfolk Navy Yard. Johnston ignored this telegram.

The next day, May 2, Davis had Lee send Johnston a telegram asking if he could delay his withdrawal a few days. Johnston ignored that also. Instead, he wrote out the order for the immediate evacuation of the Yorktown line. Through faulty organization, the men did not move out of the muddy lines until the night of May 3-4, leaving behind some thirty heavy guns, some of which had been newly sent. This was during the time when families were contributing metal utensils and churches their bells to be made into desperately needed cannon.

On Sunday morning, May 4, when McClellan had at last mounted the heavy batteries in position to throw 176 tons of metal a day, the front from the York to the James was empty of enemy troops. Not one sound greeted his pickets at daylight when they began their cautious actions "to stir up the enemy." At headquarters where General Barry, chief of artillery, was preparing a final ride along the lines before the great bombardment that was to open Monday, the yell swept back from the front, "The Rebs have gone!"

The men felt a natural disappointment, a sense of anticlimax, as they had looked forward to being witnesses to "the splendid sight" of the bombardment. McClellan's supporters in the army feared that his "enemies, who are getting very bitter, will use it as an argument against him that he has allowed them to escape."

McClellan, indifferent to the opinions of his enemies, was probably relieved. He had achieved precisely what he wanted. The road was open to Richmond with the York River open for the supporting navy. The navy would build a supply base on the Pamunkey River, a tributary of the York, scarcely twenty-five miles from the Confederate capital. Near his planned base a railroad had recently been built from the York River to Richmond, and it would be a simple matter for his resourceful engineers to build a spur directly to the wharves on the Pamunkey.

His advance was further assured by the evacuation of Norfolk, made necessary by Johnston's withdrawal; and as soon as the *Virginia-Merrimack* was scuttled the James River would be clear all the way to Richmond. With gunboats on both his flanks, there was really nothing that could halt his army in its sixty-odd-mile march to the Rebel citadel.

None of these significant developments coincided with McClellan's grandiose declarations about the "great battle" to be fought at Yorktown nor with the government's urgency for battle action, and Lincoln only grew more impatient for the nonbloodletting victor to engage the Rebels in the field. Nothing so stirred the public as reading newspaper accounts of men killing each other in battle. Even the most barren victories could, by omitting mention of the corpses and mangled bodies of Union men, give an illusion of "crushing the rebellion."

McClellan was on the way to giving the people the reality of crushing the rebellion by approaching the single overwhelming decision that would lead toward a settlement. However, McClellan's devious dealings with Lincoln and Stanton in his approach to his objective was hardening the mold of divided command. As he advanced to the climax of his campaign, this seemed unimportant to McClellan. It seemed unimportant with Johnston retreating before him and the Confederate defensive operations in eastern Virginia thrown into chaos by Johnston's having broken off communications with Lee and Davis.

The Johnston Era

CHAPTER THREE

Lee Plays at Machiavelli

JOHNSTON did not communicate with Richmond from his May 1 arrangement of evacuation until May 7, when his army had struggled through the mud to the crossroads village of Barhamsville, near the Pamunkey River about thirty miles to the east of Richmond. On May 5 Johnston had been forced to halt his columns at Williamsburg, the drowsing old colonial capital sprawled across the main highway to Richmond, and fight a rearguard action. He did not notify his government of this engagement, though it swelled into a fair-sized battle with both sides sustaining about two thousand casualties.

The authorities in Richmond learned the details from the clusters of mud-splattered soldiers, lightly wounded, ill or exhausted, without arms and their faces gray, dragging their way through the streets already crowded with apprehensive civilians. With the soldiers came caravans of fugitives who, abandoning their homes and farms, fled from the enemy's approach in carriages, wagons, on horseback and on foot. While the city absorbed this forerunning impact of war, Davis and Lee were desperately trying to meet the chain of emergencies set in motion by Johnston's withdrawal, without knowing even what intentions Johnston had for his own army.

Johnston's May 7 message told nothing of where he expected to make a stand, nor anything about his plans. Somewhat ominously, Johnston expressed apprehension over Richmond's safety with McClellan establishing a base on the Pamunkey under protection of his gunboats. Since Johnston must have foreseen the inevitability of McClellan establishing such a base when he proposed a defense at Richmond, this isolated intelligence seemed to indicate that he had no plans for fighting anywhere. It also indicated that Johnston had separated his army so completely from the total operations that he

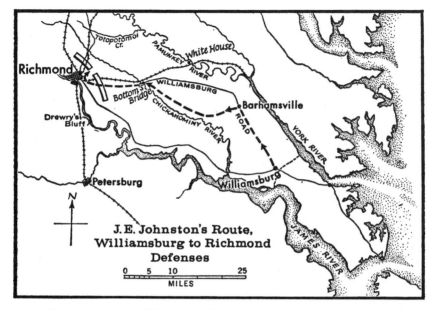

J. E. Johnston's Route,
Williamsburg to Richmond
Defenses

seemed unaware of Richmond's acute, immediate danger from one of the repercussions of his privately made evacuation. As soon as the *Virginia-Merrimack* was scuttled, the James River would be open to the enemy's gunboats all the way to the Richmond docks.

Had Johnston's orders to General Huger to evacuate Norfolk been carried out, the James River would already have been opened. When Johnston, at Yorktown, had failed to answer Davis's wires, the President had sent Randolph and Navy Secretary Stephen Mallory to Norfolk to discover what preparations had been made for removing the ordnance, ammunition and stores from that doomed port city on the south side of the James. Just after they arrived, a staff officer from Johnston had reported to General Huger with orders for the immediate evacuation of Norfolk and the Navy Yard. As they found no imminence of danger there, Randolph and Mallory had countermanded Johnston's order and given Huger the written authority to delay evacuation until portable stores were moved and the *Merrimack* scuttled.

Huger turned the job over to the navy and supporting services, and prepared to march his soft-bodied garrison troops to safety.

Benjamin Huger, an Old Army man in his late fifties, had received no specific orders from the commanding general for his troops. He was simply to "withdraw." As others who had known Lee in the Old Army, Huger wrote him for instructions. Lee, with no hint of Johnston's plans for Huger, ordered his division to Petersburg, south of the James, twenty miles from Richmond. Thus, when Johnston's May 7 message arrived, Huger's column was moving west over the flat, peanut-growing country and the busy groups in Norfolk were working against time, while Lee, Randolph and Davis were urgently directing their attention to the completion of a river fort that might protect Richmond from the gunboats due to come steaming up the James any day.

Though only eight miles from the War Department building across from Capitol Square, this fort was one of those operations which, falling between functions of various bureaus, had dragged along for months under no single authority. Officially listed as Fort Darling, the sheer cliff on the south side of the James was never called anything except Drewry's Bluff, as the site on the property of Colonel Drewry was known locally.

At this bluff the south-flowing James bent sharply to the east for a short stretch and then again to the south. In this elbow of the river an earthen fort had been under haphazard construction since 1861, mostly by the farmers of Chesterfield County. Since their property was endangered, they had contributed their services and money to digging deep gun positions to face the bend in the river. If boats laden with stone were sunk to narrow the channel, gunboats in making the turn would come broadside to the gun positions — much like ducks rising in a shooting gallery — where the ships' guns would be ineffective against the high elevation. However, the volunteers lacked the facilities for sinking boats laden with stone in the channel, as well as the heavy timbers necessary to complete the fortifications.

Just before Johnston evacuated Yorktown, a group of worried citizens of Richmond had visited the site, and their alarm had inspired Thomas H. Wynne, chief engineer for the city's defenses, to write War Secretary Randolph a bill of charges on the specific needs being neglected. Randolph sent the letter with a strong endorsement to the chief of the Engineer Bureau. Danger was then too close for the Richmonders to be satisfied with endorsements passing through the maze of government offices.

While Johnston was beginning his retreat, a committee was formed to see that the work on the fort was completed, and another committee from Virginia's General Assembly appeared personally in Davis's office demanding to know what could be done. This visitation achieved results. On May 5, as Johnston was fighting at Williamsburg fifty miles away, the project became the personal charge of Custis Lee, the general's oldest son and a West Pointer who was to chafe four years as the President's aide-de-camp.

On May 8, while the emergency work was being rushed and General Lee and President Davis were taking trips down the river to gauge progress on the fort, Johnston wrote Lee a second letter. This message complained of the lack of recognition of his authority in the area, and charged Lee with, among other malfeasances, giving directions to troops under Johnston's command. He apparently was referring to the units of Huger's garrison abandoned at Norfolk on Johnston's order of evacuation. He wrote, "My authority does not extend beyond the troops around me. I therefore request to be relieved of a merely geographical command."

This threatening gesture of "resignation" revealed an infantilism in Johnston's relations with the war offices. If he seriously wished to be relieved of command, he would have tendered his resignation to the commander in chief, and at that stage Davis might have accepted it. If he had wanted Lee to endorse the request, he would not have written on at some length about matters of future concern. Johnston, knowing he had acted uncooperatively, had now turned aggressive and accused Lee of not cooperating with him.

After delivering his threat, he complained that the government had not furnished him with information on the other departments of his command, though he himself had broken communication with Richmond. He demanded to be informed "without delay" of the position and number of troops in the Fredericksburg area.

As Johnston doubtless expected, Lee did not refer in his reply to the threat of resignation nor reveal any personal reaction. He did practice an evasiveness wholly unsuspected by Johnston. Laboring to protect Richmond while in the dark about Johnston's plans for the army, Lee had opened a direct correspondence with Johnston's subordinates in the Valley and in middle Virginia. Without authority and skirting the thin ice of protocol, Lee was working privately to effect some correlation between the scattered, static forces neglected by Johnston. To Johnston's complaints Lee, with no hint of what he was doing, gave a literal answer which also managed to constitute something of a rebuke.

"I do not recollect your having requested information relating to the other departments of your command to be forwarded by any other means than the usual course of the mails, and supposed the commanders were in direct correspondence with you." Johnston, receiving what he considered to be an acknowledgment of his authority, asked no more about middle Virginia nor offered any information about his own plans. Dragging his dispirited army ever closer to Richmond, he answered Lee's letter merely by insisting that his authority be recognized in the Valley and in the Fredericksburg area.

2

At the end of his exchange with Lee, Johnston seemed to be beginning to prepare the war office for the evacuation of Richmond, much as he had developed a campaign of preparation for announcing the evacuation of Yorktown.

On May 8, he wrote Lee the strange message, "We depend upon the *Virginia* for defense of the James River. The batteries on the south side [of the James River] are useless." Since Johnston knew nothing of the work being rushed on the south side at Drewry's Bluff, he seemed to be saying that the ascent of the Federal gunboats up the James River would force the abandonment of the capitol.

Two days later he wrote, "A concentration of all our available forces [at Richmond] may enable us to fight successfully."

The next day, May 11, the *Virginia* was scuttled, and the following day the Federal gunboats started unopposed up the James River. Whether or not Johnston learned of this immediately, that day

(May 12) he wrote Lee asking what plans had been made for supplying his army in the event that Richmond fell. Of any plans that he might have had for fighting, he said nothing.

Lee evidently conveyed Johnston's defeatist attitude to Davis, for on May 14 the President called a cabinet meeting. By then hysteria was in the air, and the imminence of evacuation was accepted throughout the city. As Johnston's stragglers and the groups of dispossessed families poured into Richmond from the east, civilians jammed the railroad depots to the south, and lines of carriages, foot travelers and horseback riders flowed across the bridges over the James and to the road to the west. Jefferson Davis, a brave man of unyielding determination, had been so infected by the defeatism that he told the glum-faced cabinet members the purpose of their meeting was to consider the next line of defense after Richmond was abandoned.

The President's military adviser was shocked by surprise, and emotion burst through the composure to which his companions were accustomed. Lee had no intention of abandoning the city without a fight.

"Richmond must be defended," he said in an unusually strong voice.

The President could have dismissed his protest with a word, and there would have been the beginning of the end. But because of the unwonted passion in the voice of one general without command, the group around the President somberly agreed to defend the city. There remained the detail of their ability to defend against the gunboats.

The next day the guns in the unfinished fort at Drewry's Bluff, supported by a brigade of Huger's division which Lee (without Johnston's permission) had hurried from Petersburg, turned back the James River fleet of the U. S. Navy. No deathless lines were given history, such as "Damn the torpedoes, full speed ahead"; and no hero emerged to be forever associated with a decisive action. Yet, nowhere in the war did so few accomplish so much in the significance of the course the war followed.

Night came to the capitol of the Confederacy on May 15 with a sigh of relief. The agricultural Southerners, in and out of the armed forces, held in that first year an almost superstitious awe of the boats carrying big guns that shot at people. In Richmond on that Thursday night, the tense citizens shed their fears of this enemy they could not get at. Suddenly their apprehensions were reduced to the danger of enemy soldiers on their land. Though the people by no means minimized this danger, soldiers presented an understandable menace.

But there was no respite for the military authorities. While the hastily gathered defenders at the unfinished river fort were standing off the gunboats, Joe Johnston, not waiting for the outcome, moved his army across the Chickahominy River, the last barrier between Richmond and the enemy. The swampy Chickahominy coursed in an arc from north to east of Richmond, growing broader where it crossed the Williamsburg Road at Bottom's Bridge, twelve miles due east of the capitol. With every man in the war offices expecting Johnston to make his stand at the Chickahominy, the uncommunicative general did not even pause. When Johnston had said he wanted to defend Richmond, he meant literally that.

On May 17, his advance units limped into the old breastworks built during the first months of the war, three miles east of the city. Manifestly dismissing any consideration of maneuver, he was beginning the immobilization of his army where the only possible action was defense against a siege. As Johnston himself had steadily maintained that in such a contest he lacked the weapons to contain McClellan, and as conditions at Richmond were the same as they had been at Yorktown, what plans could he have had?

Johnston did not inform the War Department even of his whereabouts. Postmaster General John Henninger Reagan, upon hearing on the streets that the army was withdrawing toward Richmond, had ridden to the east to look up friends in Texas regiments, and found them making camp on the outskirts of the city. When he told Davis, the President refused to accept the civilian's report. Mounting a horse, Davis rode down the steep hill of Shockoe Valley and then went galloping through Church Hill, the old, original section of Richmond. With no suburban transition, the shady streets led abruptly into the country, where farms were interspersed with heavily brushed woods. All too soon the agitated President came upon the camps and was directed to the commanding general's headquarters.

Johnston received him with the icy courtesy that one would extend to an enemy during a truce. The tall, lean Mississippian with his erect carriage, smartly turned out with coat and waistcoat of Confederate gray, towered above the spruce little general who was inevitably referred to as "bantam" or "gamecock." The clash was quickly over. When Davis asked Johnston for his plans for the defense of the capital, the general simply refused to commit himself.

Davis seemed more frustrated than angry. There was the possibility that Johnston, who liked to refer to his "father's Revolutionary sword," felt a social advantage over the *arriviste* from the new South. Davis was an extremely self-aware, practically self-made gentleman, and the loathing between the two men dated back to West Point, where awareness of class lines had produced other lasting personal antagonisms. Whatever the cause, Davis, usually described as autocratic, acted like a baffled schoolmaster with a recalcitrant pupil.

Back at his home in the gray-stuccoed dwelling called the White House, Davis again showed his bafflement in handling Johnston. He wrote the general a note demanding that he state his intentions, and had it delivered by Colonel Custis Lee, who was to receive the verbal answer. The President's dignified aide-de-camp returned with the information that General Johnston refused to commit himself. By then frantic, Davis had Colonel Lee's father write Johnston that "the President wishes you to confer with him about your future plans, and for that purpose desires you to see him at his office." This note was not acknowledged.

On the same day, Lee received a disturbing telegram from Major General Thomas J. Jackson, the commander of the Valley forces with whom Lee had been quietly developing a separate action. Johnston, his peninsula "campaign" over, was asserting his authority over his distant subordinates.

3

Lee's correspondence with Jackson had begun back on April 21 when, with Johnston at Yorktown, the Richmond authorities had received the unsettling news that McDowell's corps was advancing south from Alexandria to Fredericksburg. As no one in the war offices suspected that McDowell was being permitted to venture only that far south of Washington, every one assumed that the Federal corps — under McClellan's orders — was advancing on Richmond from the north as part of a two-pronged assault. Lee was the only one who did anything about it.

Johnston was not consulted. He had already established his primitive concept of concentration, which consisted of the futility of attempting to match mass with Federal mass at a given point of defense. Lee's concept of strategy was to prevent the enemy from massing, to keep McDowell away from Richmond. In the desk-general's first attempt to practice his theory of disrupting the enemy's prearrangements, Lee hoped primarily to immobilize McDowell at Fredericksburg. But his plan involved opposing four separate Federal forces aggregating more than seventy-five thousand troops, more than in Johnston's army combined with Magruder's and Huger's. To accomplish this, Lee must work with twenty-one thousand troops scattered in four forces and fixed in defensive positions.

In his unauthorized move to remedy the absence of a directing control for the uncoordinated forces from Fredericksburg to the Alleghanies, Lee had to tread softly to avoid arousing Johnston's protests at any intrusion in his area of authority. To the men he must work through, Lee was limited to suggestions, in which he avoided the appearance of conflicting with their commanding general's authority.

The key man Lee selected for his machinations, Jackson, was at that time known principally for his eccentricities and personality clashes. As one of Jackson's clashes, which had led to his threatened resignation from the army, arose over a breach in the proper procedures involving his own area of command, this might indicate a rigidity about regulations. But Lee had seen enough of Jackson's correspondence to others to perceive a more fundamental attitude: the Valley general was chafing to seize the initiative for the purpose of disrupting the enemy's plans.

At that time the Federal forces in the Valley, commanded by politically appointed General Banks (former governor of Massachusetts), totaled about twenty thousand, including a division detached from McDowell. A force of nine thousand commanded by

General John C. Frémont threatened the Valley from the west, and Blenker's ten thousand, also detached from McDowell, were wandering vaguely around between the separate forces. Banks and Jackson were both in the Valley for the purpose of observing the other. The vital line in Jackson's correspondence which Lee had seen was, "If Banks is defeated, it may greatly retard McClellan's movements."

What Jackson was saying was this: when he had assaulted Kernstown with his small force, on March 23, his aggressive action had held Shields's fine division temporarily in the Valley; an attack large enough to be successful would not only prevent Shields from rejoining McDowell, but would insure McDowell's remaining at Fredericksburg. Without being personally acquainted with the thirty-eight-year-old Jackson, Lee recognized a soldier who thought with his own aggressive cause-and-effect strategy. That was all he had to go on when he tentatively opened the correspondence on April 21. And that was all he needed.

Jackson's total force, of all arms, approximated about eight thousand troops, and all the infantry above four thousand consisted of recent recruits, most of whom had volunteered in order to avoid the April 16 conscription act. A large proportion were poorly armed, and some had no weapons at all. His cavalry was commanded by a regional hero, Turner Ashby, a "when knighthood was in flower" type of partisan leader, whose undisciplined Prince Ruperts aroused in Jackson a smoldering disapproval. That this unimpressive force, under their weird commander, figured neither in Davis's worries nor Johnston's immediate plans made it possible for Lee and Jackson to develop their intuitive collaboration.

Two other generals under Johnston's authority, Richard S. Ewell and Edward Johnson, were included in the plan Lee and Jackson discreetly evolved during the last part of April and the first week of May. Edward Johnson commanded a small scratch force in the Alleghenies and Ewell commanded a division of eighty-five hundred of all arms east of the Blue Ridge, between Jackson and Fredericksburg. There was yet another unit, a brigade, at Fredericksburg, which Lee did not include in the operations designed indirectly against McDowell. He did, however, build this force at Fredericksburg into considerably more than an observation unit.

Through diplomatic dealings with the military department commanders in North Carolina, South Carolina and Georgia, Lee was able to gain their cooperation in transferring to Virginia a brigade from one department, a brigade and two regiments from another, and a couple of batteries and a detached regiment from around Richmond. From these he formed three brigades totaling twelve thousand, which, supported by artillery, he placed in McDowell's path. Though not a formidable force, it was no longer an isolated unit to be brushed aside, and Lee put it under the able command of Brigadier General Joseph R. Anderson. A West Pointer, Anderson had operated the cannon-producing Tredegar Iron Works before the war, and he was a superior, energetic executive as well as a soundly trained soldier.

Having put this obstacle in McDowell's direct path, Lee encouraged Jackson to combine with Edward Johnson and Dick Ewell to assault Banks. First, while Ewell was replacing Jackson's division on Banks's front in the Valley, Jackson and Johnson would unite to fall upon Frémont in the mountains and dispose of him. With that Federal threat removed, Jackson would return to the Valley from the west and join Ewell for the major attack on Banks.

On May 8, as Johnston was demanding of Lee that his authority be recognized, the first phase of the campaign was completed. On that day Jackson, with Johnson, turned back Frémont's advance units, under General Robert H. Milroy, at the inconspicuous Battle of McDowell. By May 17 Jackson had returned to the Valley, had united with Ewell and was preparing to move against Banks. Banks had been deceived by the apparent quiet on his front and, assuming Jackson to be harmless, had already sent Shields's division on the march eastward to join McDowell. It was at this point that Johnston made the unwelcome intrusion into his own area of command.

On May 13, as he neared Richmond with no pursuit from McClellan since Williamsburg, Johnston had reopened correspondence with his neglected subordinates, Ewell and Jackson. In his inclination toward a mathematical concentration, he sent Ewell an order to follow any Federal troops east if they left the Valley. As following this order would, with Shields then starting east, wreck the carefully matured plan, Ewell courageously told Jackson he would ignore the order if Jackson, as his immediate superior, would give him the authority. Jackson wrote out the authority with the proviso that it would not obtain if superseded by a later order from Johnston to the contrary. On May 17, Johnston sent the superseding order. Knowing nothing of the conditions in the Valley, he wrote, "We want troops here; none, therefore, must be kept away unless employing a greatly superior force of the enemy."

When Ewell glumly showed the message to Jackson on May 20, Banks was already in retreat northward, where he was pausing at the town of Strasburg on the Valley Pike. Jackson could not accept the order which meant, as he said, "that I must hide my army in these hills," and be content with supinely observing the enemy. Buttressed by Ewell's loyal stand, he violated all his own principles of adhering to regulations and sent a wire directly to Lee. "I am of opinion that an attempt should be made to defeat Banks, but under instructions just received from General Johnston I do not feel at liberty to make action. Please answer by telegraph at once."

It has always been assumed that Lee, on his own authority, wired Jackson to proceed with the offensive. Though some hours after Jackson sent the May 20 telegram, he put his army in motion on what became the famed "Valley Campaign," no record of the message from Lee has been found. There is a possibility that later that day Ewell showed Jackson two new letters received from Johnston, written on May 18, and which, according to the usual time required for delivery, could have reached Ewell on May 20. In these letters, Johnston had reconsidered his orders and reversed his earlier position.

"The object you have to accomplish is the prevention of the junction of General Banks' troops with those of General McDowell." On this new position, Johnston wrote, "The whole question is whether or not General Jackson and yourself are too late to attack Banks. If so the march eastward should be made. If not (supposing your strength sufficient) then attack."

Whenever these letters did reach Jackson, they provided him with authorization from his commanding general, and made it unnecessary for Johnston to be made aware of Lee's activities in his area of command. Actually, the ultimate objective of Jackson and Lee extended beyond Johnston's orders. Jackson followed Lee's suggestion "to drive him [Banks] back toward the Potomac, and create the impression, as far as practicable, that you design threatening that line." It was this move toward the Potomac that comprised the range of the collaborators' strategic intentions.

In his postwar account Johnston wrote that when Jackson asked him for instructions, "They were given at once, and were to advance and attack. . . ." This, of course, was not strictly true. In Johnston's nonconceptual thinking, he was divided between building numbers at Richmond and (after Jackson suggested the attack) in holding the Federals away. Though he finally gave his permission for the attack, after the offensive force had been developed, his sporadic orders had been contradictory, sometimes discretionary and sometimes arbitrary, with a day-to-day type of thinking that could not direct subordinates with a singleness of purpose.

Had the commander of the detached forces not possessed Jackson's initiative (and few did) the Valley Campaign would never have developed to the stage of attacking Banks. Had the commander been less determined than Jackson, or had he lacked Lee's support, the attack would have been abandoned and Ewell headed east before the letters of approval reached Jackson by way of Ewell. Jackson's single-mindedness and determination not to leave the initiative with the enemy made possible the execution of the Machiavellian devices which Lee resorted to in order to introduce strategy in the Confederate defenses.

4

Lee had been able to exercise his unsuspected gifts for behind-the-scenes manipulation because Davis had been too distracted to direct his attention to the Valley and Johnston too preoccupied with bringing his woebegone army to a haven. But such separate lines of command were unhealthy and, when Jackson took off down the Valley on May 20, Lee was reduced to the functions of an expediter of Johnston's demands. Along with performing the chores of correlating the inadequate and autonomous supporting services, Lee was forced to the paperwork of effecting a concentration near Richmond that violated every principle of warfare he believed in.

No sooner had Johnston gathered all the reins in his hands than he began to draw toward Richmond the twelve thousand troops under Joseph Anderson which Lee had assembled in front of Mc-Dowell at Fredericksburg. This was tantamount to announcing to the enemy that the force in middle Virginia held no intention of collaborating with Jackson in the Valley and that the assembling for defense at Richmond awaited McClellan's initiative.

McClellan, himself waiting for McDowell to move south, had advanced slowly and divided his army into two prongs, to make juncture with McDowell. One division from McDowell's troops had been sent to McClellan before he left Yorktown, and McClellan's army now took position outside Richmond with approximately one hundred thousand troops, more or less equally divided into five infantry corps. Two new corps were commanded by generals of his choice, Fitz-John Porter and William B. Franklin, men in their late thirties whom he had known at West Point.

When Stanton had promised to release McDowell, he had made the stipulation that McDowell move due south from Fredericksburg in a line where he would be in "a position as to cover the capital," and McClellan could give him no order that "would put him out of position to cover" Washington. McDowell was to retain independent command of his force, subject to McClellan's orders for cooperation, and a letter from Lincoln gave McDowell the authority to judge the extent of his cooperation. Finally, McClellan was to prepare to welcome McDowell by extending a right wing to the north of Richmond to establish contact with McDowell's left.

The extension of this wing forced McClellan to divide his army across the Chickahominy, where the sluggish stream was widened by the heavy spring rains into from half a mile to a mile of deep swamp. Five miles northeast of Richmond, near the village of Mechanicsville, the Chickahominy turned from a north-south flow into a nearly due east course for several miles before bending in an arc to the southeast and crossing the Williamsburg Road at Bottom's Bridge, twelve miles due east of Richmond. McClellan sent two of his corps across Bottom's Bridge on May 23, and their van approached the crossroads of Seven Pines, about seven miles from the streets of Richmond. The three corps of Porter, Franklin and oldtimer Sumner advanced along the north bank of the river toward Mechanicsville, Porter, in the lead, fanning out to the north.

Between the two wings ran the Richmond and York River Railroad which, crossing the river at Dispatch Station, was connected by the new spur with McClellan's base at White House Landing, on the Pamunkey River, about twenty miles east of Richmond. The White House plantation had been the home of Martha Custis when she had married George Washington, and the property had been inherited by her great-great-grandson, "Rooney" Lee, General Lee's son and a colonel in Stuart's cavalry. Mrs. R. E. Lee had been in residence there when the Federal troops took possession, and, through those gallantries typical of McClellan, the partly crippled lady had been ceremoniously escorted through the lines. McClellan, fearing nothing from Johnston, had remained a week at the landing, where there had been erected a small city of supply, two square miles, connected by boat with Washington and New York, and by rail and road with his advance forces on both sides of the Chickahominy.

When he advanced Porter's corps toward Mechanicsville, only five miles northeast of Richmond, McClellan, as open in his intentions as was Johnston, in effect was announcing to the Confederates that he was disposing his army to join McDowell coming from the north. This move was more dreaded by Lee than an attack from the east. Fifteen miles north of Richmond the Chickahominy thinned out into little branches near its rise, and provided no water barrier to enemy movements to the west. There the enemy could operate against the Virginia Central Railroad, the South's essential link with the Valley, and McDowell's move from Fredericksburg exposed this line of communication to destruction.

There was nothing Lee could do about it when Johnston shifted Joseph Anderson's twelve thousand men to Hanover Junction, where the Virginia Central crossed the Richmond, Fredericksburg and Potomac Railroad no more than twenty-five miles from Richmond. Not only did this move leave the railroad tracks unguarded to the west, but Johnston was gradually shifting the troops southward, between the highway and the R.F.&P., ever nearer to Richmond.

Worse, Johnston stationed a detached brigade, newly arrived from North Carolina, on the railroad east of Hanover Junction, near Patrick Henry's old town of Hanover Court House. These four thousand green troops, commanded by a civilian volunteer, L.

O'Bryan Branch, comprised one more of the units which Lee had been able to shift from the North Carolina Department when General Burnside's inland threat from New Bern had shown no signs of life. Isolated from Anderson and potentially on McClellan's line of communication, Branch's position invited attack.

What Johnston planned to do with this troop disposition Lee had no way of guessing. Davis had again ridden out to Johnston's headquarters house where, like a reporter prying when he wasn't wanted, the President had received a "no comment" to his questions on Johnston's plans. The Richmond authorities could not even be certain he planned to defend the city at all.

Johnston's main army (53,688 according to his May 21 report) was placed at an angle facing the Federal advance at Seven Pines to the east and guarding the Chickahominy River crossings to the north, from New Bridge to the bridges leading to Mechanicsville. But the soldiers were not put to work fortifying the weak lines which had been little more than sketched on the terrain during Lee's first hasty defensive preparations for the whole state in the spring of the year before. The only digging going on was in nearby Oakwood Cemetery for the daily burials of men who succumbed to camp diseases.

Davis's later disbelief in Johnston's willingness to fight was planted during those wet days at the end of May, when the harassed men in Richmond must have considered the probability that Johnston would already have prepared for a withdrawal if it were possible, as at Yorktown, to retire through Richmond against the government's wishes. But, with Lee having gained the President's confidence and at hand, probably Davis would have relieved Johnston of command had he tried to evade the fight at Richmond. And, however Johnston might refuse to include the commander in chief in his confidence, there was no mistaking the firmness in his attitude regarding his plans for *the defense of Richmond*.

Knowing that he would be forced by the authorities and eventually by McClellan to fight at Richmond, Johnston was goaded to break his inanition — though not his silence — by a misunderstanding of the enemy's intentions.

5

Unknown to the Confederates, on May 24 McDowell at last received orders from Washington releasing his troops from their desuetude. The Jackson-Ewell attack on Banks had not come in time to hold Shields's division in the Valley. Resting from their march to Fredericksburg, these good troops were to move with McDowell to complete McClellan's pincer on Richmond.

With timing that no one could have planned, it was also on the 24th that Banks went in hasty retreat down the Valley to Winchester, with Jackson driving to cut him off. The day before, Jackson had fallen upon a detached Federal force at a supply depot at Front Royal, where he was potentially on the rear of Banks at Strasburg. This fatuous political general, slow to catch on to what was happening, barely pushed by Jackson to make it into Winchester at the end of the 24th. Jackson crowded behind with the obvious intention of delivering a full-scale assault the following day.

When news of this reached Lincoln, he immediately wired McDowell to suspend his movement on Richmond and to return Shields to the Valley. McDowell, perceiving this order to be the purpose of Jackson's movement, protested to Lincoln, and pointed out that it was too late to save Banks. It was. On the 25th, Banks was defeated at Winchester and fled northward in disorder. His loss in wagons was so heavy that he became endeared to the lean-rationed Confederates under the sobriquet of "Commissary" Banks. On the 26th, he crossed the Potomac.

At this point, Jackson had only achieved a local success that need not have been of military significance. However, acting on Lee's suggestion of creating the impression that he intended threatening the Potomac line, Jackson put his hard-marched troops down the Valley Pike to Harper's Ferry. This hazardous move was more dangerous to his own army than to the Federals. His combined infantry had numbered no more than sixteen thousand before losses from casualties and straggling, and he was placing tired troops in a pocket which the enemy could close on all sides.

For all the risk, moreover, the only persons deceived by his threat were Lincoln and Stanton. Though unsuspected by the Confederates, these were the only two who counted. At that point Lincoln and Stanton had assumed complete direction of the strategy and tactics of the Federal forces in Virginia. McClellan and all his generals had been reduced to the status of technicians executing the decisions of the two lawyers.

Stanton again turned poltroon and sent panic-stricken messages to governors all over the United States. Infected by his partner's terror, Lincoln wired McClellan he believed Jackson's offense was a "general and concerted" move that would not have been undertaken if the Confederates were determined to make "a very desperate defense of Richmond." He then ordered McClellan either "to attack Richmond or give up the job and come to the defense of Washington. Let me hear from you immediately."

As McDowell had earlier, McClellan knew the Confederates had succeeded in imposing on Lincoln, and he was angered by the President's preemptory order written out of that deception. Writing his wife, "It is perfectly sickening to deal with such people," he showed in the same letter that he was irritated with himself for all the explanations he had written Washington. To Lincoln he sent an exasperated telegram, stating that Jackson's movement was designed to prevent reinforcements being sent to him, and correctly reported, "The mass of the rebel troops are still in the immediate vicinity, ready to defend it."

In his reply, Lincoln made the unequivocal statement that he considered his civilian's judgment of military matters equal to that of the trained soldier. "That the whole of the enemy is concentrated on Richmond I think can not be known certainly by you or me."

Having dismissed the judgment of the general on that ground, Lincoln then revealed that, like Davis, he had not progressed beyond the preference for giving equal value to all points rather than primacy of value to a significant point. Apparently feeling the need to soften his second withholding of McDowell, Lincoln promised to strengthen McClellan "all I can consistently with *my* view of due regard to all points." (not his italics)

No hint of this disharmonious exchange involving McDowell reached the Confederates. When the Richmond war office learned that Shields's travelers were returning to the Valley, it never occurred to any of them that 75,000 Federal troops, exclusive of the

Washington garrisons, would be immobilized by the flight of poor Banks. With Shields returning from the east, with Frémont's reassembled army in the Alleghenies, and with another force from north of the Potomac all converging on Jackson, a ten thousand-man division under Blenker was in motion and unaccounted for. (It turned out that Blenker was never accounted for: he always arrived at a place where the action was over.)

As far as the Confederates knew, McClellan had not been diverted by Jackson's sideshow. They expected McDowell, minus Shields, to come on to Richmond with the knowledge that Jackson's and Ewell's divisions were entangled far away in the Valley. It was here that McClellan, without intention, acted to confirm their fears over McDowell's juncture with the Federals north of the Chickahominy, and inadvertantly forced Johnston to act.

McClellan, by nature no improviser and with his mind fixed on the expectation of McDowell's corps, could think of nothing except waiting until that part of his army was returned to him. Regarding McDowell's arrival as only postponed again, he improved the waiting time by clearing the way for McDowell's passage in a move that also eliminated a potential threat to his suppy base.

By late May Johnston had drawn the three brigades under Joseph R. Anderson south from Ashland, closer to Richmond, leaving Branch's brigade in its isolated position at Peake's Turnout, a railroad siding ten miles east of Ashland. The first action in the unplanned concatenation was McClellan's disposal of Branch's detached force.

This juicy assignment went to a devoted McClellanite, Fitz-John Porter. Forming his twelve thousand troops, with cavalry, as carefully as if he were taking on a corps, Porter fell hard upon the four thousand North Carolinians, whose war experience had been limited to observing the supine Burnside at New Bern.

Forty-one-year-old Branch, a peacetime lawyer and U. S. Congressman, was one of those natural leaders without military training, and in this first test he showed more valor than discretion. Under the best handling, his inexperienced men could not have contained Porter. As it was, the more bravely the men fought, the more mangled their units became. By the time they sensibly fled for their lives, the brigade had given up several hundred prisoners.

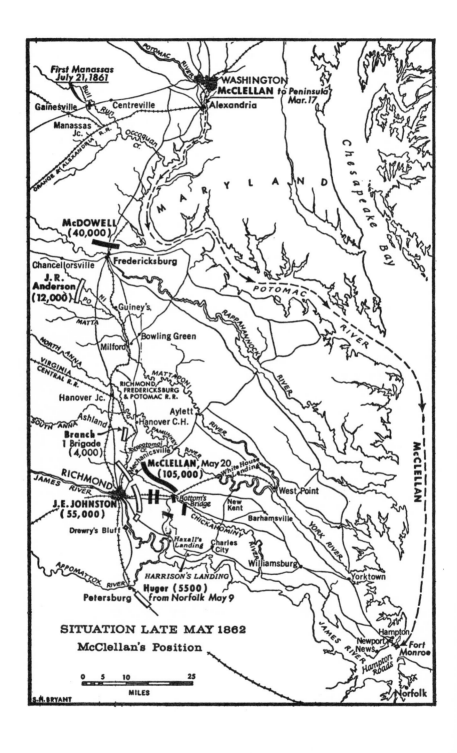

First Manassas
July 21, 1861

WASHINGTON
McCLELLAN *to Peninsula*
Mar. 17

Gainesville
Centreville
Alexandria

Manassas
Jc.

ORANGE & ALEXANDRIA R.R.

Occoquan Cr.

M A R Y L A N D

McDOWELL
(40,000)

Chancellorsville
Fredericksburg

J.R.
Anderson
(12,000)

Guiney's

Bowling Green

Milford

NORTH ANNA

VIRGINIA
CENTRAL R.R.

Hanover Jc.

SOUTH ANNA

Ashland

Branch
1 Brigade
(4,000)

MATTA

PO

NI

RICHMOND,
FREDERICKSBURG
& POTOMAC R.R.

MATTAPONI

Aylett
Hanover C.H.

PAMUNKEY
RIVER

Mechanicsville

McCLELLAN, May 20
(105,000)

White House
Landing

West Point

RICHMOND

JAMES RIVER

J.E. JOHNSTON
(55,000)

Bottom's
Bridge

New
Kent

Barhamsville

CHICKAHOMINY

Drewry's Bluff

Haxall's
Landing

Charles
City

Williamsville

YORK RIVER

APPOMATTOX RIVER

HARRISON'S LANDING

Huger (5500)
from Norfolk May 9

Petersburg

Yorktown

JAMES RIVER

Hampton
Newport
News
Fort
Monroe

Hampton
Roads

Norfolk

Chesapeake Bay

POTOMAC RIVER

RAPPAHANNOCK
RIVER

McClellan

SITUATION LATE MAY 1862

McClellan's Position

0   5   10   25
MILES

S.H. BRYANT

The Federal soldiers, as eager for action as the Confederates, whooped joyously into the charming town of Hanover Court House, where the tavern associated with Patrick Henry faced the faded pink brick buildings of the court-house group.

The little-known "Battle of Hanover Court House" combined with a totally unrelated movement on the same day, May 27, to force Johnston's hand and to change the course of the settlement in Virginia. While Richmond was absorbing the news of Branch's predictable disaster, the war office learned that McDowell's corps had started southward and had reached Guiney's Station on the R.F.&P. Railroad. Forty miles from Richmond, McDowell's van was separated by only twenty-five miles from Porter's victorious occupiers of Hanover Court House.

As the Confederates saw it, the long-dreaded juncture was only a matter of miles and hours. Actually, however, McDowell was only giving his troops some exercise, and the temporary destination of Guiney's Station was in no way connected with Porter's occupancy of Hanover Court House. Hence, because Johnston had carelessly placed Branch at Peake's Turnout, because McDowell had decided to exercise his men, and because the Richmond war office did not know that Lincoln had assumed command of the armies and was immobilizing McDowell, Joe Johnston committed himself to the one action most shunned both by him and by McClellan — a battle.

Since a fight could not be avoided, he made the overnight and secret decision to attack one part of McClellan's divided army before McDowell arrived.

CHAPTER FOUR

Seven Pines

JOHNSTON'S original plan was to attack McClellan's wing north of the Chickahominy, on May 29, and no action in the war was planned with such slovenly thinking or prepared so carelessly. Johnston's aversion to details, especially anything involving paperwork, was typical of him, but the amateur quality of the assault plan looked like the work of a man whose heart was not in what he was doing.

South of the Chickahominy, where at that time McClellan had no more than thirty-six thousand scattered infantry, Johnston left idle the larger portion of his available troops, about thirty-five thousand men. Most of these, under Longstreet and Daniel Harvey Hill, were from his old Manassas army. For the assault north of the Chickahominy, where the Federal corps of Porter, Franklin and Sumner totaled fifty-seven thousand, Johnston was to *attack* with twenty-nine thousand infantry. More than that: the assault was to be made by two separate forces who not only had never operated together but had never seen each other.

One of these was a new division, formed, after Branch's May 27 debacle, of Branch's victims of Hanover Court House and the three brigades under Anderson. Ambrose Powell Hill, brigade commander in Longstreet's division, was promoted to major general to command the new division. Powell Hill had never laid eyes on the troops whom he was to lead in an offensive maneuver.

The whole assault was to be directed by Gustavus W. Smith, Johnston's second in command, in the unofficial role of "wing commander." While A. P. Hill was attacking from the north, Smith was to make a forced crossing of the Chickahominy at the Mechanicsville bridges and the Meadow Bridges. Smith's assault force was to be formed of his own division, under Chase Whiting, and two brigades from Magruder's Yorktown "army." Though Magruder accepted with good grace his nebulous status of division commander in Johnston's army, he could not get along with the overbearing Smith as wing commander, and so his troops were detached from his command for the assault. Neither Smith nor Whiting, who were engineering officers, had ever led troops in combat.

Johnston — and probably Richmond — were saved from the consequences of this suicidal attack by two little-recorded incidents. McDowell, having ventured as far as he dared under his orders, marched his limbered-up troops back to Fredericksburg. Stuart immediately reported the movement to Johnston's headquarters, on the night of the 28th, in time to rescind the order for the assault the next morning.

On the following day, Johnston, having worked himself up to the point of ordering an assault, decided to exploit the separation of McClellan's army and to attack south of the Chickahominy. Reports from D. H. Hill, on the Williamsburg Road east of Richmond, convinced Johnston that the Federals were vulnerable in the area of their advance at Seven Pines and Fair Oaks.

McClellan had grown negligent before Johnston's continued lack of enterprise, and his two infantry corps, made up of thirty-six thousand men, were indifferently disposed in the heavily wooded country between the Williamsburg Road and the Chickahominy. There were no works at all and few troops between Fair Oaks Station on the York River Railroad and the river, where the Grapevine Bridges connected the separate portions of the army. Johnston's plan, simplicity itself, was to overwhelm the two corps south of the river before help could arrive from the other three corps on the north side.

Of the suspended battle of the 29th Johnston said nothing to Davis or to Lee, nor did he mention that he was organizing a new attack for the 31st. Through Lee, he ordered Huger's division to come by train from Petersburg, and these troops camped on the night of the 30th at Oakwood Cemetery on the eastern outskirts of the city. Magruder's brigades returned to their original lines along the Chickahominy to the east of Richmond, and Smith's division under Whiting began to withdraw from the Meadow Bridges. With all this troop movement, it was impossible to keep the knowledge of "impending action" from the clerks in the War Department.

Lee could not endure being uninformed and sent a tactful, verbal inquiry by Colonel Armistead Long, a personable staff officer of Old Army background. To Lee's offer of his services, Johnston answered civilly enough that Lee would be welcome at headquarters but that the only service he could perform would be to send reinforcements. For what purposes he did not tell Colonel Long.

Such was Johnston's determination to keep his battle private that he extended his secretiveness to his own command. Those of his generals who received written orders were given instructions for their own objectives without being told the whole plan, and by some of his later statements Johnston even misled himself.

2

The night before May 31, nature literally showered its blessings on Johnston's plan. A violent downpour during the night turned the sluggish Chickahominy into a torrent that washed over the bridges and completely separated the two parts of McClellan's army.

Major General Keyes, commanding the Federals' Seven Pines–Fair Oaks front, said later that Johnston had been given the opportunity to destroy two-fifths of McClellan's army. That is, the high losses in casualties and prisoners and in artillery and supply could have eliminated the two corps as military factors.

Johnston's orthodox plan of attack was unaffected by the changed conditions. His assault plan had been dictated by the geography of the area, where two roads from Richmond formed the lines of advance. The Williamsburg Road ran due east for seven miles to Seven Pines. North of it, Nine Mile Road ran in a paralleling loop first northeast and then southeast for eight miles to Fair Oaks Station, continuing its final mile to Seven Pines.

McClellan's lines were drawn from south of the Williamsburg Road to north of Nine Mile Road. His picket lines were advanced about three quarters of a mile to the west, toward Richmond, from his main line running between Seven Pines and Fair Oaks. Though the assault would be delivered simultaneously along both roads, the

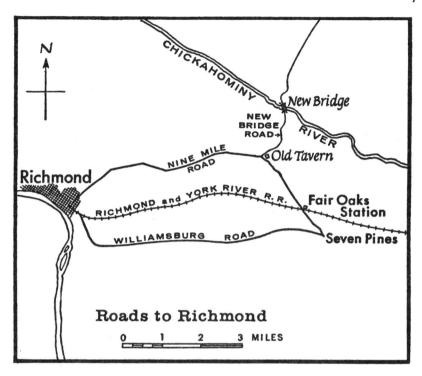

line of advance along the Nine Mile Road to Fair Oaks offered the greatest potential. There the envelopment of the Federals' unanchored flank would cut the troops off from the river and insure their destruction.

The northernmost point of Nine Mile Road was two and a half miles from Fair Oaks, where a road turned off north to the New Bridge at the Chickahominy. At the turnoff for the New Bridge Road stood an ancient tavern referred to by both armies as "Old Tavern." From this tavern, which marked the outer lines of Johnston's defenses, Nine Mile Road sliced at a forty-five-degree angle through screening woods to the clearing around Fair Oaks Station.

Between the Chickahominy and White Oak Swamp the flat land drained poorly, and few farms were maintained in the marshy, wooded countryside. The stretches of timber were made as dense as jungles by the rank vines and briars that come to eastern Virginia in the spring. The rain of the night before had turned the ground into a bog, and parts were in flood. Across the Williamsburg Road, where the Federal lines reached southward to the edges of White Oak Swamp, this smaller though equally ugly version of the Chickahominy provided a strong flank. But across Nine Mile Road at Fair Oaks, the Federal position simply drifted off through the brushy, spongy ground toward the Chickahominy.

To favor Johnston's chances further, both corps south of the Chickahominy were led by political choices of Lincoln and Stanton. The front-line corps was commanded by fifty-two-year-old Erasmus Keyes, who was to resign from the army before the end of the war. His division commanders were Silas Casey, soon to be transferred to a desk job, and Darius Couch, who would be transferred to the West.

The weakly led corps of fifty-seven-year-old Samuel P. Heintzelman had good combat leaders in command of its two divisions — one-armed Phil Kearny, the only general officer not from the Regular Army, though of considerable war experience, and Joe Hooker, a coarse man who would in time maneuver himself into a brief day at the top. Heintzelman's corps was in reserve. Some of his troops had not advanced from Bottom's Bridge and others were no closer to Seven Pines than Savage's Station, one stop east of Fair Oaks on the York River Railroad.

In Keyes's corps, Casey's division formed across the Williamsburg Road, about one thousand yards west of Seven Pines, with his line reaching from near the edge of White Oak Swamp on the south to and beyond Nine Mile Road on the north. Behind Casey, Couch's division formed along the one mile stretch of Nine Mile Road which ran between Fair Oaks and Seven Pines. Couch extended slightly to the north of Nine Mile Road through the clearing at the Fair Oaks railroad crossing. East of Seven Pines, toward Bottom's Bridge, construction of an unmanned third line had been begun by work details.

Around the crossroads of Nine Mile Road and the Williamsburg Road at Seven Pines was one of the few large clearings in the area. Casey's main line at the Williamsburg Road was formed where a strip of woods cut across this clearing on the west, and from this timber Casey's men cut what they then called "abatis."

Later in the war abatis came to mean sharply pointed sticks fixed in a base, like spokes in a wheel, placed as an impediment in front of earthen works. At Seven Pines the troops used the word abatis for a cluster of trees felled in the direction of the enemy. Where the entangled branches and trunks were interlaced with briary vines, twenty-five yards or so of such an abatis formed a position in which the troops fought.

Parts of Casey's line were strengthened by rifle pits, and to the south of the road a pentagonal open fort — formidably called "Casey's Redoubt" — was constructed as a position for six guns. Though such works would later be considered primitive, at that time they presented a considerable hazard to advancing troops. In addition, they gave relatively inexperienced soldiers a sense of protection and a definite line to defend.

Near Seven Pines there were more abatis in a second line, very strong in the woods south of the crossroads, and there the working parties of Couch's division had started digging earthworks. The Federal officers later claimed they had lacked the time to finish either line. There would have been time had the men worked with a sense of urgency. Also, troops were not as physically strong then as they became later and, not having formed the habit of throwing up works wherever they halted in the enemy's vicinity, the men were less inured to the pick and shovel. Casey's men took the time to build a fine camp close to the front line, fitted with luxuries that became a wonder to the Confederate soldiers.

While Keyes's and Heintzelman's corps, with their vast stores, were thus exposed to the Confederates, McClellan was sick in bed at his headquarters on the other side of the river — to paraphrase the Revolutionary verse: "Nor dreamed of harm/as he lay warm . . ." — thinking of when McDowell would come.

Ignoring the enemy while embroiled with his own government, McClellan had allowed himself to assume that he alone possessed the initiative for the battle "to terminate the war" — and practically forced the initiative upon Johnston.

3

Johnston's great opportunity failed to inspire him to make a written battle plan. The assault was to be entrusted to forty-one-year-old

James Longstreet, the powerfully built, self-assured friend whose skillful handling of troops had caused him to rise steadily in Johnston's esteem. Longstreet's "wing," consisting of D. H. Hill's division and his own six-brigade division, was to lead the attack on two roads — Hill on the Williamsburg Road toward Seven Pines and Longstreet himself on Nine Mile Road toward Fair Oaks.

The newly arrived division of Benjamin Huger was to support Hill, and Longstreet was to be supported by Smith's division, under Whiting, then returning from the Meadow Bridges above Richmond. With Smith's wing dissolved, Magruder's six brigades were to guard the Chickahominy crossings and were to constitute the reserve for the attack on Fair Oaks. A. P. Hill's new division, then shifting southward to a position at the Meadow Bridges, did not figure in Johnston's plans. Of Johnston's twenty-four available brigades, seven were assigned to D. H. Hill for the Seven Pines attack and eleven to Longstreet for the Fair Oaks attack, with six in reserve close or relatively close to Nine Mile Road.

Longstreet was the only general with whom Johnston discussed his troop dispositions, in a conversation at Johnston's headquarters house the night before the battle. While neither man ever divulged what transpired, Johnston admitted — in an epic understatement — that there had been a "misunderstanding." The things Johnston failed to make clear or Longstreet failed to understand were the objective of the assault, Longstreet's area of responsibility, and the road on which Longstreet was to attack.

In Johnston's plan, Longstreet was to advance down Nine Mile Road to the area of Old Tavern, deploy there, and attack when he heard Hill's assault open on the Williamsburg Road. Hill's orders were to carry Casey's lines at Seven Pines, opening his attack when Huger's first brigade established contact with one of his brigades on the Charles City Road.

The Charles City Road, branching off from the Williamsburg Road, ran at an angle to the southeast and was about one and one half miles south of Hill's position at the point where Huger's advance brigade would make contact with the brigade, Robert Rodes's, detached from Hill. When Huger approached, Rodes's regiments were to cross the flooded countryside, waist deep in spots, to rejoin Hill. Then Hill's division would advance, its firing providing Longstreet's signal.

To Huger, on whom the opening of the battle thus depended, Johnston had sent two notes the night before. In the first he showed his desire for Huger's three brigades both to protect Hill's flank and to support the attack, if both were possible. In the second he stated that the primary assignment was to protect Hill's flank from any turning movement that might originate in the White Oak Swamp area. The Charles City Road passed through the swamp, and south of Seven Pines was separated from the Williamsburg Road by two and one half miles of bog made impassable by the night's downpour.

Huger's marching orders were clearly to leave his camp at Oakwood Cemetery, near Nine Mile Road, and move "as early after daylight as possible" by a farmer's lane across country to the Williamsburg Road, and thence onto the Charles City Road to Rodes's brigade.

Major General Benjamin Huger, of distinguished South Carolina lineage, was one of the Old Army men who had had all the initiative trained out of him. Then fifty-six, he was a stocky man, growing into middle-aged thickness, somewhat pompous, and not a quick thinker. His troops, though containing some individual leaders of promise, had long been sheltered in garrison duty, and Huger himself seemed characterized by the cadence of garrison life. But, a stickler for following orders, he was dependable in executing routine assignments involving troop movement, and not long after daylight came at four-thirty his lead regiment was moving down the slope from the cemetery.

Turning south into the muddy cross-country lane, the head of the column soon came to a halt where a creek crossed their line of march. Gillies Creek was normally a fordable little stream running between steep banks covered with vines and wild ferns. Now, the rainfall had raised the waters above the banks, flooding a network of small tributaries. But it was not the waters that halted Huger's advance; other troops were there, the halted columns stretching as far as Huger's men could see. They were Longstreet's troops, 14,000 of them, followed by baggage wagons, reaching to Nine

Mile Road and beyond to its beginning on the edge of the city. The columns of fours were halted while a footbridge for the troops was being built.

Neither Longstreet nor Huger was nearby and, since none of the officers at the creek knew anything about the general orders, Longstreet's men insisted on crossing first because they had gotten there first. They "took precedence," as Longstreet wrote in his report, without mentioning that the early opening of the battle depended upon Huger's arrival on the Charles City Road.

Huger's troops, new to Johnston's army and its ways, stood watching while fourteen thousand men crossed the bridge in single file and got their wagons over. With the way open at last, Huger's men crossed the creek and followed Longstreet's route to the Williamsburg Road. Arriving there, Huger's men saw with surprise that Longstreet's brigades had cleared the road. Having held Huger up for hours, Longstreet's division now waited on the roadside for Huger's men to pass.

The morning was well advanced, perhaps nearing noon, when Huger's lead brigade turned off the Williamsburg Road onto the Charles City Road. It was around twelve-thirty, eight hours after they had broken camp, that Huger's bewildered van came in view of the nervously waiting Rodes, and the chain of action for the assault was at last put into motion.

4

Robert Rodes was a thirty-one-year-old Virginia civil engineer, trained at the Virginia Military Institute, whose fierceness in combat gave him the fastest rise of any non-West Pointer in the infantry. He was a tall, bony-faced man with long tawny hair and a piratical mustache which did nothing to soften the resolution in his mouth and chin. He hurried his Alabama troops across the mile and a half of boggy ground, in which the battle-equipped men slithered and sank, with parties breaking off to save comrades from drowning.

When D. H. Hill saw the Alabamians struggling toward the Williamsburg Road, he had grown too impatient from the long delay to wait for Rodes before ordering his other three brigades forward.

Few agree on the times of action in any battle, but Harvey Hill said he ordered the advance at one o'clock.

When his assault opened, Hill was in command of the field. Longstreet and his staff had left Nine Mile Road, but had not yet reached the Williamsburg Road. He and Huger were holding a staff meeting in a house between the two roads. Huger's orders for supporting Hill had made no mention of Longstreet, but Longstreet was determined to establish his authority and informed Huger that he was senior officer by date of rank. Though this was not true, the South Carolinian finally accepted Longstreet's claim of authority, despite the fact that Huger's written orders had come from the commanding general. As Huger rode ahead to join his troops on the Charles City Road and Longstreet's resting troops were put in motion toward Seven Pines, D. H. Hill's division became heavily engaged.

Harvey Hill was one of those men who become very combative when drawn into action. Both intelligent and literate, he had difficulty in accepting the fact that others might be equally endowed and was known for his caustic, outspoken criticism. Just short of forty-one, a former professional soldier who had turned educator in his native North Carolina before the war, Hill suffered a chronic spinal ailment which, he said, made him irritable. He was small, delicately made and, when not bent from back pains, carried himself erect. Though not formal in his manner and a good companion among friends, his expression was austere, and, when excited, his tongue was harsh.

At that stage of the army's development, when the performance of inexperienced troops was disproportionately determined by the qualities of leadership, Hill's gifts for combat were invaluable. The level of performance had little to do with the troops' courage in going into battle: most of the men on both sides were all too willing to fight. Under the impact of battle, the men had neither learned to look after themselves nor to operate in groups, and they needed firm control to advance under fire as effective units. When units lost cohesion, individuals might rush blindly forward to become dead heroes or rush blindly away to leave gaps causing disorder in other troops.

Cool in his determination, Hill maintained a wide range of view, his perceptions were sharp and he was quick to act. In not waiting until Rodes formed on his right, he sent his three brigades forward perhaps a little too quickly. The first brigade deployed alone into the dense woods north of the road, the men suspecting that somewhere in the green and shadowed maze, obstructed by the grotesque shapes of hanging vines, they would be met by the bullets of Casey's unseen skirmish line. The white-faced men, their uniforms darkening with sweat, could hear nothing above the noise of their own floundering through the matted underbrush covering the ankle-deep mire.

This brigade was the new command of thirty-one-year-old Samuel Garland. A graduate of V.M.I. and a soldier of promise, Garland had been with the troops only one week — succeeding Jubal Early, its regular commander, who was recovering from a wound taken at Williamsburg. Behind Garland, and blocked from view by the woods, a supporting brigade was also without its regular commander. Its senior colonel was George B. Anderson, a thirty-one-year-old North Carolinian and West Point graduate. Anderson, like Garland, was a promising soldier, but he was only temporarily in command.

Confusion came quickly to the two separated brigades. On the eastern edge of the woods Casey's skirmish line was established about a thousand yards in advance of his main line at the abatis, with a clearing between the two belts of woods. Green Federal troops had been rushed forward to support the skirmish line, and on contact with the gray figures approaching through the vines, the men broke and ran. Garland's advancing regiments quickened their stumbling advance and overran their own skirmish line. The skirmishers, a Mississippi battalion, not wanting to halt and reform behind their fellows, intermingled with the advancing regiments. The uneven lines came bursting out of the woods, and the excited men, yelling wildly, started to run across the wet clearing toward Casey's abatis.

With Casey's skirmish line having evaporated, its supports were fleeing through the abatis and beyond. Several hundred sick in the advance camp rose from their beds and, joined by the usual skulkers, took off after the fugitives heading for the distant rear. This panicky movement gave an impression of rout that did not reflect the true condition of Casey's front line. However, it brought confusion to the field and incited Garland's disordered regiments to rush pell-mell at the abatis.

There Casey's regiments stood firm and poured a sizable volume of fire into the advancing troops, as the six guns in the redoubt on Garland's right opened with case shot. These pointed projectiles contained about seventy-five lead slugs which sprayed a small area. The Federal gunners were amazed that the Confederates did not falter before the blasts that ripped gaps in their lines. Actually, the men were trying to claw their way into the outer fringes of the abatis where, though close to the enemy's infantry, it would be safer than the clearing.

The regiments had overlapped and in spots had bunched, and brought no concerted force to penetrate the abatis. Young Sam Garland, in his first command, decided the flanks of the abatis must be turned. Sending his staff officers with orders to the left, he rode to the right near the Williamsburg Road. Since Rodes's brigade had not yet advanced south of the road, Garland found his flank being torn and the North Carolina regiment on the flank without a commander. Colonel Duncan McRae, who was ill, had collapsed.

Personally re-forming the regiment, Garland sent an order to push through the abatis. Then he looked around for somebody to deliver a hurried call for reinforcements to Colonel Anderson. He was alone. None of his staff officers had returned from the left, and his couriers were wounded, lost in the woods or had had their horses shot from under them.

During his excitement Garland must have sent a message without remembering it. Colonel George B. Anderson received an urgent call, and his brigade began deploying on the left to turn the abatis. Such a feat as the passage of lines in battle had never been rehearsed in Johnston's army. When Anderson's right regiments advanced, the troops on Garland's left went forward with them, more as a crowd than as battle lines. However, the added weight and pressure along the whole line — even of isolated fragments — began to push the enemy back.

While Garland and Anderson started advancing through the abatis, Rodes's brigade came up south of the road and confronted the redoubt. The ferocious-looking Rodes kept firm control of his regiments (his colonels reported that he personally sent them in), and brought up the first Confederate artillery battery. With the help of sharpshooters who found perches in the leafy branches of the trees and picked off gunners and artillery horses, Rodes's four guns began to silence the guns in Casey's Redoubt and a section on the road.

By then, Harvey Hill had discovered that the Federal flank did not extend southward to White Oak Swamp. Between the swamp and the open flank Hill sent in his fourth brigade, under Brigadier General Gabriel James Rains, to take the redoubt in reverse. Against little opposition, this movement succeeded, and Confederate troops on both sides of the road suddenly swarmed into the enemy's camp. The exultant men captured the guns and turned them on the Federal troops falling back on Couch's earthwork lines at Seven Pines.

Their lines fragmented from casualties and with only a semblance of order, the Confederates on both sides of the road began to fight their way toward Seven Pines. Couch's division was receiving reinforcements from Heintzelman's corps, when Hill's troops north and south of the road advanced separately and without coordination.

North of the road the mingled forces of Garland and Colonel Anderson received timely support on their flank from the first brigade of Longstreet's division on the field. This was well commanded by Brigadier General Richard H. Anderson, a forty-year-old Regular Army man from South Carolina. Parts of these combined forces swept across the clearing to Nine Mile Road between Seven Pines and the railroad.

South of the Williamsburg Road the regiments of Rodes's Alabama brigade found the going tougher in advancing from the captured redoubt to the dense woods south of the crossroads at Seven Pines. Short of the woods, the regiments were halted by a galling fire on the right flank, where Rains's brigade should have been.

Rains was an old-time army man unsuited for combat, whose specialty had not then been exploited. He was fascinated by torpedoes, and on the retreat from Williamsburg had agitated both armies by sowing land mines in the road behind the withdrawing columns. When McClellan protested at this "barbarous warfare," the Confederates agreed, and Rains was ordered to desist fooling with his contraptions.

When Rains refused to move forward with Rodes, claiming a threat on his right, Rodes's shattered units were forced to cling for survival to the edge of the woods. There the men waited for support, while Rains in effect took his brigade out of the fighting.

At that stage of the battle, between two-thirty and three o'clock, Harvey Hill's division alone was fighting the bulk of Keyes's corps, supported by Kearny's fresh division from Heintzelman's corps. This was never intended by Johnston. But since no simultaneous attack was being delivered at Fair Oaks, three fourths of Couch's division had shifted along Nine Mile Road toward Seven Pines to extend Casey's right, as Kearny came up on the left in front of Rodes's single cut-up brigade.

At some point during the action, Longstreet came on the field and assumed command of the battle.

5

In assuming command of the one half of the projected battle at Seven Pines, Longstreet did not assume direction of the field. The big fellow never admitted that he felt something was wrong in concentrating thirteen brigades (approximating thirty thousand infantry) on the single, narrow front at the Seven Pines crossroads, and maybe he did not.

For all his confidence, Longstreet had commanded troops in combat only in the limited action at Williamsburg. Though he had handled his brigades with the poise of an old campaigner, the enemy had been coming at him in relatively open country and he needed only receive attack. In the jungle-like brush surrounding the clearings at Seven Pines, troops vanished as soon as they left the road, and it devolved upon him to direct the total action. The terrain may have been sufficient to confuse him in commanding his first real battle, especially as he misunderstood the objective.

He did not seem aware that a simultaneous assault, to be led by him, had been planned for Fair Oaks. He acted as though he thought the drive at Seven Pines constituted the whole objective and that Smith's division on the Nine Mile Road was merely to support his left. What he actually thought during the battle is impossible to hazard, for his actions reflected only a confused state of mind.

It has always been hard to associate inner confusion with Longstreet because of his unruffled presence on a battlefield. His heavy features were stolid, and above a bushy, chestnut-colored beard his blue eyes looked at the world with aggressive self-reliance. Free of any nervous habits and exuding physical well-being, he put others at their ease with a bluff, male humor. But, within this reassuring exterior, Longstreet's mind labored in faulty response to the situation he found at Seven Pines.

When he arrived near the field where the battle was well advanced, Longstreet did not immediately consult Hill. For some reason he thought of Huger's three brigades then marching cautiously along the Charles City Road toward the fringes of White Oak Swamp. First Longstreet ordered three of his own brigades, half the division, to turn off into the Charles City Road and follow Huger. He assigned this half division to Cadmus Wilcox, without informing him of the purpose of marching behind Huger.

When the handsomely trained brigade of George Pickett approached the field of action, Longstreet ordered Pickett to move through the woods left of the road to the York River Railroad. At the railroad tracks the Virginia regiments of the flamboyant professional soldier, within a few miles of his family's home, fidgeted in idleness while the battle raged to their right. The disgusted Pickett was guarding the tracks, though for what purpose it was never explained.

After these four brigades had been shunted away from the battle, Longstreet received an urgent message from Hill asking for support in what had become a very lonely fight against two and one half corps. It was then that Longstreet sent his first brigade, Richard Anderson's, into action to support Garland. A well-liked, reserved man who had experienced difficulties with the bottle, Dick Anderson led his troops that day with a high-keyed alertness. In moving forward on the left of the disordered advance, he reacted quickly to the looseness developing in the Federal line on Nine Mile Road, and on his own initiative devised a local attack north of Seven Pines.

The appearance of rout that accompanied Casey's withdrawal had caused the Federal flank to contract on Nine Mile Road north of

Seven Pines, and Anderson detached a half brigade under Colonel Micah Jenkins to strike this flank. Twenty-six-year-old Jenkins, a brilliant and scholarly graduate of The Citadel, was one of the most gifted natural soldiers to volunteer with the Confederates. He had with him two South Carolina regiments from Richard Anderson's fresh brigade, and the Georgia regiment of Colonel G. B. Anderson's brigade which had been farthest on the left of the Garland-Anderson line.

Jenkins's three regiments fought their way to Nine Mile Road, halted to dress the line, and then drove obliquely southward back to Seven Pines — "scouring the road," as Harvey Hill called it. By then the Federal defenses were in such confusion that Jenkins's half brigade cut like a projectile through the midst of four divisions — the remnants of Casey's, most of Couch's, Kearny's in support of the Federal left, and Hooker's coming up.

At Seven Pines, Jenkins turned east down the Williamsburg Road, and drove between enemy forces one mile in the rear of the Federal troops still fighting at Seven Pines. At this point, almost surrounded and without supports, Jenkins began to bring his cut-up regiments out. Groping through the dusk, his men exchanged shots with passing Federal units falling back from Seven Pines.

During Jenkins's isolated drive, Longstreet received another call from Hill. This was for help on his right, where Rodes's mangled brigade was hanging on for support that was never coming from Rains. Longstreet sent forward his only brigade then on the road.

This had been A. P. Hill's brigade until four days before, and the Virginia regiments, who had demonstrated their zest for battle at Williamsburg, had been brought to an advanced stage of efficiency and morale by Hill's training. The brigade was commanded by its senior colonel, James Kemper, a boyhood friend of Hill's from Culpeper, Virginia, and one of the politically appointed officers who was to develop into a good soldier. Kemper was destined to be the sole surviving brigadier of "Pickett's Charge" at Gettysburg, where he was brought off the field severely wounded: "a thousand fell where Kemper bled. . . ."

In his first brigade command, Kemper advanced his troops into the miry brush then obscured by smoke. Even before the smoke gathered, the brigade commanders could not see their separate regiments through the vines. Rodes's scattered remnants were fighting in clusters, the furious Rodes himself was wounded, and Kemper deployed his regiments evidently without a clear objective. The peak of the battle was past before he moved up and, perhaps in uncertainty, Kemper did not commit his troops to vigorous or full-scale action. In his report Harvey Hill said, harshly, that Kemper did not become engaged at all. More accurately, Kemper did not become significantly engaged.

The action was obscured from Longstreet's vision, but he correctly assessed that it was hanging at the Seven Pines crossroads. With no other troops at hand he thought fleetingly of the half division under Wilcox he had sent down the Charles City Road behind Huger. For the moment he must have considered some turning movement of the Federal flank in the jungle south of the cross-roads, without being aware that the flooded morass of White Oak Swamp was well nigh impassable from the Charles City Road. Evidently he wanted to trust the movement to the known Wilcox rather than to Huger, for Longstreet sent Wilcox an order to halt Huger and take the lead.

Cadmus Wilcox was a plain-featured, plainly dressed, "no foolish-ness" type of professional soldier of the great West Point class of 1846, which included George Pickett, Powell Hill, Hill's intimate friend and former roommate George McClellan, and, among others, Stonewall Jackson.

Uncertain from the beginning of the purpose of his march be-hind Huger's three brigades, Wilcox did not understand it at all when orders came to march past Huger's halted columns and take the lead. And, hardly had this been accomplished when another or-der came from Longstreet directing Wilcox to return to the Wil-liamsburg Road. Again Huger halted, Wilcox turned his columns about and marched past the puzzled soldiers who had only that day joined Johnston's army.

The half division under Wilcox retraced its course about a mile when a courier from Longstreet brought an order to countermarch and continue down the Charles City Road as before. By this time Wilcox was irritated beyond trying to understand. The three bri-gades, led by Wilcox's Alabama regiments, were closing in on Hu-ger for the second time when yet another order came. Wilcox was to lead his three brigades across country to the Williamsburg Road.

The six thousand soldiers, who had done considerable marching since five that morning, sloshed through the bogs toward the sound of the firing. Sometimes after five in the afternoon, Wilcox's lead brigade reached the rear of the action. After Wilcox deployed his Alabamians, they made contact with the periphery of the fight on Hill's right without accomplishing anything. By the time the other two brigades went into position out of battle range, it was all over.

Huger, adhering to his written orders from Johnston, at last completed his interrupted march in protection of Hill's right. In the shadows of White Oak Swamp, separated from the unseen fighting by two miles, he was not engaged by the enemy, nor did he try to stir up any trouble. A more resourceful leader than Huger would have been bewildered by the goings-on of the army he had only joined that day, and the regulations-minded old soldier acted on the discretion in Johnston's written instructions which advised that "a strong reserve should be retained to cover our right."

At four o'clock, during Wilcox's countermarches on the Charles City Road and at least an hour before his first brigade would start across the mire to return to the Williamsburg Road, Longstreet shifted his attention to the left. This was about the time that Brigadier General Richard Anderson was pushing against Keyes's line north of Seven Pines, and Colonel Micah Jenkins was forming his half brigade for the flanking drive south along Nine Mile Road. Whatever Longstreet may have known of the progress of Dick Anderson's attack beyond his own limited view of the field — and there is no record that he knew anything — he decided the time had come for Smith's division to move from Nine Mile Road to the support of his left flank. Obviously forgetting that Pickett's fresh brigade was posted on the railroad tracks, available for a forward movement on Anderson's left, Longstreet sent a message to Johnston for reinforcements for his left.

It was this four o'clock message, Longstreet's only communication with the commanding general all day, which revealed his belief that the assault at the Seven Pines crossroads constituted the whole battle. While he had thirteen brigades available at Seven

Pines, he seemed to expect that the five brigades of Smith's division should already have appeared on his left. His message said that "he" was driving the enemy and needed Smith on his left to sustain the "drive."

When Longstreet sent the message, the enemy was not being driven, nor — except for Casey's break — were the Federals driven as a force at any time during the day. Trickles of individuals flowed toward the rear, units floundered about in disorder, and after dusk the last regiments withdrew about a mile east of the Nine Mile Road line between Seven Pines and Fair Oaks. But at four o'clock the troops in the worst plight on the field were Rodes's regiments south and west of Seven Pines. There the Federal line, reinforced by Kearny's division, had not budged and before the day ended inflicted casualties to 57 per cent of Rodes's brigade — three out of four men in some regiments.

Longstreet's four o'clock message, misrepresenting his own front and showing his unawareness of Johnston's plan for Fair Oaks, brought no reinforcements. No significant change came to the battle before the fighting faded off with the coming of night. Except for the support of Dick Anderson's brigade in the advance north of the Williamsburg Road, Longstreet might as well have not been on the field. Hill started the battle with four brigades and — with Anderson compensating for Rains's brigade — the battle was finished with four brigades.

That was what Johnston had originally planned, with possible support from Huger on the right, but in conjunction with Longstreet's six and Smith's five brigades attacking simultaneously at Fair Oaks. Johnston never reproached Longstreet for scattering his brigades uselessly on the wrong road, because the commanding general entered into collusion with Longstreet to suppress the facts in order to conceal the "misunderstanding" over his battle plans. It is possible that Longstreet may never have known he was on the wrong road, since for his part in the collusion he was permitted to justify his deranged battle by placing the blame on Huger.

6

Longstreet originally planned to spread the blame for his failure at Seven Pines between Huger and his poker companion Gustavus Smith, on the basis of his four o'clock message stating that the continuance of his drive depended on reinforcements from Smith. He wrote Johnston a week after the battle, on June 7, that Huger's slow movements "threw perhaps the hardest part of the battle upon my own poor division. It is greatly cut up . . . our ammunition was nearly exhausted when Whiting [Smith] moved, and I could not therefore move on with the rush that we could had his movement been earlier. . . ."

Unknown to Longstreet, Johnston himself had been in command on Nine Mile Road, and this criticism of the slow movement not only reflected on Johnston, but exposed the "misunderstanding." When Longstreet submitted his official report a few days later, no mention was made of the Smith-Whiting movement at all, nor of his four o'clock message calling for help from Smith. Gustavus Smith was asked by Johnston to suppress any reference to Longstreet's four o'clock message in his report, which Smith obligingly did.

With Johnston himself therefore in the clear, he permitted Longstreet to write his own version of the battle — even though this fiction was a complete contradiction of Johnston's battle plan. Indeed, Johnston went to some lengths in an effort to corroborate Longstreet's version, denying that he had ever planned to attack on both roads and claiming that the crowding at Seven Pines was what he had intended all along.

With this support from the commanding general, Longstreet was free to concentrate on building a case against Huger, outside the clique of the old Manassas line army. At the same time this scapegoat could be used to explain what Longstreet must have come to recognize was the weird sequence of orders by which he wasted the half division under Wilcox.

In his official report Longstreet wrote, "The division of Major-General Huger was intended to make a strong flank attack around the enemy's position and attack him in rear . . ."; but, as Huger did not get into position, Longstreet was obliged to send three brigades

"to support the one of Major-General Huger's which had been ordered to protect my right flank." In one sentence Longstreet stated
both that Huger's *division* (of only three brigades) had been ordered
to attack the enemy's rear and that one *brigade* had been ordered to
support his right flank, and the failure of Huger's division to get into
position for the attack around the enemy's rear forced Longstreet to
send half of his division to support one of Huger's brigades protecting his right flank. On the face of it, this made no sense, as Huger
had needed no support, nor received any from Longstreet, in protecting a Confederate right where not one shot was fired.

Then contradicting this use of the three brigades with Wilcox,
Longstreet wrote, "The only reinforcements on the field were my
own brigades, of which Anderson's, Wilcox's and Kemper's were
put in by the front on the Williamsburg Road, and Colston's
and Pryor's [the other two with Wilcox] by my right flank;
Colston's just in time to turn the enemy's flank." Written within ten
days of the battle, this report was submitted along with the reports
of the other generals engaged, which stated that Kemper gave only
indecisive support to Rodes, that Wilcox at the end of the day got
on Kemper's right to no effect, and that neither Pryor nor Colston
was deployed on the field, let alone having turned the enemy's flank.

This imaginary accomplishment on the right was submitted in
place of the original line about his "poor, cut-up division," with its
ammunition exhausted, not being able to advance when Smith moved
late. In point of fact, Colston, Pryor and Pickett had not fired a shot
among them, and Wilcox sustained only sixty-six casualties, whereas
Rodes — truly "cut-up" — suffered 1100 killed and wounded, with
only five missing. But this new line, that went into the official report,
attributed to Huger's slowness the failure of the mythical advance to
achieve complete success. However confused Longstreet may have
been about what had actually happened on the battlefield, in building
his case on Huger's alleged slowness, he recorded outright lies which
he and Johnston, who endorsed the report, knew were lies.

"After waiting some six hours for these [Huger's] troops to get
into position, I determined to move forward without regard to them,
and gave orders to that effect to Major-General D. H. Hill . . . I
have reason to believe that the affair would have been a complete

success had the troops upon the right [Huger's] been put into position within eight hours of the proper time. . . ."

As Longstreet reported that his movement started at two o'clock,
after a six-hour wait for Huger, he stated indirectly that he was in
position at eight o'clock. By all records as well as the time sequence
of the developments, at eight o'clock his troops were crossing Gillies
Creek, where Huger was kept waiting, and Hill was fully engaged
before Longstreet's first troops neared Seven Pines *behind* Huger.

The flat lie about the time element was all too well known to
Johnston, for his whole battle plan had been disrupted by Longstreet's crossing of Gillies Creek at eight o'clock. Yet Johnston confirmed Longstreet by writing in his report that Longstreet "was
ready to commence operations at eight o'clock . . ." on the Williamsburg Road, but ". . . unwilling to make partial attack, instead
of the combined movement which had been planned, waited from
hour to hour for General Huger's Division." Johnston put this in his
report in the face of his two written orders to Huger which, making
no mention of any "combined movement" with Longstreet, went
into detail about Huger's support of Hill's right on the Charles City
Road.

Their corroborating reports took care of Seven Pines, along with
Huger, who was never able to get Johnston's support in holding a
court of inquiry to disprove the charges against him. But there was
still the other half of the attack, at Fair Oaks, and this became Johnston's own battle.

CHAPTER FIVE

Fair Oaks

SHORTLY AFTER sunrise on May 31, Johnston was unexpectedly joined by Major General Gustavus Smith in the headquarters room of the house he occupied several hundred yards north of Nine Mile Road. A proud, handsome man, Smith was clean-shaven above a dark fringe along his jawbone and a jutting chin beard that emphasized the force of his clearly defined features. Smith had not been included in the conversation with Longstreet the night before, and he had received no orders for the day beyond those for his division. Since his division remained under the temporary command of their mutual friend Chase Whiting, Smith told Johnston that he had come to establish himself at general headquarters. By implication, he was making himself available in his capacity as second in command.

Gustavus Smith was one of the big names from the Old Army and not modest about his reputation. He had left the army for the quicker success of civil engineering and at the beginning of the war was street commissioner of New York City. As a Kentuckian, Smith had not made his personal decision until after the First Manassas, but such was the esteem in which the forty-year-old engineer was held that Davis immediately appointed him major general with date of rank to give him seniority to all general officers in Virginia except Johnston and Lee. Smith soon became one of the intimates who enjoyed the social aspects of army life at Johnston's headquarters during the long hiatus and regarded himself as a privileged friend of the commanding general.

When preparing for the postponed attack of the 29th, Smith was recorded as showing a "physical indisposition" that was not described. Earlier in the year Johnston had mentioned that Smith's health was "precarious." It is not known if Smith's health influenced

Johnston in giving him no responsibilities for the May 31 assault. It may have been no more than thoughtlessness on Johnston's part in ignoring the sensibilities of the proud Kentuckian.

The result was that Smith became history's witness to events that would otherwise have remained inexplicable. Unlike Johnston, who did not always keep copies of his own orders, Gustavus Smith had the deadly habit of keeping a record of everything. He was also businesslike in obtaining written depositions from other participants and using official records to substantiate and complete his own records. Only by this chance were the events revolving around the commanding general brought to light years later, including the facts that Longstreet had advanced on the wrong road and that a collusion blackened the name of Major General Huger.

2

At around six o'clock on the morning of May 31, while Johnston was amiably discussing his battle plans with Smith, a staff officer of Whiting's arrived at headquarters with the day's first message. Whiting had moved out promptly with Smith's five brigades at daybreak from north of Richmond, turning off from the Mechanicsville Turnpike, as ordered, across country to Nine Mile Road. On reaching the entrance to the road, Whiting found it clogged with Longstreet's troops. Supplying no details, Whiting's message merely asked that the road be cleared for his passage.

Reading this message, Johnston assumed that Longstreet's troops blocked the road in their movement forward. Johnston directed Captain Mason, his assistant adjutant general, to write Whiting a message to quiet his impatience, explaining that "Longstreet will precede you." Though six o'clock was getting late for the entrance to a road to be blocked, Johnston sent no one to investigate Longstreet's progress.

Two more hours passed before another communication was received at headquarters. This time Whiting came himself, looking for his immediate superior, Smith. Whiting told Smith that the road was still blocked by Longstreet's troops, and he was growing alarmed. Smith told Whiting he would send an aide, Captain Beckham, to learn why Longstreet was delayed.

Before sending Beckham, Smith turned to General Johnston and asked him where Longstreet could be found. This was at eight o'clock — the hour when Johnston wrote in his report that Smith's troops as well as Longstreet's were in position to commence the action. Johnston told Smith and Captain Beckham that Longstreet would be found with his division farther advanced down Nine Mile Road, unless he had personally crossed to the Williamsburg Road to confer with D. H. Hill.

Beckham left headquarters, and another hour passed with no word from him. By then it was time for Huger to have established contact with D. H. Hill, and tension began to enter into the waiting. But Johnston sent no officer from his staff to investigate.

At nine o'clock a courier arrived at headquarters with a note for Smith from Captain Beckham. The message read that he could not find Longstreet *or his division* on Nine Mile Road. An hour before, Longstreet's division had been blocking Whiting's entrance to Nine Mile Road. Beckham added that he was riding across to the Williamsburg Road to look for the assault commander and his missing division. Without comment, Smith handed Johnston the note.

The commanding general was shaken. He said Beckham could not have ridden far enough down Nine Mile Road. Then he turned to one of his aides, Lieutenant Washington, and ordered him to ride down Nine Mile Road until he found Longstreet. By then the road was clear for Whiting, but Johnston had grown uneasy. He ordered Whiting to hold his troops where they were, at the beginning of the road, until they heard from Longstreet.

Another hour passed with no word from Lieutenant Washington. No word was to come from Lieutenant Washington that day. Dutifully following Johnston's orders, he had ridden past McLaws's picket line at the New Bridge Road turnoff and on into the Federal picket line. There he was happily welcomed, a staff officer of the enemy's commanding general captured.

The next message to arrive was another note from the enterprising Captain Beckham. Received around ten o'clock, this note read that Beckham had located Longstreet's headquarters on the Williamsburg Road. There his division, with its luggage wagons, was halted to allow Hill's brigades to advance. This was evidently the halt for the

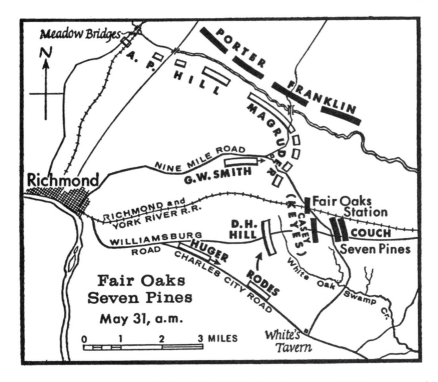

Fair Oaks
Seven Pines
May 31, a.m.

passage of Huger's brigades, for Hill already occupied the ground from which his troops would deploy into action.

After reading this message, Johnston forgot himself for one moment and muttered, "I wish all the troops were back in camp."

Why did he not order them back? It is impossible to imagine that he never thought of calling off the attack. Not knowing Huger had been halted by Longstreet, he perhaps feared Hill's troops would be committed before he could send an aide who would find Longstreet. Perhaps he also thought of all the explanations he would have to make to Davis and Lee. How would it look on his record?

Then, too, he would never again have such an opportunity to catch part of the enemy's army isolated from the main body by swollen waters. His belief that the bridges across the Chickahominy could not be used may have been the deciding factor.

Since Longstreet was on the other road, his troops, with Hill's and

Huger's, could contain a large portion of the enemy, and Johnston himself could direct the Fair Oaks attack. Smith's division of more than ten thousand would outnumber the regiments from Couch's division at Fair Oaks, and reserves could be drawn from another fifteen thousand in Magruder's command. Johnston decided to salvage his assault by assuming personal command of the Nine Mile Road movement.

Johnston told Smith then that the "misunderstanding" with Longstreet may have been his fault, and later he asked Smith to make no reference to it. Once Johnston had made his decision, he seemed anxious to rid himself of Smith's presence. At the time, Federal guns were engaged in routine firing from across the Chickahominy. Though Johnston did not believe the river to be passable, he ordered Smith to take two brigades to the river bluffs to resist any attempt of the enemy to cross. Since these brigades were from Smith's own division — leaving the other three under Whiting — Johnston was pointedly reducing Smith to his official rank of division commander, as well as getting rid of him at headquarters.

When Johnston later filed the report claiming that the salvage effort was his battle plan from the beginning, he wrote glowingly of Smith, whom he had also asked to eliminate from his report all references to the morning's proceedings with Whiting, Captain Beckham, Lieutenant Washington and the like. In his later narrative Johnston embellished his version by stating that Huger's delay of the forward movement "disappointed me greatly, and led to an interchange of messages between General Longstreet and myself for several hours." The first and only "exchange" was Longstreet's four o'clock call for support.

During the day of the 31st Johnston did not know enough about what Huger was doing to be "disappointed." He obviously presumed Huger to have marched ahead of Longstreet according to his original intention, and he expected the contact of Huger's lead brigade with Rodes's brigade to open the action on the Williamsburg Road. Assuming that Longstreet would add the weight of his six brigades to the seven already on the field at Seven Pines, Johnston sent no staff officer to discover the actual conditions on the road two miles away. He turned his attention to advancing the remaining troops along

Nine Mile Road, to be ready at the point of assault when the signal from Hill's guns was heard.

With Smith, the unwelcome observer, out of the way, Johnston ordered Whiting to advance his three brigades to the New Bridge Road turnoff, two and one half miles from Fair Oaks. As soon as Whiting had started forward, Johnston and his staff moved ahead to establish advance headquarters near the New Bridge Road. There they found a house ideally located south of Nine Mile Road across from the Old Tavern at the turnoff into the New Bridge Road.

McLaws's brigade, of Magruder's division, still held their picket line across Nine Mile Road, and Whiting still had Johnston's written order of the night before: "Should there be cause of haste, General McLaws, on your approach, will be ordered to leave his ground for you, that he may re-enforce Longstreet." As McLaws obviously was not going to leave his ground to reinforce Longstreet more than two cross-country miles away on the Williamsburg Road, Whiting may have held some question as to Longstreet's whereabouts — especially as Johnston had written him only a few hours before, "Longstreet will precede you."

Chase Whiting was another famous West Pointer, who was not backward about advancing his opinions to anybody. He was also a member of the happy clique around Johnston, having served as engineering officer on Johnston's staff during the period of First Manassas. As soon as his van drew up behind McLaws's picket line, Whiting and his staff went into the room in the farmhouse where Johnston had established his new headquarters. Nothing of his conversation with Johnston was recorded, for Smith was then absent on his assignment of observing the waters of the Chickahominy.

Some time between twelve and one o'clock this bad penny, accompanied by his full staff, turned up at the new headquarters. General Smith offered no explanation for having left his bootless assignment, though he probably reported that the two brigades were posted in readiness to repel any amphibious assault. Most likely Smith's curiosity had gotten the better of him, and he was determined not to be shunted off by transparent devices. His return was accepted in silence, and the by then somewhat large gathering settled down to continue the wait.

As two o'clock came and went, the atmosphere in the downstairs front room must have grown clammy with tension. At two-thirty Johnston could endure no more of the strain. Regardless of what the officers might think, he had to know what Longstreet was doing. Evidently lacking faith in his own staff officers, he asked Smith if his chief of staff, Major Jasper Whiting, might be permitted to ride across country and try to learn from Longstreet what was happening.

After they heard Major Whiting's horse gallop away, the silence descended again. Then, shortly before three o'clock, it was broken by the arrival of a group of visitors. At this inopportune moment in the fortunes of Joe Johnston, General Lee with several members of his staff entered army headquarters.

3

The appearance of the handsome majestic soldier at this time could only have been an embarrassment to Joe Johnston, suffering his tenth hour of waiting for his battle to commence. More recent than the warm memories reaching back to their apple-cheeked days as classmates at the Military Academy on the Hudson were those of Johnston's curtness and evasiveness with his old friend, Johnston's stiff reminders of his areas of authority and this final slight of committing the army to battle without taking Lee into his confidence.

When Lee had left the city, he knew no more about the battle than any other observant citizen in downtown Richmond. All knew a battle had to come, and from the troop movements late Friday afternoon and in the early morning it looked like this Saturday might be the day. Armistead Long, the staff officer closest to him at that period, recalled that Lee had left his office because he was restless and wanted to be on the field if anything was going on.

When Lee began the five-and-one-half-mile ride along Nine Mile Road to Johnston's new headquarters, there were abundant signs that a battle was impending, if not already opened. The soldiers' camps were abandoned, and along the road he passed those individuals who inevitably get misplaced in any advance, the thrown-away equipment, blanket rolls and haversacks, and the litter in the wake of a forward movement. Near the new headquarters house,

Whiting's three brigades were ready to go in. When Lee dismounted in the clearing around the farmhouse, he heard what he took to be the rattle of muskets in the direction of the Williamsburg Road. Then, when he entered the room where the general officers waited, no one could have missed the strain in the atmosphere.

Since Johnston did not offer any information, Lee tried a feeler, and said he thought he had heard rifle fire when he had ridden up.

Johnston dismissed that. "It's only cannon fire," he said, without elaborating. Cannon fire was commonplace when two armies were in position, as some battery was always target-practicing on the enemy.

This particular cannon fire was, as Johnston knew, coming from the Williamsburg Road. Little artillery was used at Seven Pines, very little at the opening, and none of the generals at Johnston's headquarters felt the rumbles they had heard carried enough weight to indicate a full-scale action. Johnston said later these distant rumbles had prompted him to send Major Whiting to Longstreet at two-thirty.

Lee did not pursue the point. The President's military adviser so unobtrusively took his place among the silent generals that neither Smith nor Porter Alexander, acting chief of ordnance, mentioned his presence at headquarters. His staff officers crossed the hall and joined friends of their own rank on the other side of the house.

Bespectacled Colonel Marshall, a kinsman of the chief justice and himself a lawyer, found a seat beside Dr. Gaillard, Smith's chief of surgery. Unlike the tight-lipped generals on the other side of the house, Marshall and Gaillard passed the time in agreeable conversation. While they and the other staff officers were talking, all of them plainly heard the sound of the musket fire Lee had mentioned to Johnston.

This musket fire, which was to serve as the signal for commencing the action on Nine Mile Road, was not heard in the room where the generals waited. An acoustical freak caused by the muffling bog of the ground blocked off the sound. While the rifle fire could be heard distinctly all around the house, and even in the rooms on one side of it, it was not heard on the side where Johnston outwardly controlled his growing agitation.

The forces set in motion by Johnston were not of the nature to attract good fortune, but this acoustical trick cost him the possibility of achieving success with his salvage plan. Major General Keyes said of the Federal Fair Oaks position, "If Johnston had attacked there an hour or two earlier than he did, I could have made but a feeble defense comparatively, and every man of us would have been killed, captured, or driven into the swamp or river before assistance could have reached us."

Yet, this natural freak was only able to remove the possibility of success from Johnston's salvage battle because of his own secrecy and slothfulness. Had the staff officers known the musket fire was a signal, they would have told the generals, and had Lee known even that much, he would not have accepted Johnston's dismissal of his impression. Had Johnston not been so determined to keep Lee in the dark, he could at least have sent staff officers to investigate the possibility that Lee was right. During the interminable afternoon, there is no evidence that Johnston bestirred himself or his staff.

Nor, while waiting for the signal of musket fire, did Johnston send forward reconnaissance parties or seek in any way to establish the condition of the Federal troops at Fair Oaks. Though he might have explained this as part of a desire to surprise the enemy, a reconnaissance between two and three o'clock would have revealed the enemy lines around Fair Oaks to be abandoned.

By three o'clock Couch's division, contracted near Seven Pines in support of Casey's right, was all entangled, except a half brigade that was cut off from the division by Jenkins's slicing drive around the Federal right on Nine Mile Road. Under Brigadier General John Abercrombie, these regiments, with a battery, began to retire beyond the abandoned Fair Oaks line. Somewhere between three and four o'clock Abercrombie's detached segment left the field and started north toward the unsafe bridges over the Chickahominy.

Scarcely in the history of warfare had a general blundered into an opportunity of this magnitude. Johnston needed only to move forward the three idle brigades at hand and his deranged battle would yield a stroke that appeared to be "genius," confirming his admirers' estimate of his greatness. But the long waiting and his ignorance of what was happening at Seven Pines had reduced the general to stupefaction. He learned no more about the lines immediately in his front than those on the Williamsburg Road.

Johnston was aroused from his stupor shortly after four o'clock when Major Jasper Whiting brought the note from Longstreet calling for support on his left to keep his drive going. This note caused Johnston's first action of the day and the final action of military irrationality.

4

Longstreet's message gave Johnston to understand that the enemy was being driven and all that was needed to secure success was support to his left flank. From this Johnston assumed that Longstreet's left was overlapped by a Federal line extending from Seven Pines to the Fair Oaks area. His purpose, based on this assumption, was to hurry troops into the woods to the right of Nine Mile Road and to move them forward obliquely and establish contact with Longstreet's left.

Other troops were to advance along and to the left of the Nine Mile Road, extending a continuous front to overlap the Federals supposedly at the Fair Oaks end of the Federal line. It was a logical tactical move in the absence of any knowledge of the position of Longstreet's left or the enemy's disposition on his own front, and Johnston was too eager to get troops into action to take time for reconnoitering.

Shortly after Johnston received Longstreet's message, President Davis and his entourage were seen riding into the clearing. Alexander believed Johnston hurried away from headquarters to avoid Davis, and this observation has been usually accepted to mean that Johnston wished to avoid Davis's presence. It seems more likely he wished to avoid any questions from anybody. He was anxious to get away from Lee and the whole gathering at the headquarters house. Davis's appearance served as a spur to get as quickly as possible to the field, where he was in sole command and beyond explanations. There was something impelled about his rush to his horse and the quickly spoken orders to Smith to advance the three brigades under Whiting.

When the advance regiment moved out down the road with a tinkling of tin cups, canteens and bayonets, Johnston was excited by the hope that his support would not be too late to sustain the "drive" which Longstreet threatened might falter. He grew very cheerful in the break from tension, and rode forward with the advancing troops as if awakened from the day's long nightmare.

Afterwards Johnston disavowed his command of the Fair Oaks field. He tried to make it appear that Smith took the troops into action, and the management of Smith's division at Fair Oaks was certainly nothing any general would want to claim. At the basis of Johnston's disordered movement was his intentness on establishing contact with Longstreet's left — or where, from Longstreet's message, he assumed it to be — and this made him careless about everything else. Without trying to advance any guns with the infantry, he sent the first brigade off the road into the dripping woods to the right to feel its way toward the supposed area of Longstreet's left.

This tough brigade, commanded by the herculean John B. Hood, strained forward in release from the twelve-hour wait. The professional Hood had no way of knowing that, in terms of a flank extending toward him, Longstreet had no left. After Jenkins had "scoured" Nine Mile Road from midway to Fair Oaks back to Seven Pines, Hill's left flank had coiled back upon itself. Hood's eager troops were wasted in groping through a gap between the fighting at Seven Pines and Fair Oaks.

When Hood's brigade was swallowed up in the woods, Johnston was riding beside Whiting immediately in the rear of Whiting's own brigade. This was advancing along Nine Mile Road into the clearing at Fair Oaks Station, where the railroad crossed the road. Whiting's brigade was commanded by its senior colonel, Evander McIver (pronounced "McKeever") Law. Another of the brilliant young scholarly products of The Citadel, Law was an unfriendly rival of Micah Jenkins. In less than one month Law would, alongside Hood, lead this brigade in the first of its many epic charges. Under the uncertain command of Johnston or Whiting or both, Law sent his own Alabama regiment across the railroad tracks to dispose of what Johnston took to be a fragment of a Federal brigade retiring from Fair Oaks to the Chickahominy.

Johnston was partly right. It was the half brigade under Abercrombie, cut off from Couch's division, and it had been retiring to the Chickahominy. In his retiring movement Abercrombie had, as they said, "found friends."

The Federal troops nearest the swaying bridges on the north side of the Chickahominy belonged to the corps of Old Army man "Bull" Sumner. Sixty-five-year-old Edwin Sumner was not to develop to meet the increasing demands of top-flight corps command when both armies became professional, but he possessed a bellicose determination that would not let any unsafe bridges keep his troops out of a battle where they were needed.

Around two-thirty — at just about the time Johnston sent Smith's chief of staff to find out what was happening with Longstreet — Sumner started John Sedgwick's division over the swaying bridges. Incredibly, he got some guns across too, the men pulling the dismounted pieces through the muck. Old Sumner came along himself. Sedgwick's van was moving away from the Chickahominy when Abercrombie turned his withdrawal into a stand between four-thirty and five o'clock.

Abercrombie, a sixty-four-year-old professional from Tennessee, had barely placed his half brigade in line when Law's regiment came at him. North from Fair Oaks a narrow road ran to the Chickahominy, and along the east side of this road there was a wide stretch of cleared fields in which sat the small Adams house. Abercrombie's half brigade, with its battery divided into two sections, faced west on both sides of the house to command this marshy field. Stumps protruding out of the mire made this ugly terrain for an unsupported regiment to charge across, and Law's troops slipped and stumbled back from the blasts of the unsuspected guns and the concentrated rifle fire.

As Whiting contended, there was nothing so formidable about the ground that his brigade, attacking in unison, could not have carried Abercrombie's position along the Adams house. Pettigrew's brigade was deploying off the road to the left to support and extend Whiting's brigade under Law. But Johnston had his mind on a quick disposal of these supposedly detached Federals, to get on to Longstreet, and another partial attack was hurried forward. These troops too fell back from the artillery supported by rifle lines.

Though these actions were relatively brief, both assaults were carried forward in the abandoned violence with which Southerners, bent on hurling the enemy back off their land, charged in those days. Having developed none of the protective instincts of the "old soldier," the men rushed forward in the exultant spirit expressed by their high rebel yell. When their front was broken by metal — and Whiting's regiments left many writhing and still figures in the mud of that cleared field — the men reverted to the civilian reactions which would direct them to safety as individuals. They retired from the fields in fragments that gave the appearance of disorder.

Experienced officers could quickly have reorganized the units. But the line and field officers, mostly civilian volunteers elected by the men, knew no more than the soldiers. They depended on rallying the troops by appeals to their spirit which sent the men back before the units were reorganized. One doomed assault was initiated by an unidentified officer who rode to the front yelling, "Charge that battery!"

While Whiting's brigade — under Law and/or Whiting and/or Johnston, and/or anonymous persons — was being cut up piecemeal, everything in Johnston's battle began to fall apart. When Law's own regiment had first passed over the railroad tracks at Fair Oaks Station, Johnston, Whiting and their staff officers were approaching the tracks along Nine Mile Road. At that point the mounted men were in a clearing with a fringe of woods behind them and, beyond the field on their left, dense woods stretched all the way to the river. Whiting, for some reason, suspected enemy troops to be in the woods toward the river. Perhaps Abercrombie's stand seemed too determined for unsupported troops and, fearing that Federals must have made it across the Chickahominy, he protested against crossing the railroad. Pointing to the woods beyond the field on their left, he said that enemy troops there would be on the rear of Law's brigade.

Johnston, in cheerful humor, pooh-poohed the idea. "Oh, come, General Whiting," he said, "you're too cautious."

As if his words were a signal, artillery fire blasted from the woods and shell fragments broke across the road. The group drew back to the fringe of woods to survey the situation, and that about marked the end of possible reconstruction of the Confederate action at Fair Oaks.

5

The Federal action, except for the time element, was comparatively clear. Sumner, on the field, put part of Gorman's brigade and part of Dana's on either side of the Adams house, facing due west, and got in action the six guns of Kirby's U. S. Regular Army battery. The guns sank up to their axles in mud with every recoil, and foot soldiers had to push the pieces out for another shot. There were only ten guns going, but these were ten more than Johnston had carried forward.

Sedgwick's third brigade, under Burns, with parts of Gorman's, were turned off the road from the river into the woods on the Confederate flank. Their position faced due south. When Sedgwick's division was deployed, the Federals then had at least as many men on the field as in Smith's full division, with a significant difference in the deployment. While Smith's five brigades were separated, all the Federals, in good order and led with clear purpose, were fighting at the same time on solid lines that more or less spontaneously formed an inverted L. Within this angle, the disordered Confederates were fighting in two directions.

It seems reasonably certain that Whiting's brigade, all its regiments finally in action under Law, continued its fight with Abercrombie's half brigade and the more than one brigade from Sedgwick. Pettigrew's brigade came out on Law's left and caught it from front and flank, though the troops pushed forward toward the Adams house line. These two brigades took the full weight of the Federal fire and were mangled beyond further effectiveness before any support came up.

At this stage Johnston, by his own admission, could not rid himself of the delusion that he was engaging only the half brigade that had been retiring toward the Chickahominy. Some time later, whether or not under Johnston's orders, Hood's brigade floundered back out of the woods from its futile groping for Longstreet's nonexistent left. In the dusk, these good troops could do no more than contribute thirteen wounded to the casualty lists in the disorder along Nine Mile Road.

Before Hood's men made their bewildered reappearance off Law's

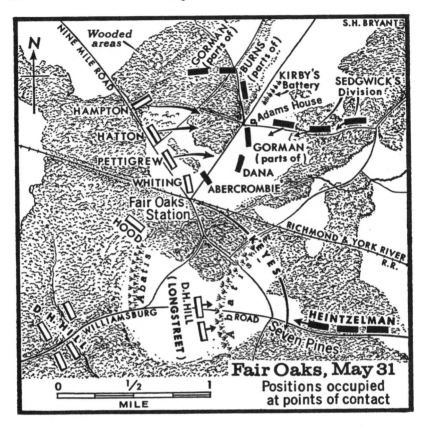

Fair Oaks, May 31
Positions occupied
at points of contact

right, General Smith began sending in reinforcements to Law and
Pettigrew on the left. Whether Johnston ordered it or Smith took
the initiative, Smith had brought forward his two brigades from
their watch of the Chickahominy where the bridges had been swept
away. The one point where the generals corroborated one another
was that Smith took the responsibility for sending in these last two
brigades, under Robert Hatton and Wade Hampton. He directed
Hampton to turn off Nine Mile Road into a woods lane about three
quarters of a mile from Fair Oaks, to follow this north until he
passed the line of Pettigrew's brigade and then turn east to come
up on Pettigrew's left. Hatton was directed to follow Hampton in
support.

As with every unit all afternoon, beginning with Law's single regiment, the brigades moved forward separately. First Hampton and then Hatton moved into the angle of cross-fire at the head of the inverted L. Light was failing then. The soldiers could not see the enemy in the woods, though at places they were firing at one another only twenty-five yards apart. To complete the confusion, the brigade leaders fell before their troops got in position. One of the reasons for the obscurity about the action of these two brigades, and Pettigrew's also, was that none of the officers filed reports.

Robert Hatton was shot from his horse and killed as he led his brigade out onto the open field south of the woods. Hatton was a native of Ohio who had been a lawyer and U. S. Congressman in Tennessee, and he had brought well-trained Tennessee regiments to Virginia.

Johnston Pettigrew was severely wounded and, believing he was dying, insisted that his staff leave him. In a later counterattack, the unconscious general was captured and sent to a Federal prison. Pettigrew was a learned and revered North Carolinian with a compelling enthusiasm, and one of the most admired officers with the troops in Virginia.

Wade Hampton, the massive South Carolina grandee, was one of the richest men in the South, one of the most chivalric, and one of the toughest. In the same same field, he caught a bullet in the foot. With no vainglory, as he had no military ambitions or even liking for the army, Hampton always acted with a combative determination to get on with the unpleasant business. Refusing to leave the field, he dismounted and called on Dr. Gaillard to remove the bullet then and there. Dr. Gaillard performed the operation in the dying light and, on his way back to Smith's staff, was himself struck by a shell-fragment. That night another doctor amputated his arm.

Before Hampton returned to action several weeks later, Smith's division had been dissolved, and no one had any interest in reports on an action better forgotten.

Neither Johnston or Smith, on Nine Mile Road, had any notion of what went on after Hampton and Hatton moved to support Pettigrew. By then, between six and seven o'clock, Johnston had finally come to accept the inevitable conclusion that he was fighting Federal troops from across the river. He sent an urgent message to Smith to order forward a brigade from Magruder's fifteen thousand idle troops. McLaws's brigade, two and one half miles from Fair Oaks all day, was advanced too late to accomplish anything.

In the general disorder, President Davis so far forgot himself as to order forward a brigade from Magruder's command. These Mississippi troops, who were later to win fame under their then senior brigadier, William Barksdale, got close enough in the gathering shadows to lose a few men from stray bullets. By then, any possibilities of driving the enemy were past. Johnston never brought forward any guns, the positions of the enemy were not established, and the individual soldiers were fighting blind.

After sunset, Johnston went riding across the cleared field in some desperation of his own, and a shell knocked him from his horse. He was severely wounded and in deep pain, though not unconscious. When his slight figure was gathered on a stretcher, President Davis hurried to his side. Apparently forgetting their differences, Davis leaned over the wounded man with an expression of concern and asked if he could do anything. Johnston shook his head and was carried from the field.

That was the end of Johnston in Virginia. It was well for him to go that way, taking a wound gallantly in action. Because of this circumstance he never had to face the failure at the climax of his long campaign against McClellan. In time, he would come to believe that only this wound in the gathering darkness had prevented him from leading his army to a decisive victory. Consoling his spirit with this palliative would have done no harm except that his refusal to face and present the facts — coupled with his support of Longstreet's cruel fiction — made it impossible for Johnston to be understood as a general in his last battle in Virginia.

He left an impenetrable secret his thoughts and feelings after his shocking discovery that Longstreet was on the wrong road, and the subsequent discovery that, with no Longstreet left flank existing, he had permitted two brigades to become entangled with more than a division of the enemy. Perhaps he was never certain about what happened north of Fair Oaks Station where he had been trying to hurry troops forward, too late, when the blow removed him from the bedlam of the field. After he was removed the fighting faded off, as it would have had he remained.

6

Of the dying fight on the evening of the 31st, after Johnston was wounded, the Federal reports were more complete. Triumphant Sedgwick and others made somewhat extravagant claims about "routing" Rebels in counterattacks in the deepening twilight. In fact, despite the violence of the disordered Confederate advances, casualties were too low for the units to have suffered sizeable or sustained counterattacks. Routed troops in knee-deep bog would yield large numbers of prisoners, especially with darkness coming on, and Smith's four engaged brigades reported only 109 men missing. Smith's approximately 8000 engaged reported a total loss of 1283 killed, wounded and missing — 15 per cent casualties, as compared to D. H. Hill's 33 per cent reported casualties at Seven Pines.

Sedgwick had every reason to feel proud. As he reported, Abercrombie had been hard pressed and under severe attack when he rushed his first regiments into support. As his building weight gradually turned the tide, and as Law and Pettigrew's leaderless men ceased trying to charge, local counterattacks undoubtedly met little organized resistance and withdrawing units did not maintain good order. There is no evidence that they fled the field.

After dark, Smith's four brigades withdrew from the swampy area where they had engaged the enemy and, with Hood's brigade, took position at the western edge of the clearing west of Fair Oaks Station. When daylight came, Sedgwick's men remained in their defensive line extending on both sides of the Adams house, east of the road running from Fair Oaks to the river. Burns's brigade was brought out of the woods west of the country road and extended the defensive position. During the day of June 1, when the rest of Sumner's corps came over with more guns, the Federals became aggressive and invited battle. As this was refused, and Smith's division (minus three brigadiers) withdrew farther west on Nine Mile Road, Sedgwick and his officers grew more convinced of the decisiveness of their fight the evening before.

Aside from the Federals' colored impressions of their prowess on May 31, Fair Oaks was a distinct, though unexploited, Federal victory. The result of Johnston's Nine Mile Road battle was a disorderly repulse, from which no opportunity existed for a resumption of the attack with reasonable hope of success the following day.

In the poorly directed and anticlimactic fighting during the next day, at Seven Pines, with Smith in command of the army, Smith's division was kept out of action and connected with Magruder's command along the Chickahominy. After this June 1 fighting, the Federals reestablished the positions they had held in the Seven Pines area before all the futilities, which cost the Confederates six thousand casualties. The Confederate opportunity to exploit the isolation of McClellan's two corps had passed before the sunset of May 31.

7

Long after the war Johnston came to believe that *"only darkness"* (his italics) prevented the success of his advance on May 31. He stated then that if Smith had not been in command on June 1 the Confederate tide would have rolled on to complete his defeat of the Federals.

Johnston made no such claim in his brief official report to the War Department. In that he wrote, "Had Major-General Huger's Division been in position and ready for action when those of Smith, Hill and Longstreet moved, I am satisfied that Keyes' Corps would have been destroyed. . . ." Johnston knew that Smith's corps had moved at five in the afternoon, because he had led it. On writing his report, Johnston counted on Smith's silence when he joined Longstreet in focusing on Huger. It was later, after Smith, drawing on the official records, had published the whole story, that Johnston turned on Smith for exposing him.

When Johnston submitted his report on June 24, he was not yet at ease with his concocted version and wrote in extreme reticence. In the later elaborations of his personal narrative, he ignored the available records (as well as the facts he had suppressed) and wishfully built a case of "might-have-beens" for his lost opportunity in Virginia. To his admirers, then and since, the picture soldier became the great general of *ifs*. His supporters were convinced that the charming gentleman, who made himself so appealing to subordinates, must have fought as good a battle as he talked *if* only fate had not invariably intervened at some high hour in his destiny.

One of Johnston's most persuasive alibis was that Lee, succeeding him, drew to Richmond all those troops from the South Atlantic for which he had "repeatedly" petitioned the President. This gave the generally accepted impression that Lee, after refusing to withdraw troops from the South Atlantic states for Johnston's desired "concentration," got them for himself. Johnston stated that Lee received thirty-seven thousand reinforcements from Georgia and the Carolinas, including brigades of six thousand and seven thousand, sizes no Confederate brigade ever approached during the war.

The dates of arrival in Virginia of the troops from the South Atlantic garrisons show that all withdrawals were made during Johnston's command except one Georgia brigade which went to replace Jackson's Valley losses and a brigade on loan from North Carolina. Though all the arrivals in Virginia were not immediately available to Johnston, he drew directly to his command the sixteen thousand troops formed, with Field's Virginia brigade, into the division under A. P. Hill. At least one thousand of these were wasted in the useless casualties that befell Branch's isolated brigade on the Virginia Central.

On the day Johnston was wounded Ripley's brigade of 2300 arrived in Richmond from South Carolina, and was sent to Seven Pines on June 1. After Lee assumed command, Ripley's 2300 were brigaded in D. H. Hill's division as partial replacements for the 3000 casualties Hill sustained at Seven Pines.

Also while Johnston was in command, Lee brought two North Carolina brigades to Virginia to operate south of the James, on guard at Drewry's Bluff and Petersburg. After Lee assumed command, he incorporated one of these, Ransom's large brigade, into Huger's division in exchange for Wise's small brigade, which had been detached from Huger south of the James River. The difference in numbers between Ransom and Wise only partly compensated for the three thousand casualties sustained at Seven Pines and Fair Oaks outside D. H. Hill's division.

South of the James, Wise's brigade and the remaining North Carolina brigade (Walker's) were joined by Daniel's brigade, sent on loan from North Carolina, and the three were formed into a temporary division under Theophilus Holmes. This incompetent legacy from the Old Army, commanding the department south of the James, only brought his makeshift division to the periphery of one action with Lee, reporting fifty-one casualties and, as General Early charitably reported, "Holmes' Division was really of little avail during the battles."

Except for these troops wasted with Holmes, Lee fielded in the army at Richmond actually fewer men than Johnston had, while McClellan's 5000 losses were considerably more than replaced by McCall's well-trained division of 9500, drawn from what had become McDowell's troop depot. (Later, other units from the South Atlantic were released to the Virginia theater, after Lee's battles had caused Burnside to abandon his inland threat from New Bern and shift his force to Virginia.) Lee added approximately twelve thousand to his force by the strategy and the boldness which enabled him to combine at Richmond with the survivors of Jackson's Valley campaign and Lawton's Georgia brigade which had gone to Jackson as replacements.

It was not numbers. In Johnston's fight on Nine Mile Road, he had used fully only four of eleven available brigades (not including the four brigades in A. P. Hill's division), while in Longstreet's undirected fight only five of the thirteen available brigades were fully employed. Even including the brigades that touched the edge of the action to no purpose, Johnston fought his big battle with less than one half of the available force and a minuscule part of his artillery. This is the immutable record against which the *ifs* and *mights* must contend.

As cold as the record were the words of the analytical Alexander. Stating that the battle was "phenomenally mismanaged," he wrote, "It must be admitted that at Seven Pines our prospects, had Johnston not been wounded, would have been dismal."

That was not a charitable epitaph for a general's departure from an army. Impersonal Alexander was not appraising the man's attractive traits or the soldier's sundry gifts: he was appraising the chances of his country's independence under Joseph E. Johnston as a commanding general. On that basis, it seems an accurate appraisal.

Joel Cook, correspondent for the Philadelphia *Press*, considered the misdirected shell that struck Johnston as "the saddest shot fired during the war. It changed the entire Rebel tactics. It took away incompetence, indecision and dissatisfaction and gave skilful general-ship, excellent plans and good discipline."

8

There was a postscript to the Johnston phase of the year of the settlement. When on June 1 the army devolved on Gustavus Smith, the "big name," as Longstreet called him, suffered a total collapse of his faculties. Smith was removed from the field in a state which he described as paralysis, and which today would probably be diagnosed as traumatic shock.

After his recovery, Smith received a number of departmental assignments before finally resigning from the Confederate armies. As related to the period of the settlement, Smith passed from the scene with his superior, Joe Johnston.

Smith's collapse had nothing to do with his not remaining in command. President Davis had told General Lee on May 31, as they rode into Richmond together in the darkness from Fair Oaks, that he would be given the army the next day.

Out of a mixture of consideration and unfamiliarity with Johnston's plans, troop disposition and officer personnel, Lee did not exercise his authority over Smith on June 1. For practical purposes, Lee assumed command of the army after the May 31–June 1 Battle of Seven Pines–Fair Oaks (each side calling the battle after the sector in which it had been successful).

The respective positions of the armies were the same as before the battle, except that McClellan retained Sumner's corps south of the Chickahominy and, shaken out of his careless disregard of the enemy, put his troops to erecting strong lines from White Oak Swamp to the Chickahominy.

The Johnston phase ended with the Confederate troops backed up around Richmond, according to Johnston's preference from the time of his arrival on the peninsula. This was the situation — with McClellan alerted and digging in for the beginning of siege operations — which Lee inherited along with the loose organization of Johnston's forces. And everybody was still waiting for McDowell.

A Single, Controlling Hand

CHAPTER SIX

End of Retreats

I N A MODEST house owned by the Widow Dabbs, set back on the north side of Nine Mile Road about one and one half miles from the edge of Richmond, fifty-five-year-old General R. E. Lee at last enjoyed the gratification of running up the General Headquarters' flag. Without fanfare he assumed responsibility for a military community larger than the capital outside which its camps spread in an area to the northeast and east about five by six miles. On June 2 Lee had a flatly worded special order read to the troops, in which he appealed for "the cordial support of every officer and man" during the "temporary" absence of Johnston. It went unobserved that the troops were for the first time addressed as "the Army of Northern Virginia." Lee's designation of the army was significant, for it indicated where he expected it to fight.

As soon as he escaped from the hateful desk job in Richmond, Lee began planning ways in which the enemy could be evicted from Virginia speedily and thoroughly. The attitude behind his planning was different from the defensive purposes of Davis (who had wanted to call the troops "the Army of Richmond"), but in talking with the President Lee limited his discussion to the immediate objective of lifting McClellan's siege. Most of all, he *talked* to Davis, and after Johnston's icy rejections of confidence, the President was so relieved to be working in a harmonious relationship that he accepted Lee's plans without question. More important, he turned over unquestioningly to Lee the details of execution.

Officially, Lee was given no more authority than Johnston, as general in charge of the Department of Northern Virginia — north of the James River at Richmond. However, Lee retained some of his authority from his days as military adviser and could order troop movements as long as he exercised discretion. Perhaps the most important gain won by Lee's unfailing consideration of Davis was the President's trust in his discretion. Lee had demonstrated a sensitive awareness of all aspects of the whole and a tactful skill in achieving cooperation with men who could be difficult — including the President himself. In his first letter to Davis, on June 5, he wrote, "Our position requires you should know everything & you must excuse my troubling you." In that letter Lee developed his thoughts freely, as if speaking in unguarded conversation, and after that Davis never asked him a question during this period of their relationship.

In this letter, Lee suggested his fundamental strategy and committed himself to seizing the initiative. "I am preparing a line that I can hold with part of our forces in the front, while with the rest I will endeavor to make a diversion to bring McClellan out." By maneuver, he intended to pry McClellan out of fixed positions, nullify his siege guns, and attack him in the open.

Even before he wrote the President, Lee had sent specific instructions to Major Stevens, the army's chief engineer, to construct defensive positions along the existing lines east of Richmond. By this Lee implied that the area of maneuver would be north of the Chickahominy, where Johnston had originally planned his attack. At first, however, Lee did not commit himself completely to an offensive so close to Richmond, but studied the possibility of strengthening Jackson for a counterinvasion from the Valley. As Lee wrote Davis — a further expression of his basic purpose — "This would change the character of the war."

Jackson himself was eager to mount an invasion of the North, but in the first week of June he was entangled with two separate enemy forces, and his army was in hard case. Moreover, Lee was forced to consider the element of time. In any joint operation with Jackson, they must move before McDowell came down on their flank and before McClellan advanced appreciably closer to Richmond. And before he could move a step, Lee had to organize his heterogeneous collection of troops into an army. He therefore had to calculate to a hairline the shortest time in which he could prepare a joint movement and the longest time he dared risk before McClellan began his siege approach.

2

Though General Lee knew nothing of McClellan's troubles with Washington and their effects upon him, he correctly assumed that the Battle of Seven Pines would do nothing to disturb McClellan's conviction that he held the initiative nor to change his deliberate method of approaching Richmond. McClellan shared the view of the Richmond newspaper which, back in May, had commented bitterly: "McClellan will advance by regular approaches and the Confederate generals, who never attack anybody, will meet him with regular defenses."

Two weeks after Lee took command, McClellan wrote his wife, "I shall make the first battle mainly an artillery contest. As soon as I gain possession of Old Tavern, I shall push them in upon Richmond . . . and then I will bring up my heavy guns, shell the city, and carry it by assault."

Assuming a passive enemy, McClellan planned very soundly in advancing to Old Tavern, the turnoff from Nine Mile Road leading to the New Bridge on the Chickahominy. By holding the Old Tavern-New Bridge line the Confederates controlled the high bluffs on the southern bank of the Chickahominy, making it possible for their inferior cannon to command potential river crossings from New Bridge west to the Mechanicsville bridges. The loss of the Old Tavern line would force the evacuation of Magruder's gun positions at New Bridge and seriously cramp the Confederate defensive positions between the river and Richmond.

Of course, McClellan's phrase "carry it by assault" was merely a heroic manner of speaking. He still expected, as Lee predicted, to advance from position to position until his siege guns forced the evacuation of the city. Within this purpose, McClellan's thinking had grown inflexible as a result of his fixation with McDowell's arrival.

His true feelings about the expected juncture north of Richmond are obscure. Well after the event, he wrote that his army was split across the Chickahominy only because of orders to extend a wing to meet McDowell, and that this forced him to maintain the base at White House Landing, when his preference was a base on the

James. Yet, from his first proposal to Lincoln for a waterborne approach to Richmond, McClellan stated that his objective was a base on the York or its tributary, the Pamunkey.

When his army left Yorktown, McClellan's first move was to the Pamunkey, and before June he had never mentioned the James. He seemed unalarmed by the division of his army even after Johnston attacked the portion south of the Chickahominy, and nothing indicated dissatisfaction with his own selected base at White House Landing. Indeed, for moving siege guns to the front, the York River Railroad gave him facilities that could be found nowhere else. From the evidence, the idea of abandoning the enormous base built at the White House would seem to be a later development, as in early June he received more positive assurances that McDowell would join him.

In response to McClellan's insistent calls for reinforcements, Stanton advised him on June 7 that McCall's 9,500-man division from McDowell's corps would be sent him immediately by water. McDowell wrote cordially, "For the third time I am under orders to join you, and this time I hope to get through. . . . McCall goes in advance by water."

McCall's division began to disembark at the White House June 11. The next day McClellan wrote Scranton requesting that the rest of McDowell's corps also come by water. At some length he described the practical difficulties of extending his northern wing to make the juncture with McDowell by the overland route. At this turn, it appeared that McClellan was no longer certain of what he did want or of what he could get. He knew that Lincoln and Stanton would never remove McDowell's command from the line between Richmond and Washington, and, in extending the wing north of the Chickahominy, he could not have been unaware of the problem posed by this pincer to the defenders of Richmond. Also, some force north of the Chickahominy was necessary to protect the White House base. Not until this message to Stanton did he hint that he objected to extending the wing, by his mention of the fighting that would be entailed in holding the passage clear for McDowell.

McClellan's objection to fruitless battles so soon after Seven Pines undoubtedly was strengthened by a message received from Stanton on June 6. "Officers of your army, some of high rank, are sending details to their wives and friends, by telegraph, of the late disasters, in respect to the number killed and wounded." As this constituted the whole message, Stanton would seem to be reproaching McClellan for the fact that his army had suffered casualties during a battle and reminding him, as after Ball's Bluff, of the political consequences of wives and friends of high-ranking officers spreading stories of killed and wounded.

By June 16, McClellan's obsession with reinforcements from Mc-Dowell outweighed his objections to fighting to make the juncture, and he wired Stanton, "Please let me know when and which direction McDowell's command will come."

During this period, as the ground began to harden, McClellan had sent Lincoln a steady stream of messages of his intention to advance on Richmond. "I shall be in perfect readiness to move forward to take Richmond," he wrote on June 7, "the moment McCall reaches here and the ground will permit the passage of artillery."

Four days later, while McCall's big division was landing, he wrote, "I shall advance as soon as the bridges are completed and the ground fit for artillery to advance."

On June 18: "A general engagement may take place any hour."

These messages, which made no mention of McDowell at all, obviously were designed to tell Lincoln what he wanted to hear. While McClellan was still playing the increasingly taxing game of appeasing the authorities as he went about his own plans, it is not at all clear where McDowell fitted in.

At the same time, Lincoln and Stanton continued to play their game of "now you have him, now you don't," and after June 12 no more was heard from Washington about either McDowell or reinforcements.

The effect of this vacillation on McClellan's nerves cannot be appraised; he attributed his inaction to the rains and the time consumed in replacing bridges. Though rain fell heavily during the first week of June and turned the Chickahominy country into a quagmire, his engineers were not long in overcoming this obstacle. By June 14 the engineering corps completed the masterpiece of

Woodbury's Bridge, over whose "level pavement" artillery trains could gallop without causing the slightest disturbance to the structure.

Despite his engineers' accomplishments, McClellan did not order his first siege guns to be unloaded from the ships until June 21. Nor were the bridges to be used at all by the heavier seacoast guns, which could be transported on the York River Railroad. While engines and traincars, early disembarked at the White House, brought up five hundred tons of supplies a day, the seacoast guns in his siege train remained on the ships.

After June 14 McClellan seemed bemused when all evidence from the other side indicated that the new Confederate commander was not waiting on his initiative and time schedule. Beginning on June 11, Jeb Stuart led 1200 troopers with two guns on a reconnaissance mission which the exuberant twenty-nine-year-old chief of cavalry expanded into a three-day, hundred-mile raid around McClellan's army. The jingling horsemen started north around Fitz-John Porter's flank near Hanover Court House, rode east toward the Pamunkey to within five miles of the White House, turned south to the Chickahominy behind McClellan's lines, and returned to Richmond along the James River below the flank of McClellan's Seven Pines lines. With military property destroyed, supplies gathered, and prisoners ridden off on captured horses, Stuart's bravura performance caused McClellan deep personal humiliation.

The effect of the publicized raid, "Stuart's Ride Around McClellan," did not alert McClellan to the new aggressiveness of the enemy, but it turned his attention to his own logistical problem. It was then that he first seemed to grow apprehensive over the exposed position of the White House base and began to explore the possibility of another, emergency base. On June 15, the day Stuart returned to Richmond, McClellan ordered surveys made of the country from south of White Oak Swamp to the James River. Three days later he opened communications with the navy about the possibility of moving transports from the White House to the James River.

While McClellan began to think defensively, he learned that Stonewall Jackson was now in position to cooperate with Lee. On

June 8 and 9 Jackson had defeated two forces on two separate days — Frémont at Cross Keys and Shields at Port Republic. As early as June 11, when brigades from Gustavus Smith's former division and Lawton's fresh brigade from Georgia were sent to the Valley, it became clear to Washington as well as to McClellan that Jackson and Lee planned some cooperative action.

Despite these indications of enemy movement, McClellan continued his methodical, unimaginative preparations for the advance to Old Tavern. His superior intelligence was reduced to that rigidity in which he could only continue to persevere in a set action without the faculty to think of new combinations.

3

By June 21, when McClellan first ordered some of his siege guns disembarked to be sent forward, Lee had completed his plans for a counteroffensive. In the scant three weeks since moving into the field, he had considered and rejected two plans involving a combination with Jackson. The first plan, a counterinvasion, proved to be physically impractical. Jackson's troops were exhausted from their four-hundred-mile march and the constant fighting, and had left some three thousand stragglers in their wake. In addition, Lee could not get any more troops from the South Atlantic garrisons.

Lee's next plan was to reinforce Jackson sufficiently for him to drive the enemy northward in the Valley, and then hurry toward Richmond for a combined move against McClellan's wing north of the Chickahominy. To this end he sent to the Valley Alexander Lawton's brigade, newly arrived from Georgia, and a new two-brigade division under Chase Whiting formed from Gustavus Smith's dissolved division. Law and Hood, the only general officers surviving unhurt from Fair Oaks, commanded the brigades. By the time these troops reached the Valley, Frémont and Shields had voluntarily withdrawn north, nearer Washington, removing their forces from a point of quick juncture with McDowell.

On June 16, the day after Stuart's return, Lee settled on the plan to move Jackson secretly from the Valley for a combined assault — a counterpincer — on the Federal wing stretched northward to receive McDowell. That day Lee wrote Jackson to keep his movements secret from the enemy and bring his command, minus most of his cavalry, on a forced march to Richmond.

To screen his movements in the Valley, Jackson had a new cavalry commander. The romantic partisan leader Turner Ashby had been killed toward the end of the campaign and succeeded by Colonel Thomas T. Munford. Young Tom Munford, a cadet at V.M.I. when Jackson was a professor, was more amenable than Ashby had been to the eccentric's iron discipline. Controlling the somewhat wayward Valley horsemen, Munford pushed hard against the enemy and blocked off all information about Jackson's army.

Along with Munford's aggressive screenings, the Federals had been put on the defensive by learning of the reinforcements that had come to Jackson. Lawton and Whiting had gone by train to the Valley, and since there was no way to keep such a move from the Federal spies in Richmond, Lee had made a virtue of necessity and moved troops as ostentatiously as possible. The more Washington was made aware of reinforcements to the Valley, the less the likelihood of McDowell being released. Though Lee could not know Lincoln and Stanton were responsible, he had observed the reflex contraction in protection of the capital.

On June 21, seventy thousand Federal troops were scattered in immobilized detachments through middle Virginia, waiting for Jackson's initiative, while the dour Valley commander was moving his army east of the Blue Ridge on the beginning of its march toward Richmond. That day Lincoln informed McClellan that no troops could be sent to him until they were sure what Jackson would do.

This was exactly one month after Jackson had started on the Valley campaign, initiating the collaboration that led to this first strategic maneuver among Confederate armies. However, though Lee had seized the initiative without the Federals yet being aware, he was combining with Jackson with a force that was an "army" in name only. As hard as he and his staff had worked to bring cohesion and efficiency to the slipshod organization left by Johnston, three weeks was simply not long enough.

4

In the beginning, Lee had encountered a defeatist attitude when he had called a conference to acquaint hmself with the general officers. Colonel Marshall had reported that "a number of officers were in favor of withdrawing nearer to Richmond." Chase Whiting, the brilliant engineer, had drawn diagrams on paper to convince Lee of "the inevitable consequences" of McClellan's advance by constructing successive parallels. Lee showed his feelings only to Whiting, by saying suddenly, "Stop, stop, if you go on ciphering, we are whipped beforehand."

This pessimism was not reflected among the troops, but morale was not high and the men lacked a sense of purpose. Fundamentally, no animating spirit had flowed from general headquarters among the collection of clans, cliques and cabals jealously guarding their own rights and asserting their own superiority in the sprawling, muddy network of military neighborhoods. Except for a very few cosmopolitans, every man was intensely place conscious, and, in their physical uprooting, all of them became primarily attached to the unit with which they identified themselves. With little provocation, a fiercer battle than that of Seven Pines could probably have been staged between adjoining divisions. As for the spirit of the army as a total entity, scarcely any could be said to have existed.

General headquarters was a remote place to the soldiers and the new commanding general only a name. To the men who had known or known of him in the Old Army Lee had fallen far below his reputation. Since his unspectacular accomplishments were obscure to nearly every one except President Davis, and since he had presented no explanations for his failure in achieving coordination between the political prima donnas in the 1861 campaign in Western Virginia, Lee was regarded as fit for no more than a desk soldier's job. Even Jeb Stuart, who had been a cadet at West Point when Lee was superintendent and held the older man in the deepest respect, wrote his wife that he was "disappointed" in Lee as a soldier.

Lee ended the remoteness of general headquarters from the army. He began by assuming responsibility for and supervising the detailed operations whose functioning created a unity of the army community. The President said that Lee brought a quick organization to the army by "the exact order, the systematic economy, and regularity begotten of his personal attention to the proper adjustment of even the smallest parts . . . the minutest details . . . of that mighty machine, a well-organized, disciplined army."

Major Joseph L. Brent, Magruder's ordnance officer, mentioned "the new impulse from Lee's headquarters." He wrote, "Very soon, and almost imperceptibly, the network of the general organization was cast over the whole army, and we were brought into a far closer connection with headquarters."

Major Brent, a peacetime lawyer who knew little about artillery, was particularly impressed by the "unheard of improvements" which Chief of Ordnance Alexander brought to the wagon trains that supplied ammunition to the guns in the field. Alexander, Brent said, "used Lee's great powers" to bring efficient supporting services to the artillery attached to each unit. Brent's strange duties were simplified when Alexander produced for Magruder's artillery twenty-five or more large wagons, with a field forge and mechanics, to accompany the reserve train.

It was this sort of small thing endlessly repeated that Lee caused to be done in all branches of the service. As soon as he approved of the plans of Major Walter H. Stevens for the defensive works east of Richmond, Lee himself directed that two hundred spades, shovels and picks, and fifty axes be sent him, and advised the chief engineer to return the tools if he did not need them.

At first, the use to which these tools were put caused considerable complaining among the Southern soldiers. Various of the chivalric volunteer officers protested that their men had come to fight and not to dig. Soon, however, the soldiers perceived the safety the lines provided in their daily rounds, and regarded the entrenchments as evidence of Lee's thoughtfulness. In this aspect of warfare, former engineer Lee was extremely advanced.

As the works grew, Lee discouraged the practice of holding large segments of troops standing under arms for long hours, and emphasized the importance of advanced lines of alert skirmishers to guard against surprise. Also discouraging withdrawals from threats, he advised commanders to fight for the ground they held unless forced back. The changes brought by the once despised works made the soldiers' lives less monotonous and more interesting. Somebody was always doing something on which all the others depended.

An oblique illustration of this lifting of boredom was a sharp decline in drunkenness, which also reflected the tightening in discipline. As officers up to the rank of colonel were elected by the troops, many of them felt they held rank by virtue of their popularity and were afraid to displease their "constituents." Under Lee it became more important to bring their units up to the new standards of the army.

Underlying all changes was the sense — felt by all officers, from platoon leaders to division commanders — that the new commanding general assumed full personal responsibility for everything in the army. No longer did officers complain of what the government did or did not do, nor were vacuums left for which no one could be found to assume authority. Obvious lacks, such as wagons for reserve trains of artillery, were not simply accepted or overlooked. Everything that should be done was done, and done with a sense of purpose.

Lee personally rode much about the lines, often with only a single staff officer. In his impressive appearance — "the highest type of manly beauty," Davis said of him — he was not yet a familiar figure on his gray horse. He began to be seen often enough to become recognizable as the leader who had assumed responsibility.

By some of the lax officers he was seen too often. If Lee felt an officer indulged in lounging about headquarters instead of looking after his lines, he never rebuked him directly, but was inclined to say something like, "I thought your horse looked in need of exercise, General." If the hint was not sufficient, that officer was marked for service elsewhere. This too was felt by the army.

The men would see him motionless on some rise of ground, his massive features blocked out against the sky, peering through glasses at the enemy's lines. To Colonel Long, the darkly elegant staff officer who rode most with him in these days, Lee would murmur, "Well, now, how are we going to get at those people?" In that line often used by Lee when studying ground occupied by the enemy he never varied from saying, "how are we going to *get at* —" the enemy? Never once did he say, "What are their plans against us?"

This spirit of aggression was also communicable. The troops felt they had come to the end of retreats.

These palpable changes could be brought quickly in the troops — the foot soldiers, their line and field officers, the gunners and men in supporting services — but not to the staff system which coordinated the action of the units in battle. Staff work was like a system of nerves that carried the impulses from general headquarters through the corporate body of the army. Only time and experience could create an effective staff system, and Lee himself did not recognize its inadequacies nor the extent to which an army would be dependent upon staff in the changing conditions of warfare since the Napoleonic methods in which he and his contemporaries had been schooled.

5

All the Confederate and Federal armies were organized on existing models, but no model was known for a general staff adequate to meet the demands made by technological advances — especially in weapons, with the greater range of the rifled musket and the higher accuracy and heavier fire power of the rifled field pieces. There was also the increased mobility made possible by railroads, for the first time a factor in warfare, with the problems attendant to their use for quickly delivered supplies and for the evacuation of the sick and wounded.

Napoleon, the American model, had not developed a highly trained staff, though his chief of staff, Louis Alexandre Berthier, was a brilliant and energetic man. The German general staff, inaugurated by Gerhard Von Scharnhorst and August Gneisenau after the Napoleonic wars, had not then displayed its operations. In the Mexican War, General Winfield Scott made skillful employment of the engineering officers on his staff — Lee, McClellan, and Beauregard — for reconnaissance, but as general in chief in 1861 he operated nothing approximating a general staff by modern standards. McClellan had nearly a year and all the facilities of a going concern to develop the staff which served his army, as well as the good fortune of having an enterprising professional, who was also his father-in-law, as chief of staff. Yet, in many aspects of operations, McClellan's staff suffered lapses.

In the army Lee inherited, the general staff had proven to be worse than useless, and it was no loss to the new commanding general that, in response to his courteous offer to retain Johnston's staff, only Captain Mason joined him as assistant adjutant general. Little to no system of coordination existed between the general staff and the staffs of twenty-five brigades, five divisions, cavalry, artillery and supporting services.

These thirty-odd separate staffs were largely congenial groups, with generals having selected their staff workers on the same qualifications that would apply in civilian life — recommendation, character, and their fitness to adapt to the military family. As the quickly developed military units were informally assembled, and as most of the generals were individualistic gentlemen who had never conceived of working in any kind of system, standards of fitness were not usually businesslike.

Social graces at the dinner table and companionable turns of mind might constitute fitness by the standards of some generals. Others showed a preference for neighbors or friends, and some selected men whom they had respected in civilian life. Magruder selected Major Brent as ordnance officer because Brent, a Louisianian who had succeeded in law and politics in California, had represented him in a financial entanglement when Prince John was garrisoned at San Diego. Brothers and even sons were not infrequently on staffs, and cousins abounded. As Lee said, this made for agreeable headquarters life rather than effectiveness, but in June there was no time, with all else, to change that.

While Lee selected his own staff on the basis of merit — which included, of course, adaptability to the life of the headquarters household — he brought no new concepts to staff functions. With all his originality in strategic thinking and the technical advances he introduced into tactical warfare, Lee produced no development in staff organization. With experience, he would develop an effective use of staff, but essentially he followed the existing methods of employing staff officers as expediters of operations he personally planned and controlled.

The standard practices of Lee's day used fewer departments than the modern staff — with their G1, G2, G3, and G4 sections — and less interrelation between the departments. Lee duplicated the functions of G1 in the assistant adjutant general's paper work, and he approximated G4 in what might loosely be called the functions of supply and logistics, though he had no G4 officer. These duties were divided among the chiefs of special services, such as quartermaster general, commissary general, and chief of ordnance.

An intelligence officer responsible for all information about the enemy, the modern G2 section, was unknown in either army. McClellan had tried to compensate for the lack when he employed the Pinkerton detectives. In time Lee was to use Stuart, the war's greatest reconnaissance cavalryman, for what amounted to intelligence operations, and he developed a system of espionage from observant natives. But in preparing for the campaign in June Lee had, in effect, no intelligence system at all.

In comparison with modern developments in staff work, Lee's most significant deficiency was the equivalent of an operations officer, responsible for plans and operations performed by the modern G3 section. While today a military force, from brigade to army, is considered to be no better than its operations officer, Lee seemed to have no idea of the necessity for one officer responsible for knowing the whereabouts and employment of every unit of his army. As the operations officer is also supplied with all available information about the enemy's forces, he maintains a moment-by-moment awareness of the movement and disposition of his own troops in relation to the enemy's.

Such a blank in Civil War staffs was not unique with Lee, though to Lee it did represent his preference for operating at the strategic level. When the later attrition in command personnel forced Lee to direct tactics, he developed at his full flowering a supreme mastery in commanding tactical operations. However, his practice was to leave battle tactics to the initiative of subordinates whenever possible, and he designed his first offensive on this method.

In making the ambitious plans for the offensive, with what he had and what he knew, Lee evidently assumed that some of the functions of an operations officer would be fulfilled by his new chief of staff, Lieutenant Colonel Robert Hall Chilton. Lee, only eight years Chilton's senior and remembering him warmly from their service together in Texas, welcomed the conscientious professional when he joined the staff immediately after headquarters was established at the Dabbs house.

Older than the others at forty-seven, Chilton had been a captain of dragoons in the Regular Army and was paymaster major when he resigned, the same rank as Longstreet. Chilton had served in the adjutant general's office before coming to Lee on June 4 as nominal chief of staff. For unexplained reasons, Chilton never took hold, and in practical terms Lee had no chief of staff.

In Armistead Long, who had been with Lee since the South Atlantic operations, Lee had a superior soldier from the Old Army, but his talents were not used to the best advantage on the staff. The thirty-six-year-old Virginian, strongly built, dark and intense-looking, was primarily an artillerist, trained in the Regular Army under General Henry Hunt. Long, a lifetime friend of Hunt's, had an even closer tie with McClellan's army: General Sumner was his father-in-law. A literate, intelligent soldier, Long was used partly as military secretary and partly to help in a hurried reorganization of the artillery.

In the loose structure of Johnston's army, each brigade carried its own battery or batteries, sometimes with other batteries attached to the division, with no field officers in command of the division's artillery. The reserve artillery of the army was disproportionately large with twenty-three batteries, about ninety guns, commanded by Brigadier General William N. Pendleton. An Episcopal rector from Lexington who had graduated from West Point a year behind Lee, Pendleton was also officially chief of artillery — "generally" in charge, the orders read. His duties were not clearly defined, and Pendleton, a hard worker, was inclined to absorb himself in fussing over details. To sharpen the artillery organization, Lee gave Armistead Long many of the duties normally belonging to the chief of artillery, and this was a poor arrangement.

Lacking the time to attempt a full reorganization of the artillery, Lee, through Pendleton and Long, could do little more than tighten the slack. Some uniformity was brought to the number of guns, men and horses to a battery; weak batteries were pulled out of line to be reorganized; heavy artillery was replaced by field-gun batteries, and a start was made toward forming a division's batteries under a divisional chief of artillery and providing a divisional reserve.

Working directly at headquarters were the three men, all from civilian life, who were to form the nucleus of Lee's permanent personal staff. Walter H. Taylor had been with Lee from the first and was to stay to the end. Taylor had attended Virginia Military Institute, without graduating, and was a successful businessman in Norfolk when he was recommended to Lee by a distant cousin of his, also a distant cousin of Lee's. Good-looking, personable, able and devoted, Taylor was listed as aide-de-camp and, on the move to the Dabbs house, was largely manager of office routine — in charge of clerks, correspondence and such. Young Taylor grew in his job more than any other man and, also growing very close to Lee, was to become assistant adjutant general of the army.

Charles Marshall, a lawyer, and Charles S. Venable, a mathematics professor, both joined Lee during the Richmond period and also were listed as aides-de-camp. They gradually worked out their spheres of special duty, Marshall replacing Long as military secretary and Venable becoming something of an informal inspector general. Taylor, Marshall and Venable were the only members of the staff to remain with Lee to Appomattox.

Along with Captain Mason, the legacy from Johnston who served with Lee only temporarily, the staff was completed with Major Thomas M. R. Talcott. An engineering officer who also joined the staff during the Richmond period, Talcott acted as liaison with Major Stevens, then chief engineer, before returning to the engineers himself.

These seven men comprised the personal staff, who lived at headquarters, ate with the general and assumed responsibility for the operation of general headquarters. Except for Mason, then assistant adjutant general, their duties were not rigidly defined, and all took turns in the transmission of orders. To this extent, most of them acted as joint chiefs of communications: they were in charge of couriers — usually individuals temporarily detached from the cavalry — and delivered verbal orders themselves during battle.

This personal staff was extended into what today would be called a general staff by chiefs of branches of the service — commissary, quartermaster, medicine, engineer, judge advocate general, inspector general, Pendleton as chief of reserve artillery, and the spectacular Porter Alexander as acting chief of ordnance.

Lieutenant Colonel Alexander, of a privileged Georgia background, had been one of the younger West Point graduates in the Regular Army most sought by both sides when war came. Just turned twenty-seven, Alexander, with an extremely high intelligence, had a restless energy, a goad to perfection, and a capacity like Lee's for taking pains over details within a broad vision. Lacking the authoritative support in Johnston's regime to exploit his powers, Alexander began to emerge after Lee assumed command. Ultimately he would be transferred to the artillery, to become the greatest cannoneer of the Confederacy and possibly of the war. Not a major figure in the mind of the army in June, 1862, nor a popular officer — he was too demanding with subordinates, too critical of superiors — this sharp-edged young man was the nearest approach to genius in the immediate group with which Lee worked.

These two groups — the personal staff and chiefs of services; with assistants, numbering twenty-odd — comprised the staff through which Lee worked to ready the army for its offensive in combination with Jackson.

CHAPTER SEVEN

"General Orders No. 75"

OUTSIDE THE Dabbs house a dust-covered officer, wearing a dingy uniform without insignia, was leaning against the yard fence when D. H. Hill rode up on Monday afternoon, June 23. As Hill dismounted, he was attracted by something familiar in the slouched figure, the eyes shaded by the brim of a cadet cap and the lower part of his face covered by a rust-colored beard. He recognized his brother-in-law, Stonewall Jackson, whom he had presumed to be in the Shenandoah Valley.

When Harvey Hill asked, "What are *you* doing *here?*" Jackson replied he had ridden ahead of his troops to attend a council called by General Lee. Hill had ridden over from his lines across the Williamsburg Road for the same meeting, and the two men went into the general headquarters house together.

Jackson did not explain that he had ridden fifty-three miles since one o'clock that morning, accompanied by a single staff officer and two civilian guides. In his mania for secrecy, he had stolen away from his own army, carrying a pass made out to an unidentified colonel. Incredibly, Jackson had no awareness of his fame. He never read a newspaper, permitted no correspondents about his army and went to no places where crowds of strangers might have admired him. At that moment the most famous soldier on the continent, he had waited in shyness outside the Dabbs house until his brother-in-law's appearance made his entrance easier.

In a downstairs room in the back of the house, Lee's private headquarters office, Longstreet and A. P. Hill had joined the commanding general. Jackson was acquainted with the other two major generals, though he was not, and never became, on intimate terms with them. With no staff officers present, Lee passed quickly over the amenities — asking Jackson if he wanted any refreshments after his long ride — and then told the four generals in explicit detail their parts in the offensive to be opened on McClellan's right wing.

Since the area to be covered would make personal direction of the battle impossible, Lee intended to compose a battle plan that allowed no margin for human deviation. Unlike Johnston in his private planning, Lee was very modern in giving each general a clear understanding of the objective and of his precise interrelated part in the total design. None of the four men said anything when Lee unfolded his purpose of attempting the most hazardous movement in warfare — the meeting of two separated forces on the field in the presence of the enemy.

These generals were not the only division commanders involved in the operation. While their forces made the offensive movement against McClellan's right wing, the divisions of Magruder and Huger were to man the defenses east of Richmond. Magruder and Huger would be sent written orders after the details of the offensive were evolved. Lee never offered any reasons for selecting the men he did for their different assignments, but the choices seem obvious enough.

Huger, under the Seven Pines cloud, had not looked enterprising in performance of his duties, and his three brigades had performed indifferently in the anticlimatic fighting of June 1. Lee proposed to strengthen Huger's defensive line, across the miry country south of the Williamsburg Road, with Robert Ransom's North Carolina brigade from Holmes's department.

Magruder, extending the front from Huger to the Chickahominy, was a natural selection for his assignment. Though his energetic command had brought good conditioning and morale in his troops, Magruder himself was excitable. Naturally loquacious, he needed constant communication with superiors when placed in a subordinate position. Armistead Long, an admirer of Magruder's "chivalric" character, believed Magruder "belonged partly to that class of men whose genius, being unshackled, was capable of achieving the most brilliant results; but when overshadowed by authority became paralyzed."

Long observed that his old comrade did not "possess the dashing nonchalant air" of the Newport period, which he had retained even on the barren plains of Fort Leavenworth, where he had bedazzled the Indians and frontiersmen with his pageants. With the loose structure of Magruder's command, in three two-brigade divisions, his thirteen thousand men would be best suited in all ways to the holding action in front of Richmond. There their commander's theatrical strain could be employed in "demonstrating."

Of the generals to lead the offensive, only A. P. Hill was an unproven quantity at division command, but in his one month as major general he had demonstrated — as did all men who advanced under Lee — that recognizable quality of responsible application beyond the minimal requirements. Armistead Long had made a mid-June inspection tour of Hill's new defensive position east and west of the Mechanicsville bridges, where Hill had replaced Magruder. Long reported: "[Hill's] defenses are as well advanced as those of any part of the line. His troops are in fine condition. . . . Hill is every inch a soldier and is destined to make his mark."

Not then thirty-seven, Powell Hill was the youngest of the four men and the most handsome. Lacking Lee's classic male beauty, he had grace and the indefinable quality of "style." His cheeks were lean, his hazel eyes deep set and intense, and he had a full beard of reddish brown. He wore his hair parted high on the right side and brushed back over his ears, quite long in the back.

At home in the social life of Richmond, A. P. Hill was emotional, highstrung, sensitive and courtly. Though not a man to invite familiarities, his manner was warm and informal, and his thoughtfulness made him a favorite of junior officers and couriers. A brother officer called him "the most lovable of all Lee's generals," and Lee was personally fond of him. Hill's grandfather had served as a colonel with Lee's father, Light Horse Harry Lee, during the Revolution.

New at his rank, A. P. Hill said little at the meeting, nor did Jackson or D. H. Hill. Longstreet seemed to be spokesman for the subordinate generals. The top soldier remaining from Johnston's regime, in which he had enjoyed such prestige and power, he was in something of a state of afflatus.

Because of his vindictiveness toward Lee in the self-defenses he wrote after the commanding general was dead, it is difficult to judge his feelings for Lee at this period. He had, naturally, been sorry to lose Johnston and in his writings referred admirably to him as the "beloved chief." Yet, later in the war, when Longstreet found himself in the West where Johnston was nominally department commander, he wrote Richmond of the urgent need for "a great mind, like Lee," and said nothing about Johnston. Longstreet's feelings for Johnston were undoubtedly colored by the personal advances he made in Johnston's command, during which period his ambitions burgeoned.

In the Old Army Longstreet had been content with the mundane duties and security of paymaster major, and he had volunteered directly into the Confederate armies rather than joining with a state's forces, seeking the same undemanding post. When necessity had forced a field command on him, he had recovered the taste for glory. Then, in the preceding January, Longstreet had turned more serious-minded following the death of three of his children during a scarlet fever epidemic in Richmond. Colonel Moxley Sorrel, his chief of staff, said that before this tragedy Longstreet, "fond of a glass, and very skillful at poker," had enjoyed convivial evenings with fellow generals in Johnston's army. When Longstreet returned to the army from the funeral, he was, Sorrel said, "a changed man." His un-relaxed concentration on the army, and Johnston's flattering prefer-ments, coincided with the resurgence of his ambitions.

When Lee succeeded Johnston, Longstreet was definitely among those who regarded Lee's career as a dubious basis for combat com-mand, and he immediately began to assert himself. At first he had tried to continue in command of the wing which had composed the Seven Pines assault on the Williamsburg Road. Acting as the out-raged superior of the man he was going to make the scapegoat, Longstreet had removed Huger's troops from that general's com-mand. Upon Huger's protest, Lee quickly restored his troops to him, and that ended Longstreet's wing. Then, according to Longstreet, he took to visiting Lee's headquarters with proffers of advice. There is no reason to doubt Longstreet's account, since he was very full of himself, and during the following year he repeatedly attempted to impose either strategy or tactics on Lee.

Lee's gentleness of command would lead Longstreet to over-estimate his influence, laying the basis for his future obstinacy and discord in command, but at the Dabbs house meeting Longstreet was satisfied that he had established the influential position he had enjoyed under the departed Johnston. Though no one exerted the influence over Lee which Longstreet assumed he did, there was no question that the new commanding general regarded the burly division commander as a dependable known factor. In addition to his self-assurance and his record with Johnston — no more was known of D. H. Hill's conspicuous part at Seven Pines than of Huger's innocence of the charges — Longstreet showed a tireless energy in the administration of his division that was reflected by the condition and morale of his troops.

However, in planning the offensive, Lee did not give Longstreet's division a post of special importance. As all through his command, he assigned equal duty to all divisions and assigned units their position according to their place on the field. By this arrangement, Powell Hill's division became the connecting hinge between the three Richmond divisions and Jackson's force, and the stranger Jackson, with whom none of the others had operated, became the key figure of the offensive movement.

2

The basic element in Lee's plan was McClellan's line of supply from the White House. Only by this line — the York River Railroad and a network of mostly poor crossroads — could McClellan maintain his advanced community. Along with ammunition and the materials of war, daily meals must be supplied to 117,000 men and forage to 10,000 horses. The approximate figure of 117,000 included his sick, those under arrest, or detached on special details. His troops equipped for duty approximated 105,000 of all arms according to his June 20 report.

Lee's purpose was to mount a successful attack north of the Chickahominy which, by driving this Federal wing eastward, would force McClellan to abandon his works in front of Richmond and cross the river to protect his supply line with the White House. Lee built his plan on the faith that by *driving* the northern wing, his troops, holding the initiative, could defeat the rest of McClellan's army in the open when those units crossed the river in defense.

As this plan was posited upon a decisive defeat of the northern wing, Lee's risk was to leave the eastern approaches to Richmond held only by Magruder and Huger, about twenty-two thousand, in order to concentrate fifty thousand infantry and artillery on the northern wing. In addition to these seventy-two thousand troops, Lee's large reserve artillery approximated three thousand, Holmes's brigades south of the James would run close to seven thousand, and Stuart's cavalry to about three thousand. The larger portion of the cavalry operated under Stuart north of the Chickahominy, and twelve hundred in scattered units patrolled the roads between the Confederate right and the James River. Lee's total approximated eighty-five thousand.

Including Holmes's brigades south of the James in the total, Lee was committing 60 per cent of his available force under his four best commanders to an operation in which the offensive force would be separated from the holding force by the Chickahominy. Excluding Holmes, the cavalry and reserve artillery, Lee was committing about 70 per cent of his brigades with their accompanying batteries to an offensive in which they would be detached from the other 30 per cent.

The assault force, fifty-thousand-odd exclusive of the cavalry, was in turn to commence the operation in two forces to form a pincer on McClellan's wing. Jackson's command, screened by Jeb Stuart, was to come in on the flank and rear from the north, while Longstreet, D. H. Hill and A. P. Hill attacked from west to southeast. This pincer movement was designed to force the Federals out of a natural stronghold on Beaver Dam Creek. As the whole plan was designed to force McClellan into the open in protection of his supply line, so the opening action was designed to turn the headwaters of Beaver Dam Creek and avoid the strong position which began at Ellerson's Mill.

Lee's plan can be traced on the map on page 154: (1) Jackson would approach, screened by Stuart's cavalry, to the east of the headwaters of Beaver Dam Creek, behind the Federal position. (2) At Jackson's approach, A. P. Hill would force the crossing of the Chickahominy against the Federal outpost at the Meadow Bridges. (3) A. P. Hill, on the Federal side of the Chickahominy, would drive the light Federal force out of the village of Mechanicsville, uncovering the bridges over the Chickahominy on the Mechanicsville Turnpike. (4) On hastily built bridges, D. H. Hill and Longstreet would cross the Chickahominy, Hill swinging to A. P. Hill's left and Longstreet to his right. (5) With Jackson approaching on the flank, the

Federal force would withdraw from the stronghold along Beaver Dam Creek; Jackson, D. H. Hill, A. P. Hill and Longstreet would drive the enemy eastward along the Chickahominy — with Jackson, bearing to his left, advancing toward the crossroads of Old Cold Harbor, on the line of roads to McClellan's base. (6) The initial action would drive the Federals east of New Bridge, where Lee's assault force would open communications with the Magruder-Huger line south of the Chickahominy.

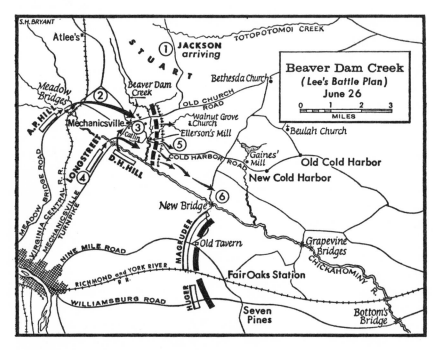

Once the Confederate forces north and south of the Chickahominy were connected, the offensive would pass the point of gravest danger, that of McClellan striking toward Richmond while the bulk and the best of Lee's army was engaged on the north side. When the forces on both sides of the river were connected, Lee planned to continue the north-side drive east along the York River Railroad, improvising the details according to McClellan's reaction. In Lee's total offensive plan, then, only the opening action had been developed in detail at the conference with his four generals.

3

In the primitive stage of liaison, Branch's brigade would be detached from Hill's division and posted at an unguarded crossing of the Chickahominy at Half Sink. Jackson would communicate his approach to Branch by courier. Branch would then cross the narrow stretch of the Chickahominy and move southward, parallel to the river and loosely parallel to Jackson's advance. When their approach became known to Powell Hill, Hill would force the crossing of the Meadow Bridges, and this action would serve as the opening of the battle. No preparations were made for communications with general headquarters: coordination depended upon the Jackson-to-Branch-to-Hill liaison to spring the trap.

Lee, having discussed with the generals all the details except time sequence, for some reason left the four subordinates to arrange among themselves the time for commencing the action. As the commands of Longstreet and the two Hills were camped in the area, the choice of day was given Jackson. At that point began the strange behavior of Stonewall Jackson that has been for the hundred years since the subject of so much discussion, analysis, and controversy.

When Jackson left his army for the fifty-two-mile ride to Richmond, its vanguard was at Frederick's Hall, a stop on the Virginia Central Railroad. Jackson's command had begun the march from its Valley camp near the Port Republic battlefield on June 18. In the pass across the Blue Ridge, at Waynesboro, the troops began to move in relays on two hundred cars, passenger and freight, of the Virginia Central. The trains would collect troops at the end of the line, ferry them to the front, and repeat the process. The soldiers, covering the cars inside and out "like bees," enjoyed the novel means of transportation.

On June 20 the advance had reached the Piedmont country at Charlottesville, and by noon of the 21st the head of the column reached Gordonsville, about sixty miles from where they had broken camp. On Sunday the 22nd the van passed Frederick's Hall, twenty-five miles from Gordonsville. In observance of the Sabbath, Jackson, a devout Presbyterian, halted the march.

While the infantry was being thus whisked across space with a minimum of walking, the artillery and heavy wagons had plodded along the roads. Beyond Frederick's Hall, however, the railroad track had been cut by Federal cavalry, and for the rest of the way the infantry would join the artillery in its more familiar method of covering ground.

On the Monday that Jackson had ridden to Richmond, the infantry was to make a daylight start on the road to Ashland, about thirty-five miles from Frederick's Hall. In Lee's plan, Jackson was to reach the Hanover Court House Road southeast of Ashland the day before the battle was to open. As Ashland was sixteen miles due north of Richmond, Jackson's march from his camp beyond Ashland to the designated battle area would be about ten miles.

When the other generals asked Jackson when he could reach the point beyond Ashland, he said the night of the following day, the 24th. He would be ready to move at three o'clock in the morning on the 25th to advance to the battle.

The approximately forty miles from Frederick's Hall to the Hanover Court House Road would not under ordinary conditions represent a difficult two days' march for Jackson's troops. But the conditions under which Jackson's "foot cavalry" averaged twenty miles a day had been in the open Valley terrain, in a familiar country over well-mapped roads, with the old Valley Pike as the main artery. From Frederick's Hall to the battle area his long columns would be moving through strange country, flat, marshy and obscured by brush, with poor roads that were mostly a series of disjointed connections of short lanes built by individual farmers in Colonial days. Few natives would have felt certain of the way ten miles beyond their own gates.

On the tortuous, unknown route — for practical purposes, unmapped — only the van of Jackson's sixteen thousand men of all arms had advanced as close as thirty-five miles to the point beyond Ashland. In the confusion brought by the speedy travel to Frederick's Hall, his columns stretched at least fifteen miles behind the advanced units. Furthermore, Jackson himself, facing another night ride, would not rejoin his troops until midmorning of the 24th. Under these conditions, for Jackson to estimate that his troops would be in position to move into action in thirty-six hours from the meeting was an unrealistic appraisal not characteristic of him.

Jackson was a low-spoken man, usually quiet and never assertive. From all that is known of the conference, the general from the Valley merely stated that he could be ready to advance to the battle area at three in the morning of June 25.

The other three generals, familiar with the brushy country, knew the hazards of its narrow roads, even without interference from the enemy. They all assumed — correctly, as of then — that Jackson's movement was unsuspected by McClellan, but Federal cavalry operated actively as far north as Hanover Court House. Since Jackson was totally unfamiliar with the terrain, Longstreet suggested that he delay the assault date for one day. This would give Jackson three days (including that Monday, the 23rd) to move his strung-out columns from thirty-five to fifty miles to the Hanover Court House Road beyond Ashland. Little latitude was allowed for closing up and resting before moving out at 3 A.M. on June 26 for the last ten miles to the battle area.

With no recorded comment, Jackson accepted Longstreet's suggestion to postpone his arrival to the 25th. When General Lee returned to the private headquarters room, the generals informed him that June 26 was the day they had agreed upon for opening the offensive.

Lee then told them he would write out the battle orders the following day and send a copy to each man, as well as to Magruder and Huger. Having been a witness to Johnston's disaster through verbal and unspecific orders, Lee planned to put in writing details down to the movements of the cavalry regiments on the roads east of Richmond and to the artillerists on the heavy guns covering the Chickahominy.

4

In what Lee considered to be specific details, he showed his inexperience. The four generals with him showed equal innocence of the difference between the strategy and the tactics, or the plan and the operation. None felt their organization to be too loose, their staff work to be too primitive, the generals too inexperienced in moving large bodies of armed units and too unfamiliar in working with one another to undertake the complicated maneuvers of Lee's grand strategy. In effect too inexperienced to recognize their limitations, the five generals did not know enough to know better. Where McClellan abandoned the initiative by conceiving of every detail that could go wrong, Lee and his generals confidently agreed to seize the initiative by conceiving only of what could go right.

None of them seemed at all concerned about the possibility of McClellan attacking the lightly manned lines to the east while their own assault force was engaged north of the Chickahominy. Only Lee's stress on reaching the north end of New Bridge showed his awareness of the risk he was taking. But there was one very curious omission made by the five generals, and by all the Confederates who became involved in the offensive: what Federal force were they attacking north of the Chickahominy and what Federal force posed the threat to Magruder and Huger east of Richmond?

Every preserved line of correspondence, every recorded line of dialogue, and every reference in battle reports and in postwar writing refers to McClellan's wing north of the Chickahominy only as "the enemy." Nor has any historian ever questioned what force Lee and his generals thought the "enemy" to be attacked consisted of.

When Johnston had attacked at Seven Pines, McClellan had had only two corps south of the Chickahominy, with Sumner's corps crossing during the battle and on June 1. Sumner remained. When Stuart's cavalry took its gaudy trip around the Federal army, Porter's corps had been posted in the area of Beaver Dam Creek and Franklin's corps farther east. After Stuart's ride on June 18, Franklin's corps was moved south of the Chickahominy. There is no evidence that this was known to Lee. It was known that McClellan had received reinforcements, in McCall's division. When Franklin's corps crossed to south of the Chickahominy, McCall's division was advanced to strengthen Porter's corps.

With McCall, Porter's force approached thirty thousand of all arms. Also on the north side were parts of a cavalry division of two thousand commanded by Jeb Stuart's father-in-law and a fellow-Virginian, Philip St. George Cooke. Lee's total force on the north side, including Stuart, some of the reserve artillery, and a scattering of engineering units, would total upwards of fifty-five thousand.

This five-to-three ratio was not in itself a particularly heavy numerical advantage for an assault that must succeed, quickly and decisively. It was a heavy proportion to commit considering that McClellan had in front of Richmond seventy thousand infantry and artillery, opposed by no more than twenty-two thousand, more than one third of which were unproven troops under Huger's dubious leadership. This proportion of more than three-to-one with McClellan's superiority in cannon represented a hazard which it seems unlikely Lee would knowingly have risked.

In addition to Huger's Old Army garrison habits — waiting for the evening gun and a visit to friends — there was Magruder's known excitability and need for guidance when acting under another's direction. With this pair isolated from general headquarters, nothing could have provided a serious check to McClellan's advancing the six miles to Richmond's streets.

Lee was bold enough to leave Richmond's defenses to these two for twenty-four hours against any numerical superiority; it would have been foolhardy to risk the capital against nearly four fifths of McClellan's army. It would have been almost unthinkable after McClellan made his short advance on June 25, the day before Lee's planned offensive.

Everything considered, it seems certain that Lee could not have known the composition of the force he was attacking nor of McClellan's strength south of the Chickahominy. Lee and his generals parted, with Jackson returning to his horse for another fifty-mile night ride, in a state of which it might be said that ignorance was confidence.

5

Unknown to Lee and McClellan, their time schedules were running neck and neck. With all of Lee's ignorance of the balance of weight of the Federal strength, he was disturbed by McClellan's advance along the Williamsburg Road on June 25. The action in itself was small and local. South of the Williamsburg Road, at the westernmost fringes of White Oak Swamp, a boggy wooded area of no-man's-land existed between the two picket lines. McClellan's limited purpose was to advance to where this last of the swampy ground would be within his lines and not at his front.

Kearny's and Hooker's divisions, from Heintzelman's corps, made a relatively heavy attack in the action variously called Oak Grove, French's Hill, and King's School-House. In the sharp fighting, costing about five hundred casualties on both sides, McClellan's troops achieved the objective of advancing their picket line with some difficulty. It was not until the end of the day that the new Federal picket line was established, facing a clearing, four miles from Richmond.

The attacking force struck the three brigades of Huger, and there again the timing was very close. Huger's three brigades, with numbers reduced by sickness and absentees to barely six thousand troops "present and equipped for duty," only that morning had had their line extended and strengthened by the arrival of Robert Ransom's brigade of three thousand brought from Petersburg in Holmes's department.

Ransom, a thirty-four-year-old professional from North Carolina, was plagued by poor health, and a strain of the martinet prevented him from winning the affection of volunteer troops. A very good soldier, he was valuable at that stage, and his North Carolina troops were well trained for regiments that had been in service only two months. The colonel of the 35th North Carolina regiment was Ransom's older brother, Matt. A lawyer and politician, with the personal appeal lacked by the West Pointer, he was to become the able and popular commander of the new brigade put into action June 25.

Two elements about the Federal advance on the Williamsburg Road caused Lee, as he wrote the President, "some anxiety." Because of the inexperience of Ransom's brigade, Lee had ridden across to the Williamsburg Road when he heard the firing grow heavy. As it turned out, the troops handled themselves more than adequately in restraining a considerably heavier enemy, and held their main line of earthworks. But the affair, as Lee saw it, "was not well managed." He was annoyed to find Huger absent from headquarters and not exercising command. Lee wrote the negligent old-line soldier an order to stay where he belonged and alert himself in looking after his lines.

The larger element of concern was the possibility that McClellan had discovered Jackson's secret advance and was acting in anticipation of Lee. This possibility Lee, in the boldness of his singly held purpose, seemed to dismiss from his mind. In his battle report Lee wrote that the Federals attacked with "the intention, as appeared by a dispatch from General McClellan, of securing his advance toward Richmond." Though this dispatch could be assumed to have been found on a captured courier, it was nowhere else mentioned. Neither Armistead Long, Walter Taylor nor Charles Marshall referred to the June 25 action at all in their writings. All evidence indicated that Lee, after returning from the engagement on the Williamsburg Road, devoted his attention to the execution of his own battle plan. General Orders No. 75 had been drafted by Lee the day before, and on the night of the 25th copies were sent to Magruder and Huger.

Lee was sound enough in assuming that McClellan was only securing a stage in his slow advance on Richmond, and "appeared to be unaware of our purpose" — the combined assault with Jackson. But McClellan had also planned an attack for the next day.

McClellan had gradually established June 26 as the day for his advance on Old Tavern, and the 25th's action was a preparatory step in the larger movement. If McClellan took Old Tavern on the 26th, his troops would force Magruder to evacuate the line along the New Bridge Road all the way to the New Bridge crossing of the Chickahominy and isolate Lee's assault force on the north bank. Lee would lose on his great risk and be unable to support the troops manning more than five miles of lines in front of Richmond with a density of no more than two men a yard. Unknown to both generals, the game had become a matter of who made the first move.

Another vital element was unknown to Lee. On June 25 McClellan did have an inkling of Jackson's approach. A captured Confederate deserter, unusually well informed for a soldier with the secretive Jackson, on June 24 gave McClellan the clearest, most detailed report he had ever received of the enemy's movements, strength and disposition.

Though no deserter was completely trusted (and Jackson contrived to have rumors scattered which caused Federal generals all over Virginia to predict his imminent approach on their sectors), other signs indicated to McClellan the probability that Jackson was moving from the northeast to strike at his line of communications with the White House. Everything depended upon the use McClellan made of the information.

The dictionary meaning of the psychological term perseveration is, "continued repetition of the same action . . . through inability to shift readily from one activity to another." McClellan could be said to suffer acutely developed perseveration. His mental processes were incapable of appropriate response to the new element of Jackson.

With his rigidified absorption in his own plans, he could not consider the possibility that Jackson might be approaching as part of a general offensive. He regarded Jackson's approach on the line of his communications as only another disruption, like the rains, to his schedule. McClellan immediately postponed his advance of June 26 and made preparations to protect his base against Jackson.

To the north of the Chickahominy he sent orders of rudimentary precaution. The cavalry was to move out toward the line of Jackson's advance, destroying bridges and obstructing roads. The guard at the White House depot, where Silas Casey had been transferred, must be put on the alert. To Heintzelman, whose corps had made the June 25 advance on the Williamsburg Road ("perfectly successful," McClellan had wired Washington), he sent orders for protecting his new line against counterattacks. With this he wired Stanton, "Have made all possible arrangements" for Jackson's attack on the "right and rear."

Actually, his major arrangement was to postpone the one movement that could have disrupted Lee's plans.

6

At the end of the day of June 25, McClellan knew he had not done enough. In his unselfadmitted failure to respond to the new development, the center of his attention shifted to considerations of his reputation. At quarter past six he sent Stanton a long telegram renouncing responsibility for what might happen.

Along with the fact that Jackson was approaching on his right and rear, he added the rumor that Beauregard had arrived in Richmond with reinforcements that brought "the rebel force" to two hundred thousand. Beauregard, who commanded the Confederate Army in the West after Shiloh, had recently taken a sick leave from the army's rebuilding camp at Tupelo, Mississippi, and, while absent, had been removed from command. A less likely reinforcer could scarcely have been conjured than this ill, out-of-favor soldier more than one thousand miles away.

Against these "vastly superior odds," McClellan promised that "this army will do all in the power of men to hold their position and repulse any attack." Then, calling attention to his repeated representations of the necessity of reinforcing his inferior numbers, he came to the crux: "I will do all that a general can do . . ." and if the army "is destroyed by overwhelming numbers, can at least die with it and share its fate. But if the result of the action . . . is a disaster, the responsibility can not be thrown on my shoulders; it must rest where it belongs."

It must be said for McClellan that when he shifted blame to another he did not pick a victim in his own command nor stoop to falsifying reports. He attacked in the open, he called the top men, and in Lincoln and Stanton he had justifiable grounds for complaint and resentment. Too much self-knowledge would have been demanded of McClellan for him to have understood that the most damaging results of their interference was the effect on him. His message to Stanton revealed that he was defeated before the enemy had struck a blow.

It was not probable that McClellan believed the enemy's force approached two hundred thousand. As Colonel Henderson wrote, if a general "can not discover from the attitude of the enemy what the odds are, he is unfitted for supreme command." Making faulty estimates was not the nature of McClellan's unfitness. When the foolish Pinkerton agents were not providing him with misinformation, McClellan made accurate estimates of the enemy's numbers. He had estimated Magruder's force at Yorktown and Jackson's in the Valley almost to the man. With his intelligence and the general information available on all fronts, McClellan would know that the five million white population of eleven Southern states, with garrisons in every one and field forces scattered over more than one thousand miles of front, could not amass at Richmond nearly twice the numbers that the United States could field from a population of more than twenty million.

The forces opposing him certainly gave no indication of possessing "overwhelming numbers." Only that day, the 25th, when Heintzelman had broken off the incompleted attack on the Williamsburg Road, McClellan himself had sent in one division, and the Confederates, backed up to the outskirts of their capital, had brought forward no reinforcements to hold their position. Nor had McClellan, on the field, shown any apprehension that large numbers would be massed in counterattack. By his military estimates, nothing suggested any need for the commanding general to face such a desperate resort as dying with his troops under waves of attackers.

Of course, McClellan had no intention of dying with his troops, nor of having his army killed off. The calamity he envisioned was not destruction of his army but the suspension of the offensive. He knew that, after eleven months of preparation, and from a position within four miles of the enemy's capital, the suspension of his offensive would require explanations. So he explained in advance, predicting the disaster for which the government was responsible.

After that, *if* he saved his army and contained the enemy, he would not be under scrutiny for halting his advance. He would be judged on the positive accomplishment of saving his army from the consequences of the government's management.

This was the position McClellan developed when he later presented the campaign, and the position he took when he wired Stanton on the evening of June 25. As he had made some exchanges with the navy prior to the 25th toward the end of convoying supplies from the Pamunkey to the James, McClellan later claimed his defensive shift was the realization of his long-cherished change of base from the White House to the James River.

However, early on the morning of the 25th, before Jackson's approach had begun to work on his imagination, McClellan had wired Stanton for "new regiments" to build up his garrison at the White House. The next day Stanton wired him, "The reinforcements will be sent to the place you request." During the day of the 26th, McClellan's chief quartermaster, Brigadier General Van Vliet, was making arrangements with Quartermaster General Meigs in Washington for the movement of five thousand men — infantry, artillery, cavalry, and baggage trains — from Alexandria to the Pamunkey River base. That knotty little item fouls the rationalization that his defensive shift was part of a purpose to abandon the White House.

There was another element in his rationalization that has been curiously ignored by both detractors and defenders, as it was by McClellan himself. That was his 101-gun siege train. Half of this was composed of the seacoast artillery which could not be moved by the heaviest gun carriages and required special equipment to haul and lift the pieces onto firing platforms. This neglected item brings an obscurity to all of McClellan's motives in front of Richmond.

As of June 25, McClellan had moved from the White House none of the forty-eight pieces of seacoast artillery, which presumably remained on the ships. Of his regulation siege guns, which could be brought forward slowly to fixed positions, he had brought up only twenty-six pieces. On June 25, ten of these — five 4½-inch rifled Rodmans and five 30-pounder Parrotts (4.2 inches) — had been placed in position north of the Chickahominy at Dr. Gaines's farm. There they had shelled the Confederate batteries on the southern bank of the Chickahominy in the New Bridge area, obviously as a part of McClellan's preparations for the artillery assault on Old Tavern.

While these regulation siege guns lacked the mobility of field artillery, their weight did not prohibit the use of dried-out roads. The Rodman and 30-pounder Parrott weighed 3450 and 4200 pounds, as contrasted with 890 pounds and 1227 pounds for the 3-inch rifled Parrott and the 12-pounder (4.62 inches) smoothbore Napoleon, among the favorite field pieces of both sides.

The seacoast artillery, which McClellan did not list separately from the siege guns in his siege train, ran in weight from 9700 pounds, for the 100-pounder Parrott, to 17,120 pounds for the thirteen-inch mortars. At Yorktown, when this seacoast artillery was brought forward, only the lightest were advanced over roads by using sling carts. The guns were mounted to fixed platforms by the ropes and pulleys in a tripod contrivance called a gin. The heavier pieces could only be brought forward on barges on Wormley's Creek, under cover of night, to be landed on wharves constructed for that purpose along the battery platforms. The neglected point in McClellan's rationalization of the change of base is that from the James River no creeks ran in the right direction for floating the guns forward on barges to battery wharves in a position to shell the lines close to Richmond. *From the James River base McClellan could not have brought forward the heaviest of the so-called siege guns on which he depended for repeating the Yorktown tactics at Richmond.*

McClellan's dependence on the York River Railroad for advancing this seacoast artillery was so obvious that Lee, almost immediately on assuming command, gave orders for the construction of a mobile, one-gun fort that became the first "railroad artillery" used in warfare. This heavy, protected gun was mounted on a railroad flatcar that could be moved by engine toward Fair Oaks Station, and there dispute the advance of the trains bringing forward the seacoast artillery.

Since the railroad from the Pamunkey was recognized as the only available means of bringing forward the guns that would have determined the campaign, and since there is no doubt that McClellan's only plan for forcing the evacuation of Richmond was by siege operations, a base on the James River would eliminate the use of the basic machinery of his operation.

That this move was regarded only as an emergency alternative was revealed in the wire McClellan had General Van Vliet send to the White House on the 26th: "If you are obliged to abandon the White House . . . you must throw all our supplies up the James River as soon as possible . . . It will be of vast importance to establish our depots on James River without delay if we abandon White House. . . ."

All messages showed the sudden preparation to evacuate the White House to be part of the defensive reaction to the threat of Jackson's approach. Just as when McClellan had discovered Magruder's fortified works on April 5, he contracted. Then he sent Stanton the wire of the impending danger.

7

When McClellan sent the message to Stanton, he had possessed no certainty that Jackson was approaching his flank. Before that night, McClellan had absorbed for weeks a stream of rumors about impending Confederate thrusts without being affected. But this newly threatened movement was not just "the enemy": it was Jackson. His sudden appearances and disappearances, along with the swirl of reports which placed him each day in a different place, gave Jackson the quality of a sinister will-o'-the-wisp. He was everywhere at once and nowhere. Whenever he actually did appear out of the mists, disaster inevitably followed. Then he was gone. A general need not be as imaginative as McClellan to have his poise shaken by Jackson.

With Jackson rumored to be on his way to Richmond, Lincoln and Stanton took their final action in supervising McClellan's Peninsula Campaign. Lincoln's wire, in reply to McClellan's to Stanton, must have come as the *coup de grâce* to the commanding general.

Saying that he was pained at McClellan's "talking of where the responsibility belonged," Lincoln added in an offhand PS, "General Pope thinks if you fall back it would be much better toward York River than the James. As Pope now has charge of the capital, please confer with him through the telegraph."

The next day McClellan learned officially that John Pope, a braggart from the Western front and a friend of the Radicals in Washington, had been placed in command of all Federal forces in central and northern Virginia, including McDowell. Thus, when McClellan warned Stanton that his army was threatened by the approach of Jackson's force from the Valley, Washington responded by informing him that a new Federal army had been formed in the area evacuated by Jackson and that McDowell would be withheld from the point of Confederate concentration.

The only possible explanation of this divorce from reason was that Lincoln had taken McClellan's scare wire literally and thought first of the safety of Washington. That Stanton supported the formation of an army for Pope where no enemy existed would appear to confirm McClellan's conviction that the war secretary actively operated against his success, though it was probably not so simple as that.

This climax in the government's blundering interference contributed further grounds for McClellan's rationalization. Yet, with all causes from without and from within, including the central motivation of protecting his status as the Young Napoleon, McClellan did rationalize in refusing to admit that he was transfixed, waiting for the blow to fall.

On that humid Thursday night in Dr. Trent's two-story frame house near the Chickahominy, he was the hero facing the "fall from high estate." That summer night in McClellan's life could have been a scene from one of Shakespeare's kings except that the hero had lost contact with the realities of his situation. He had forgotten that his objective was to restore the Union by taking Richmond.

CHAPTER EIGHT

The Early Work of a Master

WHEN THE SUN came up at 4:38 on Thursday the 26th of June, the busiest man in the two armies was John Bankhead Magruder. The day before, he had received his copy of General Orders No. 75, which, he wrote, "directed me to hold my position in front of the enemy against attack and at all hazards [and] to make such demonstrations as to discover his operations." As Magruder and his troops did not know Lee had formed his assault force of what he considered to be his best commanders, Major Brent, the ordnance officer, reported that Magruder's men felt they held "the post of honor."

"Prince John," always attentive to the amenities, had arranged for his staff to have their meals at the family table of the house in which the general had his headquarters. The officers slept in tents in the farmhouse yard, but at breakfast they sat down to a linen-covered table with china and silver. That morning the group was excited and tense. Along with the exhilaration that came at the prospect of a big offensive, Magruder and his staff had reason to feel apprehensive.

In his orders, Lee had revised Jackson's halt on the night of June 25, and instructed the Valley commander to push beyond Ashland five or six miles to make camp across the tracks of the Virginia Central (about eight miles from the battle area), and to move out at three in the morning. With Jackson's reputation for fast marches, Magruder could expect the Confederate offense to open across the river as early as seven o'clock. Instead of the welcome sounds announcing Jackson's approach, the first firing from across the Chickahominy fell on Magruder's position at Dr. Garnett's farm, commanding the approaches to the New Bridge crossing.

The day before, new heavy Federal guns — the 4½-inch Rodman rifles and the 30-pounder Parrotts from McClellan's siege train —

had opened on Magruder from entrenched positions at Dr. Gaines's farm on the north bank of the Chickahominy. Magruder's heaviest piece along the river was a 12-pounder Napoleon and his longest ranged gun was a 3-inch rifle, firing a 10-pound shell. (The pounds of howitzers and guns designated the weight of the projectile.) Magruder's two batteries had been quickly overwhelmed. After two gunners were killed, several wounded and half a dozen horses disabled, the pieces were withdrawn from the range of the heavier Federal metal. It was an ominous beginning for the morning of June 26 when the Federal siege guns across the river again forced Magruder's light batteries to withdraw from their position at the New Bridge crossing.

Originally placed at Dr. Gaines's farm to support the advance McClellan had planned for the 26th, the Federal guns were then firing only to silence the Confederate batteries. Magruder naturally suspected the heavy guns had been brought up for some reason concerning him. The fourteen hours of daylight ahead looked very long when his acting chief of artillery, Stephen D. Lee, reported "there was but little prospect of injuring the enemy's batteries" across the river.

Since Magruder's command had been absorbed into Johnston's army and the artillery organization changed after Lee had taken command, Magruder's batteries had not fared well. Colonel Henry C. Cabell, commanding the new reserve, protested to Pendleton that twelve guns were replaced by ten of inferior caliber, and Colonel Lee stressed the need of at least one heavy gun. Lee, who was temporary artillery chief, rated Magruder's fully manned batteries from "efficient" to "very efficient," but the action across the Chickahominy on the 25th and 26th bore out his stress on the need of guns of heavier calibre.

As it was too late to do anything about that, Magruder began firing those batteries stationed from Mrs. Price's farm, near the river, across Nine Mile Road at Old Tavern, and to the York River Railroad where his lines joined Huger's. At intervals he stirred up his skirmishers. As if pleased with the legend of their great demonstrations at Yorktown, Magruder's infantry put on a very convincing show, and made each bustle appear the prelude of a general advance.

For a demonstration to be effective, the soldiers had to be willing to fight, and Magruder had some soldiers from the Deep South who regarded combat as one of life's simple pleasures. There was a Mississippi brigade (later famous as "Barksdale's Mississippians") composed of the tallest, hardest, most powerful men in the army. In the 17th Mississippi Regiment thirty-five men stood more than six feet one inch, and ran to two hundred pounds and better. There were a lot of bear hunters from the canebrakes in this brigade, marksmen so accurate that at times the enemy took them to be sharpshooters. One of the gunners in the 1st Company of Richmond Howitzers, who supported the brigade, said the Mississippians liked "the racket" of guns near them, and whooped and hollered with delight.

These irrepressible soldiers were commanded by a forty-eight-year-old Philadelphian, Richard Griffith, who had lived for more than twenty years in Mississippi. A banker in Jackson with some military experience in the Mexican War, the well-liked brigadier had only three more days of life.

Magruder's command was composed of three divisions of two brigades each, and Griffith's brigade was in Magruder's own division. The other brigade in Magruder's division was composed of Georgia regiments, commanded by their state's most imposing citizen, Howell Cobb.

A planter of wealth, Cobb at forty-seven had behind him a distinguished political career. He had been speaker of the house when only thirty-four, secretary of the treasury in Buchanan's administration, and was elected governor of Georgia as a Unionist in the period of the compromises in 1850 and 1851. Some believed his moderation on secession prevented his being elected president by the Confederate delegates at Montgomery. With no great future as a soldier, the broadly intelligent man was an able administrator and natural leader. General Cobb was clean-shaven, with rather heavy features, a fine brow and serious mien.

Major General D. R. ("Neighbor") Jones commanded another of Magruder's divisions. A member of the great West Point class of 1846, he was plagued by ill health, and in seven months was to die of heart disease. "Neighbor" Jones was a stately South Carolinian with a gentle, friendly expression, and his agreeable personality made him one of the best-liked men in the army.

Cobb's fellow Georgian politician, Robert Toombs, commanded a brigade in Jones's division. Toombs, a few days away from his fifty-second birthday, was a man of violence, intemperate in all things, and some believed that his tumultuousness had caused him to miss beating Davis for the presidency. Bob Toombs was one of the most brilliant and magnetic of the secessionist leaders. He had amassed a fortune as a lawyer, built a big plantation, and won great prestige in the U. S. Congress and Senate. He possessed the qualities that would have made him a good soldier except for the impatience with discipline and great ego which made it impossible for him to subordinate himself to anyone. But he was a fighter.

Jones's other brigade, also of Georgia regiments, was commanded by George T. Anderson, Magruder's only brigade commander with Regular Army experience. Not a West Pointer, "Tige" Anderson had served in the Mexican War, after which he had been commissioned captain in the Regular Army. He had resigned two years before secession. Never spectacular and not destined to advance beyond brigadier, the steady-eyed Georgian maintained a level of dependable competence.

Magruder's third division was commanded by another professional, Lafayette McLaws, a classmate of Longstreet's at West Point. McLaws was one of those sound soldiers without flair, and his steady performance was never colored by a high moment. An enormous bushy beard half covered his broad face and his eyes peered out with something of an owlish appearance.

McLaws's two citizen-soldier brigadiers, Paul Semmes and Joseph Kershaw, were among the best of the nonprofessionals with the army. A Georgia planter-banker just turned forty-seven, Semmes, with a seignorial mustache and beard, was distinguished looking in the romantic tradition. He was the brother of Admiral Raphael Semmes, the Confederate sea raider.

From Camden, South Carolina, where his father had been mayor, forty-year-old Joe Kershaw was a lawyer and state legislator, a literate man of diligence, enthusiasm and contagious courage. Cleanshaven except for a drooping blond mustache, he had fine features and a resolute expression, and was much admired by the South Carolinians in his brigade. Kershaw's regiments were led by an unusually high caliber of field officers, mostly drawn from positions of prominence in civilian life and distinguished by gallant personal qualities.

All these troops of Magruder's command gave weight to the demonstration by their special eagerness to come to issue with the enemy. As their general had been edged further from the center of things, so the officers and soldiers had remained on the periphery since Johnston's withdrawal to Richmond. Probably every man except Magruder — who knew too much about their dangerous position — was trying to incite countermovements. To Magruder, the more racket the guns and foot soldiers made, the more nervously he looked at the climbing sun.

By seven o'clock, the hour when Magruder could begin to expect Jackson, A. P. Hill's positions were deserted along the river to Magruder's left, and the last man had gone from Longstreet's camps behind Magruder's lines. Behind Huger's lines were only the ashes of the campfires built up by D. H. Hill's brigades when they started moving away from the front between two and three in the morning.

D. H. Hill's and Longstreet's divisions had passed to the north of Richmond, and at seven o'clock were moving along the Mechanicsville Turnpike to the high bluff over the Chickahominy across from the Mechanicsville bridges. A. P. Hill's division, except Branch's brigade, had shifted up the north-south arm of the river and were massed in the woods across from the Meadow Bridges. Branch's brigade had marched on northward to the narrow crossing at Half Sink to establish contact with Jackson. At Magruder's back an unnatural silence hung over the flat farmland, emptied of troops and guns, between his lines and Richmond.

2

The sky was cloudless following a couple of showery days. After the mild fragrance of the early morning, the sun began to grow warm. The dragging hours, to nine o'clock and then to eleven — twice the time allotted for Jackson's eight-mile march — were marked by the growing warmth of the sun. By noon it was hot. Not only was there no sound of activity from across the Chickahominy, but no word had come from Lee. The commanding general had left the Dabbs house during the morning to join the troops on the Mechanicsville Turnpike.

In his "post of honor," Magruder bore out Colonel Long's impression that he lost his poise when acting under another's authority. At Yorktown, he had shown no strain when confronting McClellan's whole army alone. On the morning of the 26th, needing communication with his superiors, he denied himself the relief of writing to avoid revealing his anxiety.

At midday he gathered his staff to the family table for a gourmet dinner. No comfort came. The most light-hearted members of the staff showed the strain, and nobody had an appetite. After the failure of the meal, Magruder galloped along his lines, where the firing continued sporadically. Soldiers temporarily out of line, with no awareness of the danger, lounged in the shade of trees, laughing and joking. Magruder rode back to his headquarters house, from where he could look through binoculars to the other side of the river. The scene lay as still as a painting.

At two o'clock, the splendid "Prince John" could stand it no longer. He called his ordnance officer, Major Brent, the friend and lawyer from his carefree days at San Diego. Since Brent had given him legal counsel, Magruder was inclined to turn to the major when he needed advice. As Major Brent had none that day, Magruder's control broke and he gave his staff officer a message to take to General Lee's field headquarters. Wishing to avoid asking the commanding general what was going on, he instructed Brent to report that nothing untoward was happening on his front and leave the rest to Lee.

Leaving the New Bridge area, Brent rode through the woods as the quickest way to the Mechanicsville Turnpike and reached that road beyond the abrupt ending of the city around Venable Street. Turning northward, he passed farms, small and large, where children played in the yards, and two-storied stage taverns whose shaded balconies were deserted.

Where the ground rose in a long swell toward the bluffs overlooking the river, Brent passed the idle troops of D. H. Hill and Longstreet. The men were resting in the shade with no sign of activity. They had been waiting there since eight in the morning and, having moved out at two, some of the men were dozing. Individual officers were pacing nervously while others sat on the ground in small groups of friends. Gunners were fussing around their pieces, adjusting the horses' harnesses and inspecting the ammunition box on the caissons.

Toward the top of the rise, where the high earthen mounds of permanent gun positions stretched off on either side of the road, the artillerists stood in weary alertness in the open, the sun beating down on them. Off to one side of the road, President Davis was surrounded by an entourage of civilians and handsomely dressed staff officers — all noticeably silent. As Brent passed the group, he thought "a pall of gloom" hung over them. Beyond them he saw Lee's staff, equally subdued. Then he saw the general standing alone near the earthworks, his gaze ranging across the Chickahominy Valley.

As Brent approached the graying general, with his exterior of massive calm, Brent detected a touch of dishevelment in the usually meticulous dress. The bow of Lee's tie had slipped around a little in the opening of the collar of his uniform. When Brent reported that Magruder's troops were alerted across their whole front, and that the enemy had made no threatening moves, Lee thoughtfully perceived what was behind the message.

"I suppose you have come to find the cause of our delay, for General Magruder must be anxious. We have been waiting for General Jackson, from whom I have not heard." He paused, to stare off across the river, and then added, "I wish you to remain here until I am ready to send a message to General Magruder."

It was then three o'clock. Staff officer Brent found nothing curious in the absence of couriers arriving or being dispatched, as the commanding general and his staff simply waited for the long overdue arrival of Stonewall Jackson. (Lee had received a morning message from Jackson saying that he was running late.) From where Brent stood beside Lee, the movements that would begin the action — signaling Jackson's approach — would be clearly visible on the panorama unfolding across the Chickahominy.

From the marshy-banked bottom of their bluff, the overflowed river formed a swamp about three quarters of a mile wide. On the opposite bank the ground sloped upward to a plateau on which the crossroads village of Mechanicsville dozed. Mechanicsville itself was only a cluster of frame houses, with a saloon and a destroyed beer garden, and one fine two-story house with a "Greek revival" porch of the 1840's and a garden enclosed by a white picket fence.

The Turnpike, running through the village, became the Old Church Road on the other side, where it bore to the northeast. Three miles from Mechanicsville, hidden by timber, its eastward course ran across the direction of Jackson's march from the north. His destination was Hundley's Corner, which lay two miles north of the Old Church Road. The enemy retiring on the Old Church Road would cross Jackson's front.

Another road ran southeast from Mechanicsville across a flat open field before it dipped into the shallow valley of Beaver Dam Creek. The woods on the high bank of the opposite side of the creek could be seen as a fringe, marking the line of Fitz-John Porter's position at Ellerson's Mill. This was the position which Jackson's approach would cause to be evacuated. Past Ellerson's Mill, the unseen road took a winding course to Cold Harbor, and this Cold Harbor Road would be a line of pursuit when the enemy retired.

A third road ran north bearing to the west, toward the river crossing at Half Sink. Down this road Branch's brigade would march to herald Jackson's approach. One and a half miles west and a little north of Mechanicsville, the Meadow Bridges crossed the Chickahominy in the north-south course of the river, where on the western bank A. P. Hill's new division was waiting hidden in a fringe of trees. No direct road led from the Meadow Bridges to Mechanicsville, and Hill's troops would move by several short roads to enter the road from Half Sink about three quarters of a mile from the village.

While Major Brent was surveying the countryside, the oppressive silence was broken by rifle fire, sharp and solid, from the direction of the Meadow Bridges. The slumped figures on the plateau stirred into sudden movement. Officers hurried forward, bringing up their binoculars. Through his glasses Brent saw the dark dots of Federal pickets falling back fast from their side of the Meadow Bridges. Faintly in the distance under the crackle of rifle fire came the sound of drums and fifes. A red battle flag fluttered out of a belt of woods, and toy-sized soldiers in mottled gray swung in columns of fours out of the last angle of the roads on the zig-zag course to Mechanicsville.

"Those are A. P. Hill's men," General Lee said, as if commenting on the weather. Orders went to Longstreet and D. H. Hill to prepare to cross the Chickahominy.

On the opposite bank, the Federal regiment began to withdraw from the village, dark blue clumps moving slowly across the field toward a prepared position in the shadowy ravine of Beaver Dam Creek. East of the village a six-gun Federal battery opened with rolling blasts, and puffs burst near the road into which A. P. Hill's column was turning. More shell fire broke near the advancing columns, and several men fell in Hill's skirmish line.

A second brigade appeared behind Hill's advance and deployed to the left, taking a course north of the brigade moving on the village. Then a gun battery ran out between the infantry columns, the horses at a gallop, the gunners swaying on the iron seats, and in an incredibly short time wheeled into position. Men quickly detached the caisson from the gun carriage, plunging horses were moved back with men hanging onto the bridles. An officer's hand came down and the guns fired in battery.

A. P. Hill's advance column neared the village and began to deploy. More men dropped. Federal sharpshooters were firing from a dip in the ground east of the village. Another Federal battery, north on the plain, had opened on the second brigade. Stragglers broke off from the advance brigade, the men cringing away from the shell bursts. It was Field's Virginia brigade, and the men were going into battle for the first time.

Nearby came the shouts of officers and the muffled rattle of equipment as thousands of men fell into columns of march. D. H. Hill's troops were moving along the road cut between the high bluffs where the heavy guns were placed. The sun glinted on the rifle barrels as the van slushed through the marshy edges of the Chickahominy to the swampy water. There the column crowded to a halt. Officers began to yell back, a staff officer pushed his horse uphill off the side of the road. No pioneers had come up to lay the bridges. A line of infantry ran toward the remaining bridge supports across the swamp, and began to lay planks for a footbridge.

General Lee turned to Brent and told him to inform Magruder that he expected to reach New Bridge before dark. He could reassure his general that the bridge to his position in front of Richmond would be rebuilt and connections established for the divided army.

As Brent turned to go, three of Hill's brigades were deploying across the plateau north of Mechanicsville as far as he could see, and Hill had another battery in action. Shell bursts were breaking heavily across his front. Ominously, artillery fire rolled along Beaver Dam Creek, where the Federals were supposed to evacuate their prepared position at Jackson's approach.

Riding off, Brent had the feeling something was wrong. He decided to tell General Magruder that he did not think General Lee would reach New Bridge that night.

3

Powell Hill's movement across the Meadow Bridges was not, as Lee thought, the signal for Jackson's approach. At nine o'clock that morning, Jackson had sent Branch, at Half Sink, a message that he was then crossing the Virginia Central tracks, six miles from Ashland. According to Lee's orders, Jackson should have started his march from the railroad tracks at three in the morning. Though he was running very late, six hours behind schedule, he had only eight miles farther to go. A. P. Hill, like Magruder, had found the dragging minutes a deepening strain on his highly strung nerves. At three o'clock he could bear it no longer.

Hill had heard nothing from Branch or Jackson since early morning. He reasoned that by the time his five brigades crossed the Meadow Bridges, deployed, and cleared Mechanicsville for the passage of Longstreet and Harvey Hill, Jackson would certainly have moved eight miles.

Once somebody said that A. P. Hill made a premature assault on the Beaver Dam Creek position, and it has been endlessly repeated until accepted as fact. Hill forced the Meadow Bridges before Jackson or Branch had been "discovered" — as in General Orders No. 75 — but not for the purpose of making an assault. In anticipation of Jackson, he crossed to execute his orders of drawing the enemy from Mechanicsville to clear the river crossing for D. H. Hill and Longstreet, in order that their troops might get over before the day ended and be in position to cooperate with Jackson when he arrived.

Lee endorsed Hill's report in which he wrote, "Three o'clock having arrived, and no intelligence from Jackson or Branch, I determined to cross at once rather than hazard the failure of the whole plan by longer deferring it. . . . It was never contemplated that my division alone should have sustained the shock of this battle, but such was the case. . . ."

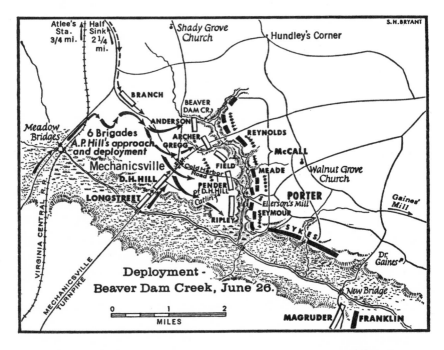

Insofar as Hill's crossing of the Meadow Bridges, before Branch was discovered, constituted a personal interpretation of Lee's order, it was an impulsive act. Yet, it was the kind of impetuosity that sometimes wins battles, and Lee did not reproach his generals for erring on the side of initiative. Hill's overeagerness was based on his concern for the commanding general's major plan. Where the new Light Division encountered trouble was in executing the part of the order which directed him to drive the enemy from Mechanicsville.

When his brigades moved away from the river, his columns came under, as he said, "a murderous fire" from the Federal guns — first from the two batteries retiring from Mechanicsville and then from mostly unseen batteries firing from the hill on the bank of Beaver Dam Creek. Having committed himself, Hill had no choice except to go forward. After the long strain of waiting, Hill, as well as his troops, was caught up in the action.

It was the first time Powell Hill had taken his new command of six brigades into battle and, a proud man, he was proud of the force he had named the "Light Division." Lithe and graceful in the saddle, he rode across with the first wave and surveyed the developing action. Hill was something of a dandy, with a variety of changes of dress, and once appeared in battle wearing a fireman-red hunting shirt. For battle he usually wore, as on that day, a simple gray flannel fatigue jacket and a black felt hat slouched forward on his forehead to shade his eyes. He undoubtedly reflected his excitement. All the men were excited, and a strong sense of communication existed between the brigadiers and "Little Powell" — as his men called him in the only affectionate diminutive given a Confederate general.

Hill had developed a quick friendship with Charles Field, the stocky Kentuckian leading the first brigade across the bridges. Thirty-four-year-old Charlie Field was a good-humored man, quick to laughter, with a broad face which reflected aggressive resolution. One of Hill's three professionals, he was at that stage the best brigadier in the division and one of the best in the army.

After Field crossed the Meadow Bridges the road bore north for a short distance along the Virginia Central tracks before it intersected another road that sliced sharply back to the southeast. After a narrow stretch through farm country, this road cut back to the northeast. About three quarters of a mile from Mechanicsville, this road intersected yet another — the road from Half Sink that slanted southeastward into the village. As Field's brigade of something over two thousand men approached this elbow that led toward Mechanicsville, the head of the column came under converging artillery fire. As the columns turned toward Mechanicsville, the regiments deployed off the road.

While the tight-faced troops began moving in battle lines over the plain, a Richmond gun battery galloped out on the field. Commanded by the scholarly, bespectacled young Willie Pegram, the gunners drew a galling fire upon themselves as soon as their battery opened. This was the battery Major Brent had seen.

Ahead, the village of Mechanicsville was cleared of the enemy. Field swung his Virginia regiments to their left, directly facing the Federal position along Beaver Dam Creek about one mile away. On his left, a Federal battery of six guns began playing over his lines, and Hill sent forward the South Carolina battery of David McIntosh (Pegram's brother-in-law) to attract the enemy gunners. At the same time Hill ordered Joseph R. Anderson's brigade to its left, moving by a different road than Field's, to take the enemy battery in reverse.

West Pointer Anderson, the progressive industrialist who owned the Tredegar Iron Works, was a good soldier. His untested Georgia regiments moved like veterans in their swing to take the destructive Federal battery in reverse. Anderson's brigade pushed north of the Old Church Road, toward Jackson's line of march.

After Anderson came the brigade of long-faced, long-bearded James Archer. A forty-five-year-old Marylander and Princeton graduate, Archer was a lawyer who had served in the Regular Army as captain. Not close to Hill, he was a capable soldier who had been transferred from a regiment in Hood's brigade to take command of Hatton's former brigade when Smith's division was dissolved after Lee took command. On crossing the bridge, Archer moved off the road in support of Field's left, drifting northward across the plain toward Anderson's right flank. Archer's brigade reached the south side of the Old Church Road, near where it was crossed by Beaver Dam Creek.

After Archer moved to Field's left, Dorsey Pender's brigade advanced from the road across the open plateau to come up on Field's right. Though his recently formed brigade was another addition to the division, twenty-eight-year-old William Dorsey Pender, Hill's third professional, was the man closest to his heart. Pender's devoutness made him a strange intimate for Hill, who was notably indifferent to religion. A dark man and as intense as Hill, Pender was both ambitious and a headlong combat soldier. His close calls in action were the only secrets he kept from his wife, with whom he shared his deepest thoughts in extremely tender letters.

Pender's brigade was formed partly of the remnants of the brigades of Pettigrew and Hampton, both of which had been cut up at Fair Oaks where Pettigrew had been wounded and captured and Hampton wounded. There had been some shuffling of regiments when Lee, to placate Davis, made an effort to brigade state regiments together. Believing in the policy no more than had Johnston, Lee entered a formal protest as a means of checking sudden upheavals in command structure, but conformed where he could in order to sustain his good relationship with the President. Thus Dorsey Pender, except for two battalions, commanded all North Carolina regiments from his native state. Pender's brigade passed to the east of deserted Mechanicsville, moving toward Fitz-John Porter's stronghold at Ellerson's Mill.

The last brigade, Maxcy Gregg's, followed the road to Mechanicsville in support of Pender. Gregg, a wealthy South Carolina lawyer, planter and scholar, was the general next closest to Hill personally. The forty-seven-year-old citizen-soldier held the passionate convictions of separatism which came to Powell Hill and the other professional soldiers only after the invasion.

His brigade was formed of equally fervid South Carolinians, mostly of privileged backgrounds; Gregg's original regiment had contained twenty-seven doctors and thirty lawyers. Gregg and his hot-bloods complemented one another, and zealous Maxcy Gregg had an aura of gallantry that made him in that June a little special among the untried generals from civilian life. With graying hair and pale, thoughtful eyes, he had a cheerful expression, and, when mounted at the head of his troops, he lacked only a lady's handkerchief on his sword (he was a bachelor) to appear the chevalier of ancient legend.

As Gregg's brigade moved toward Mechanicsville, the enemy's artillery fire was spraying the area with bursting shells and some solid shot. As neither Gregg nor his men had ever fought in a battle before — some of the soldiers watched in awe as a solid ball ricocheted through the ranks — Hill sent them in reserve where they could take cover in a declivity.

By the time Gregg reached the field and the other four brigades were deployed, it was near five in the afternoon, past the hour when there could be any reasonable explanation for Jackson's continued absence. Momentarily expecting him, Hill's lead brigades became engaged with the enemy.

4

Field and Archer had advanced across the plain between the Cold Harbor Road and the Old Church Road to the thickets on the edge of the slope down to Beaver Dam Creek. As the two lines of battle were carried forward in the momentum of advance, neither Archer nor Field moved toward the creek with the intent of forcing a crossing. Expecting Jackson on their left, they were advancing toward the enemy on their front. In that innocent phase of gallantry in the war, it was their pride to advance with ordered lines to display to the enemy their fearlessness of him. When Field and Archer neared the slopes down to the creek, the fire from the Federal batteries grew so severe that the men were ordered to move down onto the hillside to get out of the range of the guns posted on the opposite crest.

In clambering through the thickets over the brow of the hill, the men did not know the terrain. The stream itself was no more than ten feet wide, but the briary slopes on both sides ended in sheer, slippery banks higher than a man's head. On the opposite slope, Porter's infantry was formed in tiers of rifle pits below the guns on the crest.

These were formed of two brigades, those of John F. Reynolds and Truman Seymour, of McCall's division, the last units to join McClellan. Well-trained troops containing a high quality of general officers — including future army commander George Meade, whose brigade was in reserve — these Pennsylvania reserves were no more battle-wise than Field's Virginians and the new regiments with Archer. The Confederates did not know who was shooting at them. They only knew they were safer in front of the enemy rifles than the artillery, and they could shoot back.

Off the open plain and in a line with the Federal infantry, their precarious perch on the slope forced Porter's guns to overshoot. Keeping their heads down, the men of the two Confederate brigades opened a ragged exchange with the enemy's rifles, and held their position, waiting for Jackson to come up on the enemy's flank.

Farther north, on the other side of the Old Church Road, Joseph Anderson had missed the Federal battery he had been sent to take in reverse. Showing his coolness, Anderson stretched his brigade toward the direction of Jackson's expected appearance. Using the cover of a heavy thicket, he got a regiment across the creek where its banks were less steep.

During this action, shortly after five o'clock, Jackson's approach seemed imminent. Around this time the skirmish line of Branch's liaison brigade appeared out of the brush on the road from the north. In Lee's General Orders, Hill was to move out when the columns of Branch and Jackson were "discovered." As the ground lay, Jackson's columns could not have been "discovered" by Hill at all. The wood-fringed banks of Beaver Dam Creek and belts of timber lay between Hill and Jackson's line of march, about three miles to the northeast of Anderson's position.

With three more hours of daylight, Jackson's arrival would give the army the reward of Hill's anticipation. He would have to come soon, as Hill's division was fighting alone on a front of almost two miles of open plain. Because of a neglect to provide pioneers and the necessary equipment for crossing over the destroyed bridges below Mechanicsville, no troops from D. H. Hill's or Longstreet's divisions had come to A. P. Hill's support.

Around the same time that Branch's advance skirmishers were seen, one brigade of D. H. Hill's division had completed a crossing by the footbridge. Ripley's brigade, which had joined D. H. Hill the day after Seven Pines, began to form in order as the men moved up the three-fourths-of-a-mile slope from the river to Mechanicsville.

As soon as Ripley's brigade was over, General Lee left his observation post behind the breastworks and rode across the river. In the battle litter around the village, Lee learned for the first time that A. P. Hill had attacked without waiting for Jackson. However, the appearance of Branch indicated that the Valley troops were at last at hand. While Lee was talking to Powell Hill, President Davis and a large entourage galloped up and halted nearby. Grim-looking Harvey Hill had also crossed over and took yet another position near the crossroads village. The presence of these three groups around Mechanicsville seemed to bring confusion to the action.

Various accounts intended to clarify the action have only deepened the confusion. In the suspense of waiting for Jackson, no one seemed to know, then or since, who was giving orders or to what end.

5

In reconstructions of the battle, a letter written thirty-five years after the war has been used as evidence of actual disobedience on the part of A. P. Hill. Captain T. W. Sydnor, of the 4th Virginia Cavalry and a native of the region, wrote that he had warned Lee the night before of the danger of quicksand south of the Old Church Road. This was in the area where Archer's Tennessee and Alabama troops were clinging for survival to the smoky slope of Beaver Dam Creek. As a result of this warning, Lee sent Sydnor with a verbal message to Hill, after Hill had crossed the Meadow Bridges, not to bring on a general attack. According to Sydnor, after the battle Lee asked Hill in Sydnor's presence if he had not received the message during the afternoon and Hill said he had. This account has been accepted in support of the charge that Hill brought on a general attack against Lee's wishes.

A number of items make Captain Sydnor's long memory suspect, fundamental among which is the fact that Hill did not deliver a general assault. In his report Hill wrote, "Their [the Federal] position along Beaver Dam Creek was too strong to be carried by direct assault without heavy loss, and expecting every moment to hear Jackson's guns on my left and in rear of the enemy, I forebore to order the storming of the lines."

Lee confirmed this. "Jackson being expected to pass Beaver Dam Creek above and turn the enemy's right, a direct attack was not made by Genl Hill."

Around four, when Sydnor's message was supposedly sent, Lee assumed Powell Hill was "driving the enemy from Mechanicsville" — according to orders — because Jackson was coming up. At that time he had no reason to warn Hill against making an assault. Even if Sydnor did deliver a message with the warning about quicksand on the Confederate left, no attack was made by Archer in that area. The only attack ordered against the Federal position was from the Confederate right, east of Mechanicsville, and this was after Lee came on the field. It was given by Lee, President Davis, and D. H. Hill. It was this order, to Ripley's brigade, that led to the much discussed slaughter at Ellerson's Mill, in the heart of Porter's stronghold where the Cold Harbor Road crossed the creek.

Ripley was ordered in to support Pender's brigade, whose two right regiments had been mangled in moving against the obstacles at the foot of the Cold Harbor Road. Dorsey Pender, advancing on the line of the Federal regiment retiring from Mechanicsville, had pushed forward rashly on his own initiative, and his sudden change of plan had divided his force and brought disorder to the regiments' movements.

Hill's report, protecting his friend Pender, was evasive. "Pender was ordered to support these brigades already engaged and to take position on the right of Field . . ." In the same paragraph in which he stated he forebore "to order a storming of the lines," he wrote, "The 38th North Carolina . . . and the 34th North Carolina . . . of Pender's brigade, made a gallant but abortive effort to force a crossing."

Pender, addressing his report to Hill, wrote, "I was ordered by you to support General Field . . . but soon found that, by taking the direction General Field was going, left his right much exposed to a heavy fire of artillery . . . This artillery I saw obliquely to the right and further down Beaver Dam Creek than I saw any troops going. I at once changed direction of two of my regiments, so as to bring them to the right of this artillery." Pender, manfully assuming responsibility and not trying to minimize the consequences, then said he "succeeded in getting within 150 or 200 yards before we were opened upon, but when they did open upon us it was destructive . . . within less than 100 yards of the enemy's rifle-pits, [the 38th North Carolina] had to fall back."

The 34th North Carolina had swung too wide in getting into position, and did not come up until the 38th was reeling back. Intense young Pender reacted personally to this repulse and determined to silence that battery. He shifted the wobbly line of the 34th regiment farther to the right, across the Cold Harbor Road, to make, he said, "as much diversion as possible in that direction."

As no attack had been planned in the area where a hundred-yard millpond obstructed the line of advance, Pender's right flank was overlapped by Porter's left flank, strongly posted on the opposite bank of the creek. On the sharply rising hillside, Seymour's brigade fired from rifle pits, and the battery that plagued Pender was blasting away on the crest. But on Porter's left, this hill sloped away southward to the Chickahominy, and Pender formed the opinion that the Federal flank could be turned from the Confederate right.

It was at this juncture that Ripley rode into Mechanicsville ahead of his brigade, then forming for battle below the village, and here the confusion began. Roswell Ripley was a West Pointer from Ohio who, marrying into a Charleston family, had left the army and gone into business in Charleston. An opinionated man, Ripley was even more contumacious than D. H. Hill: where Hill respected some superiors, Ripley was against them all. His Georgia and North Carolina regiments had arrived on June 1, too late to participate in the Battle of Seven Pines, and the men were moving toward their first action.

About his orders at Mechanicsville, Ripley reported, "Upon communicating with General A. P. Hill . . . it was arranged that my brigade was to cooperate . . ." with Pender in getting around the Federal battery commanding the Cold Harbor Road.

A. P. Hill reported that he had asked Ripley for help "in turning the enemy's left," and had said nothing about the battery.

General Lee wrote only that Ripley "at a late hour united with Pender, in an effort to turn the enemy's left." He also said nothing about the battery.

D. H. Hill reported that Pender had asked him directly for help from Ripley. He also said that he had received "several" messages from Lee and one from Davis to send in a brigade. As Ripley's was the only one across the river, he ordered it in to support Pender.

Ripley's troops had first formed in line of battle on the hill leading from the Chickahominy to Mechanicsville. While he was moving his lines forward to turn at right angles, he reported, "I received orders to assault the enemy from General Lee and also from Major-General D. H. Hill, the latter of whom directed me to send two regiments to support General Pender, on my right, and attack the battery in front with the remainder of my force." Here nothing was said of turning the enemy's left.

In the confusion of these accounts the one certainty is that, Captain Sydnor's 1897 letter to the contrary, A. P. Hill was the only general who had not ordered Ripley to assault. Of Lee's part in the orders, Colonel Marshall wrote, "General Lee thought that, if he halted in front of Beaver Dam Creek, General McClellan might accumulate on [Jackson]. . . . He therefore considered it best to allow the attack on the strong position to proceed, in order to prevent troops being moved from it against Jackson before communication had been opened [with Jackson]."

In the orders showered upon Ripley in his first action, Lee's objective, and possibly Powell Hill's, was a flank movement designed to pin down Federal troops in conjunction with Jackson's expected appearance. D. H. Hill, cooperating with Pender, held the limited objective of taking the Federal flank battery. President Davis, caught up in the spirit of battle as at Fair Oaks, seemed to have in mind no more than a support of Pender in a general advance on the right. Judging by Ripley's reports and his actions, his only purpose was to charge straight ahead, taking the batteries by assault.

Considering that Lee, Harvey Hill, Pender and Ripley had all been professional soldiers, the blindness with which the hastily formed assault force moved forward reflected the effects of the confusion on inexperienced generals. There was no controlling command. Lee, expecting Jackson and unsettled by the long silence from the area of his approach, was trying to salvage the bad situation that had developed at the Federal stronghold — a position he had designed his first day's assault to avoid. There was nothing that could be called a channel of command from him to Ripley and Pender through the two Hills.

Pender, whose impetuosity had brought on the attack in the Ellerson's Mill area, expected support from part of Ripley's command in renewing his assault while Ripley extended his other regiments to encircle the Federal flank. If Ripley had ever understood that his movement was to turn the enemy's flank, either he forgot it or the effect of leading troops in combat constricted the play of his faculties.

In the rush, nobody reconnoitered the ground to be crossed. Pender's earlier attack had been made on both sides of the Cold Harbor Road that ran for about one mile generally east from Mechanicsville and then bent to the south along the banks of an abandoned millrace. Here it paralleled the creek before bending back to cross at Ellerson's Mill. In Pender's earlier attack, the troops on the stretch of the road paralleling the creek exposed their flank to the Federal infantry on the opposite hillside. Ripley's two right regiments, in forming to follow partly over Pender's course, shifted farther to the right of the road to pass beyond the stretch along the millrace.

In approaching Ellerson's Mill, Ripley's two regiments crossed the cultivated fields of the substantial Catlin farm, which spread from the road for about half a mile to a belt of timber. The timber marked the beginning of the rough slope down to the Chickahominy, and the covered slope offered the only approach to the Federal flank. Ripley's battle line, composed of the 44th Georgia and 1st North Carolina, extended short of these woods, and no shift in alignment was made to take advantage of the cover.

Assertively self-confident Ripley, then thirty-nine, had seen no action since the Mexican War, when his boldness had won him two brevets for gallantry. Until he came to Richmond on June 1 he had been active with the organization of South Carolina troops, and evidently had not considered the changes made since the Mexican War. His lines swept past the grove around the Catlin farmhouse in splendid array, as if advancing against smoothbore cannons and muskets accurate at little more than sixty yards. D. H. Hill had gotten no guns over to support the infantry, and the Federal gunners on the opposite plateau took their time, without danger or interference, to direct shrapnel and large grapeshot on the orderly lines of men walking into their first fire.

Beyond the Catlin outbuildings the ground began a gradual slope toward the creek, and here the men came within range of rifles that fired better than 400 yards. Under this storm of lead the numbed men stumbled through hedges and scrambled over ditches, going on like automatons toward the fringe of woods bordering the creek at the bottom of the hill. Men dropped too fast for the lines to close up, and gaps appeared. Mounted field officers and line officers fell faster than the men. The colonels and lieutenant colonels went down wounded, two mortally. A major was killed outright, and eighteen captains and lieutenants fell, killed or wounded.

On the men plunged to the abatis around the millpond in the line of their advance. Ripley recognized the uselessness of trying to go any farther. As they would lose as many men going back as they had going in, he ordered the troops to take such cover as they could find and hug the ground.

On their left, Pender's 34th North Carolina Regiment also huddled along the ground. From their inadequate cover in the slow-falling dusk, the survivors returned the fire as well as they could, chiefly to break the concentration of the rifle fire that had come at them during their advance.

Sometime before dark, around eight, D. H. Hill's first field battery moved up to their support. Captain Rhett's South Carolina gunners mercifully brought relief from what Ripley called "the storm of shell and canister which had been poured upon" the infantry. Before dark a second battery came up, and under cover of the eight guns the men of the shattered regiments climbed out of their trap when night came.

With their withdrawal, though the guns kept growling at one another, Lee's first battle ended. The enemy was strongly entrenched in the position which Lee had expected to be evacuated at Jackson's approach. As far as anyone knew, the earth had swallowed up Jackson. Lee had one worry which he kept to himself: he had not reached the New Bridge crossing to connect with Magruder. Major Brent had been sound in advising Magruder not to expect the rest of the army to establish a connection with him that day.

6

Tactically, the first battle of the Seven Days was a Confederate failure from beginning to end. Having planned for the unfamiliar pieces of the complex machine to fall into place on an exact time-table, Lee had made no preparation to assume control of the action. It cannot accurately be said that his staff work was poor; it was nonexistent. No use was made of the staff to discover why the pieces were not coming together, even after Lee crossed the river. At the Battle of Mechanicsville Lee could be likened to a future genius at a stage before his powers of execution were sufficiently developed to express his concepts.

Lee's admirers have viewed him as the complete soldier and have tended to put the blame on Jackson and A. P. Hill. In turn, Jackson's admirers have tended to blame Lee and A. P. Hill. As no legend grew around Powell Hill, between the charges of the Lee and Jackson camps the impression has been allowed to stand that "impulsive Hill" attacked single-handed the Federal stronghold where Lee wished to avoid battle. Placing the onus on Hill would seem to minimize Jackson's failure to come up or communicate, and Lee's to take command when his overly ambitious orders were disrupted. The need of a scapegoat was caused by the unwillingness of the Confederates, any more than the Federals, to accept the fact that the enemy could contribute to the failure of an action. This became particularly true as the legends grew about Lee, and at Mechanicsville the defenders overlooked one of the guilty parties, Fitz-John Porter.

After all, Hill was ordered to "drive the enemy from Mechanicsville," and in doing this his troops were drawn into action against McCall's division on Beaver Dam Creek. As he was supposed to cross the Meadow Bridges when Branch was "discovered," and as Branch was discovered around five o'clock, Hill only anticipated the signal by two hours. No one has mentioned the point that if Hill had waited and obeyed the letter of the order, he would have moved across the Meadow Bridges around five o'clock, when Branch was "discovered."

As it was, had Jackson come up at all, Hill's anticipation would have salvaged the lateness of Jackson's arrival. Then A. P. Hill would have been praised for his initiative. He would also have been praised for his initiative had Porter withdrawn from Beaver Dam Creek at Jackson's approach. For Jackson was on Porter's flank and rear at five o'clock, but Porter failed to do his part according to Lee's plan.

Along with Porter's refusal to cooperate, the army was not ready for its assignment. Among Lee, Longstreet, D. H. Hill and Major Stevens some one was responsible for the failure to provide pioneers and equipment for the troops to cross the Chickahominy, where they had waited in position for eight hours. General Pendleton, chief of artillery, remained on the Williamsburg Road, and spent the greater part of the day making a reconnaissance of Huger's front. The larger portion of the cavalry, out screening the left of Jackson's march, did not advance ahead of him or Branch to clear the way of the enemy horsemen who delayed them all day.

In the action on the Mechanicsville plain, the breakdown in communication was complete. While no critic fails to mention that A. P. Hill crossed without advising Lee that he had not "discovered" Jackson, Hill's oversight was typical of the procedures in the army that day. Jackson and Branch, the liaison, remained out of contact with both Lee and Hill, and Lee allowed himself to become little more than an anxious spectator.

After the battle, D. H. Hill, the first Confederate general to magnify the action, directed his criticism at Lee. Harvey Hill had apparently disliked receiving all those orders from Lee, and one from Davis, and he was highly critical of the 575 casualties sustained in Ripley's brigade. "We were lavish of blood in those days," he wrote bitterly.

At Seven Pines, where nothing was accomplished, Hill lost 1100 men in Rodes's brigade and nearly 3000 of a 9000 man division, a loss of higher than 30 per cent. In the adjoining futilities at Fair Oaks, four brigades of Smith's division lost 1260 men and three of four general officers, for 15 per cent losses in a very short time. The 1350 Confederate losses at Mechanicsville (nearly half taken in Ripley's Napoleonic heroics) were distributed between Ripley's men and the five brigades brought onto the field by Hill. This constituted a bare 10 per cent casualties sustained by troops engaged for upwards of five hours. At Seven Pines, Harvey Hill's friend Johnston was in command.

About Mechanicsville, the deeply religious Hill permitted bias to color him to the extent that he reported, "The three batteries of Jones' battalion, of my division . . . drove the Yankee artillery off the field." All reports agreed that the Federal guns had been driven off the plain to the Federal side of Beaver Dam Creek before Ripley's brigade had moved out. Ripley reported that he had received no artillery support during his advance. Major Jones himself confirmed Ripley's report that Captain Rhett's battery brought the first of D. H. Hill's guns into action, engaging the enemy's artillery across Beaver Dam Creek at dusk. Jones reported that his other two batteries got across so late they went into bivouac at Mechanicsville.

It was also Hill who wrote, "It was unfortunate for the Confederates that the crossing was begun before Jackson got in rear of Mechanicsville. The loss of that position would have necessitated the abandonment of the line of Beaver Dam Creek, as in fact it did, the next day." This *if* ignores the imponderables.

McClellan did not decide to abandon the position on Beaver Dam Creek until one o'clock the next morning. It is possible to assume that the assault, which placed troops 200 yards from his lines, influenced his decision in his next move. In the realm of *ifs*, had the Confederates waited on the other side of the Chickahominy until Porter withdrew from Mechanicsville — as Lee never planned — logistics might very well have prevented Lee from catching Porter. The springing of the trap had been faulty, but the initiative had been seized and pressure was being exerted on McClellan.

The casualties must be weighed against the advantages of getting A. P. Hill, D. H. Hill and Longstreet across the river and onto the field by about ten o'clock that night. Three large divisions would be in position by daylight to initiate the originally planned pursuit when Jackson at last flanked Porter out of the stronghold. On that night, as the guns died away across the narrow front and the wounded were brought out, nobody was thinking of what future historians might say. The one question in the minds of the men was, "Where is Jackson?"

CHAPTER NINE

A Study of Stress

WHEN THE FIRING faded off at Beaver Dam Creek after darkness fell about eight-thirty, Jackson was at Hundley's Corner, where he had been since five o'clock. This was two and a half miles as the crow flies from Anderson's brigade at the end of Hill's line across the Old Church Road. To have reached the battle, by his line of march, Jackson would have had to go two miles south from Hundley's Corner to the Old Church Road, make a right-angle turn there, and travel another mile to the area of Anderson's fight on the Federal flank.

Beginning at Hundley's Corner the road passed through a belt of timber, then past the cleared fields and orchards of farms as it dipped to the crossing of the narrow flow of Beaver Dam Creek where the stream faded off bearing eastward. Beyond the creek timber rose again, a little more than a mile from Hundley's Corner, and continued on the right side of the road to the intersection with the Old Church Road, screening off all view in the direction of the sound of battle.

Beyond this screen, two brigades of Morell's division occupied positions along the only line of march to the battle area. Behind the Federal flank where Beaver Dam Creek crossed the Old Church Road, these brigades of Martindale and Griffin were posted with batteries on either side of the road. Though Jackson could not know this, the Federal cavalry that had obstructed the road during most of his march from Ashland remained across his front, and he could reasonably assume that McClellan's infantry knew his whereabouts. About theirs he knew nothing. Nor did he know anything about the country that lay between him and the sound of battle.

When he arrived at Hundley's Corner at five o'clock, the battle along Beaver Dam Creek was not heavy in volume of artillery or rifles. Porter was using six batteries, about forty guns, placed at intervals on the one and a half miles of front, and Hill had in action less than half of that. Between Porter and Hill only six infantry brigades were engaged at the time, and Hill's troops were neither firing fully nor simultaneously.

As Lee's battle orders had mentioned "the enemy being driven from Mechanicsville," Jackson could have assumed (correctly, according to A. P. Hill's initial intent) that this was the action he heard in progress, although the sound indicated that the enemy was not being driven. Most important of all, Jackson had reached the area where the battle order directed him.

"Jackson will advance on the road leading to Pole Green Church," the orders had read; ". . . Genl D. H. Hill moving to the support of Genl Jackson, and Genl Longstreet supporting Genl A. P. Hill. The four divisions . . . will sweep down the Chickahominy. . . Genl Jackson bearing well to his left, turning Beaver Dam Creek and taking the direction toward Cold Harbor."

The road Jackson had followed past Pole Green Church led into a crossroad at Hundley's Corner which, if he followed it to his left, would lead him in the direction of Cold Harbor. After a short jog to his right from Hundley's Corner, the road he had been using resumed its north-south direction and crossed the headwaters of Beaver Dam Creek. Hence, if he took the road that led to the Old Church Road — and the direction of the firing — he would not "turn" Beaver Dam Creek. Only by bearing to his left in the direction of Cold Harbor would he turn the creek and execute his orders to the letter.

It was a puzzling situation for a general in a strange country, operating for the first time under Lee's orders and in coordination with commands unfamiliar to him. Clearly D. H. Hill was not coming "to the support of Genl Jackson," nor was there a visible enemy to be supported against. Two regiments from Ewell's division had sufficed to drive the enemy cavalry across the narrow stream of Beaver Dam Creek a mile to the front of their halt at Hundley's Corner. To attempt to push on to find the enemy's infantry and discover what the fighting was about he would require several hours to get his troops up over the dusty road and deployed across the cultivated fields and through the woods.

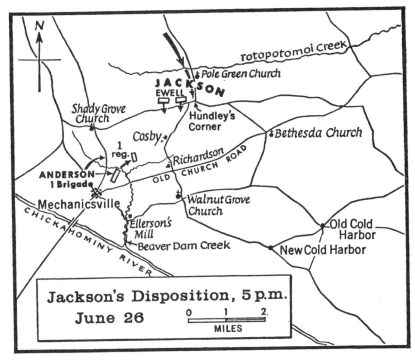

Jackson's Disposition, 5 p.m.
June 26

One sees *Jackson* on a map, and it suggests a solid mass, like a chess figure to be moved. Jackson's fifteen thousand infantry were strung out in columns of fours on two roads converging at Hundley's Corner, with spaces made in these columns at intervals by guns and wagons. His rear guard was at least more than five miles away. Winder's brigade, of Jackson's own division, "camped at Totopotomoi Creek," which placed Lawton's large brigade north of this creek. As a matter of fact, none of the brigadiers, colonels or battery captains in Jackson's own division — temporarily commanded by Winder — mentioned hearing firing on June 26. They reported going into bivouac as an uneventful detail.

Branch, with only a single brigade and no wagons, annoyed by the same tactics of the enemy's cavalry that delayed Jackson, moved only seven miles from ten until five, and all his regiments were not up until dark. Logistics would have prevented a move by Jackson in any force before seven o'clock, when only one and one half hours of daylight remained.

Considering these factors, there was no ready solution for the problem presented Jackson by the silence on his immediate front and the battle at least two hours' march away at the rate he had gone all day. At Hundley's Corner, what had gone wrong with Jackson in Lee's plan was behind him and irremediable. Having required fourteen hours to march his van fourteen miles, he arrived in no condition to deploy more than part of his force within another two hours.

Jackson became a puzzle not in that he could think of no solution but because of what he did. Without sending a message to Lee or to Hill, either to announce his presence or to discover what was happening, he ordered his troops into bivouac as they came up.

As the men started making camp, after six o'clock the firing ahead grew in intensity, and Jackson's staff saw that he looked worried. However, it was too late to do anything about it then, even if he had known what to do. The incredible thing was that Stonewall Jackson, of the lightning marches and the sudden strokes, bivouacked his Valley army without sending forward a line of skirmishers or giving an order for the next day.

The question changed from "where is Jackson" to "what about Jackson?"

2

In Stonewall Jackson's world, no general would have considered such an ailment as stress fatigue, even if he had been aware of the reactions to stress. Commanding generals, particularly Federals, recognized physical fatigue in their own troops: often this was presented as a decisive factor in explaining a failure, though a success was never explained by the opponent's physical condition. While generals themselves occasionally revealed the effects of loss of sleep and prolonged strain, a leader was supposed to be above the limitations of the flesh, and his own condition was never mentioned in a report and rarely at all. Jackson did refer in private letters to feelings of sickness in the damp, debilitating climate around Richmond, but he never understood the cause nor the nature of his undiagnosed illness.

Beginning with the opening movement of the Valley Campaign

on April 30, Jackson had been under stress continuously for fifty-eight days when he reached Hundley's Corner on June 26. Not only were his naturally limited physical powers extended over this period but his total organism was exposed to the prolonged stress of danger, sustained alertness and the urgent need of constant decisions affecting the cause he represented as well as the lives of the men entrusted to him.

In this daily call upon his resources, Jackson was supported up to a point by his body's resistance-reactions to stress — the same flow of energy that comes to any individual acting in emergency, as in physical or emotional catastrophe, or in combat. Beyond a point, continued stress began to exhaust the resistance-reactions, both mental and physiological, including a depletion of the adrenal cortex. Jackson was past this point when he led his troops on the final stage of the march to the battle area.

Jackson had been approaching stress-exhaustion when he foolishly made the fourteen-hour night ride to Richmond from 1 A.M. to late afternoon on the 23rd, and then, without rest or food — taking only a glass of milk — made the return ride through a second night from about seven in the evening until midmorning of the 24th. He was not exhausted by the rides; from physical overexertion he would have been restored by rest. His judgment had already been affected when he made the all-night rides on successive nights.

To a person in possession of his faculties, the strain to which he exposed his body would have been regarded as irresponsible. It would take a rare physical specimen to spend Sunday night and all day Monday riding, then ride all Monday night, and appear at ten o'clock Tuesday morning, without sleep for forty-eight hours, in expectation of turning in a productive day's work. Jackson was not that rare specimen. Aware of his physical limitations, he normally took good care of himself and developed habits of getting naps anywhere; church was one of his favorite dozing places.

As commander of the key unit in a maneuver, sound judgment would have indicated the need to be at his physical best, with the clearest mind and quickest reflexes. But his course of behavior violated his self-knowledge of thirty-eight years, during which he had practiced an unrelenting discipline toward the fulfillment of his ambitions. A poor mountain boy ill prepared for the curriculum at West Point, his life was characterized by an intense application based upon realism about his physical equipment. A modern doctor, in studying stress, reached the conclusion that military success is largely "the management of effort." Jackson's disregard of his own limitations represented the last flare-up before the two sleepless nights completed the drain on his resources.

Jackson returned to his army in a state of clinical exhaustion. The sickness he felt was unfamiliar and indescribable. When, after the campaign, he wrote the Reverend James Ewing, a minister friend at the Presbyterian College of Hampden-Sydney, Jackson said he had felt worse than at any time since his illness in Mexico. Confiding in no one the shameful symptoms of his disorientation, Jackson, when recovered, was inclined to blame the "malarial region" of Tidewater for his state.

Because of his explanation, the malefic effects of the country have been offered as a contributor to the unfamiliar Jackson of the Seven Days. This is superficial and specious. None of his staff suffered any harmful effects from the supposedly malarious region, not even the Reverend Robert Lewis Dabney, his forty-two-year-old chief of staff. And Dabney, jerked out of his ordered, sedentary life of small comforts, complained to heaven of the hardships he was called upon to endure. The Yankees, after weeks of camp life in the swamps, seemed uninfected by the miasmas. Jackson was becoming a clinical case before he left the Valley.

He had shown an overexhilaration from the excessive secretions of hormones when his campaign ended on June 12. Then he was euphoric, feeling invincible and inexhaustible. He wrote Lee that with forty thousand men he would invade the North. Lee, accepting this wild demand as understandable excitement, wrote him affectionately, "You must first help me drive these people away from Richmond." When the troops began their march toward the Virginia Central on June 17, Jackson began to run around, as the country people used to say, "like a chicken with its head cut off."

He left his staff and rode about on the trains from one place to another. At the railroad station at Mechum's River, when he next met his staff, he told them nothing and asked them nothing. "Shaking hands all round and saying goodbye as earnestly as if he was off to Europe," according to Captain Douglas, he vanished again. The young members of the staff, accustomed to his ways, laughed at the goings on and continued their journey in a cheerful mood.

Jackson's mania for secrecy sat less well on General Chase Whiting, newly arrived from Richmond with his two-brigade division. Whiting, who attained the highest grades until his time at West Point, had been one class ahead of Jackson, the dull plodder who did not even earn a cadet corporal's chevrons. Having a low opinion of his new commanding officer to begin with, Whiting became enraged when Jackson sent him to Staunton, on the Valley Pike, from where, without explanations, he ordered him east to the Blue Ridge. Dick Ewell, commander of Jackson's second division, had resigned himself to being told nothing of the army's plans. But Whiting, fresh from his intimacy with Joe Johnston, formed a fierce resentment for his commander.

Jackson had one confidant, his unlikely chief of staff, the Reverend R. L. Dabney. Jackson's desire for a churchman superseded his judgment when he selected this home-loving professor from the theological seminary at Hampden-Sydney. Dabney had earlier served as chaplain of the 18th Virginia and retired with camp fever, and he did not want to join Jackson's staff. Though Jackson already had a good and potentially brilliant *de facto* chief of staff in young Sandie Pendleton, the son of Lee's chief of artillery, nothing would do but the heavy-minded Dabney join him, and he enlisted Mrs. Jackson to persuade Mrs. Dabney.

The theological professor was a misfit from the first. He appeared wearing a Prince Albert coat and, on a ride with the staff, raised an umbrella over his beaver hat. The troops yelled out their usual jeers. "Come out from under that umbrella. We know you're there because we see your feet shaking." Jackson resolved that situation by turning off into a woods at a gallop. When Dabney and the staff emerged, umbrella and beaver hat were gone. The staff then outfitted Dabney in an ill-cut uniform and a cap.

Though not adapted to serve with an army, Dabney was an intelligent if inflexible man, and in camp he showed himself to be capable enough with administrative work. For Jackson to entrust to him a tired army on the march to battle was merely another reflection of his impaired judgment. When Jackson disappeared at Frederick's

Hall during the night of June 22-23, for his hundred-mile round trip to Richmond, Reverend Dabney was in effect commander of the army.

He and the staff did not get on at all. He disapproved of their high spirits and they regarded him as one of their commander's less amusing eccentricities. On the march, the young men found a hospitable home every night, where they danced to all hours. While they were too young to be physically affected, and were highly moral as a group, obviously their minds were not on business. Then, although everybody on the march knew by then where they were going, Dabney cherished the general's confidence and enjoyed getting to sleep in the feather beds at private homes, to which his position entitled him.

During Monday the 23rd, the day of Jackson's absence, the van of the army, shifting from the relays of trains to the narrow roads, advanced only twelve miles to Beaver Dam (unrelated to the historic creek) northwest of Ashland. When Jackson returned sometime during the midmorning of Tuesday the 24th, the columns of men and guns and wagons were so disordered and stretched out so far in the rear that Jackson could only order a halt for the columns to straighten out and close up.

On this day, when the troops needed a strong controlling hand, Jackson's final flare-up of unnatural energy died off. He was overcome with the exhaustion of stress fatigue. The symptoms were vague and generalized, and he at first only felt that "something was the matter with him." He thought, from the deep lethargy, that the ride had tired him, and that he could persevere through this sudden fall from physical euphoria.

His faculties resisted the effort to concentrate. The familiar mechanics of his command were seen through a blur, the tasks to be done receded at the effort to bring them into focus, and the problems assumed an unreality. While watching his troops from a chair on a farmer's front porch, fact-minded Jackson did the unheard-of thing of picking up a novel. No sense from the pages came through. Any effort to prod the mind by will further taxed his depleted system. Then, nature protected itself by ceasing to function. In the middle of the day, the commander of the army went into the house and lay down to sleep.

Jackson's force was then in particular need of the unifying drive of his presence as well as of his discipline. More than any force in Virginia, his was a one-man operation, and on this march nearly half of the infantry was composed of troops new to the army. Ewell's division was intact, but Lawton's large, new Georgia brigade had just joined the three brigades in Jackson's own division, under the temporary command of Brigadier General Winder.

An elegant thirty-three-year-old professional from Maryland, Charles Winder deserved division command judged by the ability and outstanding courage he showed in leading the Stonewall Brigade. However, his relations with Jackson were tense, and he had only recently been persuaded not to tender his resignation.

Whiting, whose half division completed Jackson's infantry, did not bother to be discreet in declaring that Jackson had no more sense than his horse.

Only an efficient staff could have brought coordination to these elements with the commanding general asleep. Instead, Jackson had placed on his force the handicap of Dabney, who, unable to function away from Jackson, blocked what could have been the competent performances of the younger men, especially Sandie Pendleton.

3

After a presumably full night's sleep in the house at Beaver Dam, Jackson rejoined his force on June 25. On this day, when he was supposed to move across the Virginia Central Railroad, his troops covered about twenty miles to Ashland. This was an average march, but Jackson didn't push the troops, and his van went into bivouac six miles short of Lee's ordered destination. Jackson's only recognition of falling short of the point where Lee expected him was to order the army to move out at two-thirty instead of three o'clock. Instead of resting himself against this early start, Jackson stayed up most of the night praying.

On the day of the assault, June 26, after starting later than the planned two-thirty, Jackson's columns crept warily forward over roads winding through tangled screens of brush, falling further behind schedule with every hour. On crossing the railroad tracks at nine o'clock, he sent, as ordered, a message to Branch. Sometime during the early morning he sent Lee a message reporting that he was running late. After that, he communicated with no one and took no measures to speed the march.

Federal cavalry burned bridges, obstructed the roads with logs, and fired from the woods. None of these annoyances represented serious resistance. Jackson approached each with disproportionate deliberation. There was no drive, no urgency in him. The soldiers were not heartened by the dingy figure, perched on the little sorrel horse, riding along the lines with his familiar, "Close up, men, push on." The soldiers in the famed Stonewall Brigade thought they were on a routine march to be on the field for the next day.

When Jackson halted at Hundley's Corner and showed himself to be disturbed over the firing, he acted no different than he had for the past two days. He had reached a stage in stress-fatigue that has been called an "apathetic plateau." In this literally overpowering apathy, he put his men into bivouac and gave in to his insistent drowsiness. In terms of his ability to function, Jackson went to sleep far sicker than he might have from many ailments that could have been diagnosed by his young staff surgeon, Dr. McGuire.

The long restful night in camp, during which Jackson presumably slept, did not lift his apathy by the next day, June 27. Though all the analyses of Jackson's performance have called attention to the slow march and early bivouac of the 26th, his waste of the morning of the 27th was more revealing of his condition. Mystery surrounds Jackson's actions from daylight until after ten o'clock.

After sunrise at 4:38, some of the officers in Jackson's normally early rising command were awakened by the sound of firing along Beaver Dam Creek. Some time after, the troops resumed their cautious march forward. In this movement, Jackson left the crossroad at Hundley's Corner which led to Cold Harbor, and moved southward on the road to Old Church Road that took him toward the sound of the firing. It could only be deduced that he had then decided to feel his way toward the action in front of him.

During the hours that passed while Jackson moved the two miles from Hundley's Corner to Old Church Road, the firing at Beaver Dam Creek sounded light at first, and then became scattered, drifting eastward across his front. The road south from Hundley's Corner, after leaving the first belt of timber, led past several large farms. On the right of the road the gracious Cosby house which sat in a grove gave the only obstruction to the view of the advancing skirmishers of Ewell's division. Beyond the Cosby property, the land sloped down to the trickle of Beaver Dam Creek, and a light force of enemy infantry was reported seen in the tangled woods between the creek and Old Church Road.

Jackson halted his column, and guns were brought forward under the direction of Major Jasper Whiting, the former staff officer of Gustavus Smith who was serving Jackson as a guide. After the woods were shelled, Ewell's skirmishers moved on through the thickets without engaging the enemy.

D. H. Hill's vanguard had then crossed Beaver Dam Creek in the battle area and was moving east toward Jackson along Old Church Road. Jackson reported that the appearance of Hill and Ewell's skirmishers caused the enemy infantry to retire. No one else reported actually seeing any enemies except some stragglers, who were sent to the rear as prisoners.

When the creeping column approached the clearing of Dr. Richardson's house at the intersection of their road and the Old Church Road, the way was open in all directions. When Jackson reached the Old Church Road, the firing had ceased entirely from the Beaver Dam Creek area on his right, where Joseph Anderson's Brigade had crossed the creek and waited for him the night before. The sounds of a running action came from the south, directly on his line of march. Jackson then crossed Old Church Road, and followed for a half mile a country lane that led into the Cold Harbor Road. This lane entered the Cold Harbor Road at a curve where, after paralleling the north-south course of Beaver Dam Creek from Ellerson's Mill, the road swung to the east.

As the curve of the Cold Harbor Road was glimpsed through the fringe of brush, dust rose from the movement of troops on the road and again Jackson's guns fired. The shells burst among the troops of Maxcy Gregg's brigade of A. P. Hill's division. Jackson and Lee's army had finally joined.

4

While Jackson's men had leisurely broken camp under their general's limp direction and crept two and one half miles, A. P. Hill had, under Lee's overnight orders, opened on the Federal line along Beaver Dam at daylight for the purpose of forcing a crossing. The return fire was not heavy, but Hill's troops had grown cautious of the trap along the creek bottom and they made sure they were not being lured into slaughter before advancing in force. The enemy withdrew before them and the bridge was rebuilt at the crossing in the somber area of Ellerson's gristmill. Gregg's fresh brigade moved forward on Porter's line of retreat.

Porter had received McClellan's order to fall back to a new position, east of Jackson's approach, at three in the morning. On beginning his orderly withdrawal shortly after, Porter left a brigade and two well-served horse batteries as a covering rear guard. Between three and seven in the morning the bulk of Porter's corps, with miles of supply wagons, crossed Jackson's front at a distance of only two and one half miles from his camp at Hundley's Corner. A vigorous three o'clock move out by Jackson would have caught Porter's corps in columns of march. Even Porter's rear guard crossed his front while he poked along, reaching the line of retreat only after Hill's advance had appeared.

At some point during the morning, not early, the silence between Lee and Jackson was broken by Colonel Walter Taylor's riding to Jackson from headquarters. Taylor went to show Jackson his approach, and it is not known at what stage of Jackson's forward movement Taylor reached him. It can only be presumed that Lee expected Jackson to march southward, although at Hundley's Corner Jackson was on a road that led to Cold Harbor, according to the now obsolete General Orders No. 75. It is possible that Lee expected Jackson to continue to wait where he was, and that Taylor rode to Jackson's camp with directions for moving southward, when he found Jackson already started in that direction. Reports of the morning of the 27th indicate another vacuum in communication.

Jackson halted his troops in the country road, at its entrance into the curve of the Cold Harbor Road, where Hill's division was hurrying after the enemy. Hill's soldiers and officers paused to gape at the "hero of the South," and Jackson's men were very impressed by the stir their general created. Shortly afterwards Powell Hill was seen riding to the front alongside his columns. Jackson on a gaunt sorrel horse — not his usual "Little Sorrel" — rode down the Cold Harbor Road to meet him. The two former classmates dismounted in the large grove of Walnut Grove Church. As they chatted, General Lee rode into the grove on his gray horse, and Hill left to ride ahead with his men.

The firing east on the Cold Harbor Road continued, light and sporadic, as Lee and Jackson engaged in an earnest conversation. Lee sat on a tree stump and the famed Valley commander stood in front of him. Jackson removed his battered old cadet cap, and his forehead looked startlingly white in contrast to his weather-stained skin and brown hair. Lee's staff, as curious as the rest of the army about the legendary Stonewall, remained at a respectful distance. None observed anything in his attitude to note.

Never diplomatic, Jackson had been irascible during the last two days of the march, and that morning he had snapped at Winder in unprovoked ill temper. With Lee evidently he showed neither coldness nor warmth. They talked briefly in low tones and, without ceremony, Jackson mounted his ugly sorrel and rejoined his troops.

Neither man recorded what orders Lee gave Jackson. At that time Lee was improvising on the original battle plan which had been disrupted by Jackson, and this is known through a wire sent Huger. During the night before, Huger had grown unnerved by the strain of facing McClellan's army with nothing between him and the city, and Lee had written him, "Hold your trenches tonight at the point of the bayonet if necessary." As morning brought no threat from south of the Chickahominy, Lee — judging from the next message he sent Huger, a telegram before noon of the 27th — believed the bulk of McClellan's army was then north of the Chickahominy. He thought McClellan was forming in force beyond Powhite Creek, (an Indian name, pronounced *pow-hite*, not *po-white*) about four miles east of Walnut Grove Church, and stretching across the river to connect with the Federal lines at Fair Oaks. In his morning wire to Huger, Lee said, "If [the enemy] should diminish his forces in front of you or show a disposition to abandon his works, you must press him. . . ."

In improvising on his original plan, since the Federals had not withdrawn from Beaver Dam Creek at Jackson's apporach, Lee intended to intercept their withdrawal and catch the enemy (force unknown) in front and flank, to cut them off from the White House. To this end, A. P. Hill would follow the line of retreat southeast along the Cold Harbor Road, maintaining contact with Porter's rear guard. Porter's withdrawal, though orderly, had been hurried, and burning wagons littered the road and more stragglers were gathered up as prisoners.

Longstreet was ordered to follow a country road that ran eastward closer to the Chickahominy and came out at Dr. Gaines's farm, from where Porter's siege guns had shelled Magruder's lines the day before. At Dr. Gaines's Lee would be connected with Magruder on the other side of the New Bridge, and they could all breathe a little easier. Longstreet would continue and extend A. P. Hill's line, attacking directly ahead.

Jackson, with his "foot cavalry," would take a road to the northeast that turned Powhite Creek and would place Jackson on the enemy's flank. D. H. Hill's division, already in motion, would proceed northeast along the Old Church Road to Bethesda Church. From there Harvey Hill would turn south, to extend Jackson's flank, and deploy across the enemy's line of retreat to his supply base. Jackson's road from Walnut Church ran between the lines of march of Harvey Hill north of him and Powell Hill following the Cold Harbor Road southeast.

It was perhaps near eleven o'clock when Lee gave the new orders to Jackson in the churchyard. The sun was getting warm and the day promised to be hotter than the day before. When the two generals parted, the army had nine hours of daylight in which to box the Federals north of the Chickahominy.

5

Lee's improvised plan, based on Jackson's performing up to his reputation, held a better chance of success than even he realized. Its scope, however, was to be more limited than he envisioned. Lee's basic purpose was still to force McClellan to withdraw from his Richmond lines in protection of the White House base or to withdraw down the peninsula in protection of the army, returning to Fort Monroe.

McClellan's anxieties had affected him more than any one could guess, and his preparations for an overwhelming artillery assault on Richmond were less advanced than Lee suspected. McClellan cherished his siege train as if it comprised a secret weapon. Since the seacoast artillery had not been unloaded from the ships at the White House wharves, McClellan was not forced to protect the White House in order to save his siege train, and he needed to move only twenty-six of the siege guns by road. McClellan's slowness had made it possible for him to abandon the White House base and continue to evade the commitment to a decisive battle.

Late on the night of June 26, when McClellan knew for certain that Jackson was on Porter's flank, he decided to change his base to the James River. The ships at the White House would transport most of his siege guns, the base personnel, and such supplies as could be hurriedly put on board. No problem would be presented by destroying the remaining supplies and installations. With the boundlessness of the resources upon which he drew, the navy could soon deliver fresh supplies and equipment to a new base on the James River. To prevent his army suffering any immediate shortage of provisions, wagon trains would move food, forage and ammunition across the peninsula.

In the early morning hours of the 27th, when McClellan planned an immediate evacuation of the White House, he ordered Fitz-John Porter to withdraw to a strong position where he could connect with the bridges to the south side of the river. His plan was to support Porter for a stand on the north side, to gain the time to evacuate the White House. During the night of June 26-27 he started moving Porter's heavy stores across to the south bank, being careful first to save the siege guns from Dr. Gaines's farm. There was as yet no indication that McClellan planned to withdraw his army from the Richmond lines. His orders were restricted to Porter's holding action, after which he was to fall back across the river on the main army.

On the 27th, while Porter was concentrating at his new position,

McClellan first began to indicate the possibility of abandoning his lines. Before three o'clock in the afternoon he wired Stanton, "I think the most severe struggle is to come. . . . If I am forced to concentrate between the Chickahominy and the James, I will endeavor at once to open communications with you. All reinforcements should for the present go to Fort Monroe. . . ."

At three o'clock, Chief of Staff Marcy wired Stanton they were being attacked by "greatly superior numbers" and ". . . if compelled to fall back, shall do it in good order, upon James River, if possible. . . ."

While these messages were preparing Washington for the worst, at 4:30 McClellan sent a message to Porter: "I look upon today as decisive of the war. Try to drive the rascals and take some prisoners and guns. What more assistance do you require?"

Did McClellan think the situation was actually less desperate than he was presenting it to Washington, or was he only trying to hearten Porter into making a strong stand? Perhaps it was partly both. Certainly he did not sound desperate in his message to Porter, and McCellan knew he had one strategic advantage in Porter's stand on the north side. Lee knew nothing of the proposed change of base. His attack would be delivered on the assumption that McClellan would be forced to protect his lines to the White House.

There is the possibility that McClellan held the hope that Porter might repeat the repulse he inflicted on the enemy at Beaver Dam Creek. Late on the 26th and through the 27th McClellan asked his generals on the Richmond line what supports could be sent Porter. Their replies were not encouraging, and gave McClellan no hint that Confederate troops had withdrawn from the front.

Heintzelman wrote, "I think I can hold the entrenchments for 24 hours with four brigades," and added that the two brigades he could detach were so "worn-out" they would not be in condition to fight if they marched any distance. General Keyes wrote, "As to how many men will be able to hold this position for 24 hours, I must answer, all I have. . . ."

On the 27th, at eleven in the morning belligerent old Sumner sent a message, "The enemy threaten an attack on my right. . . ." At 5:15 that afternoon, corps commander William B. Franklin wrote,

"I do not think it prudent to take any more troops from here at present."

A few minutes later, Hooker wrote, "Have just returned from our front, where we have nothing but a stampede . . . owing to the behavior of the troops occupying the picket lines. The first shot from a rebel was sufficient to start regiments . . ." "Fighting Joe" Hooker, whose division was occupying the lines of Casey's debacle at Seven Pines, was convinced that the enemy was preparing to advance in force. "If so, I should have not less than three brigades to spring to the defenses . . . I find Casey was whipped in detail. I desire to avoid such a disaster."

Huger's nervousness was communicated to the enemy, though Hooker misinterpreted the reason behind it. Huger was supposed if necessary to ask Holmes at Petersburg for support from Drewry's Bluff. Department Commander Holmes spent the day wiring the war office about phantom enemies landing on the south side of the James River and not only kept Walker's brigade at Drewry's Bluff, but further unsettled Huger.

Magruder had done well in his demonstrations. McClellan reported that "large forces of infantry were seen during the day near Old Tavern." Magruder had been parading his troops around again and this time he "imposed" on Sumner and Franklin.

There was not only nothing to suggest to McClellan that the Confederate lines in his front were weakened; the attitude of the generals could have led him to expect an attack on both fronts. Though McClellan seemed undisturbed by the reports, he undoubtedly underestimated the numbers Lee had drawn from the Richmond front to support Jackson's move against his line of communications.

Porter had told McClellan early in the evening of the 26th when the Confederate attack on Beaver Dam Creek was dying off, that he felt no fear of the enemy overrunning his position. Only Jackson on his flank and rear made his stronghold untenable. This confident attitude could not suggest that the enemy's superior numbers, even with Jackson, would be overwhelming if met in a position of natural strength, and the new position selected by Porter was stronger across its whole front than Beaver Dam Creek. As the new position was close to the Grapevine Bridges across the Chickahominy, this would secure Porter's rear and make it possible for McClellan to reinforce him. Despite the alarmists on his front, McClellan sent a large division from Franklin's corps to support Porter during the early afternoon of the 27th.

With all the uncertainties caused by the contradiction between his orders and his later rationale, McClellan at least held firmly to the one purpose of containing the Confederate assault north of the river on June 27.

If Porter did succeed in driving the attackers, McClellan would be prepared — as he wired Stanton — to take advantage of any mistakes the enemy made. But first Porter must hold his position until nightfall. With the evacuation of the White House base then far advanced, Lee's forces would be deployed against an objective that no longer existed.

Though McClellan had not anticipated Lee's general offensive north of the river, once it opened on June 26 he reacted with a clear head. His reaction was defensive, a contraction, but tactically he was sound in his preparations to parry and thwart Lee. Lee's improvised offensive sent his four columns of infantry on four roads to intercept McClellan where McClellan was not going to be.

CHAPTER TEN

Gaines's Mill: Battle of Decision

STONEWALL JACKSON, again holding the key assignment in Lee's design, followed another of those narrow roads that seemed to induce in him uncharacteristic caution. Vine-draped woods obscured the right side of the road and dust rose in thin clouds over the columns. The sun grew hot. At intervals across the road the enemy had thrown loose logs, as on the march of the day before. When the columns halted for men to move the logs, minié balls from unseen rifles whined through the foliage. Skirmish lines were thrown out on both sides of the road, the men clawing their way through the matted screen until the road was clear ahead.

At the foot of a shaded slope the road bore northeast, passing on the left the cultivated fields of the Cowardin farm. Soon the road forked, and the slowly moving column turned right into a rough lane slicing southeast through woods. The men rustled the brush on either side of the lane as they moved cautiously ahead. Woods roads leading to private farms crossed their passage, and after about a mile the van emerged into a farm clearing. Second-growth timber grew on the opposite side of the farm buildings, covering a slope that led down to the upper end of the large millpond of Gaines's cornmeal mill. The gaunt, dusty men halted short of the timber. After a pause, the column was turned about and the troops retraced their steps through the heat of the woods back out under the bleached sky at the fork.

This time Ewell's division, in the lead, took the left fork on its northeast course. Following this and cross-country roads, Ewell's van reached an intersection with the road D. H. Hill was using in his march from the Old Church Road to Old Cold Harbor. Ewell halted until Hill's long columns rattled past and then fell in behind his rear guard. At some distance, Jackson's own division and Whiting's two brigades followed Ewell. Instead of four columns converging on Porter, Jackson was bringing up the rear of D. H. Hill's division. Hill's five brigades had made the longer march, and had encountered fragments of the enemy's army, taking prisoners, wagons and an ambulance, without suffering delay.

Neither Jackson nor his division commanders mentioned the countermarch. Whiting mentioned "frequent halts," and Winder said it had been "a slow and tedious march." Countermarching in that unfamiliar country was not unusual. John Worsham, a member of Richmond's Company "F," a *corps d'elite* in the second brigade of Jackson's division, referred to it as a trivial detail. "We halted and retraced our steps until we came to a road [the fork] we had passed some time before." The significance of this uneventful countermarch would have been unknown except for the attention called to it by one of Dabney's anecdotes, which, emphasizing Jackson's secrecy obsession, played up the eccentricities that contributed to his legend.

Dabney said Jackson had told a local guide merely that he wanted to go to Cold Harbor by the shortest route. The shortest route was the woods road that ran southward to the area of Gaines's millpond. On the opposite side of this pond a lane led to the Cold Harbor Road east of Gaines's four-story brick mill. Porter had passed this point on his retreat, and A. P. Hill's brigades had followed in pursuit. While Jackson's men were halted, Hill's deployed lines struck Porter in his new position about one mile to the east of Gaines's Mill. At sound of this firing, Jackson asked the guide where it came from.

According to Dabney's story, the guide told Jackson the firing came from "Gaines's Mill." To this information Jackson revealed that he did not want to go to Cold Harbor via Gaines's Mill, but to pass "that place" on his right. The guide then told Jackson he was on the wrong road, and added, "Had you let me know what you desired, I would have directed you aright at first."

The suspicious element in the anecdote is this: the firing was not at Gaines's Mill, in the meaning of the mill of William Gaines. The firing was in the valley of Boatswain's Swamp, more than one mile away from the valley of Powhite Creek in which the mill was lo-

cated. It was later that the battle fought on the hill above Boatswain's Swamp began to be called "the Battle of Gaines's Mill."

Jackson's guide, a cavalryman from the neighborhood, would not
have placed the firing at Gaines's Mill when it came from a more
distant valley in the area of New Cold Harbor. No one who had
heard rifle fire in volume would have located Powell Hill's assault
in the valley of Powhite Creek, where Jackson was halted on his
road behind Gaines's millpond, as Worsham said it was "the heaviest
musketry" he had then heard in the war.

As with many of the war's humble legends, things were not so
simply explained as by a general's eccentricities and a guide's salty
reply. The significance of Dabney's story, quite outside his intentions, was its indication of Lee and Jackson failing to establish a
precise understanding of the objective.

What is known of Lee's verbal order to Jackson, given in their
brief conference at Walnut Grove Church, is contained in Lee's
telegram to Huger: "Jackson's command is . . . turning Powhite
Creek." On Jackson's woods road, he *was* turning Powhite Creek,
which runs north and south across the Cold Harbor Road at the
mill of William Gaines.

When Lee wired Huger, he expected Porter to make his stand on
the hill on the east side of the Powhite Creek Valley. But Porter,
making his stand farther east, occupied the hill above Boatswain's
Swamp. That was not shown on Lee's map.

To make it more confusing: On the assumption that Porter was
at Powhite Creek, Lee wired Huger that Jackson was turning
Powhite Creek "on the road to Cold Harbor," to be "supported by
D. H. Hill." There were two Cold Harbors. New Cold Harbor,
where A. P. Hill was fighting, was at the curve in the road to Old
Cold Harbor, where the tavern sprawled at the crossroads one mile
to the north.

D. H. Hill's orders took him to the Cold Harbor tavern, clearly
where he was assigned. The crossroads straddled the mazelike net-
word of roads to the Chickahominy crossings, to the White House
base, and to the York River Railroad on its course north of the river.
Hill was placed to intercept McClellan's presumed movements toward his supply lines and base. If it can be assumed that Jackson

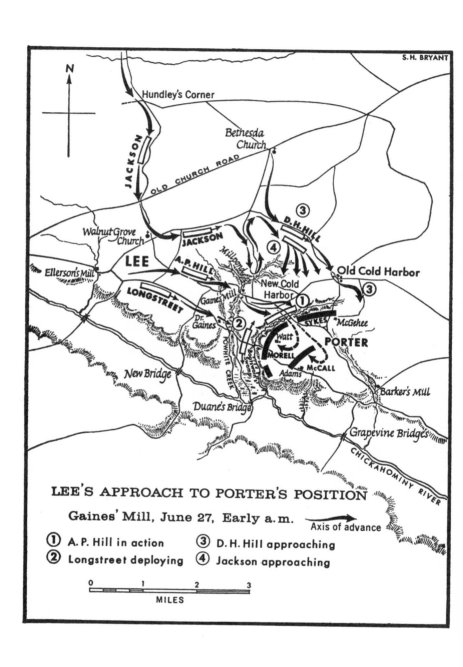

S. H. BRYANT

Hundley's Corner

Bethesda
Church

JACKSON

OLD CHURCH ROAD

③

D. H. HILL

Walnut Grove
Church

JACKSON

④

Ellerson's Mill

LEE

A. P. HILL

Millpond

Old Cold Harbor

③

LONGSTREET

Gaines Mill

New Cold
Harbor

①

Dr.
Gaines

②

SYKES

McGehee

Watt

PORTER

MORELL

McCALL

New Bridge

POWHITE CREEK

Adams

Barker's Mill

Duane's Bridge

Grapevine Bridges

CHICKAHOMINY RIVER

LEE'S APPROACH TO PORTER'S POSITION

Gaines' Mill, June 27, Early a.m.

Axis of advance

① A. P. Hill in action   ③ D. H. Hill approaching

② Longstreet deploying   ④ Jackson approaching

0   1   2   3

MILES

was also directed to Old Cold Harbor, Lee's plan would have placed the joint force on the flank and rear of Porter's presumed position, in a duplication of the plan of the day before to flank Porter out of the Beaver Dam Creek stronghold.

Jackson and Harvey Hill would have been on Porter's flank and rear had he made his defense at Powhite Creek, and without question Jackson expected to find Porter at Powhite Creek. This is made clear in his report: "The enemy had receded from Powhite Creek." At this point occurred the vacuum that would have been filled by a staff officer responsible for contact with the movements of all units.

Jackson needed only to proceed on his woods road to the south side of Gaines's millpond to have reached the Cold Harbor Road in the rear of A. P. Hill's assault. By a short march his columns could have reached the curve in the road at New Cold Harbor, then have turned north and extended Hill's line until Jackson connected with D. H. Hill at Cold Harbor tavern. Instead, retracing his march north away from the Cold Harbor Road, Jackson moved north and east until he turned south to follow D. H. Hill into Cold Harbor from the north. When Jackson reached the Cold Harbor crossroads, he was at a point of concentration of twenty-seven thousand troops separated by about one mile from the heart of Porter's position, where A. P. Hill was attacking with one division.

Jackson did not arrive on the field like a general who had simply been delayed by a countermarch and was eager to put his troops into action. When, around three o'clock, Jackson rode up to the Cold Harbor crossroads, where D. H. Hill had already deployed his division, he looked tired and ill-humored. Lethargic and peering myopically from under the brim of his cadet cap, he began a prolonged survey of the situation.

Having "receded from Powhite Creek," Porter was neither where Jackson expected to find him nor, for the second day, was he doing what Lee had anticipated. According to Lee's plans, A. P. Hill, with Longstreet's support on his right toward the Chickahominy, should be driving Porter who, with D. H. Hill on his flank and rear, should have fallen back toward the York River Railroad to protect McClellan's line of supply.

From what Jackson could see and from what D. H. Hill told him, the Federals were fixed firmly on defense with their right flank, near Old Cold Harbor, bent back to face Harvey Hill's division. Far from being driven across D. H. Hill's front at Cold Harbor, the Federal artillery had Hill deployed well back from the swampy line on their own front. At New Cold Harbor, where the intensity of the battle sounds remained stationary, A. P. Hill was obviously making no progress. He might even be sustaining counterattacks from the Federals.

In the absence of either information or orders from headquarters, Jackson had to apply his apathetic brain to resolve an unexpected situation. In his condition, nothing was more difficult than reaching a decision on a problem not readily soluble. The struggle seemed only to deepen his apathy, and time slipped away as he sat his gaunt horse in the midst of the disordered movements of troops, guns, wagons and ambulances.

Jackson's extremely reticent report gave no hint of what had been going on inside him as the hours of the hot afternoon passed and Powell Hill's division was being cut to pieces a strolling distance away.

2

Jackson reached the Cold Harbor tavern ahead of his last divisions and after Ewell's division, which was nowhere in sight. Presumably Jackson was told that Ewell had already been placed in line under Lee's orders. D. H. Hill's division, that day under Jackson's command, was deployed to the left of the road from Old Cold Harbor to New Cold Harbor. His lines, facing south, were at a left angle to A. P. Hill's assault generally from west to east at New Cold Harbor.

Powell Hill's division was fighting for the second day in a death trap at a water barrier in the bottom of a ravine. Boatswain's Swamp, which contained a high-banked stream through part of its sluggish course, roughly paralleled the Cold Harbor Road from near the tavern to south of New Cold Harbor. The swamp was three quarters of a mile to the east of the road, and the plain remained level to within about three hundred yards of the swamp. From there the land dipped with increasing sharpness to the boggy bottom, mostly covered with dense underbrush. On the opposite bank the hill rose steeply to a plateau on a level with the plain at New Cold Harbor.

The formation of the ground along the creek bed varied in the course of the swamp, changing every several hundred yards, with the valley growing shallower and the banks less steep toward the northern end. Near the Cold Harbor tavern the sides of the swamp flattened out, and the swamp, as if designed by nature to protect a defensive position, spread parallel to the road from Old Cold Harbor occupied by D. H. Hill. In effect, Hill's division was deployed on the same level of ground as the Federals, but was separated from them by the densely entangled swamp that spread at right angles to Porter's main defensive line and thus protected the front of the Federal flank.

This right-angled flank position, facing north, was held by the U. S. Regulars of George Sykes, Hill's fellow Southerner and former West Point classmate, and a cold, hard-bitten professional. Though Sykes's division did not hold a position as naturally strong as the lines above Boatswain's Swamp, his regulars were posted behind felled trees to command the open ground approaching the McGehee farm, and his powerful batteries commanded the road that ran across his front from the tavern to the Chickahominy. This road provided the only passage for Harvey Hill in trying to move up his own guns. At about the time Jackson arrived, Sykes's guns had driven off Bondurant's battery and Hill had no guns in action. His sweating troops, out of the range of enemy rifles, were close to the spray from bursts of Federal shells.

Jackson first ordered Hill to move his men into a more protected position. From Jackson's first order, he seemed to expect the Federals to be driven across his front, despite the evidence of A. P. Hill's hard struggle at New Cold Harbor. D. H. Hill was placed where he would command the road when or if the Federals were driven. In waiting for developments, Hill could occupy the enemy's attention on their flank while Jackson brought forward his own division and Whiting's two brigades. Those he planned to commit in echelon from south to north, from the left flank of A. P. Hill's attack across the gap to D. H. Hill's right flank. Then, if Lee needed support to drive home his assault, the lines would be connected for a general advance.

This uninspired reasoning would have been sound except for his failure to communicate with Lee, one mile away. He neither inquired if this movement fitted in with the commanding general's plans nor advised him of what he was doing. This and other failures to communicate might seem to support the explanation that Jackson's troubles during the Seven Days were partly caused by his unwillingness to operate under another's orders after having grown accustomed to independent command. But none of the generals knew how to cooperate. Nobody sent messages to anybody.

Lee had dispatched Walter Taylor earlier in the afternoon to find out where Jackson was, and Colonel Taylor had hurried Ewell forward. No other staff officers were sent by Lee to discover precisely when Jackson had arrived and what he was doing or to provide him with any instructions. Jackson's failure to communicate showed nothing about Jackson. What did reveal Jackson's state was his failure to assume active command of the two divisions he ordered forward.

On his staff, as quartermaster general, was a tough, rough-tongued character from the Valley, Major John A. Harman, who had operated a stage line business before the war. Though he and Jackson had experienced their personality difficulties, Harman was most efficient in handling Jackson's wagons and supplies. It happened that Harman, like Dabney, operated directly under Jackson, and he had little or no interest in any aspect of the army that did not concern his wagons. For some unexplainable reason, Jackson selected the quartermaster to carry a verbal message to the two division commanders to deploy and advance in echelon.

It also happened that the lead division on the road approaching Old Cold Harbor was commanded by Chase Whiting who, in an angrily uncooperative mood regarding Jackson, scarcely knew Harman. The efforts of the wagon trainmaster in trying to tell surly Whiting what to do led to an unprofitable exchange — "a farrago of which I could understand nothing," Whiting said about Harman's instructions — and resulted in Whiting's halting where he was. Behind him, on the road to the Old Cold Harbor tavern from the north, Winder did the same with Jackson's division.

How long they waited nobody knows. After more than enough time had elapsed for their appearance, Dabney on his own rode up the road to learn if Whiting had properly understood Harman. Then Dabney took the liberty of interpreting the general's orders and directed Whiting and Winder to deploy through the woods to their right. They were not provided with guides.

During the long wait before Whiting's skirmishers emerged from the woods nearly one mile south of the tavern, between four and five o'clock, Jackson did nothing. Nor did he send forward any instructions to Whiting, if indeed he saw the division when it appeared. Whiting, moving obliquely through the close woods and across two ravines, had drifted off course and reached the clutter of ambulances, wounded men, dead horses and wrecked gun carriages around New Cold Harbor, the backwash behind the divisions of A. P. Hill and Ewell which were out of view near the ravine bottom. General Lee, with his staff, was mounted in a clearing just to the east of the curve in the Cold Harbor Road.

From this curve in the road a private road ran southeast toward Boatswain's Swamp. Before reaching the slope down to the ravine this private road divided. One fork continued east toward the Mc-Gehee house and the other sliced toward the south, crossing the swamp where Hill had been fighting for three hours. This road ran up the Federal slope to the pleasant Watt house, whose cultivated fields and orchards spread across the plateau. Fitz-John Porter had his headquarters in the Watt house, and the most accurate designation of the battle would have been "the Battle of the Watt House Hill."

Big John Hood rode at the head of the brigade that first reached the field and from his arrival on the confusing scene all coherence went from the sequence of orders. Though Lee was gradually assuming tactical field command, he had not yet brought the action completely under his direction. From the conflicting accounts of the participants, apparently everybody was giving orders and brigadiers were acting on their own responsibility in putting their troops in as they came on the field.

According to Hood, he encountered Colonel Jones of Ewell's staff, who told him that Ewell's division needed help. Hood did not wait to report to Whiting or anyone else. He deployed his regiments as they came up and moved across the plateau toward the wooded slope. When his troops were ready to go in, they would be sent to the right of Ewell, in support of A. P. Hill's fought-out brigades.

When Whiting reached the field with Law's brigade, he evidently reported to Lee, for Evander McIver Law was sent toward Hill's right under Lee's orders. When Law was forming his brigade, the first troops of Jackson's division found their way out of the woods. These belonged to the brigade of Charles Winder, acting commander of the division. After losing his direction in the woods, Winder seemed to leave the other brigades to shift for themselves. Winder's wilted men also emerged from the woods near New Cold Harbor, and continued across the fields to the road between Old and New Cold Harbor, near where Whiting had passed. Winder saw A. P. Hill and reported to him. Hill placed him in reserve until the other brigades of Jackson's division came up.

It is possible that Jackson knew nothing of his two divisions' employment in the battle around New Cold Harbor — some brigades under Lee's orders, others under A. P. Hill's, and Hood going on his own initiative — while he waited for the enemy to be driven. Everybody else was too busy to have noticed how Jackson occupied himself from the time he arrived, around three, until after five o'clock. By then, he may or may not have learned that most of his command had been ordered into line. Dabney said that Jackson "assumed" all his units were in line, though the last was not then on the field.

At that time he apparently decided that the enemy was not going to be driven. From the increased volume of fire along the stationary line around New Cold Harbor, Lee's attack was unmistakably hanging. Around five o'clock Jackson ordered D. H. Hill to change position and prepare to open an assault on the Federal right flank behind the curve of the swamp. Then he left the crossroads at the tavern on the awkwardly gaited sorrel and rode, in his short-stirruped perch, to New Cold Harbor.

He found Lee at his informal field headquarters off the private road, and for the second time that day the two generals greeted one another without warmth.

Lee said, "Ah, General, I am very glad to see you," but the words implied a rebuke when he added, "I had hoped to be with you before."

According to Stuart's staff officer John Esten Cooke (who passed his nights writing sketches for Southern magazines), Jackson's brief answer could not be heard over the heavy rattle of musketry.

Lee then said, "That fire is very heavy. Do you think your men can stand it?"

Jackson's pale eyes, peering from under the cap's visor, ranged over the field. He replied loudly enough that time. "They can stand anything. They can stand that."

Lee then spoke to him in a lower voice and his words did not carry. Judging by the action that followed, Lee had told him to prepare for a general assault to be delivered along the whole front — from Longstreet, off A. P. Hill's right, to D. H. Hill, on the Confederate left. From Jackson's own reactions, in which he briefly asserted some personal force after twelve hours of apathy, Lee must have told him also that the situation was desperate. The commanding general stood on the verge of losing his first major battle.

3

During the afternoon while Jackson's command was getting to the field in fragments, A. P. Hill's division fought one of the longest, hardest, most unsung actions of the war. From the opening movement at daylight, his troops had been in contact with the enemy for twelve hours. After feeling out the enemy line along Beaver Dam Creek before the crossing at Ellerson's Mill, Hill moved close on Porter's rear guard to the steep valley of Powhite Creek. Expecting the enemy to make a stand on the hill east of the mill, Maxcy Gregg's lead brigade formed two regiments to advance as a strong line of skirmishers. The South Carolinians, who had seen no action the day before, rushed up the hill with the same *élan* the other brigades had shown in their advance across the plain at Mechanicsville.

At the top, just above Gaines's Mill, Gregg's regiments encountered only Porter's rear guard falling back. Leaving their camp abandoned, the Federals were retiring to a stand of pines across the plateau. While the bridges were rebuilt over Powhite Creek and a battery brought up, Gregg's advance regiments gobbled up some undestroyed supplies and, as one of the soldiers reported, "We refreshed ourselves." Then, after the guns shelled the pines where the enemy's skirmish line could be seen, Gregg's men gave themselves the glory of a picture charge — the lines sweeping across the open ground at double time.

The light Federal force fled before them and gave inexperienced Gregg a false impression of Porter's retreat. His soldiers ran after the enemy, across the Cold Harbor Road where it curved and on over the fields to the slope beyond. This sprint, in full equipment under a noonday sun, loosened the formation of the lines, and panting soldiers followed at intervals in the wake of the leaders. The fastest men caught glimpses of the enemy disappearing in the shadowed fringes of timber at the bottom of a ravine, and, without a pause, went whooping down the slope.

Immediately, hidden guns blasted from the crest of the opposite plateau, and metal burst over the irregular lines. The looseness of the lines and the speed with which the men went pell-mell down the slope saved them from heavy damage.

At the bottom of the slope, along the private road to the McGehee house, table ground descended into what one of the soldiers accurately described as "a deep, wet ravine." The soldiers had reached that part of Boatswain's Swamp north of the high-banked creek and south of the swamp that spread across Harvey Hill's front. The ravine of the creek bed, curving slightly from northeast to southwest, bulged forward toward the Confederates where Gregg reached it. By the alignment of Porter's units on the hill, the Federal lines of defense were farther back from the creek there than to the south. Where Gregg struck the ravine, only a skirmish line defended the opposite side, and those Federals withdrew when Gregg's lead regiments stumbled and slipped their way across the marshy bottom.

At the foot of the opposite hill, the winded soldiers reached a growth of young pines, screening them from the enemy, and Gregg ordered a halt for his men to rest and close up their regiments. At the bottom, though out of the sun, it was humid and breathless. While his men panted up under scattered artillery fire from the crest of the hill, and infantry opened on them from behind an abatis on the hillside, Gregg surveyed the entrenched lines on the hill, located the batteries on the crest, and knew he had found the enemy. The ruddy-faced, middle-aged scholar, as exultant as if he had run

a fox to earth, sent the word back to A. P. Hill and asked to be allowed to attack.

Powell Hill, riding forward to where the private roads branched
off from the Cold Harbor Road, was not in the impetuous mood of
the day before. He could see that the Cold Harbor Road roughly
paralleled the swamp for a mile toward Old Cold Harbor to the
north, where Jackson and D. H. Hill were expected. When Hill
halted, he could see no Confederates through the midday haze rising
over the fields between him and the tavern. First he ordered Gregg
to remain where he was, on the north side of the road to the McGehee house. Then he ordered up his other brigades, planning to deploy them to the south of Gregg, between and overlapping the
two private roads. In making those dispositions to attack, A. P. Hill
was at that time in command of the whole field around New Cold
Harbor.

Hill's front was wide, approximately three quarters of a mile, for
an attack without reserves on such a forbidding position, and his
flank was open to the north. While Hill's troops were deploying,
General Lee arrived at New Cold Harbor. Lee believed that Jackson's expected arrival would extend the enemy's line on Hill's front,
as well as provide protection for Hill's left flank. Longstreet, then
moving forward from Dr. Gaines's farm, would form in reserve on
Hill's right, between his flank and the Chickahominy. There he
would be ready to go in at the opportune moment. Lee began to
assume tactical direction of the battle when he ordered Powell Hill
to open his assault upon receiving word that Longstreet was in position.

4

Between one and two-thirty, while Crenshaw's battery formed on
the Cold Harbor Road and opened on the enemy's position, Hill's
brigades advanced down the rough, brushy slope deployed in line
of battle. From Gregg's position, neither Hill, Lee, nor the brigadiers moving their men forward were aware that Boatswain's Swamp
was much more difficult of passage south of Gregg. The banks
deepened first to form a ditch and then rose so high that the sol-

diers would have to help one another climb the slick opposite wall.

Nor did they know that A. P. Hill was to attack in the exact center of a position whose southern flank was literally impregnable. From the northern fringes of the swamp across Sykes's front, the ravine coursed two miles south, bearing to the west, and then bent back to the east below the rise of the hill at the southern end of the plateau. South of this abrupt end of the plateau, the swamp coursed across marshy, open ground to the Chickahominy one half mile away.

Federal guns posted back on the crest of the plateau and heavy guns from across the Chickahominy swept this open bog between Porter's flank and the river. The same batteries also commanded open stretches of ground that approached the front of the southern end of Porter's line, the Federal left in relation to its center at the Watt house. With his left flank impregnable and his right secured by Sykes's regulars, Porter bunched his infantry in the area of A. P. Hill's assault.

Across his whole front Porter had placed his infantry in three tiers on the hillside, behind hastily built lines of logs and loose earth packed in knapsacks. Porter's infantrymen were firing from stationary positions, which increased accuracy, and in solid alignment, which increased the density of the fire power.

The three tiers were made up, from the center toward the left, of three brigades of Morell's division, which had not been engaged the day before. To the right of center was Warren's fresh brigade of Sykes's division. This portion of the line was manned by about twelve thousand troops, with McCall's division, about eight thousand men, in support. During the afternoon, McCall was put into line at the center. Late in the afternoon, some of McCall's units were pulled out and shifted to the left, nearer the flank. They were replaced by two fresh brigades, Taylor's and Newton's, of Slocum's division, sent over by McClellan. First and last, more than twenty-five thousand men fought around the center — on either side of the two private roads.

A. P. Hill's division, after its casualties at Mechanicsville, totaled approximately twelve thousand when all six brigades were in line. Getting all six into line was the problem. From the beginning of the march down the slope the possibility of the division attacking on a

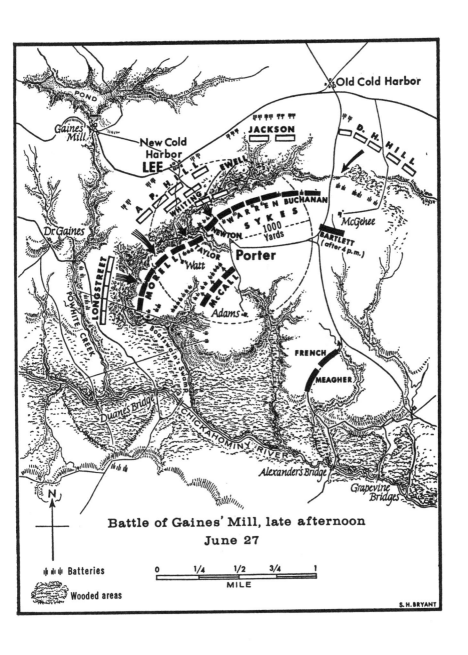

POND

Gaines'
Mill

New Cold
Harbor
LEE

JACKSON

Old Cold Harbor

D. H. HILL

A. P. HILL

EWELL

WHITING

WARREN BUCHANAN

S Y K E S

McGehee

Dr Gaines

NEWTON

1000
Yards

BARTLETT
(after 4 p.m.)

Porter

TAYLOR

Watt

MORELL

McCALL

Adams

LONGSTREET

POWHITE CREEK

BOTTOM'S BRIDGE

FRENCH

MEAGHER

Duane's Bridge

CHICKAHOMINY RIVER

Alexander's Bridge

Grapevine
Bridges

N

Battle of Gaines' Mill, late afternoon
June 27

⫟⫟ ⫟⫟ Batteries

Wooded areas

0   1/4   1/2   3/4   1
MILE

S.H. BRYANT

solid front was eliminated by the timber and thickets obstructing the view, the differences in the terrain, the varying distances to the creek and the enemy's varying distances behind it. As soon as the lines started down the slope, guns and rifles opened on them, and the farther down the slope they marched, the heavier grew the gale of canister and bullets.

Though Hill exercised a general control over the movements of his brigades, the actual attacks depended on the separate brigadiers. Partly because of the different physical conditions on their separate fronts and partly because of the inexperience of the field officers, little to no coordination was maintained between the separate brigades once the troops entered the bedlam in the wet jungle at the bottom of the hill. As it was difficult under the best circumstances to bring green troops in solid units to points of attack, the miry ravine in one place, the ditch in another and the high banks in yet another, caused the regiments in a single brigade to move unevenly in trying to close with the enemy.

Gaps created by the enemy's fire remained gaps. The men drifted to one way or another to close on their nearest fellows. The gaps became serious when the ragged lines began to cross the ravine. The men were firing then, without much to shoot at, and as a whole the soldiers were eager to get across to the opposite hill and the enemy. In their baptism the day before at Beaver Dam Creek, Hill's troops felt they never had a chance to come to grips with the enemy, and at the final stage of their assault across Boatswain's Swamp they plunged into the morass with a resolve to go all the way.

With their high screams echoing through the ravine, the determination of the attacking soldiers made their inexperienced line and field officers slow to recognize that the units were being cut to pieces separately. The range of view of the brigadiers could scarcely encompass the area of their own regiments and even the professional soldiers knew nothing of what was happening in adjoining sectors. Some units were halted before the men crossed the swamp. Others moved up to and, briefly, in places, through the first fortified lines. Parts of one regiment fought their way to the crest of the hill. With no friends nearby, the remnants fought their way back out. Each momentarily opened breech was closed by the skillful employment of the enemy reserves, and the attackers lost as heavily falling back as they had going in.

On Gregg's front, where the advance was started from across the ravine, one regiment held desperately to a position on the enemy's hill. Another, infected by the panic of several men, broke backward. By the time the regiment was rallied, solidarity had been lost. In that area Orr's Rifles lost 315 of the 537 men engaged.

Porter's three lines having absorbed the continual assaults — Dorsey Pender going in again and again — the Federal reserves began to carry the battle to the fragmented units of the attackers. Then, on Hill's left, without Jackson to menace the Federal right, the famed New York Zouaves of Sykes's division attacked Gregg in flank. As D. H. Hill, under Jackson's orders, was doing nothing on Porter's northern flank, other units from Sykes's regulars began to press against A. P. Hill's left.

Slowly the tide turned. From attacking, Hill's remnants were fighting to hold their ground. Numbers of the men under heavy fire for the first time broke under the horror which was so different from their pictures of the charges of battle lines such as they had made from Powhite Creek. In the matted brush over the marshy footing, the men could scarcely see the next company. In Branch's brigade, Branch himself lost control of his units threshing about in all directions. Some fell back, others sidled off to join another unit, and the rest took cover where they were.

Their momentum gone and the Federal pressure growing, Hill's brigades began to suffer as heavily from stragglers as they had from casualties. Some of the men were exhausted. Gregg's troops had been so tired before the assault that some of them slept behind the pine thicket, one hundred yards from the enemy's rifle lines, with artillery fire breaking around them. Countless others, too scared or too proud to cross the open field going back, huddled where they were without firing. Yet, past four o'clock, perhaps half of Hill's men stood steadily behind what protecting tree or bush or rise of ground they could find, and returned the enemy's fire.

During this disordered sequence of movements, Hill's men delivered a surprisingly heavy fire power. Two of Hill's batteries were doing far more damage than they had the day before, both against the enemy's personnel and his gunners. Even Willie Pegram, whose battery had had all except one gun knocked out the day before, along with forty-seven gunners, got up two or three patched-up pieces into action.

Though the Light Division had failed to break the enemy's front, the troops, on their second day of fighting alone while waiting for Jackson, had taken a toll of the enemy. A. P. Hill said they had done all that could be asked of men. Usually furious at any skulker from his command, "Little Powell" reproached none of the shattered, ashen-faced soldiers staggering out of the ravine.

When four o'clock passed, and Jackson had still not appeared, Lee realized that the relief of A. P. Hill had become imperative. From the heavy commitment of enemy troops, Lee believed McClellan had the bulk of his army on the field.

First, Lee ordered Longstreet to move out of his cover and make a strong demonstration to distract the enemy and draw troops from Hill's fronts. It was at this fortuitous moment that Walter Taylor led Ewell's division forward. General Ewell reported that he did not know Jackson's whereabouts nor that of the two other divisions of Jackson's command. There was no time to worry about that. Ewell was ordered in immediately on Hill's broken and imperiled left.

. Ewell began to deploy his veterans of the Valley campaign behind Hill's flank by the road to the McGehee house and extended the flank northward to stretch toward D. H. Hill's right. Before Ewell's seasoned troops were in line, the overflow of the enemy's counterthrust caught his regiments as they came up, and the fate of Lee's battle shifted off the center of Hill to include Ewell's division.

5

Major General Richard Stoddert Ewell had been Jackson's right-hand man in the Valley campaign. A West Pointer, "Dick" Ewell had come to the Confederate armies from the tough assignment of commanding a company of dragoons in the Southwest border service. Though his capacities grew with his rise to command of a division, Ewell liked it best when he could join in combat like a captain, as he did whenever Jackson was out of sight.

"Old Baldhead," as he was called, was to become the character of the army as he then was of the Valley command. With bulging eyes, sweeping mustachios, and the movements of a startled bird, he shrilled out awesome curses and bombastic plaints in a high, piping voice. His quaintness was actually the façade of a lonely, generous man of fine feelings. Ewell's once promenent family of Northern Virginia had fallen upon hard days, and his joint ambitions had been to reestablish a plantation and marry Lizinka Brown, a wealthy widow whom he had known since childhood. While the war had ruined the plantation dream, he still cherished the one of the Widow Brown.

When Ewell's soldiers pushed confidently forward through the disordered groups of Hill's troops pulling out of line the officers and men advanced with an almost contemptuous impatience to show the city soldiers how fighting should be done. Jeering at their fellow Confederates, Trimble's brigade moved through the woods and across the ravine to attack the enemy north of Gregg's survivors along the road to the McGehee house.

Isaac Trimble, about the army's oldest general officer at sixty, was a former professional who had achieved success in civilian life as a railroad builder. A native of Powell Hill's Culpeper County, Virginia, Trimble had become one of Maryland's prominent citizens. Self-confident and assertive, he was inclined to attribute to himself a wide command of battle situations and reported dispatching other brigades and even divisions to their positions on the field. However, his self-assertion made him a strong combat leader.

Even while Trimble's brigade was getting into line across the ravine, Ewell discovered the difficulties that had beset Hill's division. As he reported, "the density of the woods and the nature of the ground were such as to prevent any extended view . . . and . . . made it necessary to confine my exertions mainly to that locality." As the weight of Porter's counterattack was felt on their left, Trimble's hardened veterans locked with the enemy lines in a stand-up fight. Illusions about driving the enemy were abruptly grounded.

To the right of the road, Elzey's Virginia brigade went in and fared no better. Arnold Elzey, a thirty-five-year-old professional from Maryland and one of the dependables from the Valley campaign, went down with an ugly wound in the face and head. His men were forced to shift to defense and took positions to escape the density of fire pouring on them from the hillside. As with Hill's brigades, the regiments lost so heavily in getting close to the enemy that they lost the cohesion in which the men were accustomed to mass their fire.

After Elzey came Dick Taylor's celebrated Louisiana brigade, sporting a pelican on its flags. Probably the most colorful outfit to come to Virginia, its personnel presented an interesting contrast to the general impression that the Southern armies were composed of big plantation owners "fighting for slavery." Of the regiments in the brigade, one was all Irish, with a harp on its flag; one was formed of Acadians, the simple, warm-hearted people of the bayous; and a third was the notorious "Tigers," a battalion composed of plug-uglies from the wharves and alleys of New Orleans. The only officer who could (or would try) to control the "villainous" Tigers was gigantic Rob Wheat. The son of an Episcopal rector, Wheat was a leader of that breed of soldiers of fortune which flourished in the nineteenth century.

The big slaveholder among the Louisianians was their brigadier, Richard Taylor, a Yale graduate and the son of a United States President. Taylor, thirty-six, was a sugar planter whose only military experience had been as secretary to his father, when Zachary Taylor was a general. Widely read in the science of war, Taylor had the intelligence and personal qualities to become a superior soldier. Cold and haughty except with intimate friends, Dick Taylor was very much aware of his family connections, which included Jefferson Davis, a brother-in-law. On the march to Ashland, Taylor was stricken with a strange nervous malady which caused a paralysis of his legs, and he could not assume command of his brigade.

Taylor's brigade crossed over the littered ground where Hill's troops had caught the greatest concentration of the enemy's fire from solid lines of fresh riflemen. In passing through the clumps of Hill's shaken men, the Louisianians may have missed the commanding presence of their brigadier. Before the troops were in position Colonel Seymour, taking the brigade in, was killed. Then the lovable Rob Wheat went down, mortally wounded. The Louisianians faltered, began to fall back, and then broke to the rear in a rush.

This break, the only blight on the history of the brigade, gave the Valley troops a sobering taste of the fighting which Hill's men had stood up against. In the open country of the Valley, Jackson's men had experienced none of the effects of marshy ground and brushy timber on troops advancing. By the time Ewell had all his regiments on the field, the units were mangled and in danger of being overrun. The ferocious Tigers, who could not be controlled after Wheat's death, were never the same again.

6

While Ewell was absorbing some of the enemy's attention on Hill's left, Longstreet began his diversion below Hill's right. Wilcox, with three brigades that had been lying behind the banks of Powhite Creek, moved out toward the strongly protected Federal flank. They immediately drew fire from the batteries on the Watt house hill and from the heavy guns across the Chickahominy.

The other three brigades, nearer to A. P. Hill, had waited in a light woods, and Pickett moved his brigade forward to the edge of the clearing to develop the enemy's strength. From the volume of fire drawn along the whole front, Longstreet perceived that a demonstration would accomplish nothing. Without communicating with Lee, Longstreet decided to act on his own initiative and turn the demonstration into an assault. His division would attack precisely where the enemy wanted him to but, as he said, there was no help for it if the day was to be saved.

It was around five o'clock when Longstreet, customarily deliberate, began to prepare to advance his whole line. Pickett by that time was wounded, but his brigade continued its steady fire from the edge of the woods as the other brigades moved forward.

It was while Longstreet was forming that Whiting was sent forward by Lee to report to Longstreet for orders. Longstreet directed him to form on Pickett's left. Hood's brigade was then going into position behind Hill's lines across the road leading to the Watt house. Whiting ordered Law to form his brigade on Hood's right. When the men moved forward through the woods, regiment by regiment, Law saw that "a thin and irregular line of General Hill's troops were keeping up the fight, but, already badly cut up, [they] were wasting away from the heavy fire from the Federal lines."

When Hood and Law were advancing into position behind Hill and to his right, Ewell got some relief on his left by the arrival of Lawton's brigade. This Georgia brigade of 3500 men — about the size of the rest of Jackson's division — had arrived on the field separately from the other brigades. In the drift through the swampy woods, all the brigades of Jackson's division emerged separately, and by chance Lawton came out at a cornfield immediately in the rear of Ewell's hard-pressed troops.

Alexander Lawton, a thirty-seven-year-old native of Maryland, had entered the Harvard Law School after graduating from West Point and had practiced law in Savannah. He was Porter Alexander's brother-in-law. As he arrived on the field, Lawton heard that Ewell was in trouble. Ordering his untried regiments forward in their new uniforms, Lawton went to look for a staff officer to provide him with instructions or directions. He saw two regiments retire out of woods onto an open field in front of him, and somebody told him the enemy's fire had driven them out.

Like Hood earlier, Lawton decided to act on his own. Without advancing first into the woods, he formed his brigade in a single battle line on the fields east of the Cold Harbor Road. He excited the men, going into their first battle, by sending them forward at a run. The troops were mostly armed with new Enfield rifles and fired in a single volley when they burst into the brush. It was the heaviest single blast produced on the Confederate front until that time. As soon as the regiments reached the denser part of the woods lining the soggy creek bed, the usual difficulties in keeping alignment arose. But the weight of Lawton's Enfields tipped the balance of volume to the Confederate side in that area, and the worst was over for A. P. Hill and Ewell.

During these movements — of Longstreet, Whiting, and Lawton — Jackson rode to New Cold Harbor for his brief conference with Lee around five o'clock. The deployment of these units in getting into line was not completed until after six o'clock. It was between six and seven before a continuous line was formed from Longstreet's right to Lawton's left, nearly connecting with D. H. Hill.

When Jackson rode away from Lee, there was little left for him to do. Powell Hill had already ordered in Winder, with the Stonewall Brigade, to close on D. H. Hill's right. When Winder filled the remaining gap between Lawton and Harvey Hill, Lee would at last present an unbroken front between four and five hours after A. P. Hill's assault had opened on the expectation of Jackson's arrival.

Jackson's last two brigades, with communication lost between the vanguard and those behind, had drifted so far southward in passing through the woods to the front that the 3rd Brigade reached the field southwest of New Cold Harbor back near Powhite Creek. The 2nd Brigade appeared still farther to the southwest on the western side of Powhite Creek. The two brigades had marched almost in a circle to come on the field approximately where they would have if no countermarch had been made from the road back of Gaines's millpond.

Presumably because of the positions of these brigades on their late arrival, Jackson ordered the 2nd Brigade to support Longstreet's right and the 3rd Brigade to support Whiting in the center, where Hill's troops were being relieved. Jackson, his pride involved, avoided mention of the undirected march of the two divisions, which brought six brigades on the field in five different locations and at five different times. In his report, he stated that "Jackson's division" went in as a unit between Ewell's and D. H. Hill's.

After Jackson's brief exchange with Lee, his actions were characterized by a single sentence attributed to him by Dabney. He sent messengers to his division commanders with the words, "Tell them this affair must hang in suspense no longer; sweep the field with the bayonet."

This order has been used to indicate a directing spirit of combat that rose in Jackson. "Cheek and brow were blazing with crimson blood," Dabney recalled, "as his gigantic spirit was manifestly gathering strength." As Dabney also reported that only half an hour of sunlight remained, this placed the time that Jackson dispatched the often quoted message around seven o'clock. Lee's general assault had begun before the couriers could have reached any of Jackson's division commanders.

To cover this point, Dabney wrote, "the ringing cheers, rising from every side out of the smoking woods, told that his will had been anticipated . . ." Omitting the poetic concept of "anticipation," Jackson's famous sentence had no bearing on the battle at all.

When Jackson left Lee, he evidently made an effort to rouse himself. He rode back and forth, studying the curving front from different angles with the fierce glare ascribed to him by Dabney. As by then his command had been committed to others, there was no direction for his briefly gathered energies to take, and he could only show an animated presence. Yet, a spurious sense of accomplishment accrued to Jackson's performance at the Battle of Gaines's Mill because of the decisive part in the final action taken by troops then under his general command.

These troops, D. H. Hill's and Whiting's, were not a part of Jackson's Valley command. Whiting was on brief loan from Lee's army and had operated with Jackson only on the march to Richmond. During the battle, after sending the garbled order that immobilized Whiting on the road, Jackson had had nothing to do with his employment. Harvey Hill's division had been placed temporarily under Jackson's command that day, and Jackson's authority over Hill at Old Cold Harbor consisted mostly of restraining him during the hours when A. P. Hill's division was being cut up in its isolated action. Though these two divisions operated only technically under Jackson's command, the Battle of Gaines's Mill has usually been presented as a rise in the level of Jackson's performance during the Seven Days.

Jackson's behavior as a military commander was no different from what it had been since June 24, on the march to Ashland, when he had first revealed the effects of stress fatigue. His slow march from Hundley's Corner to the battlefield on the 27th and his bemused inaction on reaching Old Cape Harbor revealed the same muffled faculties and inability to impart energy to his troops.

7

At around seven o'clock, when Lee mounted his first general assault of the day, D. H. Hill had been pressing for some time against the angled Federal right. There Sykes's regulars had been strengthened on the flank by Bartlett's fresh brigade of Slocum's division sent from the Nine Mile Road. Hill had gotten some guns in action and was exerting a heavy, continuous pressure. Though he was not budging the regulars with their fresh reserves, he was engaging every Federal soldier and gun at that end of the line.

This placed Porter under a burden along his front. After the brigades of Taylor and Newton (of Slocum's division) were put in the right center between Morell and Sykes, Porter had no more reserves at hand. The fresh brigades of French and Meagher had crossed the Chickahominy but had not yet come on to the field. In this circumstance, while the Federal center had not yet been extended, the position was held by tiring men, their ranks thinned from casualties, and there were no replacements to help meet the solid thrust from Longstreet's division on the Federal left.

Longstreet, having everything just so before he went in, handled his brigades with the sureness that characterized the performances which built his reputation. His men, jackets black with sweat from the long wait in the sun, moved rapidly across the quarter of a mile of open ground, ignoring the shells that ripped at the flank from the Federal guns south of the river. The troops crashed into the thickets bordering the swamp with a dense burst of rifle fire.

Pushing steadily downhill toward the high creek banks, pausing to fire as they walked, the regiments were not met with the volume of canister and musketry that had showered the advances of A. P. Hill and Ewell. The metal flew thickly, but troops could live through it. Without a perceptible break anywhere, the Federal fire grew scattered in places and the feeling of solidarity was missing from the tiers on the hillside.

Major General Morell, commanding the division on the left center, and Butterfield, commanding the brigade on the left flank, believed their line had been subjected to a general assault around five o'clock, when Longstreet had made his demonstration and Whiting and Lawton had gone in to support Hill and Ewell. For this reason, the Federal generals on the left center thought they were facing fresh troops from an inexhaustible reserve when the weight of Longstreet's brigades shook their lines.

At some point, segments of the defenders began to falter. At the wrong time, regiments were pulled out of one part of the line to support another. At the creek bank, Confederates jumped into the water in pairs, throwing their rifles up on the opposite side. One pushed another up, and then was pulled out himself. On the extreme right, sturdy Wilcox started his men up the hillside. It was slow going but it was a tide, no longer a movement of thrusts that became fragmented by concentrations of fire.

With Longstreet and D. H. Hill pressing on opposite ends — and the Federal left beginning to give a little — Lee delivered the main thrust where Porter least expected it. It came over the seemingly impregnable center, at the steepest part of the hill, where Powell Hill's brigades had been shattered in their five hours of fighting.

During the course of the piecemeal arrival of the units upon the field, as Lee had gradually assumed direction of the battle, he still avoided issuing detailed orders which denied an officer the opportunity to make changes to conform with the situation as it developed in his sector. To Whiting he said, in effect: Break the enemy's line.

Hood approached after Lee had given the order, and Lee told his former lieutenant in the old 2nd Cavalry that all the fighting had not dislodged the enemy. "This must be done," Lee said. "Can you break his line?"

"I can try," Hood said.

Hood's brigade was formed on the left of Law's, the two totaling four thousand relatively fresh men. Whiting rode along the lines as the men prepared to go in over the ground where Hill's dead and wounded were strewn. Those remnants of Hill's division who continued to fire had formed behind a slight rise on the slope near and parallel to the creek. Whiting ordered his officers to send their men fast down the slope once they breasted this little rise, not pausing to fire. With fixed bayonets, the men were to carry their rifles at trail arms and place their reliance on the quickness with which they could cross the creek and approach the enemy's first and strongest line.

Law said, "Had these orders not been strictly obeyed the assault would have been a failure. No troops could have stood long in the withering storm of lead and iron that beat into their faces as they became fully exposed to view from the Federal lines."

The assault would possibly have failed anyway except for the instinct for combat leadership displayed by young Hood. Had he advanced in the blindness with which Ripley had led his brigade at Ellerson's Mill, the whole day might well have ended in failure.

From the moment his regiments began their advance, Hood, striking no gallant pose of the general inspiring his men by advancing with bared sword, moved to where he surveyed the whole field of action.

His brigade and Law's passed over the rise and plunged down the slope with a high yell. From the rise nearly to the bottom, the two lines advanced in the range of the Federal batteries, and bursting canister took a severe toll. In the thickets near the creek the men with their bright bayonets came under rifle fire from the exhausted Federal infantrymen crouched behind the earth and logs. Many of the Federal rifles had become fouled from the long firing and were useless, but the sun was setting then, and Porter's soldiers knew this would be the last assault.

On the way to the ravine, Hood's men moved through the woods while Law's brigades crossed an open field. Mounted behind his double lines, Hood saw a space widen where Law's right should connect with Longstreet's left. One of Longstreet's regiments had halted to deliver fire and, not resuming its advance, continued to fire from a stationary position. An uncomplicated, aggressive man with quick reflexes, Hood reacted quickly to do what had to be done.

With no desire to claim credit himself or to cast reflection upon another, Hood never reported that the failure of other troops to advance exposed the flank of Whiting's division. He only said he had crossed two of his regiments behind Law and threw the 4th Texas forward with the 18th Georgia in support. Actually he dismounted and, towering above most of his men, personally led the 4th Texas toward the gap.

This regiment had been his first Confederate command. The 4th Texas was not a young man's regiment. It was dominated by substantial citizens — stockmen, farmers, merchants — with forty lawyers among its 130 commissioned and noncommissioned officers. After Hood was promoted to brigadier, the assertive individualists could not agree on a native Texan to command them. They selected for their colonel fifty-year-old John Marshall, a Virginia native who, as editor of the Austin *State Gazette*, was a state political power. The lieutenant colonel was twenty-three-old Bradfute Warwick, of a distinguished Richmond background. A graduate of medical college, Warwick, while continuing his medical studies in Europe, had volunteered with Garibaldi and risen to captain. This handsome young man had, like Hood, sent his mare to the rear.

Going down the slope alone the Texans marched bent over, "turkey hunting style," as a soldier from another outfit saw them. When their line formed on Law's right at the bottom of the hill, the 4th Texas had taken the heaviest casualties in the two-brigade division. At the brushy bottom of the hill in that area, the Federal lines were the closest to the creek, no more than a few yards up the slope from the high banks. When the 4th Texas reached the creek in line with the other regiments, nearly one fourth of the men had fallen in the two brigades.

At the creek none paused to fire. Some leaped the banks, while others jumped in and climbed out. Despite their different methods of getting across, the men maintained their alignments in the battle lines and started up the hill, still without firing. Colonel Marshall fell from his horse, dead when they found him. Bradfute Warwick picked up a battle flag left behind in one of Hill's earlier thrusts. Waving it, he yelled to the men to rush the first breastworks.

The worn-out Federals behind the works had given all they had. It was clear that the screaming men coming toward them with bayonets were not going to stop. The first line of defenders left their works and started to scramble up the steep hill. At the second line they might get a chance to reload, maybe replace a fouled rifle, and make a stand with the reserve line fifty or more yards farther up the hill.

Only when Porter's troops began their withdrawal to the second line did the Texans begin firing. As other segments of Porter's first line were abandoned, Law's regiments — from Mississippi, Alabama and North Carolina — paused to aim and fire at close range. The 4th Texas had lost 250 men, half its personnel, but the 18th Georgia coming on behind gave weight to the fire.

The retreating Federal soldiers fell in droves. The reserves on the second line, seeing their companions fall by the scores, and themselves unable to fire with the withdrawing first line in their front, broke back for the crest of the hill. When the weaker second line of works was abandoned, the retreating soldiers from the first line made no effort to make a stand. Their retirement became flight.

The two brigades, the men's blood up with the chance to return the thousand casualties they had suffered, stayed on the heels of the Federals, firing rapidly and carefully. At last the Texans, with no more breath for yells, reached the crest of the slope and saw the masses of Federal troops milling on the plateau in the falling dusk. Bradfute Warwick went down there, severely wounded. He was taken to his father's house in Richmond, where he died a week later.

Though the consensus of reports agreed that the 4th Texas had opened the first wedge, sections of the line of defense beyond the creek were abandoned almost simultaneously across the front of the two brigades. Also, though the consensus agreed that the first break had been made by Hood and Law, troops from Longstreet's long line of assault stumbled up on the crest of the Watt house almost at the same time. Micah Jenkins's South Carolina regiment, which had sliced through the Federal lines at Seven Pines with such speed and power, was among the first to reach the disorder of the crest, near Hood. Further right Virginia regiments of Cadmus Wilcox came storming up onto the plateau.

Porter said the first break came in the center, near his headquarters in the Watt house. The Confederate pressure from the Federal left flank to the center was so heavy, and the defenders so fought-out, that a break anywhere would have started the whole two-mile front to give.

8

The drives to the crest were not made evenly. The first men to reach the center of Porter's force on the plateau seemed to be confronted with more Yankees than they had faced all day. Though the separated Confederate units, several with all field officers lost, found themselves in no position to exploit the break, Porter's men were equally disorganized.

Nothing like a general rout had begun. Most of the Federal soldiers were trying to establish order on regimental units. But numbers of soldiers were fleeing, dropping their arms as they ran, and some units were cut off in the suddenness of the break. In the center two regiments surrendered to Whiting's two brigades.

Then, in the failing light, Sykes's U. S. Regulars and their reinforcements began a stubborn withdrawal from Porter's right, moving slowly back in a slight arc from the McGehee house toward the road to the Chickahominy.

That had been a long, grim duel along the swamp on the Federal right flank between the two Southerners, Harvey Hill and George Sykes. They were a tenacious pair, and dour Sykes, commanding regulars, fought with the pride of an old-line soldier against volunteers. Harvey Hill showed again, as at Seven Pines, his skillful control of his units and the cohesive drive he could sustain in assault. For his final push, after more than two hours of frustration, his right was supported by the comparatively fresh brigades of Lawton and Winder. Sykes could not contain the weight thrown in late, but Hill could not break him.

With Sykes retiring southeast across the plateau, Porter could look only to withdrawing Morell, McCall and the brigades of Slocum. Porter had fourteen or more guns lined up on the plateau to blast the disorganized Confederate units breaking over the crest of the hill, and a curious episode nullified their potential destruction.

Philip St. George Cooke commanded several regiments of cavalry that had been held in reserve and the veteran professional soldier decided to break the assault force before its units formed for pursuit. Cooke, a Virginian, was Jeb Stuart's father-in-law and the father of a Harvard-educated infantry colonel, both of whom had broken off relations with him for fighting against his state. The arguments are evenly divided as to whether the cavalry charge was a bold stroke or a foolish impulse doomed to disaster.

With the light dimming and smoke drifting over the indescribable confusion on the plateau, the horses, looming out of the fog, bore down on the foot soldiers. Against some troops such a charge might have worked, but these soldiers were country boys as familiar with horses as with house pets, and they calmly stood their ground and fired. When their rifles were empty, the men thrust bayonets at the necks of the horses or at the riders trying to get at them with saber and pistol.

The charge quickly degenerated into a stampede in reverse. Riderless horses ran about with wildly flapping stirrups, horses went out of control and the riders lost all sense of direction. Their backward rush carried the horsemen into Porter's fourteen guns. Artillery horses joined the gallop and ran off, gunners were knocked down, and by the time the dust settled most of the guns had been overrun by Whiting's troops.

Porter claimed Cooke's cavalry charge precipitated his retreat. Cooke claimed his charge made possible the relative order in which Porter withdrew. From the condition of Porter's infantry, no confusion wrought by the cavalry was necessary to force a hasty withdrawal. The luckless charge unquestionably intensified the general confusion, though it also confused Lee's soldiers. Whatever the charge contributed, the action of the 5th and part of the 2nd U. S. Cavalry marked the end of the battle.

Fitz-John Porter was a hard loser. Many Confederates, in their official reports and later personal writings, paid the good soldier the highest tributes for the magnificent stand made by his troops. Porter was not at all generous. Back in May, when he had used half a corps to drive Branch's green brigade at Hanover Court House, he had attributed his victory entirely to the valor of his own men. At Gaines's Mill, where he was actually outnumbered by little more than five to four, and where he enjoyed the advantage in artillery and possibly the strongest defensive position of the war, he attributed his loss entirely to the enemy's "overwhelming" numbers and presented a picture of orderliness in his withdrawal which did not exist.

Blaming Cooke, Porter stated that the fourteen guns which the cavalry charge had forced him to abandon were the only guns lost except for two that ran off from the bridges in the night movement across the Chickahominy. Some of those fourteen guns were still firing after the cavalry charge, and the Confederates captured twenty-two guns altogether. Thousands of Federal rifles, supplies which the Confederate quartermasters were three days collecting, and several rapid-fire contraptions on a machine gun principle were gleaned from the field. Nearly three thousand Federal soldiers were taken prisoner and countless hundreds of stragglers were saved from capture by darkness.

The late arrival of French's and Meagher's brigades provided a rallying point to troops making their way through the dusk in poor order. The solid lines presented by these two brigades prevented any spontaneous pursuit by the disorganized Confederate units on the plateau. It was too dark for organized pursuit to be formed and the Confederates could not get their batteries up the hill.

Porter retired from the dark plateau southeastward to the Chickahominy, his guns using the road that ran from the McGehee house. Units slowly converged on the new bridges McClellan had built, where Sumner had crossed during the Battle of Seven Pines. The bulk of his army had crossed by daylight of the next morning, though some stragglers never got to the bridges. Brigadier General Reynolds, who had lain down to rest while his lines crept through the night, was captured asleep the following morning. Porter brought his army off the field in highly commendable order under the circumstances, but it was not the ordered withdrawal he claimed. His corps was saved from more complete wreckage by the late hour of the final attack.

Demonstrating the advantages of a strong defensive position and superior artillery, Porter's loss of 4000 killed and wounded was only half of Lee's total. Porter's total casualties were brought to about 6900 by the loss of almost 3000 prisoners.

9

Driving Porter came at the heavy cost of eight thousand Confederate casualties. This was never emphasized as were the losses at Ellerson's Mill. In the first day's fight, where the responsibility could be shifted to A. P. Hill's "impulsive attack," Ripley's losses were cited endlessly as waste of life: "335 men in the 44th Georgia alone" was frequently mentioned, without the mention that only one other of Ripley's regiments was seriously engaged, or that Hill lost little more than seven hundred out of five brigades engaged. Of Gaines's Mill, where Lee commanded, it was never stressed that A. P. Hill's division lost 2688 killed and wounded (60 per cent casualties in the regiment of Orr's Rifles) and uncounted hundreds not included on the casualty lists. These were men who suffered minor concussions from shell bursts, temporarily incapacitating injuries from blows from spent bullets, shell fragments, or falling tree branches and heavy falls the men took in underbrush and ditch. Many of these unlisted casualties, which returned to action within twenty-four hours or a few days, would have been captured had the field been lost.

The highest proportion of casualties, 25 per cent, was suffered by Whiting's two brigades. Chase Whiting dimmed his own glory by writing disparagingly of those remnants of Hill's troops through whose ranks Hood and Law passed in their late assault. Whiting accused them of not following his attacking lines up the hill, and said he doubted if any of the men passed the creek. Whiting's remarks came ill from a general who had remained idle while Hill's division splintered its strength in wearing down successive lines of defenders.

Longstreet, in observing that A. P. Hill was about the only general who did not claim credit for the breakthrough, pointed out that the success of Whiting's assault was built on Hill's five-hour fight in the swamp. "The troops of the gallant A. P. Hill, that did as much and as effective fighting as any, received little of the credit properly due them. It was their long and steady fight that thinned the Federal ranks and caused them to so foul their guns that they were out of order when the final struggle came."

Ultimately, it was John Hood's tactical initiative that sustained the assault of the two brigades then under Whiting's command. Though Law was an intelligent, determined and ambitious soldier, whose record of performance was uniformly high, he was not a professional. At Gaines's Mill, he could scarcely have been expected to exercise the intuitive tactical control of the combative Hood. It was "Hood's Texans" the army spoke of (ignoring the 18th Georgia in the brigade), and Hood's Texans, not Whiting's command, became from that day on Lee's favorite shock troops.

Longstreet, in a generous mood after the sound performance of his own troops, spoke for the majority when he said there was glory enough for all. Longstreet was a different soldier than he had been at Seven Pines, when Johnston had given him a range of responsibility that exceeded his capacities — at least in such an ill-defined command situation. Under Lee, Longstreet's part in the whole was both more definite and more limited, since he was allowed initiative in tactics within the framework of a clearly stated objective. In his appraisal of the situation on the Union left at Gaines's Mill, in forming his troops for the separate points of assault, and in delivering a thrust in coordination with Whiting, Longstreet gave every evidence of living up to the reputation he had built in Johnston's army.

Immediately following the battle Lee conferred with his laconic, unruffled subordinate, revealing by his manner trust in his dependability. For his part, Longstreet seemed secure in the niche he had won in the new commander's army, and his energies were directed to executing the orders of the leader who had won the first major Confederate victory since First Manassas.

That night, June 27, the men with Lee were not certain of the nature of the victory. Some, such as Whiting, doubted the action was a victory. Whiting believed that McClellan had permitted Lee to become fully engaged on the north bank of the Chickahominy in order to drive over Magruder and Huger.

If Lee considered this possibility, there is no record of it. Longstreet's division was near the crossing to New Bridge, connecting with Magruder, and his troops had not been hard used. Excepting Lawton's brigade, the three brigades of Jackson's division had scarcely been engaged, taking less than a hundred casualties.

More of a factor than his position to shift troops across the river was Lee's belief that he faced the bulk of McClellan's army on the north side. He might have felt less secure in the ability of Magruder and Huger to hold their positions had he known that McClellan had more than sixty thousand infantry in front of them, with his artillery containing twenty-odd of his semimobile siege guns. In a case where ignorance supported boldness, Lee evidently thought only of finishing McClellan on the north of the river or forcing him into a retreat back down the peninsula.

On leaving the grisly battlefield to go to temporary quarters at a country house near New Bridge, Lee planned to resume the action early the next morning to discover the new position to which McClellan would withdraw. He did not know that during the night Porter's corps was crossing the bridges to fall in on McClellan's main force around Fair Oaks, nor did he suspect that McClellan was abandoning his base at the White House.

According to the knowledge Lee possessed, it seemed likely that McClellan would take a stand somewhere between the Cold Harbor Road to the Grapevine Bridges and Dispatch Station. This was a stop on the York River Railroad where it crossed to the north side of the Chickahominy, eight miles east of the battleground.

For Lee and the rest of the army all this was supposition during the night where uneasy small stirrings followed the violence of the seven hours of battle. Lost units poked gingerly through the blackness looking for water. Lanterns flickered where surgeons moved to those wounded they could locate by their cries and moans. Harness and wheels creaked as artillerists moved their horses to Powhite Creek. Captains and majors, assuming the commands of fallen field officers, moved about establishing their regiments.

Jackson's wagons were not up, and poor Dabney, trying to make a bed in a cornfield, had his stomach gag at a piece of raw tongue an officer shared with him and his feelings outraged at the fiery liquid the officer offered him to wash down the tongue. It was not a happy night at Jackson's headquarters.

Throughout the army there was little feeling of elation. The men knew they had won an engagement they had had to win. For the rest, they ached with fatigue, brushed weakly at mosquitoes as they found spots on the ground for sleep, and left the next day and the next battle to the unknown fates of tomorrow.

CHAPTER ELEVEN

"Gone Away"

THE CAVALRY was given little opportunity in the Seven Days. Neither commanding general had learned the proper employment of the mounted force, and the heavily brushed country was unfavorable terrain for cavalry operations.

Jeb Stuart, restlessly enterprising and eager for combat, had hovered off the Confederate left at Old Cold Harbor during the long afternoon of Gaines's Mill, waiting to begin pursuit on the enemy's withdrawal. Watching his brilliant young gunner, John Pelham, fight two Federal batteries with one Napoleon, Stuart was diverted by a mishap to his wife's cousin, John Esten Cooke. An overshot Federal shell burst near Stuart's staff and Captain Cooke, in instinctively ducking, fell off the log on which he was sitting. When the other staff officers turned quickly to ask if he was hurt, Cooke sheepishly said, "No, I ducked too far." Stuart's laugh belled over the field, and the prolific fiction writer had provided a permanent camp joke.

In the dusk, when Porter's force began to withdraw from the front, Stuart led several regiments along the darkly shadowed road from Old Cold Harbor in the general direction of Dispatch Station. There were no signs of an enemy withdrawing, though this indicated little about Porter's line of retreat. In retiring his corps southeast from the hill along the route of the road passing the McGehee house, Porter would reach a road close to the Chickahominy that paralleled the river to Dispatch Station.

The next morning, when Stuart was summoned to the New Cold Harbor field headquarters of the commanding general, he learned from Lee that the enemy's movements had become clearer, but his intentions were uncertain. Longstreet had pushed across the plateau east from the Watt house in the first early light and found no sign of the enemy. Jackson encountered only a few stragglers in probing down the Cold Harbor Road toward the Grapevine Bridges. The Federals had obviously abandoned the north side of the Chickahominy. Leaving vast supplies, McClellan showed no intention of coming out of his works to fight in the open. Yet, no one with Lee could discover any indications of McClellan withdrawing from his lines in front of Richmond.

Across the river, Magruder had grown highly nervous as he began his third day of confronting the enemy, and phlegmatic Huger showed the strain. Short of full-scale attack, reconnaissance was impossible against skirmish lines formed in depth half a mile in front of impenetrable abatis. The four cavalry regiments on the south side, scattered from Nine Mile Road to the James River, could find no approaches on the roads south of McClellan's main line. From the Federal flank on the fringes of White Oak Swamp, strong picket lines were formed in front of obscuring obstacles on all the roads. Against the clear morning sky the Confederates would have observed any columns of dust raised by movement over the roads, and there were none then.

As General Lee viewed the Federal contraction south of the Chickahominy, unless McClellan planned to withdraw from Richmond he was under the necessity of keeping open his supply line via the York River Railroad. To discover McClellan's dispositions, Lee ordered Stuart to provide a cavalry support for Ewell's division, which was to proceed along the north bank of the Chickahominy to Dispatch Station.

Ewell, after sharing a part of A. P. Hill's long ordeal at the creek, had withdrawn most of his troops at dusk when the final assault went forward. His brigades, refreshed and re-formed, moved out in good order.

Stuart, who provided the only account of Lee's orders, gave color to his assignment by writing he was "to cut the enemy's line of communication . . . and intercept his retreat." Lee's more general report would indicate that the mission of Ewell and Stuart was rather to seize the York River Railroad and discover if McClellan intended to fight anywhere on the north bank in order to preserve his line of communications.

Stuart's troopers reached the railroad stop first, and a squadron of enemy horsemen galloped off at their approach. The Federal cavalry rode not northeast to the White House but southeast along the Chickahominy. This was in the direction of the Bottom's Bridge crossing at the Williamsburg Road. Stuart mentioned carbines and pistols being left behind. Ewell, coming up soon afterwards, complained that Stuart's cavalry had burned the small depot and an accumulation of stores. Most significantly, Stuart and Ewell found that the enemy had destroyed the railroad bridge over the Chickahominy, severing his supply line by the railroad.

Ewell, with his sound training as a subordinate under Jackson's iron discipline, decided to send back the information and wait at Dispatch Station for further orders. The men spent the time tearing up the railroad tracks. Stuart, grasping his first chance for initiative since his celebrated ride earlier in the month, decided to push on to the White House with his small command.

The total cavalry brigade consisted of six Virginia regiments, the Cobb (Georgia) Legion, the Jeff. Davis (Mississippi) Legion, a small North Carolina regiment and one Virginia squadron. With four of the smaller units on the south side, Stuart had with him about 1800 riders and a section (two guns) of 12-pounder Napoleons from the Stuart Horse Artillery under Pelham.

At this time in Stuart's small force were most of the men who were to contribute to the golden legend of the last cavalier in the first total war. On his staff were his gifted cousin Channing Price; the herculean Prussian baron Heros von Borcke; Captain W. W. Blackford, the energetic engineer of a Virginia family famous for its early emancipationist activities; and Captain William Farley, a South Carolina Shakespearian scholar with an extrordinary and deadly skill at individual scouting. Close to this group was Stuart's favorite, the good-looking and modest John Pelham, just twenty-two years old. Pelham, Price and Farley were later killed and von Borcke wounded out with a throat injury. Only Blackford survived, in another branch of the service.

Also close to Stuart were the two Lee cousins, twenty-six-year-old Fitz, colonel of the 1st Virginia, and twenty-five-year-old Rooney, the commanding general's outsized son and the colonel of what became the famed 9th Virginia Cavalry. Fitz Lee, the high liver, had been a professional soldier since his graduation from West Point. Happy-hearted Rooney, who had attended Harvard, had served two years as lieutenant in the Regular Army when, after his marriage, he resigned to work the White House plantation he had inherited from his great-great-grandmother, Martha Washington.

They were all young, none yet thirty, exuberant with animal spirits and, though intensely serious about driving the invaders off their land, rode the countryside as if off to a frolic. Sweeney, the ex-minstrel who adorned the staff with his banjo, provided accompaniment for impromptu singing. Stuart's favorite song was "Kathleen Mavourneen," written by Professor Crouch of the Richmond Howitzers. But while the men sang as they rode and made jokes under all circumstances, Stuart was one of those men who could be extremely businesslike about the work at hand without appearing to take it seriously all the time.

Such was his ebullient, inexhaustible energy that had he not laughed and danced he would have been a tyrannical driver. As it was, he worked his men hard, demanded ceaseless alertness and physical endurance. It was his way of going at the work that made his men willing to extend themselves as if in a hard game to be followed by music, pretty girls and adoration. That was in the summer of 1862, when their mounts were well conditioned and the native-born horsemen could outride any enemy cavalry they encountered.

When Stuart led his troopers jingling northeastward toward the White House, he knew that George Stoneman and William Emory — who had operated cavalry on Porter's right — were in his front with infantry and artillery. He also seems to have known that Silas Casey commanded a force at the landing. After the riders left the brushy bottomlands of the Chickahominy, the roads led over mostly flat land where farmed clearings interspersed with dense timber, and the horses' legs rustled the roadside vines. At intervals along the railroad, pickets of enemy cavalry took off ahead of them. During the late afternoon, the troopers saw heavy columns of smoke rising above the horizon in the direction of the White House.

At Tunstall's Station, only three miles from the White House, Stuart discovered a vacated fieldwork built in the two weeks since his ride. Stuart regarded this fieldwork, with other entrenchments passed along the railroad, as a tribute to his raid: he had forced McClellan to make large detachments in protection of his communications. It never occurred to Stuart nor to any of them that the bravura act had also put McClellan on his guard and, by causing him to begin preparations for a new base, had wrecked Lee's offensive plan.

Beyond Tunstall's Station, their front was crossed by Black Creek, another of the streams moving sluggishly along a miry bed between abrupt banks. A wooded hill rose on the opposite side. The bridge was destroyed. Pelham's two guns were brought up and shelled the woods, flushing an infantry ambuscade. Then Captain Farley led a dismounted party across the creek to scour the woods while Blackford hurried a detail to rebuild the bridge.

By then darkness was falling, and Stuart put his riders into bivouac. The men ate the last of the cooked rations and fed the horses the last of the forage carried in the saddlebags. During the night the sky turned red from the fires at McClellan's base, and the air was split by the explosion of ammunition magazines.

Early in the morning, Stuart crossed the whole party over Black Creek and moved cautiously over the low, brushy countryside to the plantation. Oddments of cavalry surrendered and no opposition was offered. Where a dusty road turned through a fringe of pines toward the river, the vanguard beheld on the plain about a quarter of a mile away the awesome spectacle of two square miles of a smoldering supply depot. The ribs of burned wagons showed through the wisps of smoke, there were endless lines of blistered railroad cars, and the men counted five locomotives. Most of the riders with Stuart had never conceived of such a wealth of goods. All the men were saddened to see, on a rise near the river, the charred ruins of Rooney Lee's home.

Out in the river, where barges were burning, a gunboat lay offshore. Stuart decided to eliminate the bugaboo of these floating monsters and ordered forward about seventy-five dismounted sharpshooters. The men were directed to protected approaches by an unnaturally sober-faced Rooney Lee.

The gunboat immediately sent a boat of riflemen toward the shore to meet them. Pelham ran forward one of his Napoleons, and shells burst over the deck. Back went the boat of naval riflemen, climbing aboard the gunboat under Pelham's accurate firing. The gunboat steamed off down the Pamunkey and Stuart sent the Howitzer galloping along shore beside it. Stuart had, as he said, expected to accomplish nothing by this except to dispel the men's fears of the gunboats, "so terrible in their fancy."

Then the whole command started digging through the smoking heaps for supplies. While collecting quantities of forage for their horses, the troopers came upon delicacies never before imagined. The country boys were most fascinated by what they called "dessicated" vegetables and by the cans of fishes, in a fishing country. Some of the officers treated themselves to a breakfast of lobster and champagne, topped off with a cigar. Everybody had a fine time, except Rooney Lee.

The wanton distruction of the historic White House (burned by an arsonist against the specific orders of McClellan and Silas Casey) made a deep impression of the nature of the struggle on the cavalrymen. As Colonel Will Martin wrote, "This once beautiful estate, made more interesting by associations connected with the great leader of the first Revolution, George Washington, now utterly despoiled, forcibly reminded us that we were contending against a foe respecting nothing, sparing nothing."

2

Long before Stuart, on the morning of June 29, had made his positive confirmation of McClellan's abandonment of his base, General Lee had been forced to act on deductions made from the information at hand. Before noon of the 28th, the telltale columns of dust began to rise on the south side of the James, moving away from McClellan's lines in front of Richmond. Some while later the messages arrived from Stuart and Ewell informing him of the enemy's abandonment of Dispatch Station and the destruction of the railroad bridge. Manifestly McClellan was retreating, but it was equally obvious that Lee could do nothing about it without details.

The lines in front of Magruder and Huger presented the same aggressively manned works. McClellan had posted guns along the south bank of the Chickahominy that outranged every piece Longstreet tried to bring against them. It was a strange situation, with the defending army in the open and the invading army having

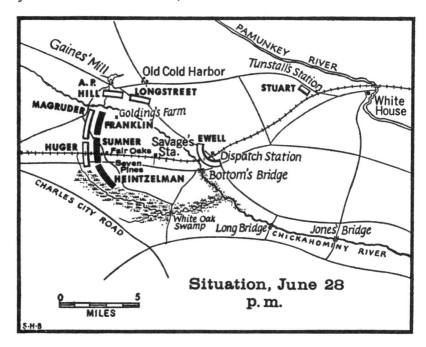

Situation, June 28
p. m.

drawn into a shell. The possibility must have occurred to Lee, as Whiting insisted, that McClellan's retreat was a ruse and the time was ripe for his trap to be sprung.

The positive element against this was McClellan's break with his supply base. Operating on the conviction that the movement indicated a retreat, Lee ordered troops with Ewell to move east along the Chickahominy to Bottom's Bridge to discover if McClellan was withdrawing down the peninsula. If he was not, and no attack was delivered directly on Richmond, by process of elimination McClellan must be moving to the James River and a new base.

None of the primitive intelligence work at that stage had discovered any evidence that McClellan was preparing a James River base. On the south side of the James, old, deaf Holmes continued to see only his visions of transports going up the Appomattox River. With no advance advice on a James River base, Lee was slow to react to McClellan's abandonment of the White House, because of his inability to comprehend the enormity of the Federal resources. Nothing in his previous experience, civil or military, had conditioned him to conceive of destroying millions of dollars' worth of property, transported and built by a vast concentration of technical resources, without significant effect on an army operating in a hostile country. That the destruction of "the canvas city" could be literally all in a day's work to a detachment of troops lay outside his calculations.

By the end of the day, June 28, when Stuart's cavalry was bivouacked three miles from the White House, everything pointed to an orderly Federal withdrawal to the James River. On this final realization that McClellan had avoided his trap, Lee never wrote a line to suggest that he was disappointed or disturbed. From his brief factual message to President Davis, he accepted the unsettling development as no more than a new tactical problem to be solved. In fact, Lee's undramatic acceptance of the withdrawal of McClellan's army built an impression that the Seven Days was the execution of a single plan toward a single end. Longstreet gave the best summation of what actually happened in his report: "The effort to draw the enemy out by cutting his base was entirely unsuccessful."

Accordingly, Lee extemporized a totally new offense, involving the shift of his operations from the north to the south bank of the Chickahominy. Since McClellan had declined to leave his works to protect the White House base, Lee rearranged his forces to catch the enemy in his withdrawal to the James.

There were few Confederates on that day who would not happily have settled for lifting the siege of Richmond and been content with the reality that McClellan was withdrawing. Lee, seeking a decision, held to the purpose of destroying McClellan's army. In a truly remarkable improvisation, before he went to bed Lee evolved the details for every division in his army to advance in the formation of a new trap to intercept McClellan before he reached the protection of the Federal gunboats on the James River.

3

In devising the new trap, Lee expected McClellan's army to be more encumbered than it was. With all his seacoast artillery and most of his semimobile siege guns shipped by the navy, McClellan had to move by road only twenty-six of those guns from his siege train which weighed as much as two tons. His four thousand wagons loaded with subsistence and ammunition, and a herd of live cattle, were moving during the day of the 28th, using the twenty-four hours McClellan had correctly estimated the change of base would gain him.

The men were to carry three days' cooked rations. Tents were to be abandoned, along with "all articles not indispensable to the safety or the maintenance of the troops." "Unnecessary officers' baggage" would be left behind. The sick and wounded who could not walk would be abandoned in the field hospital at Savage's Station, entrusted to the care of the Confederates. In a stupid act of vandalism, some of the Federal soldiers threw the medical supplies McClellan left into a useless heap that gave off a dreadful stench. Considering the needless abundance of supplies that burdened the Army of the Potomac (and this continued throughout the war), McClellan, by destruction, abandonment and help from the navy, moved a relatively mobile force.

McClellan later implied that he had planned the withdrawal of the army on the night of the 26th, after Mechanicsville, as the culmination of his preferred "change of base." He gave no orders toward that end. Four carloads of ammunition for his siege guns which were moved to the front by train during the 26th indicated his hope of resuming the regular approaches from his advanced lines. Also during the 26th Quartermaster General Van Vliet, in wiring the White House instructions for possible evacuation, had written, "This is a precautionary measure entirely."

Van Vliet went to the crux of the matter in his report: "Every precaution [had been] taken to guard against our supplies falling into the hands of the enemy, should it be found necessary for the army to fall back on the James. The Battle of Gaines's Mill rendered this movement necessary."

The "change of base" phrase demonstrates the truism that if anything is repeated often enough it becomes accepted as a reality regardless of the facts. In the sense that "change of base" was generally accepted, McClellan did not change his base at all. Rather than leave his works to defend his base, McClellan abandoned the base and withdrew from the lines to which he had been advancing since April 4. McClellan could not have changed to another base, since at that time he possessed no other base.

On deciding that he would abandon the base in preference to fighting outside his works, the precautions he had taken enabled him to load some supplies on ships, and these ships were sailing to, or already in, the James River. In the same way, the wagons were rolling toward the James River. But these supplies, being transported by road and water, were not at another base. These supplies in transit were being directed to where McClellan's army would retire. While the rationalization, as weak as it was, would make it appear that he withdrew his army because he changed his base, he withdrew his army at the sacrifice of his base and by prearrangements managed to rush supplies to the point of retirement.

In withdrawing to another river, instead of to the permanent base at Fort Monroe, even McClellan never implied that he preferred trying to take Richmond from the river bottomlands twenty-odd miles away. As Van Vliet reported, this movement had been made necessary by the outcome of Gaines's Mill, which turned out to be the "decisive" action McClellan had predicted to Washington it would be.

When Porter's battered corps limped across the bridges over the Chickahominy that night, the defeat confirmed McClellan's worst fears. After all his cries of "wolf," the numbers Lee had thrown against Porter on the north side convinced McClellan that Lee must have had something approaching the one hundred and eighty thousand to two hundred thousand men attributed to him by Pinkerton. On the night of the 27th he told his general officers the army was to retire the next day.

On the 28th he began his orderly withdrawal around noon by starting Keyes's corps on the line of the wagon train crossing White Oak Swamp toward the James River. Then Porter's corps, reorganized during the morning, started in motion after Keyes. Later Slocum's division, sharer of Porter's battle, was moved to White Oak Swamp to strengthen the guard for the wagon train's passage. The corps of Sumner and Heintzelman occupied the works to the front with Smith's division of Franklin's corps. During the night of the 28th-29th, these troops were to retire from the advanced works to an interior line.

With Lee on his flank across the river and potentially on his rear, confronted by the hazardous project of withdrawing his army from the enemy's front and moving cross-country to the protection of the river gunboats, the magnetic young commanding general had never seemed more poised. It was as if at last he was engaged in an operation in which he could use his assured skills, free of uncertainties and of conflict with his government.

The message he received during the day from Lincoln could only have hardened his spirit toward the administration. This was Lincoln's postscript about the general from the West who had been placed in command of the forces in middle and northern Virginia: "General Pope thinks if you fall back it would be much better toward York River than toward the James. As Pope now has charge of the capital, please confer with him through the telegraph." Pope knew nothing of the country in which McClellan was operating nor of the conditions of the two armies. McClellan was too outraged at Lincoln's suggestion that Pope was capable of advising him even to acknowledge the message, let alone confer with the presumptuous Pope. In this atmosphere of cross-purposes and bitter misunderstanding, McClellan wrote Stanton his most intemperate, ill-advised message of the war.

Harping again on his lack of numbers — "Had I 20,000 or 10,000 fresh troops to use tomorrow I could take Richmond" — he wired, "If we have lost the day we have yet preserved our honor, and no one need blush for the Army of the Potomac. I have lost this battle because my force was too small. I again repeat that I am not responsible for this, and I say it with the earnestness of a general who feels in his heart the loss of every brave man who has been needlessly sacrificed today. I still hope to retrieve our fortunes, but to do this the government must view the matter in the same earnest light I do. . . . As it is we have lost nothing but men, and those the best we have. . . . I know that a few thousand men would have changed this battle from a defeat into a victory. As it is, the government can not and must not hold me responsible for the result. . . ."

At the end, he added three lines which the Washington telegraph dispatcher deleted before delivering the message: "If I save the army now, I tell you plainly that I owe no thanks to you or to any other persons in Washington. You have done your best to sacrifice this army."

In finally giving expression to his feelings, McClellan undoubtedly felt justified in his charge. Yet, the unguarded expression revealed that he did regard his withdrawal as a reverse. *"I still hope to retrieve our fortunes."* More than all the arguments later written in retrospect, this release of his outrage, written after he had given his general officers orders for the retirement, reflected his sense of failure and his rejection of the responsibility for it.

Viewed in the light of this wire, the retirement of his army to the James River — this "fall back," as Lincoln realistically called it — was a compromise movement with which he instinctively tried to postpone the act of decision. For a complex of reasons afraid to commit his army to the finality of the test, for his own reputation he refused to put his army into retreat down the peninsula to the base at Fort Monroe. Such a retreat (which could be called by no other name) would constitute an admission of the unsuccessful end of his campaign, and be the end of him. The *shift* of his army to a "new base" on the James River lacked the finality of a *retreat* to Fort Monroe.

In proximity to the Confederate capital, he would still appear to be in a position to threaten Richmond. He would have moved from the enemy's front gate to his back yard. It was true that once on the James, McClellan could, as he later suggested to Lincoln, strike on the south side of the river. From there, by severing railroad connections, he could isolate Richmond from the South. This was the move always feared by the Confederates.

In 1862 McClellan's suggestion was too long-range for Lincoln's government. Two years later, when Grant gave up on taking Richmond directly, he was permitted to move south of the James on the line rejected when McClellan suggested it. Once on the south side, when his thrust failed, Grant was permitted ten months to wear down the opposition by siege operations. By the time Grant came along the government, having long since abandoned hope of a quick decision, was resigned to dragging out the war by slow attrition. McClellan was as much as anything else a victim of bad timing in his rendezvous with destiny.

Yet, had the hero image of McClellan been entirely false, he would not have possessed the self-control he did on June 28. For he had lost more than the "men" he mentioned in his wire to Stanton. He had lost control of the campaign, and it was no longer subject to his methods and time schedules. Lee had reduced his blueprint for victory to wastepaper.

Even if consideration of his reputation had been McClellan's only motive in shifting his army to the James River instead of admitting failure by a retreat, McClellan did not retreat down the peninsula. He did move to maintain his army in the heart of the enemy's country as a threat to the capital and its communications. This was not the desired thing, but it was not a small thing. McClellan, with his "Young Napoleon" status rapidly vanishing, made it as big as possible. He convinced a number of people that "the transfer of the army" was truly a strategic preference. Most importantly, he convinced himself. The finely functioning machine he had built moved in its new course as methodically as on any leisured, unmenaced advance against Johnston.

The troops which raised the dust columns observed by Lee were not moving as a defeated army. In fact, McClellan's army still possessed the potential for defeating Lee when night fell on June 28. With its powerful armaments intact, the Army of the Potomac had held Lee at bay outside the periphery of its lines and the Chickahominy flank. When darkness settled over the marshy countryside, McClellan held for the next eight hours the tactical initiative. It would be daylight before Lee tried to probe the barriers, and then the last men and guns would be gone.

CHAPTER TWELVE

The Day of "Prince John"

AT SUNRISE of Sunday June 29, a hot, close day, two of Long-street's engineering officers waded into the Chickahominy Swamp to cross by fords to McClellan's side of the river. Major Kidder Meade and Lieutenant S. R. Johnston climbed out of the mire through the thickets up the opposite hill in a silence broken only by the rustling of the underbrush. Lieutenant, later captain, Johnston was to become expert at this type of reconnaissance; it was he who would reconnoiter Little Round Top in the dawn of July 2 at Gettysburg. The two cautiously moving men parted the vines at a clearing on a rise and looked into the empty works of a Federal strong point on Golding's Farm, between Fair Oaks and the Chickahominy.

With feelings unfortunately never described, Major Meade and Lieutenant Johnston climbed down the trench walls and surveyed stretches of vacated works as far as their eyes could see. They were the first to discover that the siege of Richmond had been lifted.

Presumably couriers had followed them, for without leaving the works the engineers sent word to Longstreet. Making no to-do over this great moment in the new army's history, Longstreet sent a verbal report to Lee. When the message reached the outwardly composed commanding general, it was the first relief — for him and the troops — from the grim work of cleaning up a field which many soldiers felt was the most sickening of the war.

Because of the corpses hidden in the thickets by the creek, where the woods had been mangled by artillery, burial details worked into the second day. Most of the Federal dead were buried without shoes, as the Confederate soldiers had then grown sufficiently hardened to supply their needs from corpses. The medical corps at that stage was unequipped to handle the volume of wounded, with the uncounted hundreds of the enemy left on the field added to the more than six thousand Confederates. At intervals lightly wounded Federal soldiers appeared apprehensively out of the brush to the east where they had been hiding from Stuart's cavalry. They all seemed to fear the Confederate cavalry as "guerrillas," who would put them to death. Some wonderful conversations have been recorded between Yankees and Rebels in which the captors solicitously reassured the prisoners they would be safe. The soldiers captured by Jackson's men were incredulous that Stonewall Jackson was on the field.

Harvey Hill personally placed in an ambulance without guard, two friends from the Old Army, General Reynolds and Major Wiltze. They were moved to Richmond with the endless stream of vehicles of all descriptions in which the wounded were being taken to improvised hospitals in warehouses and dry goods stores in the city. Moving in the opposite direction service units and Local Defense Troops from Richmond came out to glean the field of food, blankets, new rifles, ammunition, and the crude machine guns — the first tried in warfare. The bottles of bonded whiskey the medical corps had particularly wanted for the wounded were all gone: the Texans had got there first.

The delayed elation came, thirty-six hours after the battle, when the news of McClellan's evacuation reached the troops by way of Lee's new orders. A. P. Hill's division, whose men were resting, had re-formed its chopped-up units. Paying their last respects to fallen comrades, the troops were quickly aroused to take again to the dusty roads after the enemy. Canteens were filled, blanket rolls and haversacks thrown across shoulders, pouches inspected for ammunition, and the lean, brown-faced men moved to their familiar places in the ranks when the bugles blew "assembly" and the company sergeants bawled out "Fall in!"

Hill's division was to follow Longstreet across New Bridge and the combined force was to hurry southeast to the Darbytown Road for their part in Lee's quickly formed plan to intercept McClellan's retreat. In the speed with which Lee acted he took no time to compose a general order for this improvised plan to catch McClellan's army on its retreat across White Oak Swamp. The basis of his new plan was the fan of roads leading east from Richmond between the Williamsburg Road and the James River. This pattern can be seen on the map on page 262.

At the top runs the east-west Williamsburg Road, across which McClellan's army had faced west in the Seven Pines area. On abandoning those lines, McClellan moved east along this road to a point near Bottom's Bridge where two roads ran southward through White Oak Swamp. Across the swamp, these roads converged into the Long Bridge Road, running at an angle from northeast to southwest and ending at New Market Heights. At Glendale, the Willis Church Road branched off from the Long Bridge Road, running south toward the river. The Long Bridge Road, McClellan's cross highway, was the key to Lee's trap.

The Charles City Road, cutting southeast of the Williamsburg Road, intersected the Long Bridge Road at Glendale, the point of densest concentration in McClellan's movement. The Darbytown Road, also cutting southeast off the Williamsburg Road closer to Richmond, loosely paralleled the Charles City Road, and intersected the Long Bridge Road south and west of Glendale. It was Lee's plan to strike McClellan in flank, from front, and from rear in the area of Glendale, where McClellan would turn off the Long Bridge Road into the Willis Church Road.

Provided with no intelligence of McClellan's movements, Lee simply assumed that McClellan would follow the available route as indicated on his map.

Huger (see map p. 271) would move from his lines across the Williamsburg Road into the Charles City Road and march directly for Glendale, on McClellan's flank. Longstreet and A. P. Hill would move down the Darbytown Road to the Long Bridge Road and turn northeast, striking at the head of the Federal army where it swung off at Glendale into the Willis Church Road. Theophilus Holmes, with his brigades from the Department of North Carolina, would cross from the south side of the James and move by the New Market Road. At New Market Heights this became the River Road. This concentration on McClellan's front and flank was planned to be coordinated on the following day, Monday, June 30.

In order to slow McClellan's march and to inflict as much damage as possible, Magruder was to move out immediately and follow

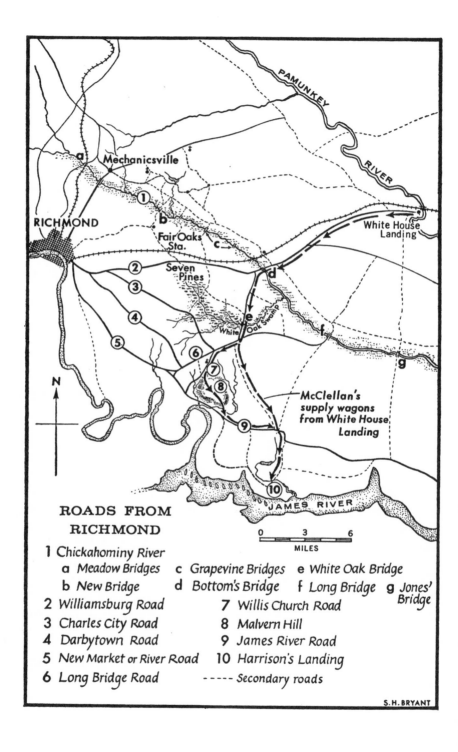

ROADS FROM
RICHMOND

1 Chickahominy River
  a Meadow Bridges **c** Grapevine Bridges **e** White Oak Bridge
  b New Bridge **d** Bottom's Bridge **f** Long Bridge **g** Jones' Bridge
2 Williamsburg Road
3 Charles City Road **7** Willis Church Road
4 Darbytown Road **8** Malvern Hill
5 New Market or River Road **9** James River Road
6 Long Bridge Road **10** Harrison's Landing
    - - - - - Secondary roads

S.H. BRYANT

McClellan down the Williamsburg Road, attacking his rear guard upon contact. To support Magruder, Jackson (with D. H. Hill continuing in his command) was to cross the Grapevine Bridges over the Chickahominy and turn east along the river, moving toward Savage's Station on the York River Railroad. All commands were to move at once.

For Longstreet and Powell Hill, whose orders for Sunday were simply a line of march to a designated point, the movement was begun sharply to New Bridge. There they crossed the river and continued over the steaming countryside of the old lines to the Darbytown Road.

The orders to Huger, Magruder and Jackson also seemed simple enough. Magruder drew in his troops from either side of Nine Mile Road to form his regiments in columns of march. Early on Sunday morning, when the humid heat was already felt, the miles of his columns of eleven thousand men and field guns shuffled forward toward contact with the enemy. Huger got off at about the same time, leaving his works and turning his van into the Charles City Road. Jackson first needed to rebuild bridges across the Chickahominy destroyed by McClellan after Porter's crossing.

Apathetic again after the brief flurry during the late afternoon at Gaines's Mill, Jackson settled down to build those bridges as if it was his primary assignment. While the Sunday hours passed without a sign of Jackson south of the Chickahominy, the burden of his inanition fell on Magruder, and "Prince John" by then was in a highly overwrought state. Clinically, his growing frenzy was the opposite of Jackson's inertia.

2

From early afternoon on June 26, when he had sent Major Brent to discover from General Lee what was happening at Mechanicsville, Magruder's anxieties had mounted. The more anxious he grew the more excited he became. During the Gaines's Mill battle on the 27th, Magruder's demonstration along his front was convincing because he was acting in earnest. His fears conjured up an Austerlitz maneuver in which McClellan, containing Lee's assault with one part of his army, would mount a parallel thrust on the holding force in front of Richmond. Seeing his troops as the victims, Magruder stirred up a nervous action along his line that was in effect an anticipation of the enemy's attack.

His own troops became infected by his threatening attitude, and his brigadier, Bob Toombs, decided the time was ripe to make good the threat on the cowering enemy. Consulting no one, the brash Georgian with an untrammeled ego sent his brigade in a charge at a segment of McClellan's line at Golding's Farm. It happened to be a strong section of the line and the enemy, though nervously alert, was far from cowering. Toombs's loyal fellow Georgians — whom he treated more as constituents than as soldiers — reeled back from the enemy's undented front, leaving four hundred of their companions on the ground.

As foolish and as unsoldierly as Toombs's attack was, it doubtless contributed its costly part to convincing McClellan's general officers that a Confederate attack might indeed be imminent. However, Magruder was a trained soldier who, with all his childish love of military pageantry, took his responsibilities seriously, and Toombs's willful action could only have unsettled him further. As he viewed his perilous situation, he felt McClellan would undoubtedly be advised of the weakness behind all his brave show. By nightfall, after Lee's battle at Gaines's Mill, Magruder expected every minute to hear the rumble of the enemy's mighty hosts moving toward him on the way to Richmond.

D. R. Jones, the stately professional who commanded one of his divisions, stated that the New Bridge had been rebuilt that night and connections established with Lee's main force on the other bank of the Chickahominy, but Magruder seems to have convinced himself that he was isolated from the rest of the army. During the long, warm night (while Porter was withdrawing his forces from the north side of the river), Magruder suffered agonies of apprehensions against which he was helpless to act. As it turned out, he was right in believing that the whole Federal army had gathered on his front.

On the morning of the 28th, the gourmet had no appetite for breakfast. Feeling sick with what he regarded as indigestion, he left headquarters around seven o'clock, presumably to confer with his doctor. When he returned around eleven o'clock, Division Commander Jones was looking for him.

"Neighbor" Jones had been to headquarters earlier and, finding Magruder absent, had decided to take some initiative. With none of Magruder's apprehension, Jones on the contrary believed the enemy was withdrawing from his front that day. He brought up two batteries close to the lines to shell Golding's Farm and ordered Brigadier General Toombs to observe the effect of the fire. If the enemy failed to show a strong defense, he was to advance. Jones had picked the wrong man for a contingent order.

Toombs was never to be convinced that any professional soldier's judgment was superior to his or that, this being the case, he should defer to what was manifestly the limitations of the West Point mind. Not only did he immediately prepare his own brigade to have another go at Golding's Farm but he ordered Colonel G. T. ("Tige") Anderson, commanding Jones's second brigade, to assault at once. Toombs assured Anderson of his support. This was taking initiative further than Jones had intended, and now, having set the sequence in motion, he reported Toombs's transgressions to Magruder.

The actions that followed were enough to unnerve a general not already in a state of tension. Magruder was under orders from Lee to initiate no assault except in coordination with a general advance, unless absolutely assured of success. Quite properly, Magruder immediately told Jones to send Toombs and Anderson orders countermanding the attack.

While one staff officer rode forward with this order, another appeared with the information that Toombs's attack had been successful. As a successful attack was not prohibited by Lee, Magruder punctiliously sent off a staff officer to inform the commanding general that his troops were carrying the position at Golding's Farm. After sending Captain Dickinson ahead to get first-hand information, Magruder rode forward himself.

He had not gone far when he met Captain Dickinson returning with a doleful report. Between the orders and the counterorders, the attack had fizzled out after clearing the enemy's rifle pits. The two brigades were back in their lines, with more of their comrades left on the stubby ground at Golding's Farm. There was nothing for it except to send yet another message to General Lee with the latest and final bulletin on Golding's Farm.

Though Toombs's self-assertiveness was stifled for a while, nothing that happened in Jones's division gave Magruder any assurance on June 28. When that night came, the third of his harrowing vigils, he was advised by Lee to observe "the utmost vigilance," and have his men sleep under arms. For Magruder there was no sleep at all. He moved about during the dark hours inspecting his lines and listening. As late as three-thirty in the morning, he detected the small sounds that indicated the enemy's continued presence across the black countryside. What Magruder was actually hearing was the last of McClellan's troops moving out.

At daylight Sunday the 29th silence lay over the countryside beyond the abatis in front of McClellan's lines, and Magruder's pickets aroused no answering fire. With more punctiliousness in the details of exchange than any of Lee's general officers displayed, Magruder dispatched one of his hard-worked staff with a message that he was going to assault the enemy's lines. In reply, Lee indulged in a little heavy-handed humor and warned Magruder to be careful not to injure Longstreet's engineering officers who were then in McClellan's deserted works.

The overwrought Magruder was too relieved to heed the joke at his expense. As a matter of fact, one of his own staff officers had brought him the news of the evacuated lines at the same time that Colonel Chilton had delivered Lee's message. In his report Magruder wrote only and unashamedly of his "great relief."

3

Magruder's constant exchanges with Lee might have indicated more than punctiliousness. Not one to abase himself before anybody, and eloquent in defending his reputation against any imputations, he treated Lee with the type of respect given a parental authority. Having known him since West Point, Magruder revealed a curious dependence in his need for communication with Lee. Though Magruder remained insistent on establishing the precise area of his own domain of command and displayed a tendency to assume direction of Huger, which the proud South Carolinian did not appreciate, as a subordinate acting under Lee's orders Prince John seemed to lose confidence in himself.

The effect of this anxiety to perform well made the extroverted man rely on energetic action, doing everything himself without thought of the physical toll. With three days of extreme tension before the 29th, and loss of sleep as well as appetite, Magruder was already in a state of unnatural excitation when Colonel Chilton rode into his camp early Sunday morning.

Chilton gave him Lee's orders for putting his troops in motion after McClellan's rear guard. Then, Magruder said, Chilton "hurried me off to see General Lee on the Nine Mile Road," all so quickly that he was forced to send his orders to his brigadiers while riding from his headquarters to the road.

Near Nine Mile Road, he was able personally to direct the immediate advance of Griffith's brigade, from his own division, to lead the way to Fair Oaks Station. The brigades on either side were to fall in behind his column. Richard Griffith, the forty-eight-year-old Philadelphian with the thoughtful expression and melancholy eyes, had only a few more hours of life when he stirred his Mississippi regiments into the movement they welcomed.

On Nine Mile Road, Magruder joined the commanding general and Lee outlined his extemporized battle plan. While sketching in the general purpose of converging on McClellan at White Oak Swamp the next day, Lee stressed the importance of the immediate pursuit. Damage must be inflicted on McClellan's rear guard of a severity to delay his movement and disarrange his plans. Magruder's eleven thousand, mostly fresh, troops, well supported by artillery, were to push vigorously between the Williamsburg Road and the York River Railroad. Lee advised him that Jackson was to cross — or, was crossing — the Chickahominy at the Grapevine Bridges to support his attack on the left, from the railroad to the river.

Magruder's "post of honor" was to change from holding a fixed position into directing the pursuit of the enemy in which he, at last, was to command an attack. Magruder understood his assignment well enough but, in adjusting to the shift in his responsibility, he misunderstood Huger's role.

Perhaps because for the past three days he had been thinking of Huger as his support rather than as an equal commanding an adjoining segment of the line, and perhaps also because the magnitude of his assignment suggested support on his right from Huger, Magruder understood Lee to say that Huger would advance by the Williamsburg Road. Lee had said that Huger was to leave the Williamsburg Road and follow the Charles City Road to parallel Longstreet and A. P. Hill in the convergence planned for the following day at White Oak Swamp. With this detail of misunderstanding, the two generals parted where the Nine Mile Road approached Fair Oaks station, the scene of Johnston's battle the month before.

At what became known as the Battle of Savage's Station, it has been the custom to make Magruder the somewhat ludicrous goat. The theatrical soldier was not difficult to ridicule and he did not control the actions of his units with the firm skill of Longstreet and the Hills. Conditioned by his apprehension over the enemy's counterthrust and worrying about the coordination with Jackson and Huger, he was too distracted to coordinate his own loosely organized command. But, if Magruder is viewed as a conscientious man straining to do the best he could within the limitations of his own temperament and in the undirected action of which he was a part, the pursuit becomes properly an illustration of Lee's specific lacks in staff work.

In the absence of an intelligence section, the commanding general assumed Federal dispositions which were, in fact, different from what he supposed. With his cavalry chief that day at the abandoned White House base, Lee had been guessing. He was making informed guesses, accurate in general, but wrong in the details of the Federal dispositions in front of Magruder.

Lee also assumed that Jackson would move up on Magruder's left to attack in coordination, because he had been so ordered. No measures were taken to discover when Jackson crossed the river and formed on Magruder's left. With no member of the staff responsible for information about the location and action of the separated units, the staff officers seemed to have followed Lee (who had no established field headquarters) and waited for directions from him. From the day of leaving the Dabbs house, with the prescribed tasks of organization behind them, the members of the staff functioned chiefly as communications officers, and on the June 29 pursuit even communication almost ceased.

In ordering Magruder to direct the pursuit, fundamentally Lee acted in his preferred method of command and, without at least a strong chief of staff, the method was impractical under the circumstances. In turning over the field to Magruder on the assumption that Jackson would cooperate (though he had not cooperated at all on the first day and inadequately on the second), Lee assumed McClellan's rear guard would be weak and desirous of avoiding large scale action. When he ordered two commands totaling more than thirty thousand troops to attack the Federal rear guard, Lee expected to force a return of McClellan's marching columns and halt the progress of the retreat.

However, McClellan had left nearly half his infantry, with strong artillery support, posted in two lines directly across the routes of advance of the pursuing forces. While half his infantry, the bulk of his artillery, and all his wagons were moving southward from the Williamsburg Road across White Oak Swamp, two and one half corps had merely withdrawn eastward from their works and taken new positions still facing west to Richmond.

The reports of the Federal corps commanders whose troops were engaged, Sumner and Franklin, did not in any way treat Magruder lightly. Franklin mentioned the "severe contest" and Sumner referred to the "great obstinacy" of the fighting. The Federal reports read like a different battle from the standard accounts that have been presented of Magruder.

In fact, it *was* a different battle from those accounts which, as the usual versions of Mechanicsville, tend to divert attention away from Lee's responsibility at the expense of another. As Powell Hill was impetuous at Mechanicsville, so John Magruder was too excited and worried on the pursuit to handle his own command with maximum efficiency. Yet, as it turned out, Magruder's inadequacies saved Lee from suffering a severe repulse.

4

A South Carolina regiment of Kershaw's brigade, of McLaws's division, were the first troops to occupy the abandoned Federal works at Golding's Farm. Under Magruder's orders, during the morning the other regiments of Kershaw's brigade came up and advanced by Nine Mile Road to the evacuated Federal camps around Fair Oaks Station. There the soldiers paused to gape at a plushness in army life beyond their visions. Along with barrels of meat, boxes of crackers, and real coffee, were camp chests, trunks, bags, and standing tents, some of which had furniture in them. The men were allowed little time to forage for food before they were advanced across the railroad.

To the north of Fair Oaks the angling course of the Chickahominy sliced sharply from northwest to southeast. The space between the railroad and the river gradually narrowed until the two met, forming the apex of a triangle, about six miles east of Fair Oaks. This geography was very important to Kershaw, because of the expected support from Jackson from the Chickahominy.

As the river coursed in toward Kershaw's left, Jackson's movement after crossing the Chickahominy would verge toward the line of Kershaw's advance. To avoid the danger of firing into Jackson's troops, Kershaw moved cautiously toward contact with the unseen Federals by bearing south of the railroad.

As his skirmishers crept forward through the entangled woods, light firing was stirred up from the thickets across their front. When the feeling movement had progressed slowly about a mile, rifle fire suddenly grew heavier from the left, where Jackson was expected. Then artillery fire opened from their left front to send metal fragments bursting among the troops. As Kershaw believed this to be the collision with Jackson he had feared, he halted his men.

Instructing the troops to hold their fire, Kershaw sent a regimental battle flag to the front to be waved on the railroad. The firing, if anything, increased. It was the enemy, only one mile east of Fair Oaks, and not Jackson. At about the same time Magruder ordered Kershaw to fall back.

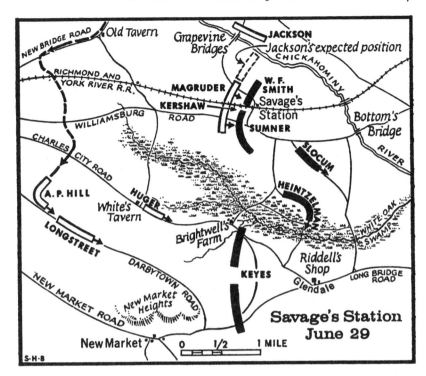

Magruder had decided to wait for Jackson to cross the river and take a position on Kershaw's left before further engaging the enemy. This sensible precaution was followed by sending off Major Bryan to the Grapevine Bridges to learn when Jackson might be expected. Since he mistakenly expected Huger to move on the Williamsburg Road, he sent his lawyer-friend, Major Brent, to General Lee to ask that Huger come up in support.

According to Brent, General Lee appeared incredulous at the report that the Federals were making a stand in strength. Believing the enemy columns to be hurrying to cross White Oak Swamp, Lee asked Magruder's staff officer if he personally had observed the enemy's numbers and formed an opinion of his own. Brent refused to be drawn in and repeated woodenly, "General Magruder has instructed me to say that he finds the enemy in strong force in his front."

Brent recorded that the commanding general looked at him with an amused expression, "as if he appreciated the loyalty that declined to express an opinion contrary to the message that I bore."

As it happened, Brent's message was a true statement of the facts. Lee made no effort to corroborate it. The commanding general told Brent he would have to recall two of Huger's brigades from another important duty. If they were not engaged by two o'clock, Magruder must send them on to rejoin Huger on the Charles City Road.

While Brent was obtaining the commanding general's approval, Magruder sent another staff officer directly to Huger. Huger accompanied two brigades to the area of Seven Pines and personally announced their arrival to Magruder.

By then, Major Bryan had returned from his ride to Jackson accompanied by Jackson's engineering officer, Lieutenant Boswell. Jackson, the young men reported, was rebuilding the Grapevine Bridges and would be delayed another two hours.

The time sequences were extremely vague during the exchanges. Opening contact had been established before ten, and it was probably sometime after noon that Magruder determined to withhold his attack until Jackson got in position on his left. The enemy had been developed from the Williamsburg Road, where old Federal works stood, to north of the York River Railroad. Redoubts for gun batteries were manned at intervals across the obscured countryside. It was Magruder's plan to envelop the Federal front when Huger and Jackson extended his line to the right and left. At least, that is what he wrote later.

At the time Magruder may have been waiting on Jackson because Lee's orders for the pursuit placed Jackson on his left and, to Magruder, this superseded the instructions for a vigorous pursuit. All of his generals reported the effect on their first advance of watching out for Jackson's troops on their left.

During the wait and before all of his own brigades had moved up into position, Magruder's anxieties led him to fear that he might be attacked. Whatever compound of reasons caused Magruder's reluctance to press forward, his instinct was sound. Sumner's full corps was immediately in his front, in the area of Allen's farm one mile from Fair Oaks. Sumner was supported by Smith's division of Franklin's corps and, to his left and rear, by Heintzelman's corps, which reached to the works on the Williamsburg Road. Magruder would have been outnumbered more than two to one, with the enemy hidden in woods and firing about forty guns from Allen's farm on the Confederate right of the railroad.

Curiously, the Federal reports mentioned the Battle of Allen's Farm as an action distinct from that of Savage's Station. To Magruder's command, their own movements under the Federal artillery fire were mainly the bringing up and deployment of their brigades preparatory to the advance to be made. Magruder's brigadiers appeared unaware of their commanding general's apprehensions over the enemy's aggressive intentions.

Casualties were few. Brigadier General Griffith was struck in "a shower of projectiles" that missed every one else. Half a shell from a rifled gun lodged in his body, knocking him off his horse. An artillerist attached to the brigade saw the "desperate clinch of his fingers and the pallor of his face as he clasped his hands back of his head." The genial brigadier died a few hours later, and the command passed to white-haired Barksdale under whom the Mississippians were to gain their greatest fame.

Griffith's brigade was taking a forward position, to gain more advantageous ground, while Magruder's batteries came up with as much precision as if executing their practiced movements on drill. Captains rode ahead, pieces lurched behind galloping horses and the gunners followed as fast as they could run. To support his guns Magruder brought into action the first railroad artillery ever used in warfare.

This was the "railroad gun" designed by Lee when he first assumed command. A siege piece was mounted on a flatcar, protected by a shield formed of track rails placed at an angle, with the mouth of the gun projecting as through an embrasure. With an engine pushing the flatcar within range of the Federal lines, its firing was immediately effective. At the same time two of the batteries made their presence felt. When D. R. Jones's skirmishers moved out from the forward positions, Sumner began to withdraw his corps in ending the Federal engagement of Allen's farm.

Sumner fell back on Savage's Station. This stop on the York River Railroad was named for the substantial farm whose clearing spread on both sides of the tracks. Houses and outbuildings were serving as Federal hospitals, along with rows of fifteen-men tents in which lay the 2500 wounded who would be left behind. All during the day fires burned on the plain where supplies were being destroyed, and at intervals ordnance trains were exploded on the railroads. The heavy blasts and reverberations made men on both sides nervous. During the night before the train which had brought forward ammunition for the siege guns was run off the open bridge into the Chickahominy.

The approach to the clearing, where all the activity was taking place, was through dense woods too far back from the Federal lines to provide any protection to attacking infantry. After advancing through the woods, the troops must assault across the open fields, to where Smith's division formed in a stand of pines along a ravine. That was in the area from south of the railroad to the Williamsburg Road.

Across the Williamsburg Road the woods continued unbroken, light timber with screens of briary vines and matted underbrush. The whole front up to the clearing was obscured to Magruder's men.

When the Federals' slow withdrawal from the Allen's farm area convinced Magruder that he was not to be attacked, and as the two hours allotted by Jackson had then passed, he prepared to advance his whole line. Kershaw moved forward on the right of the railroad, with the brigade of portly Howell Cobb, of Magruder's division, left of the railroad. "Neighbor" Jones's two brigades stretched to the left of Cobb toward the river, reaching for the then overdue head of Jackson's column. Griffith's brigade under its new commander was held in reserve. Paul Semmes's brigade, of McLaws's division, moved up on the ground left by Kershaw, to support the South Carolinians' right. With everything in readiness, Magruder received a message from Huger.

Magruder's reluctant collaborator announced that, as no action was occurring on his front, he was removing his two brigades. Huger had received a message from Lee instructing him to countermarch his two brigades and resume the march along the Charles City Road, unless Magruder needed his assistance. With his field of vision restricted to a slice of the Williamsburg Road, Huger acted as judge of Magruder's need of his troops without consulting anybody.

At about the same time, Division Commander Jones sent an officer to Magruder with news from the left. Jones had received a laconic message from Jackson stating that he would not cross the Chickahominy at all that day: he had been ordered to "other important duty." The nature of this duty was never discovered.

Harried Magruder, having set his advance in motion, lost control of himself and of his separately moving brigades. In something of desperation, he ordered "each commander to attack the enemy in whatever force or works he might be found."

5

When Magruder's command began the forward movement at around three o'clock, a great opportunity was presented the Confederates on the Williamsburg Road, on the front just vacated by Huger under Lee's contingent orders. The Federals had also suffered the lack of close liaison. General McClellan and his chief of staff, his energetic father-in-law, were as preoccupied with the retreat across White Oak Swamp as was Lee, and the rear guard had been left to shift for itself.

During the morning and early afternoon, due to the slowly formed Confederate pursuit, Franklin's cool initiative had been able to bring order out of a confusion of random troop movements and conflicting assignments. Sumner, the senior officer on the field, had fallen asleep from the morning's exertions in the heat, and Franklin had had to awaken the old regular to tell him what dispositions had been made. One of Franklin's brigadiers collapsed of sunstroke.

Then, after Sumner fell back, as the Confederates were so slow to advance, Heintzelman decided there were enough troops around Savage's Station to repel any pursuit. With even less ceremony than Huger he also abandoned the Williamsburg Road and started his corps after the columns moving southward to White Oak Swamp. Thus, when Magruder's advance moved forward with determined purpose, the Confederate right flank and the Federal left flank were both open. Had Heintzelman stayed, Magruder's stretched-out line would have been engulfed on the flank, rolled up, and his command in danger of destruction.

As it happened, in moving out of the first belt of woods alert Kershaw saw that his flank was open and sent a message to his division commander, McLaws, for support on his right. Stolid McLaws had already observed Huger's troops retiring away from the battle area and in his bewilderment could only report, "Their purpose I did not understand." McLaws hurriedly shifted Semmes's brigade from its supporting position to oblique across country and extend Kershaw's right.

On the other side, Franklin and Sedgwick had been riding forward to confer with Heintzelman when they were appalled to observe a line of Confederates and a battery moving into the position where they had expected Heintzelman's corps to be. Had the two generals not ridden over for a visit when they did, the Federal line would have been outflanked. Fortunately from their viewpoint, Franklin and Sumner had more troops on the field than Magruder, and brigades were rushed over in time to meet the advance of Semmes's Georgians. Manifestly, it was not only Lee whose staff work was faulty.

With each side rectifying its flank along the Williamsburg Road, the assault narrowed to Kershaw's attack at Savage's Station on the south side of the railroad. Before the troops reached the point of assault, the men grew wilted from the long waits and slow advances under fire in the oppressive heat of the woods. Between four and five o'clock, when the lines had moved two miles to the last brushy woods between them and the enemy's position, Kershaw halted the four regiments in a declivity. Protected from the musket fire, the men took a brief rest before going in.

The forty-year-old lawyer had never before led troops in combat. Kershaw's men, for all their length of service — they had arrived in Virginia before First Manassas — had themselves seen little action under Johnston. In the 7th South Carolina about the only shot fired in anger came in a duel, when Captain Bland severely wounded Major Seibles. After the brigade had been sent to Magruder in April, it was not used by Johnston at Williamsburg or Seven Pines. The 3rd South Carolina had never come under enemy musket fire until two days before, when the regiment had advanced during Magruder's demonstrations. The regimental surgeon, Dr. William Thompson, following close to the front to observe action, was the regiment's first man killed in action. Halted between the two low rises, all the men were sweaty and tense, listening to the metal spraying through the tops of scrubby oaks like, one of them remembered, "a fall of hail."

Kershaw's clearly cut features showed only his resolution as he surveyed his lines. Paul Semmes had moved his brigade to Kershaw's right and Howell Cobb was to his left, across the railroad. What they did lay outside Kershaw's responsibility. He ordered his men to their feet and then sent them forward without exhortations or complicated orders. His voice bugled out one word: "Charge."

The men rushed ahead into the thickets, screaming their familiar yell in self-encouragement. Soldiers began to fall early in the rush. Alignment grew lax between regiments. Men drifted off the course and lost their way among the hanging vines. When the four regiments burst out into the clearing, they went straight at the fringe of pines from where smoke curled upward from the rifle fire of Burns's brigade. Despite the lack of precision, Kershaw's brigade attacked, according to General Franklin, "with great fury." The thrust pierced the center of Burns's line.

As an effective military force, Kershaw's men had little more to bring to the battle than furious spirit. Too much of the brigade strength had been dissipated by the straggling in the woods and casualties during the advance. They had no reserves at hand, and Burns did. The men in the spearhead were forced back out of their point of penetration, and in a vicious hand-to-hand stand-up fight neither line could gain an advantage. At darkness, still unsupported, the South Carolinians fell back slowly from their first experience as an assault force. They left their dead behind them.

6

North of the railroad Howell Cobb, Georgia's distinguished planter-statesman, brought no aggression or initiative to his advance. Magruder, without contact even with his own division, sent no order to Cobb to support Kershaw's attack.

To Cobb's left, amiable Jones showed neither the effects of his sound professional training nor any flash of his promise as a leader. It may have been that Jones was restrained after the unhappy results of the excessive initiative he had used on the day before, at Golding's Farm, and was motivated by the need to hold a tight rein on Bob Toombs.

Certainly Toombs himself was unusually subdued after his assertiveness had ended in minor disasters on two successive days at Golding's Farm. The act of passing over the ground again could have served as a reminder that something more was required for a successful assault than blustery courage and dismissal of the inhibitions acquired at West Point. He may have been unsettled too by Daniel Webster's son who, having known Toombs during his great days in Washington, called to him as the young soldier lay dying. In his report, Toombs never mentioned June 29.

That one half of Magruder's force remained unengaged, making no more than the negative accomplishment of employing Federal troops, reflected his lack of directing control when the assault was finally delivered. At that, more men committed would probably have resulted only in more men lost.

Kershaw's fight south of the railroad was extended by Paul Semmes's brigade which, covering his right, engaged the enemy across the Williamsburg Road. Late in the day two regiments from Griffith's brigade hurried forward to support Semmes's right flank and struck hard in the woods south of the road. None of these troops could advance, and darkness ended the action in a drawn battle.

Nothing indicated that an attack north of the railroad, between the railroad and the river, could have accomplished appreciably more against the larger Federal forces, planted firmly on defense. Certainly the assault force available to Magruder could not, at that hour, have seriously affected McClellan's retreat.

Yet, Lee held Magruder responsible for the total failure to press a vigorous pursuit. "I regret much that you have made so little progress in the pursuit of the enemy," Lee wrote him. "I must urge you, then, again to press on his rear rapidly and vigorously." In a postscript, Lee added ". . . I learn from Major Taylor that you are under the impression that General Jackson has been ordered not to support you. On the contrary, he has been ordered to do so, and to push the pursuit vigorously."

Lee seems not to have known that the reason Magruder was under that impression was because Jackson had sent him a message that he was ordered to "other important duty" and would not support him. By nightfall, Lee must have known that Jackson never crossed the river to cooperate in the attack, but he sent Jackson no messages of reproach nor of inquiry.

Jackson's unextenuated failure removed from the pursuit two thirds of the force planned by Lee and, after delaying and confusing Magruder's command for hours, exposed the attacking force to a severe repulse. Magruder, though he hesitated because of unfounded anxieties, as well as the uncertainties caused by Jackson and Huger, saved Lee's army from the effects of Jackson's torpor by not making a vigorous pursuit alone.

Magruder was the one reproached only partly because, being on the line of the enemy's retreat, Lee had given him responsibility for directing the pursuit. And he received the blame only partly because Lee remained unaware of the strong Federal dispositions set to receive the pursuit. Along with his inadequate information, Lee was fundamentally influenced by his judgment of the capacities of the two men. As Magruder had been right for the wrong reasons, so Lee's judgment was sound though based on faulty evidence. At that embryonic stage of his tactical development, Lee's ability to judge men's potential for command in correlated actions was fully developed.

General Lee had acted on his judgment in supporting Jackson to lead the movement that became the Valley Campaign. Since this heralded performance, Jackson had shown Lee nothing to confirm his earlier judgment. Jackson's Valley Campaign might well have been a flash in the pan achieved, as Longstreet said, against "second-raters." However, Lee's faith was so little shaken by Jackson's supineness on the 29th that he placed Jackson in charge of the pursuit for the following day. As far as is known, Lee never questioned the reason for Jackson spending the 29th in bridge-building.

Unlike Magruder, Jackson would never explain himself. He was one of those men of action who never subjected their own behavior to critical analyses. In his report for June 29, he made no mention of Lee's order to cross the Chickahominy to cooperate on Magruder's left. He wrote, "The 28th and 29th were occupied in disposing of the dead and wounded and repairing Grapevine Bridge . . . During the night of the 29th we commenced crossing the Chickahominy. . . ." Actually, his troops started crossing early in the morning of June 30. Whatever had gone on in Jackson's mind in his depleted state, he deemed no explanations necessary.

On the contrary, Magruder remembered his own agitations vividly when he wrote his report six weeks later. Then, in August, Magruder was concerned only with vindication of his reputation, as he no longer shared the fortunes of Lee's army. Before Lee assumed command, President Davis in late May had assigned Magruder to the Trans-Mississippi for the important command of Texas. Davis may have ordered this transfer partly to relieve Magruder of his anomalous position in Johnston's army, for the President felt warmly toward Magruder and wrote of his "skillful and knightly" combat on the peninsula. Magruder was probably retained at Richmond in order to avoid changes in command before Lee opened his offensive.

What Lee evidently perceived in Magruder was the trait observed by Colonel Long — "When overshadowed by authority [he] became paralyzed" — as reflected by Magruder's manifestly impaired judgment during the night of the 29th. While a violent rainstorm added its epilogue to the day's long action, Magruder wrote Lee a message revealing that he still could not rid himself of apprehensions about being attacked. Lee would not have understood a traumatic reaction to the three nights' vigil in the lines protecting the capital, but he suspected Magruder was in no condition to make sound decisions.

As Magruder wrote of it later, his apprehensions became localized in Jackson's whereabouts, and he could think of nothing else. Finally, at three-thirty on Monday morning, a seedy Jackson appeared at Magruder's headquarters. Jackson had been awakened by the storm. Magruder had not yet gone to bed.

Jackson informed him that his troops would probably be up by daylight. Then Magruder slept, one hour, recording that it was his first sleep in forty-eight hours.

In self-admissions, few men on either side were as honest, or as guileless, as John Bankhead Magruder. Also, what he did himself was dramatic to him. He never used an editorial "we," nor, like Lee, depersonalized his acts or decisions by reporting, "It was decided." These endearing human qualities did not inspire Lee's confidence in Magruder's ability to cooperate in execution of the trap to be sprung the following day. When Jackson was assigned to direct the pursuit, no one with Magruder could delude himself any longer that the command held the "post of honor." "Prince John" probably was relieved that his agonizing responsibility was over.

CHAPTER THIRTEEN

Between the Plan and the Execution

M ONDAY, the last day of June, brought a crisis to George
McClellan's career. The twenty-four hours he had gained on
Lee had been insufficient to move his army and wagons beyond the reaches of Lee's three-pronged assault on his columns. Lee
had achieved all he had hoped in catching McClellan in the open,
and the young general had to face the terrible prospect of having
his army cut in half. The battle he had avoided at the sacrifice of his
White House base was overtaking him on the move to the James
River.

The day before, Confederate cavalry had made a reconnaissance in force near the crucial crossroads at Glendale, where the
Federal wagons jammed the Willis Church Road on the movement
to the river. Driving off Colonel Baker's North Carolina regiment
with heavy losses was no compensation to McClellan for the knowledge that Lee had established his precise location and had felt out
the vulnerable point in his movement. Then, late on the day before,
Confederate infantry in force had prevented Kearny's division
from crossing White Oak Swamp at Jordan's Ford. Kearny crossed
in the dark, closer to the crossroads, with the information that a
Confederate division was bivouacked on the Charles City Road
three miles from Glendale.

This was Huger's division, aimed straight at the hinge in McClellan's army. During the morning of the 30th, Longstreet and A. P.
Hill, on the Darbytown Road, were approaching the intersection
with the Long Bridge Road, little more than two miles to the southwest of the slowly moving mass of wagons and men crowded at
Glendale. Farther to the south, Holmes's division was moving east
along the New Market Road toward the terminus of the Willis
Church Road, where the van of McClellan's columns approached

the river. Brought over from south of the river, Holmes's assorted force aggregated around seven thousand of all arms. Yet a fourth column, Jackson's, was moving directly on the line of retreat, approaching Glendale from the north.

Glendale was the place name for the intersection of the Charles City Road and the Long Bridge Road, where the Willis Church Road began its course to the south. There was no settlement at the crossroads, which some called Riddell's Shop after the blacksmith shop there. The action was also called Frayser's Farm for the farm on the Willis Church Road nearest the crossroads. Federal reports also referred to the engagement as the Battle of Nelson's Farm, to the west of the Long Bridge Road, and as the Battle of New Market. Some of the officers believed the Long Bridge Road from New Market was an extension of the New Market Road.

The confusion about the roads was general and not helped by the fact the the New Market Road beyond New Market Heights became the River Road and that the sign on the Darby farm, for which the Darbytown Road was named, was spelled Enroughty. The Willis Church Road was called the Quaker Road by some, though there was also a Quaker Road.

The most important road open to McClellan was one unnamed and unlisted on maps. This was a woods road, parts of it unused for years, discovered by General Keyes the night before. Near the Glendale crossroads it branched off from the Long Bridge Road to the south, loosely paralleling the Willis Church Road for several miles. To the east of Malvern Hill, this country lane divided and one branch led Keyes's corps, with guns and some cavalry, to Turkey Bend in the James River. The van reached the River Road at sunrise of the 30th. Keyes's discovery of this road began to loosen the jam at Glendale. Wagons and reserve artillery trains had been able to move during the night, if by fits and starts, over the main Willis Church Road to the river. On the 30th, parts of the wagon train could be diverted to the woods road, then cleared of fallen logs by Keyes's men, and the main road was partially open for troop movements.

Late in the morning — Franklin thought it about ten-thirty — an energetic McClellan called his corps commanders to a meeting at the Glendale crossroads. The commanding general seemed hurried as he quickly outlined the defensive positions the corps were to assume. The troops took position according to their places in the press of the march.

Smith's division of Franklin's corps and Richardson's division of Sumner's corps, the last troops to leave Savage's Station during the night before, were formed under Franklin once again as the rear guard, facing the line of pursuit.

The road these tired men had trudged through the night ran south from the Williamsburg Road until a long slope dipped to White Oak Swamp at the main crossing of White Oak Bridge. At this point, a creek ran through the swamp, and on both banks the rank growth of vines and underbrush was at its densest, like a jungle through whose interlapped branches the sun never reached to the soggy footing.

After destroying the bridge, Franklin posted his troops and guns on the opposite hill, facing practically due north. While his men were slowly taking positions, the last of the wagon train and part of the siege train were still halted in the clearing on one side of the road. At about one and one half miles from the creek, this road intersected the Long Bridge Road, then crowded with vehicles and walking wounded.

On the opposite side of the creek, Stonewall Jackson was leading the pursuit from Savage's Station. D. H. Hill's division, as vanguard, was moving slowly along a road literally covered with abandoned equipment and overtaking so many Federal stragglers that two regiments were detached to take the prisoners to the rear. Jackson had not come into view when Franklin rode to the Long Bridge Road and on about two miles to Glendale to confer with McClellan.

Though the White Oak Swamp ran in an irregular direction, and its western end slanted northward as it faded off near the Williamsburg Road, across McClellan's front at Glendale for tactical purposes the swampy area coursed west to east. The Charles City Road, skirting its southern fringes, ran into Glendale at an angle from the northwest. To meet Huger approaching on this road, Slocum's division of Franklin's corps was posted to the right of the road, facing more west than north. In this alignment, Slocum's line was almost at a left angle to Franklin, from whom he was virtually separated.

Against Longstreet and A. P. Hill, who would approach up the

Long Bridge Road from the southwest, moving mostly to the east as the road neared Glendale, McClellan placed McCall's division. These Pennsylvania reserves seemed to have been attached to Porter's corps rather than of it, and, like the proverbial stepchild, the division was given a disproportionate amount of work. Following the division's easy introduction to fighting at Beaver Dam Creek, the men had been thrown the next day into the heaviest action at Gaines's Mill. Badly cut up, the troops were somewhat shaken after the casual triumph of their first fight and were a poor choice to be assigned a crucial sector, while the two regular divisions of Porter's corps marched on toward the river to join Keyes's unfought corps.

Behind McCall's right and Slocum's left, Kearny's division stretched from the Charles City Road to the Long Bridge Road near the apex of their juncture. Hooker, the other division from Heintzelman's corps, was placed behind McCall's left and reached across the crowded Willis Church Road. Sedgwick, from Sumner's corps, was placed in reserve in the general area of Glendale.

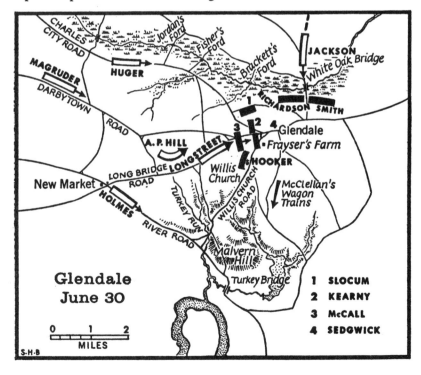

Glendale
June 30

0   1   2
MILES

S·H·B

1 SLOCUM
2 KEARNY
3 McCALL
4 SEDGWICK

McClellan had thus committed to the crossroads almost half his infantry, five divisions, with McCall supported by batteries from Henry Hunt's well-served reserve artillery. Leaving two divisions for the rear guard, with only a thin line along the swampy front between Franklin and Slocum, four divisions had been hurried toward the river. McClellan's mind was pulled toward a terminal point where his exposed columns could come under the protection of the gunboats and transports could land supplies.

With no more intention of fighting in the open on the south of the Chickahominy than on the north, McClellan's purpose in moving to the James River was to use the long-range guns of the navy as a substitute for the works he had been flanked out of in front of Richmond. In his purpose of getting as much of his army as possible to the safety of the river, his defensive arrangement was a repeat of that of Gaines's Mill — designed only to hold off the enemy. As soon as he had delivered the orders to his generals, McClellan left the scene of the impending action and rode to the James River.

2

On the 29th, McClellan had dispatched an engineering officer, Colonel Alexander, to confer with Commander Rodgers, of the James River fleet, on the selection of a landing for a new base. McClellan had in mind Haxall's Landing near the tip of Turkey Bend, one of the loops ("curls," as they were called) in the river.

The Willis Church Road, with some wandering, ran south to Turkey Bend, on its way crossing the hill whose plateau was called Malvern Hill. The western face of Malvern Hill dropped in an almost sheer cliff, and guns posted there would command the River Road — as the New Market Road had then become. By nine in the morning of June 30, Porter's corps had reached this plateau, and guns were being posted above the western cliff to cover the stretch of road leading to Turkey Bend on the line of march of Holmes's column.

When McClellan crossed Malvern Hill on the way to Commander Rodgers's gunboats, his road was packed solid with wagons creeping between the farmland on either side of the plateau and through the thickly foliaged light woods on the long, winding southern slope. Where the Willis Church road intersected the River Road it was crossed by Turkey Bend Creek, flowing into the top of that loop in the James. Keyes's corps, after its night march on the woods road, had gone into camp near the river, with guards posted along the bridge over Turkey Bend Creek.

McClellan conferred briefly with Keyes, and then joined Commander Rodgers on the gunboat *Galena*. It was here, late in the afternoon of June 30, that McClellan selected the point to which he would withdraw his army and where the army could be protected and supplied by the navy. Commander Rodgers suggested that the most practical nearby point was Harrison's Landing, about six miles downriver. What the Federals called Harrison's Landing was the wharf on the three-mile riverfront of Berkeley plantation. Formerly the manorial seat of the Harrison family, Berkeley plantation, patented in 1619, was the birthplace of Benjamin Harrison, V, signer of the Declaration of Independence, and of William Henry Harrison, the ninth president of the United States.

In the sense that the White House had been a base for operations, Harrison's Landing was not a base at all. It was simply the closest place to Richmond to which McClellan could safely withdraw his army on a river, where it could be supplied by water. McClellan made this plain in his report. He said it was Rodgers's "opinion that it would be necessary for the army to fall back to a position" downriver from Turkey Bend, and "Harrison's Landing was, in his opinion, the nearest suitable point." This exchange with Commander Rodgers, if nothing else, pulls the rug from under the rationalization that McClellan changed his base to a base at Harrison's Landing.

During the afternoon of June 30 McClellan was giving no thought to future rationalizations. Having abandoned his campaign against Richmond, his single absorbing anxiety was the salvation of his army. Of course, this anxiety embraced the salvation of his reputation, then indissolubly identified with the fate of the army. Messages sent late in the afternoon, that night, and after midnight reflected an almost hysterical state in which the commanding general seemed removed from the reality of his army's immediate danger at Glendale.

From Turkey Bend he wired Stanton, "I fear I shall be forced to abandon my material to save my men under cover of the gunboats. . . . If none of us escape, we shall at least have saved the honor of the country. . . . Send more gunboats."

Later he wired the adjutant general in Washington for fifty thousand fresh men. "That number sent at once will, I think, enable me to assume the offensive."

Calls went out for steamers to evacuate the sick and wounded. Calls were sent to Fort Monroe to hurry forward the five thousand garrison troops under Silas Casey which had been transported for safety to Fort Monroe after evacuating the White House. To stress the absence of any base on the James River, Chief of Staff Marcy wired Fort Monroe, "Please see that the men you send have three days' rations in their haversacks."

With the frantic calls for the salvation of the army when it reached the James River, McClellan left the generals at Glendale to fight their way out of the convergence of Lee's thrusts coming from three directions. Tactically, more than one half of McClellan's army was enclosed as within three sides of a box, with the open end the Willis Church Road on which the wagon train was moving and which, after the wagons had passed, offered the troops the line of march to fall in with the rest of the army and supplies. If Lee's army reached the Willis Church Road while it was still clogged with wagons, McClellan's army would be cut in half and exposed to military destruction.

The seven divisions, arranged at all angles to one another, without the possibility of initiative or freedom of movement, could do no more than resist the pressure on the three sides, to prevent any one side from collapsing before darkness came. In numbers, Lee's four forces available to press on three sides approximated fifty-five thousand infantry. After casualties, Longstreet and A. P. Hill had something less than eighteen thousand, Jackson (minus Ewell's division) and D. H. Hill something more than eighteen thousand; Huger had about nine thousand and Magruder possibly ten thousand. The seven Federal divisions approximated the same total, with any numerical superiority not significant. Neither total allows for stragglers. Lee's numbers do not include Holmes's force on the River Road, an adjunct to the main offensives at Glendale, as were the thirty-odd thousand Federal troops with Keyes and Porter.

When McClellan relinquished the initiative to Lee the fate of his army became dependent on the coordination the Confederate units could bring to the execution of Lee's trap. Since the soldiers had convincingly demonstrated their fierceness in assault and their willingness to absorb casualties ("they took a lot of killing," as the saying went), the fate of McClellan's army ultimately rested on the individual generals responsible for the execution of Lee's three-column attack.

<h2 style="text-align:center">3</h2>

The key assignment went to Benjamin Huger. Like McClellan, Lee gave assignments to commanders according to their positions in the lines of march. On the day before, when Huger had moved out of his lines across the Williamsburg Road, one of his brigades had reached to the Charles City Road, and by this physical circumstance William Mahone's brigade led Huger's division to the hinge at Glendale. Also, by the unsystematic dates of rank, Mahone was the senior brigadier in a division that contained two superior West Point-trained professionals, Ransom and Lewis Armistead.

William Mahone, a V.M.I. graduate, had been a successful railroad construction engineer who, like McClellan, had been a railroad president at the age of thirty-four. The son of a tavern keeper from Southampton County, Virginia, where he was the neighbor of George Thomas, the Federal general, Billy Mahone was outside the Old Guard. He was a small man, short and slight, with vast personal ambitions.

When Virginia seceded, Mahone had used his own railroad to run trains in and out of Norfolk to give the impression of secessionist forces arriving and contributed to the hasty Federal evacuation of the shipyards. During the war his all-Virginia brigade had not done much more than occupy garrisons until coming to Richmond for the Battle of Seven Pines, where the men had received their strange introduction to the ways of Johnston's army. The march down the Charles City Road in the late morning of June 29 was their first movement toward assault.

Little Billy Mahone, with his long, thin beard, was a hypochondriac, who had his private milk cow attached to his headquarters' wagon. Around noon of the 29th, while Magruder had been deploying around Fair Oaks, Mahone marched his lead brigade toward the enemy as if the physical well-being of his command was the prime consideration. Early in the march, Huger had gone with the brigades of Ransom and Wright to support Magruder on the Williamsburg Road, and Mahone, followed by Armistead, was in command of the march until late in the afternoon. At some time, probably around five o'clock, Mahone had moved five miles along the southern edge of White Oak Swamp down the Charles City Road when he made contact with a small party of enemy cavalry.

At this point, where the Brightwell farm spread on his right, an obscure country lane crossed his front going to his left through the thickets bordering the swamp. Mahone learned, or knew, that this lane led to Jordan's Ford, a crossing of White Oak Swamp about one and one half miles to the north. Mahone wrote in his report that "it was anticipated" that Kearny's division, of Heintzelman's corps, "would attempt its retreat" by way of Jordan's Ford or of fords farther east. This anticipation would have amounted to divination, since Heintzelman's corps was supposed to have covered the Williamsburg Road as part of McClellan's rear guard at Savage's Station, and it was around two o'clock that Heintzelman had made his unannounced withdrawal from Sumner and Franklin. As Huger had withdrawn his two brigades from the Williamsburg Road near the same time, leaving the opposing flanks open, it looked as if Huger and Heintzelman were destined to clash somewhere on June 29.

Mahone halted his column by Brightwell's farm, and skirmishers were sent into the brush to reconnoiter toward the crossing at Jordan's Ford. The Virginia soldiers, long accustomed to defensive work in garrison or lines, apprehensively parted the mottled green screens of the vines and climbed through the tentacles of underbrush foot by foot. When the tense advance reached the boggier ground near the swamp, the skirmishers beheld a similar line of dark-clothed soldiers poking their way toward them. The Virginians fired their rifles. The enemy soldiers, from the 3rd Maine, halted and returned the fire. No damage was done as the lead slugs whirred through the foliage, and the Virginia skirmishers sent back a message to Mahone.

Mahone immediately deployed his full brigade, faced them north, and two regiments pushed through the thickets. When these troops came up to their skirmishers, the enemy fell back into the shadowed density. Mahone's line crept on forward, gathering up a dozen or so prisoners, until the regiments reached the southern side of Jordan's Ford. No enemy troops were crossing, but the prisoners said Kearny's division was camped on the opposite bank.

By the time this information reached Mahone, Huger had arrived, well in advance of the two brigades removed from the Williamsburg Road. A boy from the neighborhood told Huger that Kearny's division was indeed camped on the northern side of Jordan's Ford. Huger also learned that yet another road, called the New Road, branched off from the Charles City Road farther back and ran north of the swamp past Jordan's Ford and the other crossings to the east. Fearing that Kearny might move back westward on the New Road and come at this column from the rear, Huger ordered a battery posted at the intersection and halted Wright's brigade when it came up, with orders to explore the New Road at daylight.

Between Mahone and Huger, the assault column had turned on the defensive at the first contact with the enemy. As Huger might have assumed, Kearny held no aggressive intentions. Birney's brigade, of the division, had been crossing Jordan's Ford on the line of retreat when its skirmishers encountered Mahone's. As soon as Birney saw the enemy skirmishers were supported in force, he drew back across Jordan's Ford. He then followed the rest of the division to cross the swamp further east. Birney reached the Charles City Road at ten o'clock at night about two miles beyond Brightwell's, where Huger was prepared to defend against an assault on flank or rear, and Mahone's troops slept under arms.

In the morning of June 30, Huger and Mahone began the critical day in Lee's plans with the defensiveness with which they had bivouacked. There was nothing complicated about either man. Mahone, like McClellan, had habits of success which did not promote audacity in a strange situation, and his early V.M.I. training had been sufficient to cause him to recognize the limitations of inexperience.

Old Army man Huger, not enterprising at best, had fresh in his mind the bewildering experience of Seven Pines. Huger had not on June 30 seen Longstreet's report, as he requested a copy of it on July 26. With all the June correspondence among Longstreet and Joe Johnston and Gustavus Smith, between them and the war department, and with the loose talk around Richmond and in the army, he probably had heard rumors of the blame falling on him. Certainly the new commanding general had shown little confidence in him, even scolding him once. Too set in his ways to be goaded to redeem himself by bold action, the imperious-looking, aging aristocrat went to the other extreme and acted to avoid mistakes. He'd give them nothing to blame him with a second time.

After the storm during the night, the sky was clear and pale on Monday morning, June 30, and Huger found the heat "intense." On the flat, humid countryside near the swamps, it was suffocating where the woods enclosed the road on both sides. Mahone's brigade had moved forward cautiously about one mile of the three to Glendale when the van came upon freshly cut logs obstructing the road.

The normal procedure would have been to detach foot soldiers to roll away the logs while guns were brought forward to protect the men against the enemy's rear guard. The situation awakened the construction engineer in Mahone. He had pioneers bring forward axes, picks and shovels, and parties were detached to cut a new road through the woods. Why it seemed simpler to cut down trees than to remove the logs on the road was never explained. Brash Billy Mahone, capable of aggressive action when in combat, suffered some mental lapse at his approach to the enemy.

Evidently his original purpose had been to cut a path beyond the obstructed section of the road. As soon as the troops of Slocum's division saw what Mahone was up to, the Federal soldiers continued to cut trees to fall across the Charles City Road. In this fantastic battle of the axes Mahone's men labored manfully in the heat to lengthen their swath through the woods to a mile, and then more. Over the fields where the armies were gathering, the sound of axes rang out as Slocum's men lengthened their obstructions. During this "advance," Huger rode to the front and apparently approved.

When noon was passed and the van had moved forward barely

two miles since daylight, Huger sent Lee a message that the road was obstructed. By implication, he would go into action when it was cleared. Around two o'clock, Mahone's road passed the last of the obstructions and the lead brigade emerged from the end of their tunnel into an open field. The enemy's picket fired a round and fell back. Huger, riding to the front, saw Slocum's division posted in an open hill, its line extending across the Charles City Road and into the thickets of the White Oak Swamp on the Confederate left.

Huger deployed Mahone's brigade while a battery was ordered forward through the newly cut passage. Armistead's brigade, and Ransom's farther back, merely halted. Wright's brigade was at that time moving east along the New Road north of the swamp, viewing the abandoned camps of the Federals who had crossed over during the night.

At two-thirty the gun battery was in position, and opened on Slocum. Rifled guns on the crest of the rise in the open field immediately answered. At last Mahone and Huger had established contact with the enemy.

4

The sound of Huger's guns was welcomed on the Long Bridge Road where, northeast of the Darbytown Road intersection, Longstreet and A. P. Hill had been waiting since noon to hear the opening of Huger's action. In preparation for the joint assault, Dick Anderson's brigade, under the temporary command of Colonel Micah Jenkins, had earlier advanced strong skirmish lines on both sides of the road, driving in the enemy pickets and uncovering the defensive position occupied by McCall's division. McCall was posted about two thousand yards from the Glendale crossroads.

Where Longstreet and Hill waited to advance, the Long Bridge Road cut to the northeast, slicing between low sharp banks covered with sweet-smelling vines. The ground was mostly flat, with timber thick on the left and cultivated fields on the right broken by thin belts of woods. Farther to the right, the woods grew densely toward the Willis Church Road, less than two miles to the east.

In a small clearing to the right of the road, General Lee was passing the time in pleasant conversation with Longstreet and A. P.

Hill. Lee had begun the day with Jackson on the Williamsburg Road, holding another of the conferences no one overheard. Observers reported Jackson had nodded as if to indicate his understanding and seemed emphatic in his manner and vigorous in his movements. Lee, evidently making no inquiries about the inaction of the day before, had talked only of Jackson's part in closing the trap at Glendale. Then Lee had ridden over to the Darbytown Road, joined the marching columns as the van reached the Long Bridge intersection, and waited with Longstreet and Powell Hill until Huger's guns were heard.

As Huger had sent him the earlier message that the road was obstructed, on hearing the guns Lee assumed the road was cleared and the assault opening. Magruder had reported that, in marching from Savage's Station, his van had been halted by A. P. Hill's rear guard on the Darbytown Road. Lee had dispatched Magruder an order to rest his men where they were and to be prepared to support Hill and Longstreet after their assault developed.

During the quickened movements across the hot countryside, President Davis, who had ridden out from Richmond, rode forward to Lee's advanced position. At Mechanicsville Lee had, in effect, ordered Davis off the field, but on the Long Bridge Road the two men had a more good-natured exchange over the President's presence. The tension of the first battle was lacking. Lee knew the location of every unit, six hours of daylight remained, and there was an air of relaxed excitement when the first Confederate batteries ran forward to open on the enemy and to signal Huger that their advance was ready to move out with his.

At the blasts of the guns, A. P. Hill rode up to the President and the commanding general with a display of social ease. Telling his superiors they were in his area of command, Hill said they were subject to his orders and must withdraw from the danger zone. While General Lee and President Davis were graciously "obeying" Hill's orders by backing their mounts off a few paces, Federal batteries answered Longstreet's guns and shells burst over the roadside near the group. At Hill's admonitions, Lee and Davis withdrew farther back.

The rapid fire of the Federal guns was the only answer to Longstreet's batteries. Huger's position was little more than two miles away by air line. Across country thick timber rose between the Long Bridge Road and the Charles City Road in that area, with a wet ravine from the swamp deepening the obstructions, but the generals could plainly hear Huger's single battery isolated from the roar of the Federal guns, and no increase came to his volume. Nor could the men's straining ears detect any sound of rifle fire.

Longstreet's division was deployed, with Branch's brigade from the Light Division on the right, and the firing between the skirmishers grew sharper and heavier. Except for that tentative action on the Long Bridge Road, nothing indicated any movement against any part of McClellan's angular defensive lines.

Jackson should by then have been pressing in the rear guard toward Glendale. As he had only seven miles to go to his crossing at the White Oak Bridge, signs of his advance on Glendale from the north were overdue by three o'clock. Again the vacuum of an operations officer was revealed. Lee sent no one from his staff to discover what either Jackson or Huger was doing, and no one on the field thought of such a thing.

5

When the Federals' rifled guns began to hurt the batteries of Longstreet and Hill, apprehension crept into the atmosphere with the unanswered questions about Huger and Jackson. At that point, the silence from Lee's subordinates was broken on one front by an enterprising young cavalry officer. From the River Road area of Holmes's assignment, a courier arrived from Colonel Rosser.

Tom Rosser had been with Pelham in the West Point class of 1861 and, on resigning before graduation, enlisted directly with the Confederate armies and not with the troops of his own state, Virginia. For this reason, the tall, powerfully built horseman had been a little slow to come to the attention of Jeb Stuart, who had a fine eye for potential leaders. It was just before the Seven Days that Stuart got him commissioned colonel, and gave him a Virginia regiment of raw volunteers. During the 29th and 30th, black-haired young Rosser had operated his new troopers to the west of the Willis Church Road, between the church and the River Road.

When Longstreet had first begun to deploy in line of battle, his right had reached the area where a dismounted company of Rosser's cavalry was engaging the skirmishers in front of the main Federal line south of Glendale. The eager young colonel told Longstreet that his pickets on the River Road had reported enemy troop movement. Longstreet, concentrated on getting troops in line while listening to hear Huger's assault open, ordered Rosser to reconnoiter with his whole regiment. Soon Rosser sent back a message to Longstreet that his reconnaissance parties had discovered the head of the Federal "retiring column moving hurriedly and confusedly in the direction of the James River." Rosser had observed the movement of the wagon train across Malvern Hill. Preoccupied, Longstreet ignored the message.

Rosser made the same report to Holmes. As his troops were halted at New Market Heights at the intersection of the Long Bridge Road, the Federal movement was across his front. Having taken a strong defensive position at New Market Heights, Holmes seemed not to be certain of what his assignment was, though it would have made little difference if he had.

Old at fifty-seven and deaf, Theophilus H. Holmes, who had been a classmate of Lee at West Point, was one of the Old Army relics whom time had unfitted for war. Early receiving the high rank of lieutenant general because of his rank as field officer in the Old Army, Holmes had been sent to his native North Carolina to organize the state troops. In this capacity he became commander of the department between the James River and the Cape Fear River in North Carolina and, hence, commanded the brigades moved up to the south side of the James when Huger crossed to the north side for the Battle of Seven Pines.

In the shuffle, Holmes had received Wise's small brigade from Huger in exchange for Ransom's large, professionally led brigade. The two full-sized brigades remaining with Holmes were potentially among the best that came to Virginia, commanded by superior professional soldiers in Junius Daniel, who had just passed his thirty-fourth birthday, and John G. Walker, approaching forty. The last of those troops had crossed the river to the New Market Road the night before.

Though Holmes claimed his infantry presented no more than six thousand on the field, he carried thirty guns, mostly well served.

By the necessary system, the talent and vigor in his command were stifled by this inept regular, who ignored the information sent him by a young cavalry colonel, who was later to become a major general with Jeb Stuart.

Finally, Tom Rosser sent the intelligence of the Federals crossing Malvern Hill to Lee. The commanding general left his field headquarters where he had been waiting for the battle to develop and rode off toward Malvern Hill to make a personal reconnaissance.

When Lee reached the River Road around four o'clock, McClellan's wagons were moving fast across Malvern Hill, nearing the end of the line. Lee may not have ridden close enough actually to see for himself. Major Kidder Meade, the doughty reconnaissance engineer, was on the ground and had convinced Holmes that the enemy was moving toward the James River. Holmes reported he "found the commanding general just returning from an observation of the enemy's position." Holmes told Lee he was moving forward six rifled guns, in three sections, with the 30th Virginia from Walker's brigade in support. The rest of the division was being put in motion to move up. Lee directed Holmes to open fire on the enemy's column as soon as his troops were in position, and turned his horse back to the Long Bridge Road.

The wasted hours had permitted McClellan's train to break the jam and clear the crossroads at Glendale. Still, if Holmes could delay the movement of the tail of the column, the bulk of the Federal Army could yet be caught. But the attacking columns must move fast.

Instead, when Lee rejoined Longstreet and A. P. Hill, the situation was not materially changed from when he had left. The artillery fire was steady, the skirmishers were heavily engaged, and the generals were still waiting for Huger to develop his assault and to hear from Jackson. Also, Longstreet had ordered Magruder to move from his reserve position on the Darbytown Road over to the New Market Road where Holmes was advancing. In Longstreet's mind Magruder was to protect his right; according to the order Magruder was to support Holmes.

With Magruder's tired troops crossing over to the New Market Road, Lee had at hand no more than eighteen thousand of two divisions to deliver the assault, and the Light Division had already borne the brunt of two attacks. Unless these two divisions attacked then, McClellan's army would pass unharmed between three columns totaling more than fifty thousand troops.

It was then approaching five o'clock. As A. P. Hill had at Mechanicsville, Lee reasoned that while Longstreet and Hill became engaged, Huger or Jackson *must* joint in the movement. He ordered Longstreet to open the assault.

6

The attack of the two divisions toward the crossroads was a soldiers' fight. Longstreet, in command of a field for the second time within a month, turned his own division over to Brigadier General Richard H. Anderson. The quiet forty-year-old professional from South Carolina, neither a spectacular soldier nor anything of a character, had never built a public reputation and was not widely known even in the army. In Longstreet's command, however, Dick Anderson was deeply respected as a soldier and liked as a man, and he was highly regarded by Lee.

For his direction of the division on June 30, Anderson was not singled out by Longstreet from the other brigadiers in the general praise in the report, but in the reorganization after the Seven Days Anderson was promoted by Lee to major general and given a division. The mild-mannered, gentle-eyed Anderson could become extremely tenacious once his troops engaged the enemy. That he was unable to exert skillful control of the six brigades could be reasonably explained by the terrain and the circumstances.

The timbered country, with its sudden dips and rises, gave Anderson some of the same difficulty in viewing the field that had troubled A. P. Hill and Ewell at Gaines's Mill. Then, the contact had been sustained so long between the lines before the assault was delivered that the movements forward were uneven and disjointed. Anderson's own brigade under young Jenkins, which had originally established the enemy's position and had been engaged for some while, seemingly did not receive an order to advance when Kemper's brigade moved forward on his right. Kemper's brigade, in turn, outran everybody.

In Kemper's line of march, the battle lines crossed two thin belts

of woods with a field between and then emerged on a broad cultivated plain. The men grew excited at driving in the enemy's picket
lines and when they broke out into the open, the Virginians began
to run, yelling at the tops of their lungs.

In the woods on the opposite side of the wide clearing, McCall had
a curious defensive position. Two gun batteries were placed in front
of heavy timber, with the infantry supports in the woods immediately behind the guns. In front of his infantry and guns and to the
left squatted the small Whitlock house, one story and dormer.
Around this house fence rails and logs had been built into a rude
breastwork, and an advance line there formed a projecting flank.

After their long hours of waiting at the Whitlock house, the sudden rush of Kemper's screaming soldiers, preceded by their own
fleeing pickets, stampeded the regiment of Pennsylvania reserves out
of the works and across the field. The men fled toward the rear in
one of those inexplicable panics, hurtling through all the reserve
troops who got in their way.

Kemper's exultant Virginians ran the faster, bursting through and
over the gun batteries and the infantry line in the woods. Kemper
and the colonels, growing more anxious with each yard covered,
saw they had no support on either flank. The soldiers were deaf to
the officers' shouts.

In the woods, the front runners were halted by heavier fire on
their front. As the winded sprinters came up behind them, more like
groups in a disorderly crowd than a brigade, minié balls began to
rattle through the foliage from both flanks and up and down.
Hooker's division, covering the Willis Church Road, had taken a
position in the forest and their fresh lines were relatively solid. The
happy chargers, finding themselves hemmed in and being fired upon
from all directions, took cover wherever they were. At all angles to
one another, the men began to shoot mostly at smoke drifting out of
thickets.

The officers panted up and tried to restore order to their units. It
was a slow process. Dozens of the soldiers wandered into the Federal lines, and individual Virginians and Pennsylvanians were surprised to find themselves shooting back to back. Curiously, Kemper's
killed and wounded were few. The fight was too confused in the
smoky woods for the Federals to take advantage of Kemper's dis-

order; and Hooker's lines were not clear of McCall's fugitives. About one hundred of Kemper's men were lost as prisoners. For its effect on the assault Kemper's brigade because an isolated wedge, on the Federal left, fighting at that point for its own survival.

As Jenkins did not advance in force on Kemper's left, on the right Branch's brigade, the only unit from Hill's division deployed with Longstreet's troops, was a victim of uncertainty in the purpose of its employment. Longstreet reported that Branch had been placed "to guard" the right at the time Micah Jenkins first became engaged. When Dick Anderson· assumed command of Longstreet's division no orders were sent Branch to advance when Kemper rushed ahead. His North Carolinians were deployed in the woods in back of the Whitlock house, and the ground there grew rough as it sloped down to a ravine parallel to the Willis Church Road. Later, when an order to advance reached Branch from A. P. Hill, Hooker's division extended across his front and overlapped his flank. Branch's men engaged the enemy without making a vigorous thrust.

The nearest to a break came on the left of the road, where Wilcox's Alabama regiments overran Randol's six-gun battery. Two waves of infantry had broken in direct charges into the canister blasting at them from Randol's pieces and Thompson's on Randol's right. After the second wave had subsided, the attackers, leaving their dead on the field, temporarily took cover to re-form. Randol's covering infantry charged out to rout what they assumed to be Wilcox's demoralized survivors. The 4th Pennsylvania Reserves, of General Meade's brigade, unexpectedly ran into sheets of fire and broke backward. Immediately Wilcox's re-formed lines charged behind them. The guns could not fire through the screen of their own men, and the pursued and the pursuers rolled over the batteries almost as a single force.

General Meade, future commander of the army, fell wounded. Reserves came up from Kearny, and the battle over the guns resolved into one of the infrequent bayonet fights of the war. It was savage action in that clearing in front of the brush on Nelson's farm, officers and men going down with as many as three bayonet thrusts in their bodies. Some were knocked senseless by rifle butts. In the melee, the guns were lost to McCall, along with the barren ground, and Kearny's supporting division was shaken.

Wilcox's Alabamians, taking fearful casualties and disordered, could do no more than hold the position of their advance, nearly a mile short of the crossroads. To Wilcox's left the brigades of Winfield S. Featherston and Roger Pryor (a prewar duelist) came up to widen the front of the assault, extending Kearny's division. Kearny called on corps commander Heintzelman for help.

To Wilcox's right, and right of the slow advance of Micah Jenkins, Pickett's brigade changed directions to move to Kemper's relief. Pickett's was Longstreet's last brigade and Pickett was out with the wound taken at Gaines's Mill. Colonel Eppa Hunton, of the 8th Virginia, led the brigade forward. Absorbing casualties in crossing the open field and losing direction when Confederates from other units fell back through their lines, the brigade entered the woods without Colonel Hunton. Ill, he had fallen from exhaustion. A Pickett staff officer turned the brigade over to Colonel Strange and he tried to bring order to the deranged battle in the woods.

In moving to support a line of Kemper's fighting in his front, Strange found a line of Federals behind him. Beginning to fight in groups, with little purpose beyond survival, the men of Pickett's brigade became embroiled with a fresh unit from Sedgwick's division. Longstreet's brigades were being met by divisions. Four Federal divisions from three corps were absorbing the thrusts across the uneven lines, and more supports were moving to Glendale.

The sun was going down, with nothing heard from Jackson or Huger. Featherston's left, stretching to turn the Federal flank, reached little more than a mile from Huger's position. Instead of Huger supporting Featherston, a Federal brigade was drawn from Slocum's division — the one facing Huger — to hurry to support Kearny on the Long Bridge Road. Then two brigades were drawn from Richardson's division, one of the two divisions holding the rear guard against Jackson, and moved to the Glendale front. The equivalent of four fresh divisions were massing at McCall's broken lines.

7

With the massing strength, the Federals began to mount counterattacks at isolated points. The hard thrusts of Longstreet's brigades had been delivered without cohesion across the whole front, and with little strength on the right where Pickett was battling to rescue Kemper. As the momentum went from the assault, segments of the disordered advance were forced to take positions of defense.

In Longstreet's execution of Lee's general plan, in expectation of supports from either Jackson or Huger, he had withheld Hill's Light Division to deliver the decisive blow. With no support arriving and more Federals coming to his front from the area where Huger and Jackson were expected, Longstreet could only employ Hill to bolster the troops of the spent assault as the men turned to defending themselves against the enemy's fresh forces.

Grimly, Longstreet ordered A. P. Hill to commit his division. With the sun setting, the brigades of the Light Division went in fast. Pender went along the road to the right and Field to the left. Gregg went to the left of Field and Archer to the right of Pender. These were the troops on whom the dusk fell only three days before in the slaughter-pit of Boatswain's Swamp, and the men went forward with their high yells as eagerly as when they moved out the first day across the fields at Mechanicsville. Powell Hill held only one brigade back against emergency.

General Lee had ordered Magruder to return from the New Market Road, but obviously it would be too late for him. His men had marched twenty miles in the heat, fumbling through woods roads to cross to Holmes, and the van would not get back to the Darbytown Road until after dark. On the River Road Holmes was doing nothing. Toward Glendale, in the unexplainable collapse of his trap, Lee watched a ragged battle in which his men had ceased to advance and in some sectors were fighting on defense. The uneven center seemed vulnerable to counterattack.

The commanding general said nothing when Powell Hill committed his last brigade, Joseph Anderson's, to support the center. In the falling light, Anderson's troops pushed ahead astride the road, behind Field and Pender.

Toward the field headquarters, an exultant group of soldiers from the 47th Virginia approached the generals. These were men of Field's brigade, the first in the open at Mechanicsville, who had been forced to huddle in the thickets of the creek bank against the fire from McCall's three tiers of riflemen. Now the no-longer-green soldiers were proudly bearing their first trophy of war, Brigadier General George A. McCall himself.

After the break in his lines around Randol's gun battery, McCall had been off collecting troops to stand with Kearny's supports, and Field's brigade had advanced farther than he had calculated. Screened from the soldiers by the hanging vines, as they were from him, the general rode into an opening in the woods where the Virginians were re-forming their lines. McCall reported later that Field had attacked with such impetuosity that seventy or eighty of his Pennsylvanians had been borne along bodily in the rush, and not one Confederate had paused to collect the Federals as prisoners.

There were not enough Confederates. Sedgwick's division, somewhat confused by the "torrent" of McCall's fugitives through its ranks, had the weight to hold the center, and when Kearny's right began to go, Heintzelman got the brigade from Slocum's division up in support.

When Heintzelman moved the brigade from Huger's front, he said, "I rode far enough on the Charles City Road to see that we had nothing to fear from that direction." Huger had not only failed to attack; his brigades remained so passively out of danger that Federal troops from the one division in his front had been used to contain Longstreet and Hill. Huger had not even demonstrated. When the rifled Federal batteries answered his guns at two-thirty, a few casualties were caused in Mahone's brigade, and these roadbuilders were immediately withdrawn to the safety of the woods. There they remained until night fell, and silence slowly came to the countryside where the brigades of Longstreet and A. P. Hill had attacked so magnificently and to so little purpose.

Routing the division that had humiliated them the first day, capturing fourteen guns, the no more than eighteen thousand men had engaged upwards of forty thousand from first to last. But, when it was all over at nine o'clock, the crossroads were still open. The Willis Church Road had been cleared of the wagon train for the night passage of the seven elevenths of the infantry that should have been cut off, and by morning McClellan would have completed his crossing of the peninsula.

8

At nightfall Lee's outward composure reflected none of his frustration at McClellan's escape from the perfect trap. The escape held a quality of the miraculous. The Federals had fought without a field commander. When McClellan had abdicated the battlefield, he had not given responsibility to any subordinate; he had established a signal system via Malvern Hill by which he could be contacted on Commander Rodgers's ship. Showing that he did not want to be around when Lee struck, McClellan seemed to operate on the principle that if he didn't look maybe Lee's army would go away. The miraculous part was that, in spite of the laws of probability, two of Lee's three converging columns had failed to act.

There had been nothing complicated required in coordination, nothing of the first day's grand design. The three columns were on the ground, with ready communication open between them and plenty of time for the execution of simple assignments. The limitations in Lee's staff work contributed to the way the battle had been fought, and looseness in command had wasted Magruder, but the plan was sound and simple enough to have succeeded, as had Gaines's Mill, despite the lack of operational control.

McClellan escaped for the same reason he got in the fix — human failings. As he was trapped by his own human failings, he escaped by the failings of Huger and Jackson. All other elements were minor. The inanition of these two men lost Lee his greatest opportunity to wreck an army of the enemy.

Of Holmes Lee had obviously expected little, though an enterprising officer of ordinary competence would not so completely have wasted the day. Waiting passively on defense until four o'clock while the only action within three miles was the enemy's wagon train scurrying across his front, when Holmes then sent forward six guns to shell the column he marched his brigades down the River Road as if he had the whole country to himself.

The dust raised attracted the attention of Porter's men on the western face of Malvern Hill. Porter sent thirty guns toward the edge of the cliff overlooking the River Road, among them pieces from Tyler's battalion of heavy artillery belonging to the siege train. At ten o'clock those guns were halted after crossing White Oak Swamp and had just reached Malvern Hill when Holmes's columns came swinging down the road below them.

While Holmes's guns were being posted, the general went into a nearby house for the purpose, he said, of transacting some army business. During the absence of the deaf general, Porter's thirty guns opened from the Malvern Cliff and the gunboats joined in from the river. The gunboats fired shells so large Holmes's soldiers called them "lampposts." Most of the shells from the cliff on one side and the river on the other exploded near the batteries. A couple of pieces were knocked about, several men were hit and a number of horses went down writhing and screaming.

Though the sudden bedlam looked like catastrophe, little actual damage was done. It happened that the 125 gallantly uniformed volunteers, who were attached to Holmes as a "cavalry battalion," were mounted near the six guns, and when a caisson burst with a flash of red and white rockets the riders took off in a body like a good start in a race meet. When the horsemen rushed past a battery brought up from Petersburg, some of the gun crews became infected, cut the traces from the artillery horses and, leaping on their broad backs, took out after the cavalrymen. This panicky movement, local though it was, was sufficient to break the ranks of the infantry columns packed on the road, and the soldiers ducked to the cover on either side. At this moment Holmes, having finished his business in the farmhouse, came out, cupped his hand to his ear, and said, "I thought I heard firing."

It was the only firing he heard during the day. The Federals, calling the action "the Battle of Malvern Cliff," thought Holmes's purpose was to attack with his division, and George Sykes, commanding the division supporting Porter's guns, declared that his position could not have been taken from the River Road. That was not Holmes's assignment. He was supposed only to delay the retreating column by artillery fire on the road crossing Malvern Hill.

By the time Holmes's guns were in position, the last of the wagon train was passing to the river and he could have accomplished nothing. His losses were fifty-one casualties, only two of whom were killed, when he withdrew his troops out of the range of siege guns and ships' guns. Except for that of Ransom's brigade with Huger, this constituted the sole contribution of the troops Lee used from the North Carolina department, which Joe Johnston counted among the enormous accretions Lee drew to his army.

During the afternoon the normally untemperamental Holmes showed himself to be in a testy, uncooperative mood. When Major Brent reported to Holmes and asked where he wanted Magruder's troops, Holmes very rudely told Brent he knew nothing about reinforcements from Magruder, and brusquely refused to discuss the matter. Evidently the Old Army man, years past response to combat, did not take kindly to operating a column in another general's department. In his report he never referred to the "commanding general" by name. He did mention that His Excellency, the President, had expressed approval of the defensive position he selected at New Market Heights. As Davis was his friend, Holmes was sent to the noncombat command of another department, the Trans-Mississippi. There his failures spread over a wider area and in time he was relieved.

As for Huger, the scapegoat of Seven Pines had no excuses for military behavior that was, after all, unexplainable. In his report, Huger said his orders had been to follow the enemy down the Charles City Road, and this he certainly did. Lee made no comment on the report. Within two weeks, Huger was relieved of command, and sent to noncombat duties in the ordnance department. For a time he served in the Trans-Mississippi with his contemporary Holmes and never again commanded troops. This pair of relics were obviously peacetime officers who proved under the test of combat to have passed an age of usefulness in the field.

In assigning troops for duty largely on the chance of their physical location, Lee assumed, within limits, an equality of performance from all his divisions. When his force had been molded into the Army of Northern Virginia that created the legends, this method was usually effective. In the Seven Days, Lee included such a dubious performer as Huger in this method partly because he regarded the movement down the Charles City Road as a simple assignment.

Even though Huger was directed at the hinge of McClellan's columns, Lee planned this attack to exert a pressure in the center that would expose the defensive columns to the main assaults delivered on either side by the Longstreet-A. P. Hill force and the Jackson-

D. H. Hill force. On this point, Mahone reported that their orders had been "to proceed down the Charles City Road for the purpose of cooperating with other forces of our army now pursuing the retreating enemy. . . ."

In arranging this cooperation, Lee obviously expected to strike McClellan's army when its columns were disordered. Before one o'clock, with wagons still jamming the roads, the Federal units were confused and not well arranged for defense. Hooker reported he did not know McCall's division was on the field, partly in his front, until eleven o'clock. Heintzelman reported that his divisions, Hooker and Kearny, as a result of the reshuffling of alignments, were not in position until "the afternoon." As any action from Huger by one o'clock would have caught the Federal forces in the disarrangement of Lee's calculations, Lee placed no demands on Huger beyond the most rudimentary competence.

As late as four o'clock, two of Sedgwick's brigades had been run ("double-quick," as they called it then) to Brackett's Ford, between Slocum's right and Franklin's left. This came in response to an alarm that Jackson was shifting his attack from White Oak Bridge to Brackett's Ford. A move by Huger even then would at least have kept reinforcements from Glendale when Longstreet broke McCall's line. It had not been Jackson at Brackett's Ford but Wright, of Huger's division, returning to the Charles City Road after his tour of the abandoned Federal camps north of the swamp. Wright moved to another ford and the two Federal brigades ran back to meet Longstreet's advance.

The failure to exploit Wright's position at Brackett's Ford fell on Jackson as well as on Huger. In depending on Jackson after three straight failures, Lee apparently expected the muffled potential to assert itself in a straight-on combat assignment of pursuit and attack. With all the complications surrounding the earlier movements on the Chickahominy, and with no reports in, Lee did not perceive that all of Jackson's failures were of the single nature of inanition. In fact, with the reports in, it has been the custom to review each of Jackson's failures separately and to provide each with a separate set of explanations. In this way, his inaction at White Oak Swamp has been studied as if different from the failures that began on the march to Ashland.

His torpor at White Oak Swamp was the same as that of the day on the march when, after trying to read a novel, he had given up and gone to bed in the middle of the afternoon. His performance at White Oak Swamp stood out in dramatic relief because there, in the crisis of Lee's plans, his failure was complete, disastrous and unredeemable. Yet, it was only the ultimate illustration of the effects of stress-fatigue.

9

Stonewall Jackson, awakened by a rainstorm around midnight, appeared in wet clothes at Magruder's field headquarters near the Williamsburg Road at three-thirty on the morning of June 30. Until daylight about an hour later, when his troops started crossing the Grapevine Bridges, the general sat by the campfire drying his clothes. At the first light in the sky, Jackson mounted his famous Little Sorrel and rode to the crossroads where the road from the Grapevine Bridges intersected the Williamsburg Road. The night before, he had sent orders to Colonel Munford to have his regiment of the 2nd Virginia Cavalry at the crossroads at daylight. When Jackson reached that point, Munford was not there. Soon he was seen approaching from half a mile away, with no more than fifty bedraggled-looking troopers.

Tom Munford was the energetic young colonel whom Jackson had left in the Valley to work a screen in front of the enemy until the infantry columns neared Ashland. He was then to follow with his own regiment. During the night the storm had scattered his horses, the animals breaking the picket lines and plunging off through the dripping woods. It was shortly after sunrise before the men rounded up the fifty horses that, saddled and mounted, now approached the crossroads where a stern Jackson awaited them.

"He was in a bad humor," Munford wrote later. Jackson had said: "Colonel, my orders to you were to be here at sunrise."

Munford explained his misadventure in the strange woods, and Jackson said, "Yes, sir. But, Colonel, I ordered you to be here at sunrise. Move on with your regiment. If you meet the enemy, drive in his pickets."

As Munford started out with his skeletal force, individuals, pairs and small groups of his lost riders began to straggle out of the woods to fall into their places. Shortly two couriers galloped up with the message that his men were straggling badly. Harassed Munford rode back to the general and repeated in detail how the storm had scattered his horses. Jackson said, "Yes, sir. But I ordered you to be here at sunrise and I have been waiting for you for a quarter of an hour."

Munford, "seeing that he was in a peculiar mood," then sent his adjutant back to halt his missing men as they appeared and form them before moving forward. The small mounted force with Munford continued on the line of the enemy's retreat at about the pace of the following infantry.

After his attention to the cavalry, Jackson did nothing to hurry D. H. Hill's division, acting as his vanguard. The inactivity of the day before — marching down to the Grapevine Bridges to pursue the enemy, standing around for hours, then returning anticlimactically to their camps — seemed to have cooled off the hard fighters in Hill's brigades. The officers and men appeared more interested in the signs of the enemy's retreat than in the pursuit.

Ripped overcoats and slashed blankets formed part of the miry footing. Before the column turned off the Williamsburg Road into the road to White Oak Bridge, the men saw hillocks of foodstuff still smoldering in the clearings on their left, around Savage's Station. Axes, picks, shovels, partially burned wagons and pontoons, unexploded ammunition cases and discarded small arms would require weeks for the supply bureaus to collect. As the columns moved down the White Oak Bridge Road, a drove of deserted mules was gathered from the woods and sent to the rear. At every house along the road, Hill's men found wounded from the battle of the day before at Savage's Station. Out of each deep thicket clumps of Federal stragglers emerged, giving themselves up, until the prisoners numbered a thousand.

In light humor at the evidence of the enemy's precipitate retreat, an officer told Jackson the enemy was surrendering too easily; the government would be embarrassed by having to feed them. Jackson had grown more cheerful and, with a smile, said, "It's cheaper to feed them than to fight them."

His good spirits remained despite the indifferent marching — it took the van more than seven hours to cover barely seven miles. Jackson was smiling, Munford recorded, when he reached the plateau that looked down a long slope to the White Oak Bridge. It was then a little after noon, and Jackson saw evidence of a hastily abandoned camp. More wounded were left, more mules, and Munford's small force had cleared this side of the swamp of enemy skirmishers. Franklin had only completed the crossing at ten o'clock, burning the bridge, and Jackson could see halted wagons on the opposite plateau and lines of resting infantry behind three gun batteries in a cleared field on the left of the road. Here was a situation to arouse the combative instincts of any soldier.

On the flat bottomland stretching along both sides of the creek rose a murky jungle of small trees draped by creepers and heavy vines. On the opposite hillside timber grew on the Confederate right of the road. Above the swamp on Jackson's side the hill was partly open ground, with thin belts of second-growth timber scattered on the plateau. To the right of the road a declivity ran through a fringe of woods. Jackson ordered up twenty-eight guns and, behind the cover of Munford's cavalry, used the declivity as a passageway to move the guns off the road. Trees were cut for clearance and shortly before two o'clock the seven batteries, in position and hidden from the enemy, opened fire.

This sudden cannonade, the heaviest used by the Confederates until then, broke over the exposed enemy batteries on the opposite plateau and fell among the startled soldiers lying down. As in most such cannonades, the impression of havoc was greater than the actual damage. A couple of guns were knocked about, horses were killed and casualties struck among the men, but the appearance of disaster was given mostly by the troops hurrying out of range of the bursting metal.

While Jackson's gunners fired rapidly, another battery was sent down the road to flush any sharpshooters who might be lurking in the woods across the creek, and Munford's cavalry regiment galloped downhill to the crossing. The timbers torn from the bridge had been thrown in the water, where some floated and some stuck in the miry bottom, making a passage look difficult to Munford. Jackson rode forward, excited at the apparent ease of overcoming the one physical obstacle between him and the enemy. When Munford told the general he did not think they could cross, Jackson waved him on and said, "Yes, Colonel, try it." The horses threshed and threaded their way across the entangled mire to the opposite bank. When Munford got over, there was Jackson, with Harvey Hill, right behind him. The general called to him to charge up the hill and take the enemy's guns.

Munford went gamely ahead until rifle fire halted his horsemen. Then Federal guns opened from the woods on the right of the road. To get out of range, Munford swerved his men to their left, and rode downstream until they reached a cowpath about a quarter of a mile from the bridge. Here the horsemen recrossed the creek.

Jackson and Harvey Hill returned by way of the broken bridge. On his quick trip, Jackson learned that the enemy troops and batteries he had observed in the clearing on the left represented only a small part of the Federal forces massed to contest the crossing. Indeterminable numbers were hidden in the woods on the right. By the time he returned to his own plateau, the enemy's rifled guns were already finding the range of his batteries. Even as his gunners changed the direction of their pieces, Jackson, the former artillerist, recognized that his batteries of smoothbores could not silence the longer ranged Federal guns. There was not going to be any easy crossing at the White Oak Bridge.

The enemy's evidence of disorder in the retreat was not reflected in the steady strength exhibited across the swamp. Infantry could not cross the swamp in force without a bridge and, with the enemy's artillery commanding the crossing, no bridge could be built. Soon the Federal gunfire began to break over the battery at the crossing, designed to keep the woods clear of sharpshooters, and it was only a matter of time before those guns would be wrecked. Jackson sent an order to recall the battery. That was his last order of the day. It was then approaching three o'clock.

Gunfire and light musketry could be heard four miles away, where Longstreet had commenced his action in response to Huger's battery opening at two-thirty. Jackson sat down on a log in the woods to the right of the road and there the apathy, through which he had briefly broken, reclaimed him. Gone was the good humor of his approach to the field and the flare of excitement at making the crossing. The picture of stupor, he slumped on his log while his subordinates hurried to various parts of the field to try and effect a crossing of the creek. As on June 26, when he reached Hundley's Corner, Jackson's depleted organism reacted to a not readily soluble problem by rejecting it.

10

At some period during the afternoon Jackson wrote a short letter to his wife, showing the turn of his thoughts to home. "I do trust that our God will soon bless us with an honorable peace, and permit us to be together at home again in the enjoyment of domestic happiness. . . ." She must put aside fifty dollars for church purposes. "I would like very much to see my darling, but hope that God will enable me to remain at the post of duty until, in his own good time, He blesses us with independence. . . ." He mentioned that her sister's husband, D. H. Hill, was with him.

Harvey Hill was down at the creek, trying to hold a detachment at the work of rebuilding a bridge. Hill had gotten skirmishers across the creek, where they were picking off enemy sharpshooters in the woods and protecting the working party from rifle fire. But the gunfire from the enemy's artillery kept breaking over the crossing and Hill could not hold the men to their work. The aggressive spirit was lacking.

Tom Munford sent a message that the cowpath crossing he had used was negotiable for infantry. He had skirmishers on the south bank of the creek, and the enemy appeared unaware of their presence. Jackson paid no attention to the message.

Then Wade Hampton appeared in person. Recovered from his wound and his former brigade incorporated in the Light Division, Hampton had been given temporary command of Jackson's 3rd Brigade after Colonel Fulkerson had fallen mortally wounded at Gaines's Mill. (Later Hampton would be transferred to the cavalry, where he was to find his proper sphere.) The massive South Carolinian had been an individualistic type of bear hunter: instead of shooting the beasts, he had fought them with a knife. Using his woods experience, he had found a crossing farther to the left, where the solid footing of the approaches would support a foot bridge for the infantry. Jackson told him to build the bridge.

Hampton had men cut trees on the plateau, where the sound would not attract the enemy, and carry the logs to the crossing. He returned and told Jackson the bridge was ready. Jackson sat for a moment as if he had not heard him. Then he arose and walked away.

Early in the afternoon Brigadier General A. R. Wright, of Huger's division, completed his trip north of the swamp where the New Road intersected the White Oak Bridge Road slightly behind the position of Jackson's guns. Ambrose Ransom Wright, called "Rans," was a thirty-six-year-old Georgia lawyer who had enlisted as a private, was later elected colonel of the 3rd Georgia and had recently been commissioned brigadier. Since daylight he had conscientiously performed his useless reconnaissance from the rear of Huger's column on the Charles City Road to the flank of Jackson's, gathering prisoners, commissary and quartermaster supplies, and entrenching tools and some medical stores that had not been dumped into a useless mess. He reported to Jackson.

Jackson told him to return along the swamp and try to effect a crossing, as the enemy was "in large force and obstinately disrupting the passage over White Oak Bridge." Wright began his trip back with no other assignment than to find a crossing by which he could rejoin Huger. After a mile, his local guide showed him the lane to a crossing.

The bridge had been destroyed, and on the other side felled trees blocked the woods road. Knowing nothing of the country or of the alignment of the two armies, Rans Wright got two companies of skirmishers across the creek and followed the men as they climbed over the fallen timber along the road. On the edge of the swamp, he saw enemy pickets facing him behind a rail fence in back of a ditch. He ordered his men to open fire and advance. The enemy pickets, surprised, withdrew, and Wright's Georgians and Louisianians ran forward and seized the ditch.

From there Wright looked from the edge of the swamp into a meadow, where hills rose to his right. Along the crest of the open hill he looked at batteries and batteries of artillery and lines of infantry. He was in back of Slocum's division, which faced Huger's other three brigades to the west. Without knowing it, Wright had crossed Brackett's Ford, between Slocum on the Charles City Road and

Franklin at White Oak Bridge. He was no more than one mile from the crossroads of Glendale. Around four o'clock, this one brigade without artillery was at the heart of the Federal position.

Unknown to Wright, two brigades with supporting batteries were running from Sedgwick's division at Glendale toward the ditch occupied by his two companies. Franklin assumed that Jackson was shifting his attack from the White Oak Bridge to Brackett's Ford. It was the highest hour of opportunity for the execution of Lee's plan. Slocum was not aware of the presence of Wright's skirmishers across the swamp in his rear. Wright, without one gun, was very aware of Slocum's batteries commanding the meadow he would be forced to cross. Besides, where would he go? His orders were to rejoin Huger.

Wright was a tall, well-proportioned man, vigorous from early life on a farm and very soldierly-looking in his hard-worn uniform. But his previous experiences in the war had been limited to small, independent assignments, and he had no practical concept of the interlocking of large bodies in the maneuvers of armies. Simply deciding that he could not effect a crossing at that ford, Wright withdrew his skirmishers back across the creek. Unaware that two enemy brigades were massing near the spot he had vacated, Wright resumed his westward march. Three miles farther on, he found a cowpath that led to another ford, Fisher's, and this he crossed without incident. At dark he reached the Charles City Road near Fisher's house, halted his brigade and reported to Huger.

At the same time, Jackson was sitting down to supper with his staff. While chewing, he nodded drowsily and his head fell forward. After a moment he shook himself into wakefulness and said, "Now, gentlemen, let us at once go to bed, and see if tomorrow we cannot do something."

This was Jackson's one admitted recognition of his collapse in command. His staff, unaware that they were watching a case of clinical exhaustion, were bewildered at their leader's stupor. None seemed to realize that, through Jackson's inertia, Lee's great chance had come and gone. Jackson was at that stage too removed from the realities to recognize that tomorrow was too late.

When Jackson and his staff went to bed, Franklin withdrew from the White Oak crossing and marched on toward the river.

Only the dead were left on Frayser's Farm and Nelson's Farm and the Whitlock woods near the deserted crossroads at Glendale.

II

A mild controversy has continued over whether Jackson could or could not have crossed White Oak Swamp. This is a fruitless *if*. He need not have crossed the swamp in order to effect the battle. Infantry, even attempting to establish a bridgehead at Hampton's footbridge, and infantry and guns supporting Wright at Brackett's Ford, with the continuation of the bombardment at White Oak Bridge, would beyond speculation have profoundly affected the action at Glendale.

The threat of the pressure at Brackett's Ford would have retained there the two brigades Sedgwick had sent from the center and then recalled, as well as the brigade from Slocum later moved to support Kearny's right. The threat on Franklin's flank would have retained the two brigades he sent late to support the center.

In the realm of speculation, the big *if* would have been the consequence of five less brigades at Glendale when McCall broke, at the same time that pressure presented threats on the right and rear. The issue was not dependent on what Jackson might or might not have achieved: the issue was decided by his physical inability to do anything. General Franklin said, "It is likely that we should have been defeated . . . had General Jackson done what his great reputation seems to make it imperative that he should have done."

CHAPTER FOURTEEN

The Last Day

O N THE HOT, clear morning of July 1 the generals gathered on the roads near Glendale, where stillness lay over the battle-fields. Lee could not hide the effort in self-control required by the familiar façade he presented to his generals. D. H. Hill, no admirer, said, "He bore grandly his terrible disappointment of the day before." Longstreet, writing of this fine period in their relationship, said, "The disappointment . . . in the failure of the combination ordered for the 30th was noted by those who were near him, while the composure with which it was borne indicated the grander elements of character, and drew those who knew his plans and purposes closer to him."

The composure was entirely on the outside. The galling frustration had to be released, and Lee directed it to the enemy. He no longer thought as a strategist. He thought only of striking McClellan once more before he got away.

In the strategy of Lee's plans, McClellan was already away. Nothing remained except an aggressive pursuit that might inflict sufficient punishment to prevent the bulk of McClellan's army from reaching the protection of the gunboats. No reconnaissance had been made of the enemy's line of retirement. Stuart had not returned from the White House, and Lee lacked the cavalry for a reconnaissance in force. From maps and a general knowledge of the country, Lee and his generals assumed McClellan would make a stand on Malvern Hill, the one strong position between Glendale and the river.

D. H. Hill possessed some first-hand details of the strength of the natural fort of Malvern Hill. The Reverend L. W. Allen, an observant citizen of the neighborhood, had given Harvey Hill a disheartening description of commanding heights, difficult approaches, and an open plateau on which McClellan's guns could sweep in a vast half circle. Hill, having nothing to prove about his combativeness, ventured to give Allen's description to Lee, adding, "If McClellan is there in force, we had better let him alone."

It was Longstreet who answered. Laughing, he said, "Don't get scared, now that we've got him whipped."

As Lee said nothing, Harvey Hill formed the opinion that the commanding general shared Longstreet's attitude and believed the enemy to be demoralized. Lee's actions seemed motivated more by his own suppressed frustration than by an appraisal of the enemy. Standing on the road down which McClellan had slipped through his fingers, Lee seemed not to think beyond getting the available troops at hand formed in some order to push after McClellan in force. In his tightly held impatience to achieve one concerted action, he ignored the probabilities in the caliber of performance that could be expected from the generals.

The only two, Longstreet and A. P. Hill, who had consistently fought their troops with maximum effectiveness, were both unavailable. Their divisions were cut up and exhausted. Between two and three in the morning, the men had been pulled out of line and relieved by Magruder's travelers of the day before.

"Prince John" himself had then reached such a high state of nervous excitement that many observers thought he was drunk. The day before, his agitation had been so apparent to his staff that Major Brent had acted as their spokesman in inquiring if the general felt all right. When Magruder asked why Brent thought he might not feel well, the solicitous major said he had never seen him act this way before.

"What have you seen me do different from my usual habit?"

That was Brent's opening. "Well, General, I hope you will pardon me but I have never seen your usual calmness so much lost by an extreme irritability, sometimes exhibited without an apparent cause, and hence I inferred you must be feeling badly."

"Well, Major, you are right," Magruder had replied with the simple candor that aroused affection in those who knew him intimately. "I am feeling horribly. For two days I have been disturbed in my digestion, and the doctor has been giving me medicine. I fear he has given me some morphine in his mixture, and the smallest quantity of it acts upon me as an irritant. Besides that, I have lost so much sleep that it affects me strangely. But I fully appreciate your kindness in speaking to me, and I will endeavor to regain my self-control."

Then, after already having marched his troops hard, he had spent a maddeningly useless day hurrying to support the uncooperative Holmes, and finally shuffled back through the dusk and early evening to arrive after the battle was over. He personally supervised the placing of his worn-out men on the ground evacuated by A. P. Hill and Longstreet. He slept one hour, his second hour's sleep in seventy-two, and was up at sunrise and on his horse without breakfast. Major Brent brought him some bread, which the great gourmet ate while sitting in the saddle.

Lee, having previously passed over Magruder for the pursuit, now chose the unnaturally exhilarated man as one of the two generals to cooperate with Jackson. The other was Huger. During the morning of July 1 Huger had already shown that his performance the day before represented all that might be expected of him. In the early morning he had advanced two brigades, Armistead's and Wright's, toward his right — on the ground where Featherston had fallen wounded in stretching Longstreet's left the day before — for an attack *that* day. While he was preparing this movement, twenty-four hours late, Huger learned by a message from Longstreet that the enemy was long gone from his front.

When Lee was planning his assault, heavy-girthed Huger had not ridden as far as Glendale, where the other generals were gathered. But Lewis Armistead, in advancing his brigade two miles on a "blind road" in feeling for the enemy, had reached the Long Bridge Road on the battlefield of the day before. Seeing Lee nearby, Armistead reported to the commanding general. Lee ordered him and Wright, whose brigade was following, to cross to the Willis Church Road to join Jackson and Magruder in the movement on Malvern Hill. By this impulsive decision, the two brigades went forward separately, detached from any command. Huger, undisturbed about the disappearance of these two brigades, was approaching the then crowded crossroads with Mahone and Ransom, and the movement forward had started before Lee ever saw him at all.

Jackson, with four straight failures since his arrival at Richmond, had that morning, after rebuilding the bridge over White Oak Swamp, crossed Whiting's two brigades, followed by D. H. Hill's division and his own division, again in the rear. One of the points of speculation over Jackson's performance during the Seven Days has been his sparing of his own division during the battles and marching. Jackson's division sustained only 208 casualties, one tenth of one per cent of the losses. If he did feel his own division had been hard used in the Valley, and preferred to hold it in reserve, this use of his troops was unrelated to his personal behavior.

Riding at the head of Whiting's column, Jackson passed the Glendale crossroads early in the morning, moved through the lines of Magruder's troops and halted a short distance down the Willis Church Road. It was there that Lee, accompanied by Longstreet, rode over from the Long Bridge Road to meet him. Magruder was then beginning to form his resting troops into columns of march, and A. P. Hill, very solicitous of his men, remained with his own brigades. Lee made no references to Jackson's failure to force the White Oak Bridge crossing, and Jackson offered no explanations. Their brief conversation was limited to the simple plan of advance.

Jackson was to lead the pursuit down the mostly south-running Willis Church Road toward the point where it turned obliquely to climb the rise of Malvern Hill. On contact with the enemy he would presumably deploy according to the enemy's disposition. Ewell's division, having returned from Bottom's Bridge, had rejoined Jackson's force. Jackson's right was to be supported by Magruder and the two brigades from Huger's division, those of Armistead and Wright.

Considering Jackson's failure to cooperate with Magruder only two days before at Savage's Station — indeed, his failure to cooperate in any action — and Lee's dissatisfaction with Magruder's performance at Savage's Station, this loose arrangement could have represented no more than a hurried effort by Lee to advance his freshest troops. In the same hurry, the crude logistics employed in troop movement would have been recognized by an amateur. Nineteen brigades from the commands of Jackson, Huger and Magruder — thirty thousand men in columns of four, with guns and ambulances — would permit rapid movement only in the vanguard on the single, narrow road. At this stage of getting troops in motion on a pursuit, Lee, despite D. H. Hill's opinion, could not have been committed to an assault against a forbidding position which he had not yet reconnoitered.

Wanting to attack, he would seem to have ordered the advance more in hope of developing the possibilities than in determination to attack regardless of the conditions. In his self-confident opportunism, Lee perhaps felt he could exploit any segment of the terrain or weakness in the enemy's disposition after his force was deployed on the field. This supposition is based both on his limited orders, restricted to pursuing the enemy, and on his subsequent behavior. But the men moving out understood the purpose to be an assault, although detailed orders had not then been evolved.

2

As Lee surmised, McClellan had taken a defensive stand on the ramparts of Malvern Hill only because his army could not escape without a fight. The last of his four thousand wagons had not reached the River Road until the end of the day before. Seven serpentine miles of a sandy road lay between the train and the entrance to Berkeley plantation, with another long mile on an early-eighteenth-century road to the river landing. McClellan had hoped the seven divisions left at Glendale would hold another day, in order to complete the removal of his supplies to Harrison's Landing on July 1.

His generals had retreated from Glendale during the night before receiving orders. McClellan wrote Adjutant General Thomas at 2:45 the morning of July 1, "I was sending orders to renew the combat tomorrow, fearing the consequences of farther retreat in the exhausted condition of the troops . . . when I learned that the right [Franklin at White Oak Bridge] had fallen back after dark and the center was following."

As a matter of fact, Slocum withdrew from the Charles City Road without notifying his pickets. Mahone claimed he failed to suspect that Slocum was gone from his front because of the presence of the pickets, who later surrendered.

During the morning of July 1, McClellan wired Thomas that his army had retired to the new position, Malvern Hill, and said, "I dread the result if we are attacked today by fresh troops. If possible, I shall retire tonight to Harrison's Bar, where the gunboats can render more aid in covering our position."

He wired Flag Officer Goldsborough at Fort Monroe for "every combat or other armed vessel suitable for action to be sent at once to this vicinity. . . ." He excused his urgency on the grounds of "the extreme exhaustion under which I am laboring." In every message, he said that his army was "wearied" and "worn-out."

Call it "change of base" or any other euphemism, McClellan was frantically seeking the sanctuary of the river, sending pleas in all directions to save his army. He covered every message with the excuses of the troops' physical collapse and the enemy's overwhelming numbers. "We have failed to win only because overpowered by greatly superior numbers," he wrote of the Battle of Glendale.

His officers knew the army had been attacked only by the divisions of Longstreet and A. P. Hill, combining scarcely eighteen thousand, and knew they had not been overpowered by anybody. Heintzelman and Sumner had been reluctant to leave the field at Glendale. Franklin had withdrawn the rear guard at White Oak Swamp on the sensible assumption that Jackson and Huger could not be depended upon to remain inert the second day. Had McClellan commanded on the field, he could have supported Franklin in a holding action along the swamp and with the nearby corps of Keyes and Porter delivered a heavy counterattack the next morning down the Long Bridge Road. Observers on his staff believed this to be a great opportunity for McClellan.

Keyes and Porter were already posted from Malvern Hill to Haxall's Landing to save the passage of the wagon trains. What was McClellan saving the wagons for? Supply wagons were to support the army in the field, away from a base. The navy could have erected a new base on the James River without the presence of one soldier. Then, what was he saving his army for? His casualties were already passing the Federal losses at the two-day Battle of Shiloh, the combined losses of both sides at Seven Pines, and it looked like he might be confronted with another battle.

On July 1 McClellan wrote, "we only failed to win," when he had not tried to defeat the enemy since, on the approach of Jackson on

June 25, he had decided to withdraw from Richmond rather than fight to preserve his line of communication with the White House. On the impregnable position of Malvern Hill, within a few miles of transports, he was concerned only with making one more holding action until the army could reach final safety under the gunboats. Yet, with his heavy guns making a fort of those heights, his army could not be considered in danger from a pursuing force in which every brigade had been engaged and whose artillery was demonstrably inferior.

McClellan's course had been charted when he first wrote Washington, at Jackson's approach, that he would sell his life as dearly as possible in saving the army against the defenders of Richmond. But he was only saving himself from the commitment to a battle for decision.

In actuality the campaign forced upon him had already become decisive. In saving his army from commitment to a decisive battle, he was not saving it from a decision. The campaign had been lost with his first backward step from Richmond, and it could have been retrieved only by turning upon Lee in the open. Shunning a battle in the open, McClellan, with his extraordinary capacity for self-delusion, had convinced himself that he was achieving a worthwhile objective in reaching the James River.

In making this achievement the more heroic by recounting the obstacles overcome — the men "completely exhausted" and the losses "very great" in the "very severe" fighting — he seemed not to realize he was attributing superhuman qualities to the enemy. By implication, Lee's men were not exhausted, though most of them had marched twice as far as the bulk of McClellan's army and borne the more taxing strain of assault. Having been "severely punished" in each assault, as McClellan correctly stated, here they came on as if unaffected by their heavier losses in the severe fighting.

McClellan could not explain the Confederates' supposed freshness by the imaginary numbers Lee had to draw upon, for his soldiers knew they had been fighting the same troops all the way. Nor is it likely that McClellan believed Lee's cut-up, poorly fed troops were in better shape than his. He was playing out his role of the "nation's savior" with, at last, no one to blame except the fates as represented by Lee's malevolent and disembodied pursuers.

For once his enemies in Washington were uninvolved. True, he suffered the effects of what had gone before — the autocratic interferences, the cat-and-mouse game over McDowell, the enmity of the secretary of war and the current machinations of the Radical cabal in trying to get him removed from command. The effects had removed McClellan from the realities of his assignment in an attempt to protect his status, but his retreat to the James River could not be blamed on any acts of the government.

Washington rallied to his desperation. Ships were rushed to Harrison's Landing with supplies, five thousand fresh troops were on their way and messages were dispatched to Halleck in the West for possible reinforcements. The government had done its worst before. McClellan's attempt to postpone his date with destiny was entirely his own response to a counterthreat, and in rationalizing the postponement his actions had become directed by the delusion of achievement in reaching the James.

In drawing up his still powerful army on Malvern Hill, McClellan did not act like a general who feared to be overwhelmed. With his army all together again and the wagons safely on their way to a new base, he seemed relaxed as he assumed more control than on any previous field. Late the night before, on learning that the troops were withdrawing from Glendale, he had ridden from Haxall's Landing to Malvern Hill to give instructions for the posting of troops to Chief Engineer Barnard and Brigadier General Humphreys of the engineers. During the morning, with his staff and several general officers, he rode over the field inspecting the lines and the posting of the guns.

His front line, facing north, stretched across the plateau for about one half mile on the flat, cultivated lands of the Crew and West farms. The Willis Church Road, climbing the steep slope to this crest, crossed between the two farms. On the left the Crew house and its outbuildings perched near the edge of the cliff which, facing west, commanded a wheat field below — on the Federal flank — as well as the River Road beyond. Porter's corps was formed from the Crew house to the Willis Church Road, with sixty guns sweeping all approaches up the quarter of a mile of open hillside.

On the right of the road, where the West house faced the Crew house, stretched Couch's division of Keyes's corps, with its right sup-

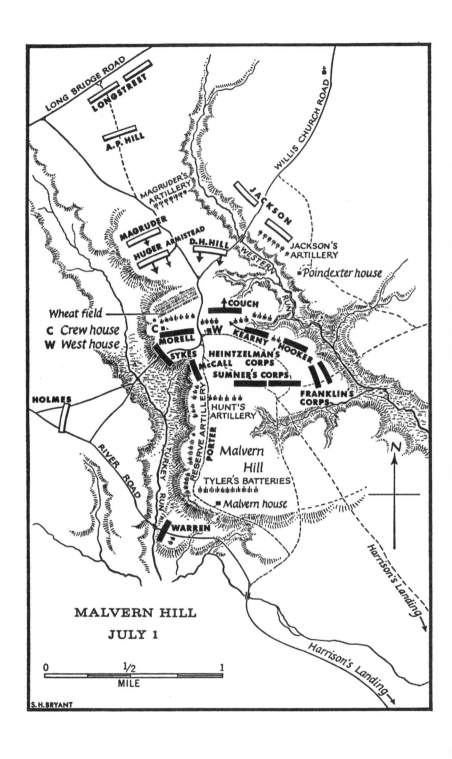

LONG BRIDGE ROAD

LONGSTREET

A. P. HILL

WILLIS CHURCH ROAD

MAGRUDER'S
ARTILLERY

JACKSON

MAGRUDER

HUGER ARMISTEAD

D. H. HILL

WESTERN

JACKSON'S
ARTILLERY

Poindexter house

RUN

Wheat field
C Crew house
W West house

COUCH

C.
W

MORELL

KEARNY

HOOKER

SYKES

HEINTZELMAN'S
CORPS

McCALL

SUMNER'S CORPS

FRANKLIN'S
CORPS

HOLMES

RESERVE ARTILLERY

HUNT'S
ARTILLERY

PORTER

TURKEY RUN

Malvern
Hill

TYLER'S BATTERIES

Malvern house

N

WARREN

RIVER ROAD

MALVERN HILL

JULY 1

0   1/2   1
MILE

Harrison's Landing

Harrison's Landing

S. H. BRYANT

ported and extended by Heintzelman's corps. On Heintzelman's front the ground rolled away to the right in rough undulations toward Western Run, another of the marshy banked creeks. At Heintzelman's right, Western Run, angling to the southeast, was about one and a half miles across from the bluff near the Crew house. Heintzelman was in turn extended and supported by Franklin's corps.

Sumner's corps was posted in reserve on the right side of the road, considered the more vulnerable by McClellan and the engineers who had reconnoitered the ground. Franklin's corps, turned to front northeast behind Western Run, faced heavily entangled woods on the opposite side of the stream, which provided protection to approaching troops.

Brushy woods also crossed the base of the hill on the right side of the road, giving advancing troops protection closer to the slope there than to the slope rising to the Crew house. Seven divisions were committed to the West house side of the road to two on the Crew house side, as the Federal generals reckoned the bluff to the west of the Crew house formed an unassailable flank. However, the open level of the compact field made possible the quick shifting of troops and gun batteries.

The superb artillerist Colonel Henry Hunt had the guns from the artillery reserve strategically posted, some in line and some in reserve on the Crew house side of the road. Across the whole front, the batteries consisted mainly of rifled Parrott guns, deadly in massed fire against the shorter ranged Confederate smoothbores. Along with the rifled guns were batteries of bronzed Napoleons for antipersonnel fire. On the right of the road, to greet any enemy infantry emerging from the woods that grew at the foot of the slope, Hunt posted a murderous battery of 32-pounder Howitzers (6.4 inch).

Most comforting of all to McClellan was the presence of fourteen of Colonel Tyler's siege guns — 4½-inch Rodman rifles, 8-inch Howitzers, 30-pounder Parrotts, and two of the long-ranged 10-pounder Whitworths. With the range of the siege guns, Hunt placed them safely back from the front lines around the seventeenth-century red brick Malvern house, the former mansion serving as a hospital. McClellan must have felt fairly confident to commit to battle those cherished weapons, as none could have escaped capture in a breakthrough. The gun crews had toiled hours to haul those heavy pieces by teams from the Chickahominy, and it had taken the men all of the night before to get them into position.

Satisfied with his survey and the enemy's slow pursuit not having developed, McClellan returned to Haxall's Landing and his true interest. He conferred once more with Captain Rodgers to, he said, "select the final location for the army and its new depot."

With the base then selected, McClellan returned again to Malvern Hill, where the opening firing had commenced. The commanding general gave command of the Crew house front to Fitz-John Porter and established himself on the other side of the road beyond the West house, "seeing more cause to feel anxious about the right." McClellan was there, not issuing orders, when the gray figures were glimpsed in the woods beyond the base of the hill, the columns of men moving under great bursts of fire from the Federal guns.

3

McClellan's army, with its nearly year-old organization, had shown itself capable of a self-operation not possible in the hastily assembled groups commanded by Lee. Lee's heterogeneous force depended totally on his leadership, and on that hot Tuesday the new commanding general was feeling the strain of striving to effect coordinated action between units in which one or more of the parts continually failed to cooperate. Lee asked Longstreet to ride along with him toward the enemy's position, and Longstreet said that Lee was "feeling unwell and much fatigued."

While they were riding with Jackson's advancing columns, Lee showed a flash of his inner frustration to Jubal Early. Brigadier General Early, just recovered from the wound taken at Williamsburg, had been assigned Elzey's brigade in Ewell's division after Elzey was wounded at Gaines's Mill. A West Point-educated Virginia lawyer and strong prewar antisecessionist, Early was one of the bitterest haters of the forces invading his land. An aggressive man, Early told Lee he was worried that McClellan might escape them.

"Yes," Lee said with strong feeling, "he will get away because I can not have my orders carried out."

Lee was referring to what had already happened. Since at that time the pursuit was progressing according to Lee's hurriedly given orders, the remark could indicate that he held no strong hope for the pursuit. Longstreet inferred that, after viewing the enemy's position, Lee was undecided about attempting an assault.

The sequences of Lee's study of the enemy's positions on Malvern Hill are not clear. From Glendale the Willis Church Road ran two and a half miles to the foot of Malvern Hill. A scant half mile before the wooded base of the hill was reached the upper stream of Western Run crossed the road and angled southeast in forming the line of flank on McClellan's right. The usual minor jungle lined the creek banks and grew very densely for about a mile to the right of the road. To the left of the road, the large clearing of the Poindexter farm stretched between the fringed banks of Western Run and the forest to the north. At around ten o'clock Whiting's two brigades, leading Jackson's force, turned left off the Willis Church Road about a half mile from Western Run and moved down to the Poindexter farm from the north. Whiting reported that he was deploying at eleven o'clock.

Behind Whiting, Harvey Hill's five brigades followed the road to Western Run and turned right, off the road, the men forcing their way through the mesh of vines until they reached the edge of the woods near the foot of the hill. Around noon, Hill's troops were going into position on the approaches to the foot of the Federal right side of the slope. From Ewell's division, Taylor's brigade formed to connect with Whiting and D. H. Hill. Ewell's other brigades and all of Jackson's division began to turn off into the woods on both sides of the road as they came up and moved to reserve positions behind Whiting and Hill.

Also around noon Armistead's and Wright's brigades, separated from Huger, came onto the field by themselves. Armistead, in the lead, had not followed Jackson's long columns on the Willis Church Road. On his own initiative he had moved through a loosely parallel woods road that brought him out on Hill's right while Jackson's troops were still crowding the main thoroughfare. In finding a crossing over Western Run through the barrier of entwined creepers and vines along the creek, Armistead emerged in a protecting ravine. Using its cover as a passage, Armistead and Wright reached the bottomland beyond Hill's right, looking up at the Crew house about one mile away on the Federal left side of the slope.

All of this movement, beginning with Whiting's turn off the Willis Church Road, had been made under constant artillery fire from the crest. Damage was not heavy, but casualties came steadily in the bedlam of the shattered woods and gun batteries were brought forward with extreme difficulty. The Confederates observed that the heaviest fire came from the Federal right, in the West house area, and recognized that McClellan regarded the approaches from either side of Western Run as his more vulnerable front and flank.

Whether it was before Whiting began to file toward the Poindexter farm at ten, or while the troops were moving to positions, some time late in the morning Lee and Longstreet took their sober-ing look at the enemy batteries ranged on the heights. Then Lee said that he would reconnoiter to their left — the Federal right — and ordered Longstreet to accompany Magruder and the two brigades with Huger to their position on D. H. Hill's right. There he was to make a reconnaissance of their front and report to Lee "the feasibility of aggressive battle."

After Longstreet rode off on his assignment, there is little to indicate what Lee did. Staff officer Long said he made "a careful reconnaissance," without stating where he reconnoitered. As Lee never revealed any knowledge of the ground, and as he parted from Longstreet to ride across the Federal right, it can only be presumed that he made a cursory tour of the Western Run area where Jackson was forming. Later in the afternoon he was seen with Jackson in the yard of the Smith house, where artillerists were moving their guns from the Willis Church Road into a cross-country lane. As this was well after Longstreet had returned with his report, nothing suggests any communication between Lee and Jackson about a possible assault on the Federal right.

The famous collaboration which later developed between Lee and Jackson was not working at Malvern Hill. Lee may have retained faith in Jackson's potential capacities, but on July 1 he asked nothing that would employ his initiative or judgment. It was on this day that Longstreet emerged as the "Old Dependable." Showing no wear or tear from the five days of fighting, cheerful and combative, the big soldier made an enterprising start on his responsible assignment.

The responsibility Lee gave him at Malvern Hill laid the basis for Longstreet's belief in his ascendancy over the commanding general.

As Lee never again fielded an army composed of such undependable parts, his future reliance on Longstreet was largely on his dependability as a field commander of his own troops and he did not turn to Longstreet in any sphere of strategy. This happened to be the area of Longstreet's ambition, though the results of his suggestions at Malvern Hill had been most unhappy. While he could not be held accountable for the chain of mishaps, Longstreet, with his own troops uninvolved, had been very sanguine in his opinion of what could be accomplished. It is true he never erred on that side again, but Lee never asked his opinion again.

When Longstreet returned from his reconnaissance trip around noon or somewhat later, his comprehensive report contained two parts. First, Magruder had not followed Jackson on the Willis Church Road. On Lee's map the road read "Quaker" Road, and Magruder had been ordered to proceed down the Quaker Road. This Magruder had done. He had consulted three privates of the Henrico (County) Southern Guard, men who had grown up in the neighborhood, and one of them, S. B. Sweeney, had accompanied him as a guide. Later, Magruder presented notarized depositions from the three natives stating that Sweeney was qualified to know the Quaker Road when he saw it and had guided Magruder upon it.

The road was little used, led away from Malvern Hill, and poor "Prince John" revealed his shattered condition when he continued on a vanishing pathway on which obviously no troops had moved before him. He would be forced to retrace much of his march and could only reach the Malvern Hill front by a country road that, running off from the Long Bridge Road, intersected the Willis Church Road at the foot of the Crew house slope. As Armistead and Wright had taken a position on D. H. Hill's right, where Magruder had been ordered, Lee sent Magruder orders to come up on the right of those brigades of Huger's. Except that it would be after three o'clock before Magruder's men began reaching the field, no harm had then been done.

The second part of Longstreet's report concerned his findings on the feasibility of opening an aggressive battle. The intersection of the Willis Church Road with the unnamed road which Magruder was to follow formed the apex of a triangle at the bottom of Malvern Hill. Armstead and Wright had formed in their ravine to the

Confederate right of the unnamed road. Back of Armistead and off the road, Longstreet had discovered a clearing that rose to an elevation as high as the Federal hill at the Crew house. Longstreet climbed this elevation and, with what was evidently some excitement, surveyed the whole Federal position.

By counting batteries, he estimated eighty Federal guns in the tier across the crest (a very close appraisal) and located the batteries of the siege guns in the rear, though he could not count those. He did not attempt an estimate of Hunt's reserve batteries between the front tier and the Malvern house, which were then silent. He observed that most of the visible batteries were trailed to Jackson's approach toward the Federal right. As Longstreet absorbed this scene, he envisioned the effect of forty or sixty massed guns firing from where he stood on the flank of the Federal batteries. In conjunction with this cannonade, he saw that the Poindexter farm provided ground for eighty to one hundred guns on Jackson's position. Massed guns on these two positions could bring an overwhelming crossfire to bear on the Federal batteries.

This was a heady moment for Longstreet. Stimulated by acting in effect as Lee's second in command, he translated the picture in his imagination into reality. Longstreet believed the crossfire of guns from the two positions could throw the Federal batteries into disorder and open the way to an infantry assault up the quarter of a mile of open hillside. "The tremendous game at issue called for adventure," he later wrote of the decision that sent him riding back to Lee with the suggestion for massing guns on the Poindexter farm and on the clearing behind Armistead.

Longstreet did not state as a fact that the Federal batteries would be thrown into disorder. However, his conviction convinced Lee of the probabilities of disordering the enemy's guns sufficiently to permit his infantry to make one more effort to wreck McClellan's army short of the James River. Lee accordingly gave the orders to move up the guns and told Colonel Chilton to write an order to go to the division commanders.

Lee's order was the product of an exhausted mind, directed only by his goad to strike the enemy before he slipped away. Chilton, with curiously unmilitary wording for a professional soldier and awkward wording for anybody, wrote: "Batteries have been estab-

lished to rake the enemy's lines. If it is broken, as is probable, Armistead, who can witness the effect of the fire, has been ordered to
charge with a yell. Do the same." It was signed by the assistant
adjutant general.

When the couriers rode off with copies of this order around one-
thirty, command ceased on the field. The malfunctioning parts of
the whole were left to operate without a single guiding control. Lee
remained on the Willis Church Road behind Jackson's lines, probably to see what Jackson did with himself. Longstreet was sent to
the elevation he had discovered to supervise troop dispositions, as
Magruder came up, and the posting of batteries. He was not given
and did not assume responsibility of the field. The assault hung on
the decision of a brigadier who, by chance of being separated from
his division and by the chance of march, occupied a position with
the clearest view of the Federal lines.

4

Lewis Armistead, forty-five, and the son of a U. S. Army general,
had resigned from the Old Army with the rank of captain, about
average for his class. He had not graduated from West Point, leaving, the story went, for hitting Jubal Early on the head with a sugar
bowl. He was a warm man, with many friends in the Old Army,
and a bold fighter. In the Mexican War he had twice been brevetted
for gallantry, and Pickett, when he later became Armistead's division
commander, called him "the bravest of the brave." Appointed colonel of the 57th Virginia, Armistead had operated on Huger's minor
fronts and had not been commissioned brigadier until April. Suddenly he was the key figure on the field.

Armistead made no reference in his report to having received
orders to advance with a yell when he decided the Federal batteries
were disordered. Soon after his troops were in position, he sent back
for gun support, and this seems unrelated to Longstreet's plan for
massing forty or more guns in the clearing. Armistead was only one
hundred yards from the fence across the Crew property, which
stretched over the bottomland beyond the foot of the hill. Along the
slope of Malvern Hill, sharpshooters from Berdan's regiment were
firing from behind stocks of wheat, and across the whole front skir-

mish fire crackled intermittently. Rans Wright, sharing this isolated position with the joint force of about 2500 men, also seemed unaware of any general plan when he brought up the first battery to support the infantry.

This was Grimes's battery, of Huger's division, and it contained only two rifled pieces. These guns opened sometime around one o'clock and Lee's order did not go out before one-thirty. Moorman's battery, also of Huger's artillery, joined in with Grimes's section, and the main effect of these six guns was to draw fire of about forty Federal guns to Armistead's position.

While the gun crews and artillery horses of Grimes and Moorman were falling under the bursting fragments of heavy shells, by some one's order Willie Pegram brought in his rebuilt battery from A. P. Hill's division. By the time Pegram's gunners were firing with any effectiveness, Moorman began to retire. A solid shot banged into one of Grimes's two guns, and the surviving cannoneers drew off the other piece. Before long, Willie Pegram had only one gun going. Pegram, who had left the University of Virginia as a shy, retiring scholar, had found his true vocation in the handling of heavy weapons in action. His spectacles clouded by smoke, Pegram was serving the single piece himself around three o'clock.

About this time, Longstreet appeared near the elevation and Armistead asked him for more artillery support. Longstreet said he would send two batteries, but, Armistead reported, "If sent, I never saw or heard of them."

At this point, Longstreet's accounts begin to grow vague and contradictory. Yet, placed in the context of his actions in relation to the action on the field, his two versions are very revealing.

General Lee had sent Chilton to lead Magruder to position on Armistead's right and, as Longstreet wrote in his 1896 narrative, "I left that part of the order to be looked after by General Lee's recognized staff . . . and I was ordered back to locate the batteries." He wrote that he found only eight guns posted and that Magruder told him he would supplement these by thirty guns under Colonel Stephen D. Lee, chief of Magruder's reserve. "With this understanding I went back to headquarters, made my report, and was permitted to go back to my command proper."

In the report he submitted to Lee four weeks after the battle

Longstreet wrote, "A little after 3 P.M. I understood that we would not be able to attack the enemy that day, inasmuch as his position was too strong to admit of it." He does not say he reported this to Lee, or that he reported to Lee at all. Lee, in his report, makes no mention of Longstreet except that he "took no part in the engagement" — referring to his division.

If Longstreet did report to Lee in the Smith yard off the Willis Church Road, he could not have told him both that he understood no attack would be made and that Magruder said he would supplement the eight guns on the elevation with thirty of his own, since this implied Longstreet's expectation of the opening of his suggested cannonade. Then, as Longstreet wrote in his narrative that his orders were "to locate the batteries," he would scarcely consider that he had executed these orders by hearing Magruder say he would order up his guns. At three o'clock neither Magruder nor any of his troops had reached the field, and Colonel Lee's batteries were far back among the toiling columns of foot soldiers.

Whatever were the actual details of Longstreet's actions after he reached the elevation around three o'clock, both of his versions — against the background of the developments — indicate that he recognized the quick, complete failure of the artillery crossfire and removed himself from any further participation in the plan he had suggested. When Longstreet left the elevation, as he wrote later, eight guns had been posted, but eight guns were not firing. He was there at a time to observe the disastrous effects of the Federal counterfire on those guns. After seeing that, for a certainty he did nothing to post any batteries or attempt to bring any on the field. Whether or not he reported to Lee, Longstreet left the field and joined his own command.

By the time Longstreet talked with Armistead, Jackson's guns had, for their part in the crossfire, already revealed they could accomplish nothing. Two batteries, one from Jackson's division and one from Whiting's, opened the firing planned for a mass cannonade. They were soon silenced. Two more batteries from Jackson's division took a closer position to the enemy, under the screening and partial shelter of the woods bordering Western Run, and these guns managed to maintain a fire. One of the batteries was commanded by William Poague, a young Virginia lawyer destined to become a superior battalion commander and then regarded as highly by Jackson's command as was Pegram with A. P. Hill. But eight guns where eighty were planned could contribute nothing significant toward preparing the way for an infantry advance.

From between one and two o'clock, when Grimes's two guns opened behind Armistead, and the three o'clock period when Longstreet left the clearing, Lee and Longstreet separately realized that the attempt to disorder the Federal batteries was futile. In the collapse in command, neither of them thought of their own reserve artillery, more than eighty guns and some of the best batteries in the army, commanded by General Pendleton.

Pendleton's reserve seems to have been forgotten through the whole campaign. During the north side fighting, Pendleton moved the train of guns up in support of Magruder. During Savage's Station, the aging rector had a fever and the day, he said, "passed by me as a quiet Sabbath." During Frayser's Farm, he "employed the forenoon in ascertaining the movement in progress and adjusting to them the arrangements of my own command." These arrangements did not include advancing any batteries. The afternoon, while Wilcox's and Field's infantry were dying in front of Randol's battery, "was given to making sure of three large rifle guns for use" the next day. The next day, July 1, was spent "by seeking for some time the commanding general, that I might get orders. . . ." Lee was less than two miles from Glendale on the main road. The rest of the day was devoted "toward ascertaining what could be best done with a large artillery force, and especially if any position could be reached whence our large guns might be used to good purpose."

Pendleton was one of the generals who have to be quoted to be believed. As an impossible *if* to suggest the significant effect of one individual on a battle, the total nature of Malvern Hill would have changed if Pendleton had had his eighty guns in position and Hunt had been off with the Federal reserve. It was true that Lee gave Pendleton no orders; neither did McClellan give Hunt any. While Lee, in his exhausted preoccupation, and Longstreet, in the quick deflation of and withdrawal from his second-in-command status, never thought of the reserve artillery, "Granny" Pendleton — as he was referred to by irreverent youngsters — never explained exactly

where he did look for those gun positions. No one saw him anywhere near the battlefield.

Here is revealed the awkwardness of Lee's necessarily hasty reorganization of the artillery, which made General Pendleton nominal chief of artillery and used Colonel Long to perform many of
the actual functions. Long, working through chief of ordnance Alexander, made sizeable achievements during the three weeks of reorganization, but he was given no authority when the army took the
field. At Malvern Hill, no one was responsible for bringing forward
guns, and fifty batteries were available exclusive of Pendleton's reserve. When the few guns in action proved ineffective, the crossfire
was simply written off as a failure.

As it was in Longstreet's official report that he wrote, "I understood we would not be able to attack the enemy that day," Lee evidently gave the impression that no assault would be made. From all
other contemporary reports it must be inferred that Lee, accepting
the failure of the crossfire and fiinding no way to get at the enemy,
had yet not reconciled himself to McClellan's escape. Not planning
any attack on the heights, he would not abandon hope that some
opportunity might develop.

Longstreet, in his 1896 narrative, described an action which has
usually been accepted as fact with no supporting evidence. He wrote
that Lee sent for him to ride with the commanding general "in
search of a route by which the enemy's right might be turned."
After a hasty reconnaissance, he wrote that Lee ordered him to move
up the reserves, his division and A. P. Hill. While the two divisions
were being put in motion toward the point of a turning movement,
the sound of battle on Magruder's front caused them to halt.

Longstreet made no reference to any of this in his report. He
stated that at five o'clock he had received a message from Magruder
calling for reinforcements. Longstreet wrote in his report that he
then ordered A. P. Hill to Magruder's support. Substantiating this,
Hill reported that the two brigades he started toward Magruder's
position were the only brigades of his division who moved after
being relieved in the line before dawn. None of Longstreet's brigadiers reported any movement at all on July 1. Beyond the fact that
neither Lee nor any of the generals involved reported the beginning

of a turning movement to the enemy's right by those two fought-out divisions, Jackson had seven fresh brigades in reserve in the area from which such a movement could be made.

Omitting this unlikely episode, the probability is that Lee would have fought no aggressive battle at Malvern Hill except for two separate circumstances unrelated to his plans or intentions. One circumstance was the existence of the one-thirty order for a general advance at a yell from Armistead's brigade. When the crossfire failed to disorder the Federal batteries, Lee apparently assumed the order no longer applied, or forgot about it. The other quite isolated circumstance was that Berdan's skirmishers, elated at the apparent success of their guns' execution, made a spontaneous advance against Armistead's line. The sequence that followed brought on a general assault.

5

The heavy shells that created such damage to Grimes's and Pegram's cannoneers standing in the open were less effective against the infantrymen huddled in woods. The exploding fragments from Civil War shells were large and few as compared to modern shrapnel, and many of the contact shells penetrated the earth fairly deeply before the burst, which was partly or wholly smothered. The men could see the solid shots coming, like bowling balls in the air. Canister and grapeshot fired point-blank were the deadly antipersonnel weapons against troops assaulting in the open.

Long-range gunfire on Armistead's and Wright's troops in the wooded ravine bore hardest on the nerves, and both generals complimented their men on standing steady under the avalanche. In the inescapable casualties, the proportion of wounded to killed was much higher than against rifle fire or canister. Where five wounded to one killed was about average in battles, under long-range gunfire the proportion would run as high as twenty-five wounded to one killed, with a number of the wounded actually injured from falling branches or a blow from a spent fragment.

When Berdan's sharpshooters advanced against Armistead's front sometime after three o'clock, the Virginia regiments, far from being badly hurt, were relieved at finding an enemy at whom they could shoot back. Not only did they shoot, but three of the regiments came storming out of their wrecked woods to get at the other foot soldiers. Berdan's relatively thin line retired rapidly. The Virginians, keyed up at their release, ran after the enemy sharpshooters before their own officers could hold them back. The men ran a quarter of a mile before their uneven lines halted, beneath a rise on the approaches to Malvern Hill, to straighten their lines and reload.

Gray-haired Armistead, a well-knit man who always stayed right up with his troops, joined the men under the little brow and immediately saw it would be suicide to go nearer the enemy batteries. As it would be equally suicidal to return without Berdan's sharpshooters screening them, Armistead decided to remain there in the advanced position. This action was entirely local, although Armistead drew parts of Wright's brigade forward on his right. Then Rans Wright joined Armistead and the two brigadiers looked over the situation.

It was getting on to four o'clock, and the generals agreed they could hope for nothing in artillery support. Wright said that "further demonstrations against the enemy in his stronghold were utterly futile and highly improper" for their small force, and he and Armistead "ordered the firing to cease." Thus far, the only result of Berdan's impulse was that parts of two brigades had advanced closer to the enemy, where the men would have held their precarious lodgment until retiring at dark.

Then Magruder rode close to the battle lines and was given the battle order Chilton had written at one-thirty. " . . . Armistead, who can witness the effect of the fire, has been ordered to charge with a yell. Do the same." The Confederate artillery firing was nearly all over when Magruder reached the field, and he had never known anything about the supposed effects of the massed crossfire. He saw that Armistead had made an advance, with or without a yell, and the unstrung Magruder evidently wanted to make a charge. After receiving Lee's reproaches for Savage's Station — unjust, as he thought, with some grounds — and two days of exhausting marches to no purpose, topped by being told — again unjustly — that he was on the wrong road, Prince John was impelled to heroic action.

Since his ordeal had begun in the early morning of June 26, Magruder had not appeared so exhilarated. Indeed, his high excitation looked like drunkenness to those observers quick to judge their fellows. Magruder could not have taken much more than a passing glance at the field, swept by fire from the practically unchallenged Federal guns, before rushing off a staff officer to Lee. There is no record of the message Captain Dickinson delivered to the commanding general, but Lee's answer makes it evident that Magruder represented Armistead's local action as a successful advance and also gave the impression that his troops had arrived in force.

Thinking with the hope that would not die, Lee seized the opportunity of an assault without investigating the actual conditions confronting the general known to be, at the least, mecurial. Quickly he gave an order for Magruder which Captain Dickinson thought it wise to put in writing.

"General Lee expects you to advance rapidly. He says it is reported the enemy is getting off. Press forward your whole line and follow up Armistead's success. I will have Mahone's brigade in the place just occupied by Colonel Anderson. Ransom's brigade has gone on to reenforce General Cobb. . . ."

The references to the two brigades with Huger, Mahone and Ransom, moving to support units of Magruder's indicates that Captain Dickinson's message to Lee contained details of troop movement. The report that the enemy was getting off probably had come from Whiting, who had mistaken some distant movement he observed on Malvern Hill for a section of wagons and troops in retreat. If Longstreet had been riding with Lee, he would have known (as he never did) that this order was sent to Magruder, and would not have introduced the episode of a turning movement having been halted at hearing Magruder's unordered battle open.

Before Dickinson returned, Magruder had looked at the sad artillery situation and was told by Armistead that Longstreet had promised to send up two batteries some while before. Magruder rushed off an order for Colonel Lee to hurry forward the reserve guns. When Dickinson brought Lee's message, everything became reduced for Prince John to those orders: "General Lee expects you to advance rapidly. . . . Press forward your whole line . . ."

Gun or no guns, the infantry must advance at once. His own six brigades, separated in moving from the Long Bridge Road and suffering heavily from stragglers who simply could walk no farther, were coming up at intervals with none yet in position to attack. Nevertheless, General Lee expected him to advance *rapidly*, and the commanding general would be given no cause to reproach him as he had for not pursuing vigorously at Savage's Station.

Mahone's brigade had come on the field, crossing the front by the ravine, where they had encountered soldiers taking their ease under the shellfire, their backs propped against the front wall of the ravine. These were the regiments of Wright's brigades that had not joined in the rush after Berdan's skirmishers. These resting regiments would join Mahone to begin the assault, gathering up Armistead's advanced regiments on the way.

Magruder's point of attack was the area of the Crew house, about three hundred yards west of the Willis Church Road, the point McClellan considered invulnerable. Just west of the Crew house and outbuildings, the bluff sliced steeply down to the wheat field below, on Magruder's right, and near the house this bluff cut around Malvern Hill in a sheer cliff to the front, on the slope Magruder was facing. Magruder's purpose seemed to be to get his men across the wheat fields, both on the Malvern Hill slope and on the bottomlands to the west, to reach the clifflike rises to the west and to the western end of the front. He evidently figured the men would be safe from the guns on the crest once they started climbing the cliff.

At quarter to five o'clock he gave the order to attack.

6

In response to the glory of the charge, three brigades alone rushed across the open field through the merciless gale of metal, Armistead's advanced regiments joining their fellows with Wright and Mahone as they rushed by. Bareheaded, Rans Wright waved his hat on his swordpoint. Under the late sun, the rays glinted on the bright rifles most of the men carried at trail arms, as they were not close enough to the enemy to shoot. Half a mile and more they struggled ahead, the lines of puffing soldiers thinning with every stride that took them nearer the gun batteries. Far behind, where Willie Pegram's one gun fired, Magruder's brigades were deploying onto the field.

The survivors of the open passage reached the bluff to the west, no more than three hundred yards from the batteries, and Armistead's men clambered under the brow of the cliff on the front. Those who had not been struck down or fallen out had won a partial safety from the guns, but Porter's corps of infantry was waiting for them behind the batteries. And not one of Magruder's brigades was yet moving to their support.

The next movement came unexpectedly on their left, where the Willis Church Road crossed between the farms. D. H. Hill's brigades, emerging from the protection of the woods, were moving toward the open slope in the cohesive lines Hill always brought to attack.

Harvey Hill had been talking to Whiting, sitting his horse with his leg thrown over the pommel and smoking a cigar, when he heard the sudden yells raised by Mahone's and Wright's troops. No part of a signal, the high scream was merely the battle cry the men always gave when going in. As the screeching came from the direction of Armistead, the designated signal giver, D. H. Hill assumed the one-thirty order was still in effect and galloped back to order the assault he believed to be doomed. With his right across the road, the bulk of his battle line advanced on the left of the road in the area of the West house.

Against Hill's compact regiments, the Federal batteries got in their destructive antipersonnel work, the grapeshot and canister spraying in lead slugs as though fired from giant shotguns. It was, as all through the Seven Days, Confederate infantry against Union guns, spirit against iron, and spirit was not enough in the open ground to be crossed. At the foot of the slope, halfway to the guns, the toll grew heavy.

On reaching the effective range of the enemy rifles, the brigades began to halt where the undulations of the ground gave the men places to hug the earth. Only Colonel John B. Gordon, the ramrod Georgian taking in Rodes's brigade, tried to breast the iron storm. At two hundred yards from the gun muzzles his Alabamians were being cut to pieces where the Federal rifles of Couch's division crackled through the rolling smoke. Then he and his men too took such shelter as they could find.

With all the casualties sustained, the impetus of their rush brought Butterfield's brigade to the support of Couch's left, along the road, and two fresh brigades from Sedgwick's division replaced segments of Couch's right. D. H. Hill sent back a desperate call to Jackson for reinforcements to hold his line of advance.

Jackson had shown no more initiative than on any other day. To protect the eight guns in action, Whiting's two brigades — the heroes of Gaines's Mill — were drawn in a line from the Willis Church Road across the Poindexter farm. Later supported by Trimble's brigade from Ewell's division and the brigade from Jackson's division temporarily under Wade Hampton, these troops were never engaged. With nothing to protect the guns from, the soldiers of the four brigades spent the hot afternoon crouched in hollows and along the edge of woods protecting themselves from the plunging fire of the enemy's batteries.

When Harvey Hill went forward, Jackson evidently did not consider his troops to be included in the order to advance, and sent no orders to Whiting. Chase Whiting, in his resentment against Jackson, did nothing without orders. The soldiers west of Western Run remained awed observers of the fate of their fellows with Harvey Hill.

When Hill's call for support came, Jackson had already ordered forward brigades from Ewell's reserve division. Ewell's men moved onto the crowded Willis Church Road into the backflow of the battle. Looking at the ashen-faced soldiers, their mouths blackened from powder, groping their way to the rear, Ewell's survivors of Gaines's Mill were not inspired with any enthusiasm to hurry. Early's brigade did not reach the field until after dark.

Late, Jackson moved out Trimble's brigade from Whiting's left, and doughty old Trimble hurried his men to the darkening slope where Hill's fragments were making their way out. Trimble wanted to have a go at the guns, but Harvey Hill talked him out of it. Enough blood had been sacrificed at those batteries.

While Hill's lonely assault was being repulsed at heavy cost and Huger's three thinned brigades continued to fight from the perch under the brow of the Crew house hill, Magruder sent forward the first of his brigades, Cobb and Barksdale of his own division. According to the Federals, the Georgians and Mississippians advanced in beautiful order under their red flags, the essence of the drama of the charge.

At the same time Colonel Lee was trying against desperate odds to bring his batteries into line. The rough, narrow passage of his lane was in the direct fire of the Federal batteries, and men and horses fell before the guns reached the clearing. Heaving and straining through the obstacles, the cannoneers brought four howitzers and two rifled guns into a clearing, and opened fire.

It could not be expected that howitzers would do much damage at the distance. Yet, with all the difficulties that beset the few Confederate batteries that got into action during the afternoon, Federal officers reported casualties among their troops. Brigadier General Butterfield, with Porter's corps between the Crew house and the road, complimented his men on the patience with which they endured the enemy's "severe" artillery fire.

General Lee had ridden over to Magruder's field headquarters when he heard the advance of Mahone, Wright and then Armistead. When he reached the field, judging from a later remark, he must have been appalled to discover the actual conditions. Fewer than eight guns were in action; the remnants of three isolated brigades clung to the brow of the distant hill almost under the gun batteries; two brigades advancing to their support were faltering under the gunfire from the crest, and Magruder's other brigades were drifting to their left — away from the point of attack — fumbling wearily forward through the woods.

Magruder reported that Ransom's brigade had refused to advance in support of the other three brigades from Huger's division. Ransom wrote him, at 5:45, "General Huger is present and directed me to say that . . . any order to officers or troops of his command must pass through him." His Old Army training remained unimpaired as Huger revealed he was still determined not to expose himself to any mistakes by acting without specific instructions.

Lee sent Huger an order to advance Ransom to Magruder's right. Seeing McLaws's two good brigades drifting in the woods, Lee tried to straighten them out to oblique to the right. He sent a hurried message to Magruder: "The commanding general directs that you press the enemy on your right.* McLaws is going in fresh."

---

* The reproduced order in *Official Records*, volume XI, part 2, page 678, reads, "press the enemy's right." The enemy's right was on the opposite side of the plateau, toward Western Run. If Lee's message actually did read "the enemy's right," Magruder understood the intended meaning to be his own right.

McLaws's two brigades, Kershaw and Semmes, combined no more than 1500 rifles when, drained by stragglers, the men reached the foot of the hill. Misjudging directions in the woods, the brigades had not obliqued far enough to the right and the lines emerged in the wheat field on Magruder's left and Harvey Hill's right. By then Cobb and Barksdale had ceased trying to advance their weakened lines and halted where the field was strewn with the dead and wounded of those who had gone before them. "Tige" Anderson's brigade went no farther. With no support on their right, and Hill's shattered regiments retiring on their left, McLaws's small force contributed nothing except more casualties before the men were pulled back.

On their left, Toombs's brigade of "Neighbor" Jones's division straggled out of the woods behind the melee on Hill's front, with the only result that of causing an altercation — which led to a challenge from Toombs — between the irascible Hill and the undisciplined politician.

When the sun had gone down and dusk was gathering over the field, Robert Ransom brought the only brigade to the support of the first attackers, still fighting around the edge of the hill near the Crew house. On sheer determination, the remnants of Armistead, Wright and Mahone had climbed and fought their way to within seventy-five yards of the guns, close enough to pick off gunners and horses.

One group came over the crest, near enough for an artillery officer to start shooting with his revolver, and Colonel Hunt ordered that battery back for safety. The accurate rifle fire from the fragmented groups around the edge forced back Griffin's brigade, with more than five hundred casualties, and stood off three supporting regiments that were rushed to their front. Six times men carrying the flag of the 62nd Pennsylvania fell. Six times Armistead gathered his men for one more assault.

The four brigades, after Ransom came up, were the troops Huger had wasted the day before, and the men, from brigadiers to privates, seemed impelled to vindicate themselves. In glory, in its meaning to them, they did. One year and two days later, Armistead led his same brigade to the enemy batteries on another hill, at Gettysburg, and fell mortally wounded with his hand on a Federal gun.

Generous Colonel Hunt later reported, "The battle frequently trembled in the balance. The last attack was very nearly successful [and] we won from the fact that we kept our reserves in hand for just such an attack. . . ." Contradicting Porter, who characteristically claimed "driving . . . the disordered . . . retiring masses . . . with the bayonet . . . ," Hunt stated to the Joint Committee on the Conduct of the War, "I cannot say that our victory was so very decisive."

Hunt himself brought the greatest disorder to the retiring troops on the front of the slope by opening on them with the 32-pounder howitzers at close range. On Porter's area along the brow of the crest, Armistead's survivors and the six hundred men remaining in the combined forces of Wright and Mahone spent the night where they were. After nightfall detachments of soldiers went in search of water and of their wounded, guided by the cries and groans in the darkness. Soon the men saw the lanterns of enemy parties moving toward their wounded. General Wright said, "Friend and foe freely mingled on that gloomy night in administering to the wants of wounded and dying comrades."

Confederate losses over the whole field exceeded five thousand; the Federal were less than three thousand.

7

After any failure Lee, as commanding general, invariably assumed full responsibility. That night he could not forbear to ask Magruder why he had attacked.

Captain Lamb, a cavalry courier who had worked that day with Magruder, had just spread a blanket on the ground for the general, to whom he was to become loyally attached. He heard Magruder answer Lee forthrightly, without apology. "In obedience to your orders, twice repeated."

It was not in Lee to say that he had ordered the attack because Magruder's message had led him to believe that Armistead had advanced in force and that Magruder's command was in position with artillery support. Nor could he explain to his contemporary and college mate that execution of an order to attack assumed the assaulting force to be ready and its commanding general in control of the units. Unmanageably excited himself, Magruder was incapable of exerting control over separate moving bodies. Ten available brigades had attacked in three weak and isolated advances, with a certain uncanny timing inadvertently achieved when D. H. Hill had attacked during the interval between Magruder's first and second advances.

Lee, not conceiving the role of an operations officer who would have spared his decisions based on inaccurate information and ignorance of his units' condition, worked to develop the subordinates whose cooperation, through initiative and discretion, could be depended upon in his system of careful strategic planning and loose tactical control. Something in his character made it necessary for Lee to work with men who wanted responsibility and were capable of assuming it. In the collapse of his great plan, Magruder could not be singled out, nor any one, nor any combination of individuals. Lee had gone after McClellan with what he had had, and only the soldiers had been ready.

After Lee left Magruder, there is no record of his talking with any other general that night. By then, judging from his subsequent reorganization, he had developed doubts about Jackson. When he regrouped his forces, the bulk of the army was given to Longstreet's command, and Jackson was returned to detached duty with only his original Valley force — his own division and Ewell's.

Later, when bad blood had developed between Longstreet and A. P. Hill, and Jackson was to go into action, Hill was transferred to Jackson. With this independent force Jackson began to perform up to and even beyond expectations. Because his Valley magic was recaptured in independent command, detractors attributed his Seven Days' failure to an unwillingness to work, as was said, "in harness" with others. But when Jackson resumed independent command, he had recovered from the apathy of stress fatigue. When next he operated under Lee in cooperation with others he demonstrated, along with willingness, the highest aptitude of any of Lee's generals for achieving concert of action.

That night, in the midst of the horrors of Malvern Hill, few would have predicted a brilliant future for the glum-faced general who had been such a disappointment. Not even his staff offered any explanations. The Reverend Mr. Dabney, himself full of complaints at his hard use, recorded that Jackson had made his way "slowly and wearily" to the rear when darkness fell. His colored servant had prepared a pallet in the confusion of wagons and stragglers, where the general, after taking something to eat, fell asleep while the Federal guns still roared.

The continuing blasts from the crest of Malvern Hill long after nightfall convinced some of the experienced men that the enemy would retreat again in the morning. Stillness gradually settled over the slopes where Harvey Hill's men had charged late in the afternoon and where Jubal Early's late-arriving reinforcements were bivouacked among the dead. Early was sure he heard the rumble of heavy wagon wheels moving toward the river. At one o'clock Jackson's division officers, having brought some order to their units, awakened the general to ask if he had any orders for the morning.

"No," Jackson mumbled, "I think he will clear out in the morning."

The general, famous for his starts "at earliest light," returned to his pallet with that summation of the last battle of the Seven Days. Though no one on the field was aware of it then, the campaign was over.

CHAPTER FIFTEEN

Aftermath

THE SEVEN DAYS Battle Around Richmond officially lasted six days, from June 26 to July 1. An attempt has been made to count McClellan's limited action of June 25 on the Williamsburg Road as the seventh day, but the series of battles was recognized by the participants as the execution of Lee's General Orders No. 75. In Lee's orders to his troops after the battles, his reference to the Seven Days read, "The battle, beginning on the afternoon of June 26th, above Mechanicsville . . ." While this established Mechanicsville as the opening action, Malvern Hill, the last battle, was not the last day. July 2 was the day McClellan ended his retreat at the river and could constitute a seventh day in the completion of Lee's counteroffensive.

June 2 began with a heavy mist over the slopes of Malvern Hill, where the rows of dead and wounded outnumbered the survivors of Armistead, Wright, Mahone and Ransom on their lonely perches on the hill below the Crew house. The only fresh troops on the field were the men of Jubal Early's brigade, in sole command of the silent wheat fields. Behind Early every road and lane from the battlefield was jammed with wagons, ambulances, gun limbers and caissons, and thousands of stragglers asking where their regiments were. In front of Early, along the crest which the Federal guns had occupied, an unmenacing body of cavalry observed the awakening Confederate camp. Behind the horsemen Early saw some infantry. As all the fearsome batteries were gone, it was apparent the remaining force was there only to cover a retreat.

When the Confederate details advanced on the hill in search of wounded, the cavalrymen fired a few perfunctory shots. A Maryland regiment in the woods along Western Run answered the fire. When the cavalrymen backed out of rifle range, the firing immediately ceased. Soon Federal parties ventured forward looking for their own wounded. "The parties from both armies," Early wrote, "gradually approached each other and continued their mournful work without molestation from either side, being apparently appalled for a moment into a cessation from all hostile purposes by the terrible spectacle presented to their view."

It was a ghastly field, and at ten o'clock the rain began to fall, heavily, steadily, drearily all through the day. Fundamentally, the men of both armies had had enough of fighting. Critics have pointed out that the disorder of Lee's army exposed the scattered forces to a counterattack that could have carried McClellan's army all the way into Richmond. One fresh Federal corps could have advanced down Malvern Hill and created chaos in the area. But even if the Confederates had not fired a shot, no force could have moved through the jam of vehicles and men on those soupy roads as far as Glendale. In any case, McClellan did not have a fresh corps.

Dragging through the mud of the River Road, McClellan's army was "greatly exhausted," according to his medical director. One fifth of the men were sick when the army reached Harrison's Landing. The Sanitary Commission rushed medical supplies, tents and nurses to the plantation landing. After 6000 men had been shipped away on transports, Dr. Jonathan Letterman reported that 12,795 sick remained in the camp. Scurvy was breaking out before the men reached Berkeley. Dr. Letterman wrote that the "full effects" of the hardships of the Seven Days had not been reached when the army arrived at the river. Though sick were not listed as battle casualties, the bulk of these medical casualties of the campaign were as lost to McClellan as were the wounded and added a burden to the movement of the normally overweighted army.

It could just as well be said that a fresh corps with Lee could have routed McClellan's weary columns strung out in the mire of River Road where the army could not bring the big guns into action. The dependables of Longstreet and A. P. Hill were started vaguely on a pursuit after the enemy cavalry had vanished from Malvern Hill. But by the time the attenuated men had slushed two miles through the rain, it was pointless to try to push them farther. Longstreet himself, with none of the cheerfulness with which he had confidently started the day before, showed a churlish ill humor.

The rain turned the weather so cold that General Lee had a fire lit in the Poindexter house, where the parlor served as an indoors headquarters. Jackson joined him there, sitting in front of the fire. President Davis came, and Jeb Stuart reported in person for the first time since he had ridden away from the army on the morning of June 28, the day after Gaines's Mill.

Stuart and Lee's handling of him have also come in for criticism. In following McClellan's line of communication toward the White House, Stuart could not have halted short of the Pamunkey River base, which he reached during the morning of the 29th. With the uncertainty of the location of the Federal units, he could not have abandoned the north side of the Chickahominy that day. In fact, the next day Lincoln personally wired General John A. Dix, who had replaced Wool as commander at Fort Monroe, on the assumption that the north side had been abandoned by the Confederates.

In urging action north of the Chickahominy, Lincoln believed the reports of the thoroughness of the evacuation of the White House, commenting that the enemy would have "nothing to subsist upon." On the contrary, Stuart's troopers were living high off the hog and — while collecting valuable material of war — the abandoned food supplies might have been a reason why Stuart was not in a hurry to leave. Chiefly, he received no orders from Lee to return until a message from Chilton arrived at three-thirty on the morning of July 1.

Stuart commented that Chilton omitted the time the message was sent, and figured out it had been written around nine o'clock on the night of June 30, after the Battle of Frayser's Farm. The only reason Lee offered for not ordering him back twenty-four hours sooner, after Savage's Station, was that he had kept the cavalry guarding the lower fords of the Chickahominy. None of them knew that Silas Casey's five thousand garrison force had embarked at the White House nor the size of the force with Stoneman's cavalry, which had fallen back to Williamsburg.

The criticism suggests that Stuart's cavalry, if present on the 30th, would have prevented the uninterrupted passage of McClellan's wagon train from White Oak Swamp to Haxall's Landing. Considering the guns and troops devoted to protecting this cargo, it seems doubtful that 1800 horsemen, armed with carbines and forced by the brushy country to operate on the roads, could have seriously impeded the wagons' passage.

Also, as Lee himself later gave "the want of timely information" as one of the reasons for his failure to destroy McClellan, this has been accepted as implying that Stuart might have supplied it — if properly employed by Lee. By the time Stuart could have reached the army after the 29th, Lee suffered no significant want of information on the enemy's movements.

Apart from the details, however, an impression remains that Stuart was not employed as effectively as he might have been. This impression is perhaps suggested by the effectiveness Stuart's cavalry showed later, when it had grown larger, when Lee was perfecting all his techniques, and Stuart was operating in open country.

On July 1, after making a customarily early start, Stuart reached the White Oak Bridge area in midmorning, when Jackson's command, to which he was assigned, packed the roads in the pursuit to Malvern Hill. Stuart was forced to retrace his route cross-country to the River Road west of the Malvern Hill area and did not reach the vicinity of Haxall's Landing until dark. After reporting to Lee in the Poindexter house on July 2, he pushed his troopers after the enemy. As a comment on what the cavalry might have accomplished on those enclosed roads, like tunnels through the woods, his riders were halted by two regiments of Daniel Sickles's infantry.

Stuart stayed on the heels of the retiring column, gathering up more discarded equipment and prisoners, the stragglers who could no longer keep up. When the rainy darkness gathered, Stuart's advance troops reached the entrance of Shirley plantation, the home of Lee's mother. Shirley was divided from Berkeley by Herring Creek and, as McClellan had established Herring Creek as one of his flanks, Stuart could go no farther. He did know where McClellan was, and this information he sent back to Lee.

Between Herring Creek and Kimages Creek on his flanks, and under the reassuring guns of the gunboats on the river, McClellan's drenched army came to its final halt on a plain which, one of the men said, had been "reduced to paste" by the passage of wagons and boots over the wheat fields and meadows. Transports began to land urgently needed food, as some men had received no rations for forty-eight hours and all had been badly fed compared to the accustomed diet in camp. That was the condition of McClellan's army one week from the day when, investing Richmond on two sides within five miles of its streets, he had planned to advance his lines on Nine Mile Road as a decisive step in his siege approaches.

In his relief at saving the army, the next morning McClellan wired Lincoln, "I have succeeded in getting the army to this place on the banks of the James River. I have lost but one gun, which had to be abandoned because it broke down. (The Confederates had captured more than forty on the battlefields.) An hour and a half ago the rear of the wagon train was within a mile of camp, and only one wagon abandoned. . . . I have not yielded an inch of ground unnecessarily, but have retired to prevent the superior force of the enemy from cutting me off and to take a different base of operations." In the last part of the last sentence, McClellan told the simple truth: there was nothing about a "change of base."

Later in the morning when he wired Stanton, McClellan had sufficiently recovered his poise to recapture the illusion that he had achieved a grand maneuver. In this self-delusion, he appeared actually to believe he had maintained his position of savior of the Union and that the government, in recognition of his achievement, would become more responsive to his demands.

"To accomplish the great task of capturing Richmond and putting an end to this rebellion, reenforcements should be sent to me rather much over than much less than 100,000 men. I beg that you be fully impressed with the magnitude of the crisis in which we are placed. We require action on a gigantic scale — one commensurate with the views I expressed in a memorandum to the President submitted early last August, when first ordered to command the Army of the Potomac. . . ."

McClellan refused to accept the reality that his retreat from Richmond, called by any other name, marked the end of his campaign to bring the war to a settlement. Yet a strain of wistful desperation ran in his harking back the previous year, when he had gone to Washington as the Young Napoleon and Lincoln had appeared to accept his plans for a decisive campaign. With the strain of desperation, his detachment from reality was reflected in a request for more than one hundred thousand reinforcements. Only the day before, Lincoln had written McClellan, in reply to his request for fifty thousand men at once, that the idea of sending him any considerable force promptly was "simply absurd." At the great house of the plantation where the Harrisons had enjoyed their long days of power, George McClellan retired into a world of his own.

2

While McClellan was convincing himself that his campaign had experienced a temporary digression, Lee had recognized within a week that it was all over. On the night of July 8, he ordered his troops to withdraw from their positions around Berkeley and away from the proximity of the enemy. On the various approaches to Richmond separate segments of the army built camps for a period of rest. There families could send or deliver boxes of food from home and garments to replace the worn uniforms in which the men had marched away. The next day General Lee rode on back to the quiet of the Dabbs house and began the reorganization for future campaigns.

"Prince John," with a final flurry of written representations, left for Texas, and on its boundless prairies managed to reestablish the elegance of his cuisine. Huger and Holmes vanished without fanfare. Longstreet's brigadier, Dick Anderson, was promoted to assume command of Huger's division; Lafayette McLaws took over most of Magruder's; Holmes's makeshift command was variously disposed of, with two of the brigades returning to North Carolina. Judgment was suspended on Jackson, as he was temporarily returned to semi-independent command. With Longstreet emerging as the big man, A. P. Hill revealed the most superior qualities as a combat soldier. His high-strung temperament needed control before his judgment could be trusted, but his very impetuosity could be useful, and he handled the well-conditioned troops of his new command with sureness at all times. D. H. Hill, who showed himself, as expected, to be a hard, skillful fighter, had been restrained by Jackson's torpid touch, and his enlarged division went on semidetached service.

The reorganization went forward rapidly during July, with most of the recuperating army retained in its camps between Berkeley and Richmond. Boastful Pope, with his new army in middle Virginia and the support of the Radicals, was threatening the Virginia Central while issuing proclamations and taking the first punitive measures against the civilian population in Virginia. Pope was the general Lee wanted to get at. He sensed that McClellan was through ("McClellan . . . is uneasy in his position") and a move against the fire-breathing Pope would, as Lee wrote, "change the theatre of war" to the frontier. There his army could threaten Washington. But as long as McClellan's army, also recuperating, remained on the James River, Lee could not move his army to northern Virginia. Lincoln and Stanton took care of that.

Lincoln had come down to Berkeley plantation on July 8, to interview McClellan and his generals, and probably to look at the army. McClellan, off in his private realm, took the occasion to hand the President a letter of what amounted to instructions on the policy of the war and how to prosecute it. Basically, he opposed the war policies of the Radicals as reflected in Pope's behavior, such as taking war to the civilian population and in running off slaves — "forcible emancipation." He particularly deplored the drift to Radical attitudes, with the introduction of slavery as an issue.

Not accepting the reality that he was an ex-hero and, hence, in no position to instruct the President, McClellan also failed to recognize the rise of the Radicals' power. McClellan's views already belonged to another time, an abandoned phase. Lincoln made no comment on the document, but the questions he asked would have indicated to anyone not as bemused as McClellan that the President had given up on the Peninsula Campaign.

Back in Washington, on July 11 Lincoln appointed a new general in chief of all the armies. General Henry W. Halleck, a military theorist of demonstrated unfitness for field command, was brought in from the West where his most significant contribution had been to stifle the aggressive Grant. He was a weak, fatuous man who essayed a politic role without the adroitness to play both sides against his own security. There seems little doubt that Halleck was brought on to Washington by Stanton to do a hatchet job on McClellan.

Halleck, having no stomach for the work, blundered through the drawn-out negotiations to bring the end with unintentional cruelty. His appointment was not announced to McClellan, who read of it in a newspaper from home.

To make it more difficult for McClellan to comprehend what was happening, Stanton had written him shortly before Halleck's appointment, "Be assured that you shall have the support of this Department and the Government as cordially and faithfully as was ever rendered man to man, and if we should ever live to see each other face to face you will be satisfied that you have never had from me anything but the most satisfying integrity."

In apparent support of this verbal assurance, Burnside's force abandoned its operations on the North Carolina coast and came by transports to Fort Monroe to cooperate, as McClellan was allowed to think, with the Army of the Potomac. It was during this period that McClellan had advocated the move to the south side of the James River, which Grant would be permitted to try two years later. Probably, at that point, nothing suggested by McClellan would have been acceptable. Besides, Lincoln and Stanton were determined to return the army to the Washington area, where they had wanted it all along.

With such increasing evidences of the way the wind was blowing as Lincoln's evasiveness about the employment of Burnside, the blow fell on August 3. Halleck signed the order directing McClellan to move his army from the peninsula to Aquia Creek. McClellan then understood that the purpose of the withdrawal was to transfer his army by units to Pope, Stanton's man. He wrote his wife that the government would probably "take the earliest opportunity to relieve me from command and get me out of sight."

McClellan also made a prophecy. "They are committing a fatal error in withdrawing me from here, and the future will show it. I think the result of their machination will be that Pope will be badly thrashed within ten days. . . ."

Within fifteen days after Lee was able to leave the peninsula to move his army against Pope, the darling of the Radicals was routed at Second Manassas and retired within the Washington forts. A victorious Confederate army was back on the Potomac, and the military situation was back precisely where it had been when McClellan was first called to Washington the year before.

3

There was a basic difference in the total situation: the period of the attempted settlement was over. Arbitration by arms had already drifted into a policy of subjugation by total war, soon to be followed by the expediency of the Emancipation Proclamation. This war measure did not "free the slaves." Ostensibly addressed to the Confederates, it only threatened uncompensated emancipation by force in the unoccupied regions in rebellion if the Rebels did not lay down their arms by January 1, 1863.

As a threat, it was meaningless. Most Federal forces had already put the policy into practice, as had the British during the Revolution. With subjugation per se the end, the obvious point of vulnerability in the Southern states was the plantations' labor supply. And where blacks were pitted against whites the threat of uprisings created uneasiness behind the lines, diverting manpower for the protection of isolated families or causing the abandonment of plantations feared to be unsafe for women and children. But the moral justification introduced with the pragmatic policy marked the end of the attempt to restore the old union; here began the Radicals' program of separating the region to be conquered from a new union.

With this program, to which the Proclamation appeared to give sanction, also began the indissoluble association of slavery and rebellion, with its implication that men fighting to be free of a political union were fighting to prevent the freedom of other men from slavery.

To Lee, and the other nonslaveholding, nonpolitical-minded professional soldiers among his generals, the changing policy only confirmed their convictions of the finality of the struggle to which they had committed themselves and their families' futures. Nor was the attitude behind the ruthless and wanton destructiveness of the enemy's soldiers on their land calculated to impress them with elements of morality in the invasion.

Lee's generals knew that former brother-officers in the U. S. Army, including Southerners, were no more dedicated to emancipation of slaves than they themselves were dedicated to maintaining slavery. No general in the war showed more contemptuous hatred of

Negroes than did Sherman, and his attitude typified that of a large proportion of Federal soldiers. Yet Sherman and other generals, and Lincoln himself in the late phases of the systematized destruction of total warfare, justified the sword and the torch as instruments of retributive justice and likened themselves to the agents of a vengeful Jehovah. Logically, this judgment carried out among a people who had permitted slavery to exist should have been extended into Kentucky, Maryland and Delaware, where slavery continued to exist unaffected by the Emancipation.

On the invaded ground, among the men reduced to their primal instincts by fighting for their lives in fighting to kill others, the added element of "moral coercion" merely gave sanction to the license already prevalent. Where men lay dying in the blood-spattered thickets and shadowed ravines, on the desolated farmland and in the abandoned farmhouses, the soldiers deciding the issue knew it was a decision of force against force.

Among the few who had recognized from the first that the Confederacy was engaged in a fight to the death, Lee was also among the few who recognized that time was not on their side. The changes in Washington that coincided with McClellan's fall from favor changed nothing in Lee's personal purpose of forcing a decision by defeating the enemy. McClellan's withdrawal from Richmond, followed by Lee's defeat of Pope at the Second Manassas, simply gave Lee the opportunity to execute his underlying purpose. He carried the war to the enemy, with the incidental hope of influencing England and France to recognize the Confederacy among the nations of the world.

While President Davis had faith that the right of a people to govern themselves (now called self-determination) would win his country recognition, Lee acted intuitively on the advice sent by the Confederate commissioner in France. John Slidell, the astute ex-New Yorker, wrote the State Department from Paris that nothing would impress the leaders of France and England except military victories. In hoping to deliver these impressive victories, Lee at no time operated with the limited intention of merely preventing a settlement.

No sooner had he cleared the Federal forces out of Virginia than Lee attempted the ultimate decision of defeating the forces of the United States on their own soil. In crossing the Potomac, Lee was profoundly influenced by the necessity of victualing and supplying his tattered, hungry army, as well as moving the battleground off Virginia's farmland. But the necessity coincided with his basic strategy when Lee attempted a counterinvasion before his army had physically recovered from its exhausting campaigns.

Though the Battle of Sharpsburg (Antietam) is usually regarded as marking "the high tide of the Confederacy," it was perhaps too late for the decision Lee sought after the Seven Days. The cost of the Seven Days and the Second Manassas had come too high, both in the losses in manpower and in the physical depletion among the survivors. In the battle that terminated this counterinvasion at Sharpsburg, Maryland, the Army of Northern Virginia encountered a stroke of ill fortune when a copy of Lee's general order, containing the detailed plans of march, fell into McClellan's hands. This loss of strategic advantage gave the decision to McClellan's numbers and superior artillery. While he could not defeat Lee in the stand-up fight along Antietam Creek, the exhausting battle forced Lee to retire to Virginia and ended his attempt at the decisive campaign which could win the Confederacy's independence.

From then on, Lee exerted no significant influence over the military policy in the East. The long rearguard action began within the contracting frame of Davis's defensive policy of resistance. After the acute emergency passed with Lee's lifting the siege of Richmond, Lee never again enjoyed that complete freedom from the President's authority.

When Lee moved north against Pope and then into Maryland, the decisions, though approved by the President, were wholly his, but Davis's interference with the organization of troops began as Lee's army drew away from the vicinity of the capital. In late fall when Burnside, McClellan's first successor, began an "On to Richmond" drive via Lincoln's favored overland route, Lee's decisions were affected by Davis's considerations for Richmond. By the spring of 1863 Davis had established complete authority over the military operations in Virginia, as everywhere else, and the concentration of detached garrisons into his own army ceased to be possible for Lee.

From then until the end, the controls of the increasingly neurotic President tightened until Lee was deprived of all freedom of maneuver. At the end, he was back where he had begun, penned up in works withstanding a siege whose result was made inevitable by arithmetic.

Though in the imponderables of war events might have taken a different direction if here and there different numbers had come up on the roll of the dice, as the course of events took shape, after the Seven Days Lee never again possessed the opportunity to win the kind of victory to affect the decision. Without attributing any prescience to him, it can be seen that Lee was a disappointed general in the midst of the elation over McClellan's withdrawal from Richmond. In two sentences, taken from two pieces of correspondence, Lee gave his total reaction to the battles. "Our success has not been as great or as complete as I could have desired," he wrote his wife, and in his report, "Under ordinary circumstances the Federal Army should have been destroyed."

What he had attempted as the battle for a decision proved to be a testing ground for Lee and his army. Neither Lee nor the unfamiliar weapon of the loosely organized force were ready to achieve the "success as complete" as he envisioned in his painstaking planning. Out of the crucible of the Seven Days, he molded an army that would be man for man the greatest fighting force ever on the continent. But when the weapon was perfected, and Lee reached the full flowering of his powers of command, he would no longer be fighting off only another army, or even other armies. Lee's Army of Northern Virginia was a personally designed, hand-wrought sword fending off machine-tooled weapons that kept coming in immeasurable, illimitable quantities.

Though the change in the nature of the war was influenced by the blind clash of the two armies at Richmond in late June, 1862, when the established government finally succeeded in imposing its physical superiority upon the dissident government, the period of the attempted settlement was not even a memory. For at the Seven Days, when the Army of Northern Virginia was born, the old America died, and the Union Lincoln and McClellan tried to restore became as lost in time as the traditional society Lee sought to preserve.

Significantly McClellan passed into history as the villain of the era, in contrast with — of all people — Edwin Stanton. Victim of divided objectives and political expediency, his most singly damning weakness was the absence of the forthrightness to write his government, as Napoleon had written from Italy, "I can not serve the country unless I have your complete and undivided trust." Yet, Lincoln dealt no more forthrightly with McClellan. But Lincoln had the power to stay in office to try it his way, and his side had the strength to wear out the other. Ultimately the success of his way led to misconceptions in the new Union about its origins, when moral coercion was used to justify and distort the use of armed coercion.

On the battleground in Virginia, a more forthright American attitude was illustrated: winner take all. For Lee, who always knew that force by any name was coercion, the failure to win decisively at the Seven Days ultimately meant that he would be among those who lost everything — even the honor of the cause of independence.

Never by written word nor recorded line of conversation did Lee suggest that he ever repined the order of events that had held him away from the field until the emergency was reached. But at the heart of his tragedy was the waste of his gifts until he was forced to rush an offensive before he was ready to command or the army to be led. The opportunity at the Seven Days — as great as was the victory that brought his emergence as the giant of the war — came too late, too suddenly, for it to be more than a victory that only postponed a decision to a more dreadful finality.

Acknowledgments

I WISH TO make grateful acknowledgment to Mr. John A. S. Cushman, my editor at Little, Brown; to Mr. John Melville Jennings, director of the Virginia Historical Society, and to its staff members, Mr. Howson Cole, Mr. James A. Fleming, Mr. Virginius Cornick Hall, Jr., and Mr. William M. E. Rachal; to Miss India Thomas, former regent of the Confederate Museum, and the assistant regent, Miss Eleanor Brockenbrough; to the staff of the Virginia State Library, particularly Mr. Milton C. Russell, Mrs. Pinkney Smith, Mrs. Lewis Causbey, and Miss Eudora Elizabeth Thomas; to Colonel H. W. K. Fitzroy, director of the University Center in Virginia; to Dr. W. G. Bean, of Washington and Lee University; to Mr. Francis L. Berkeley, Jr., and Mr. Robert Stocking, of the Alderman Library, University of Virginia; to Mr. Robert Waitt, of the Richmond Civil War Commission; to Dr. W. H. Stauffer, of the Richmond Civil War Round Table; to Dr. Chester Bradley, curator of the Jefferson Davis Casemate at Fort Monroe, Virginia; to Mr. N. E. Warinner, of Richmond, for guidance on ordnance and consultations on details of the Seven Days battlefields; to Lieutenant General Louis W. Truman, deputy commanding general of the Continental Army Command, for illumination on the comparison of Lee's staff with modern procedures; to Sir John Wheeler-Bennett, of Oxford, England, for the privilege of drawing upon his background on the history of staffs; to Dr. Beverly Randolph Wellford and Mr. McDonald Wellford, for their indispensable companionship in working the fields; to Dr. Harry Warthen, of Richmond, for advice on medical aspects of the armies; to Mr. Bruce Catton for consultations on McClellan and to Mr. E. P. Long for assistance in locating the segments in McClellan's siege train. For the factor of stress fatigue in Jackson's performance, I am indebted to Dr. David Markham and Dr. Dupont Guerry, III, of Richmond; to Dr. Theodore Sanders, of St. Louis; and to Mrs. June Huntley, medical librarian of the Medical College of Virginia, for her invaluable interest in supplying a bibliography on the study of stress.

CLIFFORD DOWDEY

Bibliography

IN THE GENERAL, selected bibliography no item is included which does not relate directly or indirectly to the action of the Seven Days or the action that led to it; this excludes some good books which have been useful in developing the total background of the armies and the times. In the *Official Records*, the bulk of the material on the Seven Days is in Volume XI, Parts 1, 2 and 3. Though items from the *Southern Historical Society Papers* have not been listed separately, the volumes were heavily drawn upon for personal sidelights on battles. A separate bibliography on the study of stress follows on p. 368.

Alexander, E. P. *Military Memoirs of a Confederate*. New York, 1907.
Annals of the War; Written by Leading Participants North and South. Philadelphia, 1879.
Battles and Leaders of the Civil War, 4 vols. New York, 1887-1888.
Beale, R. L. T. *History of the 9th Virginia Cavalry*. Richmond, 1899.
Bean, W. C. *Stonewall's Man — Sandie Pendleton*. Chapel Hill, 1959.
Berkeley, Henry Robinson. *Diary*. Edited by William H. Runge. Chapel Hill, 1961.
Blackford, Susan Leigh, compiler. *Letters from Lee's Army*. New York, 1947.
Blackford, William Willis. *War Years With Jeb Stuart*. New York, 1945.
Borcke, Heros von. *Memoirs of the Confederate War for Independence.* New York, 1938.
Bradford, Gamaliel. *Lee the American*. Boston, 1912.
Brent, Joseph L. *Memoirs of the War* . . . New Orleans, 1940.
Bridges, Hal. *Lee's Maverick General — Daniel Harvey Hill*. New York, 1961.
Bushong, Millard Kessler. *Old Jube — A Biography of General Jubal A. Early*. Boyce, Va., 1955.

Caldwell, J. F. F. *The History of a Brigade of South Carolinians.* (New edition) Marietta, Ga., 1951.

Casler, John O. *Four Years in the Stonewall Brigade.* (New edition) Marietta, Ga., 1951

Catton, Bruce. *Mr. Lincoln's Army.* Garden City, 1951.

Chamberlaine, William W. *Memoirs of the Civil War.* Washington, 1912.

Chamberlayne, C. G., ed. *Ham Chamberlayne — Virginian.* Richmond, 1933.

Clark, Walter E., ed. *Histories of the Several Regiments . . . from North Carolina.* 5 vols. Raleigh and Goldsboro, N. C., 1901.

Cockrell, Monroe F., ed. *Gunner With Stonewall — Reminiscences of William Thomas Poague.* Jackson, Tenn., 1957.

Cook, Joel. *The Siege of Richmond . . .* Philadelphia, 1862.

Cooke, John Esten. *Robert E. Lee.* New York, 1875.

Cooke, John Esten. *Stonewall Jackson.* New York, n.d.

Cooke, John Esten. *Wearing of the Gray.* New York, 1867.

Dabney, Rev. R. L. *Life . . . of Jackson.* Richmond and Philadelphia, 1866.

Dabney, Rev. R. L. *Papers, Repository University of North Carolina.* (Copies used at Alderman Library.)

Daniel, Frederick S. *Richmond Howitzers During the War.* Richmond, 1891.

Davis, Jefferson. *Rise and Fall of the Confederate Government.* New York, 1881.

Davis, Rev. Nicholas A., chaplain 4th Texas. *The Campaign from Texas to Maryland.* Richmond, 1863. Facsimile Reproduction. Austin, Tex., 1961.

Dickert, Augustus D. *History of Kershaw's Brigade.* Newbury, S. C., 1899.

Donald, David. *Lincoln Reconsidered.* New York, 1959.

Douglas, Henry Kyd. *I Rode With Stonewall.* Chapel Hill, 1940.

Dowdey, Clifford. *Death of a Nation.* New York. 1958.

Dowdey, Clifford. *Experiment in Rebellion.* New York, 1949.

Dowdey, Clifford. *The Land They Fought For.* New York, 1955.

Dowdey, Clifford. *Lee's Last Campaign.* Boston, 1960.

Dowdey, Clifford, ed., with Louis Manarin. *The Wartime Papers of R. E. Lee.* Boston, 1961.

Early, Jubal A. *War Memoirs . . .* Edited by Frank E. Vandiver. (New edition) Bloomington, Ind., 1960.

Eckenrode, H. J., Conrad, Bryan. *George B. McClellan, the Man Who Saved the Union.* Chapel Hill, 1941.

Eckenrode, H. J., and Conrad, Bryan. *Longstreet — Lee's War Horse.* Chapel Hill, 1936.

Eggleston, George Cary. *A Rebel's Recollections.* New York, 1875.

Eisenschiml, Otto. *The Hidden Forces of the Civil War.* Indianapolis, 1961.

Elliott, Charles W. *Winfield Scott* . . . New York, 1937.

Evans, Clement A., ed. *Confederate Military History.* 13 vols. Atlanta, 1899.

Fletcher, W. A. *A Rebel Private, Front and Rear.* (New edition) Austin, Tex., 1954.

Freeman, Douglas Southall. *Lee's Lieutenants.* Volume 1, New York, 1942.

Freeman, Douglas Southall. *R. E. Lee.* 4 vols. New York, 1934.

Gordon, John B. *Reminiscences of the Civil War.* New York, 1903.

Govan, Gilbert E., and Livingood, James W. *A Different Valor . . . Joseph E. Johnston.* Indianapolis, 1956.

Hamlin, Percy Galtlin. *Old Baldhead — General R. S. Ewell.* Strasburg, Va., 1940.

Haskell Memoirs. Edited by Gilvert E. Govan and James W. Livingood. New York, 1960.

Hassler, Warren W. *General George B. McClellan.* Baton Rouge, 1957.

Hassler, William Woods. *A. P. Hill.* Richmond, 1957.

Henderson, George F. R. *Stonewall Jackson* . . . (American one-volume edition) New York, 1938.

Hendrick, Burton J. *Lincoln's War Cabinet.* Boston, 1946.

Hood, John B. *Advance and Retreat.* Edited by Richard N. Current. (New edition) Bloomington, Ind., 1959.

Howard, McHenry. *Recollection of a Soldier and Staff-Officer.* Baltimore, 1914.

Hunton, Eppa. *Autobiography.* (Privately printed) Richmond, 1913.

Hyams, Harold M., and Thomas, Benjamin B. *Stanton* . . . New York, 1962.

Johnston, Joseph E. *Narration of Military Operations* . . . New York, 1872.

Johnston, T. Cary. *Robert Lewis Dabney.* Richmond, 1903.

Jones, J. B. *A Rebel War Clerk's Diary.* Edited by Howard Swiggett. 2 vols. New York, 1935.

Jones, Rev. J. William. *Peronal Reminiscences . . . of General Lee.* New York, 1875.

Lasswell, Mary. *Memoirs of Val C. Giles . . . 4th Texas.* New York, 1961.

Lee, Fitzhugh. *General Lee.* (New edition) Greenwich, Conn., 1961.

Lee, Robert E., Jr. *Recollections of . . . General Lee.* New York, 1904.

Loehr, Charles T. *History of the 1st Virginia Regiment.* Richmond, 1884.

Long, A. L. *Memoirs of Robert E. Lee.* Richmond, 1886.

Longstreet, James. *From Manassas to Appomattox . . .* Philadelphia, 1896.

McCarthy, Carlton A. *A Detailed Minutiae of Soldier Life in the Army of Northern Virginia.* Richmond, 1882.

McClellan, George B. *McClellan's Own Story.* New York, 1887.

McClellan, H. B. *Life and Campaigns of Major General J. E. B. Stuart.* Richmond, 1885.

McKim, Randolph H. *Soul of Lee.* New York, 1918.

Macon, T. J. *Reminiscences of the 1st Company of Richmond Howitzers.* Richmond, n.d.

Malone, Bartlett Yancey. *Diary of . . . W. W. Pierson.* Chapel Hill, 1919.

Marshall, Charles. *An Aide-de-Camp of Lee . . .* Major General Sir Frederick Maurice, ed. Boston, 1927.

Maurice, Major General Sir Frederick. *Robert E. Lee, the Soldier.* Boston, 1925.

Moore, Edward A. *The Story of a Cannoneer Under Stonewall Jackson.* New York, 1907.

Moore, Robert A. *Diary.* Edited by James W. Silver. Jackson, Tenn., 1959.

Morgan, W. H. *Personal Reminiscences of the War of 1861-65.* Lynchburg, Va., 1911.

Nevins, Allan. *Emergence of Lincoln.* 2 vols. New York, 1950.

Nevins, Allan. *Ordeal of the Union.* 2 vols. New York, 1959.

Oates, William C. *The War Between the Union and the Confederacy . . .* Washington, 1905.

Official Records of the Union and Confederate Armies. Washington, 1880-1901.

Owen, William M. *In Camp and Battle With the Washington Artillery of New Orleans.* Boston, 1885.

Patch, Major General Joseph Dorst. *Battle of Ball's Bluff.* Leesburg, Va., 1958.

Pender, Major General W. Dorsey. *Letters.* Unpublished. Through the courtesy of the late Dr. Freeman.

Peterson, Harold L. *Notes on Ordnance . . . 1861-65.* Pamphlet, American Ordnance Association, Washington, 1959.

Pickett, Mrs. George E. *Pickett and His Men.* Philadelphia, 1913.

Polley, J. B. *Hood's Texas Brigade.* New York, 1908.

Randall, J. G. *Civil War and Reconstruction.* New York, 1937.

Randall, J. G. *Lincoln the President.* 2 vols. New York, 1945.

Reagan, John H. *Memoirs* . . . New York, 1906.

Robertson, W. J. *Biography of A. P. Hill.* Richmond *Times Dispatch Sunday Magazine,* Oct. 14-Nov. 11, 1934.

Schenck, Martin. *Up Came Hill.* Harrisburg, Pa., 1958.

Sorrel, Moxley G. *Recollections of a Confederate Staff Officer.* New York, 1907.

Smith, Gustavus W. *The Battle of Seven Pines.* New York, 1891.

Smith, William Randolph. *Diary.* Unpublished, Alderman Library.

Southern Historical Society Papers. 53 vols. Richmond, 1876-1959.

Steele, Matthew Forney. *American Campaigns.* 2 vols. Washington, 1909.

Stiles, Robert. *Four Years Under Marse Robert.* Washington, 1903.

Tankerslay, Allen P. *John B. Gordon.* Atlanta, 1955.

Taylor, Richard. *Destruction and Reconstruction.* Edited by Richard Harwell. (New edition) New York, 1954.

Taylor, Walter. *Four Years With Lee.* New York, 1877.

Thomas, Henry W. *History of the Doles-Cooke Brigade.* Atlanta, 1903.

Thomason, John. *Jeb Stuart.* New York, 1933.

Vandiver, Frank A. *Mighty Stonewall.* New York, 1957.

Wainwright, Colonel Charles S. *A Diary of Battle.* Edited by Allan Nevins. New York, 1962.

Walker, Francis A. *History of the Second Army Corps.* New York, 1886.

Warner, Ezra. *Generals in Gray.* Baton Rouge, 1959.

Webb, Alexander S. *The Peninsula* . . . *Campaign of 1862.* (Reprint edition) New York, 1959.

Welch, Dr. Spencer Glasgow. *A Confederate Surgeon's Letters to His Wife.* (New edition) Marietta, Ga., 1954.

Wiley, Bell Irvin. *The Life of Johnny Reb.* Indianapolis, 1943.

Williams, Kenneth. *Lincoln Finds a General.* Vols. 1 and 2. New York, 1949.

Williams, T. Harry. *Lincoln and the Radicals.* Madison, Wis., 1941.

Wise, Jennings Cropper. *The Long Arm of Lee — The History of the Army of Northern Virginia.* (New edition) New York, 1959.

Wood, William Nathaniel. *Reminiscences of Big I.* (New edition) Jackson, Tenn., 1956.

Worsham, John F. *One of Jackson's Foot Cavalry* . . . *A History of "F" Company.* New York, 1912.

Wright, General A. R., Tribute To . . . Privately printed pamphlet. Courtesy of General Wright's granddaughter, Mrs. Nell Wise.

Bibliography on the Study of Stress

THE STUDY of the stress syndrome was developed by Dr. Hans Selye, of Montreal, during the 1930's, and most of the writings of medical researchers in aspects of adaptation to stress were published during the 1950's. The Korean War provided a stimulus to the study of the effects of stress in combat, which spread into broader studies on the total stress syndrome. Dr. Selye's *The Stress of Life* (New York, Montreal, 1956) gives a brief history of his experiments and conclusions, and a more general book based largely on Dr. Selye's work is *Living With Stress*, by Nancy E. Gross, published in New York in 1958. Out of the growing volume of material on specialized studies in reactions to or effects of stress, the following were consulted:

Army Medical Service Graduate School. *Symposium on Stress.* Walter Reid Army Medical Center. Washington, 1953.

Bliss, E. L. *et al.* Reaction of adrenal cortex to emotional stress. *Psychosomatic Medicine* 18: 56-76. 1956.

Dickel, H. A. Fatigue syndrome. *American Journal of Nursing* 53: 725-727. 1953.

Engel, F. L. General concepts of adrenocortical function in relation to the response to stress. *Psychosomatic Medicine* 15: 565ff. 1953.

Grinker, R. R. and Spiegel, *Men Under Stress.* London, 1945.

Harms, H. E. and Soniat, Symposium on symptoms and meaning of fatigue. *Medical Clinics of North America* 36: 311-17. March 1952.

Hoagland, H. Adrenal stress response in normal men. *Journal of Applied Physiology* 8: 149-154, 1955.

Menninger, K. Regulatory devices of ego under major stress. *International Journal of Psychoanalysis* 35: 412-420. 1954.

Selye, H. Concept of stress and response in 1955. *Journal of Chronic Diseases* 2: 583-592. 1955.

Selye, H. Endocrine reactions during stress. *Current Researches in Anesthesia and Analgesia.* 35: 182-192. 1956.

Index